Rewriting Theatre

Rewriting Theatre

The *Comedia* and the Nineteenth-Century *Refundición*

Charles Ganelin

Lewisburg
Bucknell University Press
London and Toronto: Associated University Presses

© 1994 by Associated University Presses

All rights reserved. Authorization to photocopy items for internal or personal use, or the internal or personal use of specific clients, is granted by the copyright owner, provided that a base fee of $10.00, plus eight cents per page, per copy is paid directly to the Copyright Clearance Center, 222 Rosewood Drive, Danvers, Massachusetts 01923.
[0 – 8387–5259 – 4/94 $10.00 + 8¢ pp, pc.]

Associated University Presses
440 Forsgate Drive
Cranbury, NJ 08512

Associated University Presses
25 Sicilian Avenue
London WC1A 2QH, England

Associated University Presses
P.O. Box 338, Port Credit
Mississauga, Ontario
Canada L5G 4L8

The paper used in this publication meets the requirements of the American National Standard for Permanence of Paper for Printed Library Materials Z39.48–1984.

Library of Congress Cataloging-in-Publication Data

Ganelin, Charles.
    Rewriting theatre : the comedia and the nineteenth-century refundición / Charles Ganelin.
      p.   cm.
    Includes bibliographical references and index.
    ISBN 0-8387-5259-4 (alk. paper)
    1. Spanish drama—19th century—History and criticism.
2. Spanish drama—Classical period. 1500 –1700—Adaptations.
3. Theater—Spain—History—19th century. I. Title
    PQ6113.G36   1994
    862'.509—dc20   93-13479
                                                                              CIP

For Patty and Alix
Who make it worthwhile
and who show me what life is really all about

Contents

Preface	ix
1. Approaching the *Refundición*	3
2. King Sancho Revisited: *La estrella de Sevilla* and *Sancho Ortiz de las Roelas*	31
3. *Marta la piadosa*: Tirso at the Hands of Reworkers	80
4. Art and Politics: Adelardo López de Ayala and *El alcalde de Zalamea*	126
5. Future Directions	171
Conclusion	190
Appendix	193
Notes	225
Bibliography	261
Index	271

Preface

In the introduction to his masterful study of Calderón's reception in Germany and the Lowlands, a book that any reception-oriented approach needs to take into account, Henry Sullivan writes about how Calderón was (mis)understood outside of Spain:

> To audiences who applauded Calderón outside Spain, the ways in which a *refundidor* or a particular culture misunderstood Calderón's intentions were not necessarily a negative thing. The unadaptable or incomprehensible elements in the dramas could and did lead to novel and inventive artistic solutions that were of the times and for the audiences of the new playwright. The value of these reworkings to us as modern critics is beyond calculation.[1]

The *comedias* recast by Spanish writers for their own theatres in the late eighteenth and early nineteenth centuries follow the same pattern. Lope, Tirso, Calderón, and others were reinterpreted in the light of new literary, social, and political orientations. By studying the *refundiciones* [recasts] we can begin to acquire a much broader understanding not only of the *comedia*'s reception but also of the ramifications for the development of Spanish theatre.

The five chapters of this book constitute one approach to a study of the *refundición*. For every play and every review discussed, five others could have been chosen as equally representative of the *comedia*'s reception in nineteenth-century Madrid. There is a logic, however, to the plays selected. *La estrella de Sevilla* [The star of Seville] proved itself to be extraordinarily popular through the centuries, and spawned two well-known and often-performed *refundiciones*, entitled *Sancho Ortiz de las Roelas*, by Cándido María Trigueros and Juan Eugenio Hartzenbusch. *Marta la piadosa* [Martha the pious] is included because the issue of hypocrisy it raises came to the forefront in the late eighteenth century with the translation of Molière's *Tartuffe* and the ensuing plays of Leandro Fernández de Moratín. In this ambience Tirso's *comedia* was recast twice, once by Pascual Rodríguez de Arellano and once by Dionisio Solís; this latter *refundición* gave rise to Calixto Boldún y Conde's recast of 1866. *El alcalde de Zalamea* [The mayor of Zalamea], an overtly political and promonarchic Calderonian *comedia*, became the vehicle for Adelardo López de Ayala to propound in 1864 his very monarchic sentiments; López de Ayala's official roles in Parliament and in various governments is a constant subtext in his plays, and no less so in his only *refundición* of a Golden Age play. The chapter entitled "Future Directions" indicates widening definitions of a *refundición* and other approaches to performance studies. The Duke of Rivas's *El desengaño en un sueño* [Disillusionment in a dream] exemplifies another way of recasting, of incorporating dramatic material from various sources both to respond to literary/social upheaval and to comment on the source texts and the ideologies they put forth. The brief overview of a 1986 performance of *Marta la piadosa* signals how a contemporary director redefines the *comedia*'s value as he frustrates the audience's expectations and attempts to establish new norms for late twentieth century society.

The longer a project takes to come to fruition, the greater the indebtedness its author incurs. This book was conceived over a several-year period; the impetus behind it evolved from attendance at the annual Golden Age Theatre Festival at El Chamizal National Memorial in El Paso, Texas. The opportunity to see *comedia* performed over a two-week period year after year remains an exciting prospect, especially when adaptations of the classical texts many of us know well from the classroom take on new life through performance. If one play spurred my interest more than any other, I would have to admit that it was Raúl Zermeño's provocative *Marta la piadosa*. I began to ask myself the questions that led to this book: Why did Zermeño stage the play exactly as he did? Isn't his staging a vitiation of the original text? What is an original *comedia*? How is the audience reacting to the open sexuality? How has this play been transformed in the more than three hundred and seventy-five years since Tirso wrote it? I do not know whether I have reached definitive conclusions; I certainly hope not. I do wish, however, to spur continued interest in the performance history of the Golden Age *comedia*, in the social, political, and aesthetic changes the *refundiciones* reflect.

Many institutions have offered support and encouragement. Purdue University awarded me an XL Grant for summer travel to Madrid, where I spent many hours in the Hemeroteca Municipal and the Biblioteca Nacional. To the staffs of both institutions goes my deep appreciation. I am grateful to Purdue University Libraries' Library Scholars Fund for a grant to defray photocopying and related expenses. The Purdue University Humanities, Social Sciences and Education Library Interlibrary Loan Office honored untold requests with equanimity. A semester's leave from teaching duties allowed me to complete the writing. To David A. Caputo, Dean of the School of Liberal Arts, and to Howard Mancing, Head of the Department of Foreign Languages and Literatures, I give many thanks.

Friends and colleagues were there when I needed them. Catherine Larson, Charles Oriel, Howard Mancing, Djelal Kadir, Floyd Merrell, Santiago García-Castañón, and Kathleen O'Gorman all commented on versions of one chapter or another; they will find many of their suggestions incorporated into the book. Others, such as Henry Sullivan, Edward Friedman, Frederick de Armas, Daniel Heiple, Dawn Smith, Ruth El Saffar, Louise Fothergill-Payne, John J. Allen, and David Gies either heard related talks or had read my earlier articles on the topic of *refundiciones*. In either event, their comments and bibliographic suggestions have been extremely helpful. Special appreciation is due to Anita Stoll for having called to my attention and provided me with microfilm copies of two manuscripts—one completely unknown—of *Marta la piadosa* recasts located in Madrid's Biblioteca Municipal. And the necessary disclaimer: any errors, factual or otherwise, are mine alone.

A place of honor belongs to my wife and colleague, Patricia N. Klingenberg. She managed to be an understanding wife and friend, a good reader who knew how to see the big picture when I was awash in details, a valuable colleague, and an excellent mother while carrying out her own heavy academic responsibilities. *Las gracias a ti debidas.*

Rewriting Theatre

1
Approaching the *Refundición*

> Theater does not, indeed cannot ever, simply become "historical." Whenever a theater performs a piece of merely historical interest, it has already ceased to discharge its proper and preeminent function: to represent presence and nothing but presence. . . . This does not mean that the purpose of a classical theatrical program is to give authentic performances whose historically accurate style has been established by scholars. On the contrary, the characteristic value of this chapter in the history of theater is precisely the power of fusion that the present possesses as such when it succeeds in elevating past life into presence.
> —Hans-Georg Gadamer, *Relevance*

The successful classical Spanish theatre festivals of Almagro, Spain, and El Chamizal in El Paso, Texas, have increased the awareness of theatregoers and critics alike of the *comedia*'s importance as a cultural artifact and performable text not limited to traditional stagings in the manner of historical restoration. *Comedia* scholars have redirected of late their focus toward the importance of theatre production, of performed texts, and of the *comedia*'s ability to thrive and to speak to contemporary audiences. Producers, directors, writers, and actors contribute to performance studies in order to reformulate critical views with respect to staging *comedias* to audiences whose ambience is at a significant temporal and spatial remove from that of the original public.[1] This renewed appreciation of reworkings finds a solid base in one of the "old" rules of literary theory, voiced in 1957 by Northrop Frye in *Anatomy of Criticism*: "The two essential facts about a work of art, that it is contemporary with its own time and that it is contemporary with ours, are not opposed but complementary facts."[2] Recent years have seen a reevaluation of the *comedia*'s role in the nineteenth century. The focus of the present study is the *come-*

dia's fate as rewritten text in that period of literary upheaval and renovation. The *refundición*, a wide-ranging term applied here to mean recast *comedias*, has a history dating from the late eighteenth century. I will outline the *refundición*'s development and speak principally about its reception in the nineteenth-century Madrid press. The conclusions will show that Frye's statement is eminently applicable to the Golden Age *comedia*, which can speak the language of any period willing to listen and learn.

To pinpoint the origins within Spain of the *refundición* of Golden Age drama is a daunting task, primarily because the term *refundición* has never been defined adequately. The *Diccionario de autoridades*'s definition, "Translaticiamente vale comprehender, o incluir" [Figuratively, it means to take in, or include], also cites Madre María de Jesús de Agreda in her 1665 *Mystica Ciudad de Dios*:

> Mas queremos significar que las cosas están entre sí encadenadas, y suceden unas a otras: y, imaginándolas con este orden objectivo, refundimos, para entenderlas mejor, el mismo orden en los actos de la divina ciencia y voluntad.
>
> [But we want to mean that things are linked together among themselves, and follow one another; and, imagining them in this object order, we recast, in order to understand them better, the same order in acts of divine science and will.][3]

The word implies remaking, recasting, refounding something new on the basis of the old as part of a continuous historical process that implies reception and reevaluation. Within the seventeenth century, numerous Golden Age *comedias* had been reworked. Calderón's craftsmanship, exhibited in his recast of Lope's *El alcalde de Zalamea* [The mayor of Zalamea], for example, or the rewriting process, multiple manuscripts, and complicated authorship questions of *El rey D. Pedro en Madrid* [King Don Pedro in Madrid], speak to works recast within a short timeframe.[4] Audiences of one play very likely would be familiar with both original and recast versions replete with historical allusions and a common linguistic basis. Seen from the larger framework of Spanish theatre history, the *refundición* became a corrective to the *comedia* and formed part of an overall plan to regenerate interest in the Spanish stage. In the regulations set forth in the 1807 plan to reform the theatre, for example, the *refundición* is given a broad definition as well as official recognition.[5] By 1899 the *Diccionario de la Real Academia* included a definition that in itself offers multiple interpretations: "Dar nueva forma y disposición a una obra de ingenio, como comedia, discurso, etc., con el fin de mejorarla" [To give new form and arrangement to a creative work, like a play, discourse, etc., with the aim of improving it].⁶ Ideally, the *refundidores* aimed for improvement according to the poetics that formed their artistic practice. For the purposes of this study, a *refundición* is an adaptation of a dramatic text that may manifest many kinds of changes to recast the play in a new form that reflects the aesthetics of the recaster's era, or to redirect the thrust of a play in order to expand upon specific issues developed in the original. The goal of the rewriting process is often to improve the source play according to precepts contemporary with the recaster as well as to create a work of art that will communicate to the public a writer's artistic and conceivably political preoccupations often inherent in both the original and recast text.

Until recently, critical appraisal of post–Golden Age *comedia* performance history has been limited, with a few exceptions, to documentation of performance dates and occasional commentary citing a handful of reviews without a full account of the social and political atmosphere in which these performances had taken place. Nevertheless, the groundwork laid by such documentation is essential to the continued development of interest in eighteenth-, nineteenth-, and twentieth-century *refundiciones*. N. B. Adams, concerned with the *comedia* in general, and Sterling Stoudemire, in an article on Dionisio Solís's *refundiciones*, document early nineteenth-century performance dates. Archibald K. Shields, in a 1933 unpublished Ph.D. dissertation, provides the first comprehensive listing of theatre performances, including *comedias* and *refundiciones*, of the early years of the nineteenth century. Two years later Ada Coe's *Catálogo bibliográfico* details information concerning performances and reviews published in the Madrid newspapers between 1661 and 1819, covering a period previously ignored. Shields's and Coe's documents remain seminal for any history of Spanish theatre. Of equal importance concerning repertoire and performance dates are the *Carteleras*, in the *Cuadernos Bibliográficos* series, for the Madrid theatres from 1830 to 39 and from 1840 to 49, and that of Francisco Aguilar Piñal for Seville from 1830 to 39. These three publications are essential starting points in determining the repertoire during the nineteenth century (whether a *comedia* is an original or a *refundición* is not always clear, however). A necessary companion piece is the four-volume *Veinticuatro diarios: 1845–1900*, a thorough but not exhaustive catalogue for events of the Madrid artistic world announced in selected newspapers. Greater bibliographic weight contributes to Piero Menarini's multicontributor volume that has become an invaluable guide to performed *comedias, refundiciones,* new plays, and translations for the nineteenth-century Spanish stage.[7]

Studies devoted specifically to the *refundición* have become of late more prevalent. John Cook's *Neo-Classical Drama in Spain* dedicates only one chapter to the *refundición*; Alborg and Ruiz Ramón, in their respective *Historias*, pay only glancing attention to the phenomenon. The first attempt to define and characterize the nature of the *refundición* is Edward Coughlin's unpublished 1965 dissertation, in which he offers an overview of the role of the *refundición*, background on neo-classical rules and their influence upon *refundiciones*, and a chapter each on diction and meter. Because this work was produced five years before René Andioc's influential studies, none of the economic or social factors that often spurred interest in refashioning *comedias* was taken into account. Little else appeared on the topic until Ermanno Caldera's 1974 *Il dramma romantico in Spagna*, the first chapter of which discusses some of the political and social developments reflected in the *refundición*. He writes principally about Hartzenbusch's recasts (particularly about *El médico de su honra*), as well as about Trigueros's and Hartzenbusch's *refundiciones* of *La estrella de Sevilla*, both entitled *Sancho Ortiz de las Roelas* (discussed in chapter 2). Most recently, articles by Maria Grazia Profeti and Marc Vitse further testify to the *comedia*'s viability on the eighteenth-century stage as a source for new plays, and a special issue of *Cuadernos del Teatro Clásico* is dedicated to the reception accorded the *comedia* in the eighteenth, nineteenth and twentieth centuries.[8] Aguilar Piñal summarizes the reasons for recasting plays:

> La *refundición* teatral . . . no obedece a capricho o interés personal del refundidor, sino a razonados motivos estéticos o políticos. . . . La refundición supone . . . la valoración positiva de un texto dramático, pero admitiendo la posibilidad de mejora.
>
> [The theatrical *recast* . . . does not obey the whim or personal interest of the recaster, but reasoned esthetic or political motives. . . . The recast assumes the positive appraisal of a dramatic text, but admitting the possibility of improvement.][9]

In the same issue, David Gies investigates the role played by *refundiciones* during the Constitutional Triennial (1820–1823) and the Ominous Decade (1823–1833). Relying on Shields and Adams for raw data, he gives four reasons to explain the great popularity enjoyed by *refundiciones*: the writers' desire to remodel the *comedia* according to neoclassical precepts; the need to avoid censorship; a lack of talent, or laziness, on the part of writers and impresarios (a recast play cost less than a new one); and an attempt to "reform" a play according to ideological and theatrical necessities. Gies summarizes critical attitudes toward the *refundiciones*, concluding that "la preservación de aquellos 'clásicos' responde a la profunda crisis de identidad nacional que España experimenta en los años que preceden al florecimiento del romanticismo en la península" [the preservation of those "classics" responds to the profound national identity crisis that Spain experiences in the years preceding Romanticism's flourishing in the Peninsula].[10] One must always keep in mind that the *refundición* not only responded to a deep-seated need to maintain traditional values, but also that without it, the *comedia* may very well have appeared considerably less on the Spanish stage.

The notable critical writings outlined above treat the *refundición* within the context of specific historical events; how an individual recast was received requires considerably more attention than given to date. To refocus attention on dramatic texts pulled from an earlier era implies a revalorization of them, and their insertion within a new textual tradition raises questions pertaining to the traditional Golden Age canon and, naturally, to its reception by a new generation of spectators. To stage either an original version or an adaptation of a consecrated play involves the original text's reception in a new time and requires bridge-building to link past and present, to bring together, in Hans Robert Jauss's phrase, the "here-and-there of reality."[11]

Attendance at a play's performance functions similarly to a critical reading of, say, a novel. Wolfgang Iser describes the reader's participation in the interpretive process: his postulated readers continuously reevaluate the text before them by filling in gaps and indeterminacies that arise because information necessary to reach understanding is doled out during the reading process. As readers progress through a novel, each new contribution to knowledge requires an assessment of its value, and a reassessment as to its contribution to the whole.[12] These readers then bring to the process their own experience of literature (and life). To receive a text is to view it within a particular horizon, a term defined by Hans-Georg Gadamer as "the range of vision that includes everything that can be seen from a particular vantage point."[13] A "vantage point" includes the receiver's familiarity with the traditions to which the text belongs as well as concomitant expectations of what the text will or should present. Gadamer's definition provides the basis for the concepts of horizons of expectation and horizons of experience espoused by Jauss. The first of these is constituted, as Robert Holub sees it, by a " 'system of references' that a hypothetical individual might bring to any text"; that text calls upon, and depends on, the receiver's knowledge of a specific tradition.[14] The second term refers to the continuity of the reception process, "the perpetual inversion [that] occurs from simple reception to critical understanding."[15] To outline the domains of each horizon, Jauss distinguishes between effect and reception: effect is determined by the text, while reception is within the province of the receiver. "Two horizons," Jauss tells us, "are always at play in an active synthesis of understanding. In other words, the horizon of expectation evoked by the work [in the receiver] confirms or transcends the horizon of experience introduced by the recipient."[16] The text's effect is bound within its horizon of expectation; it evokes the expectation of norms common to its genre, subgenre, character traits, and the like. At the same time reception is "norm-creating," as viewers bring their experience of literature to the process of understanding and interpreting. A dramatic text is, ideally, viewed by an audience more than once in order for a more complete understanding to develop. Successive viewings, even by a new audience perhaps familiar with previous reactions to the performance, contribute to another chapter in the history of the text's reception. Out of the interchange between expectation and experience arises what I call, within the context of Gadamer and Jauss, the horizon of tradition, because these subsequent "readings" (as attendance at a play may be considered) produce a new textual tradition. What is brought to the work has not been brought before, because no one else with the same value-system has experienced the work in quite the same way at quite the same time. Even if we postulate identical subsequent audiences, their repeated attendance at the same theatrical event will formulate a new tradition of reception.[17]

Each time a classical play appears in a new production, horizons influence understanding and interpretation on the part of both creator and interpreter(s) and contribute to the formation of canons; more specifically, a successful representation becomes a building block in the development of a performance canon. Even a production that runs counter to traditional stagings in an attempt to decanonize specific stage and interpretive conventions redefines the canon. Recent studies in the history of Shakespeare performances bear this out. R. Chris Hassel, in *Songs of Death*, elucidates the performance history of Shakespeare's *Richard III*. Hassel is well aware that performance is interpretation; he discusses Laurence Olivier's film *Richard III* and questions that it is "Shakespeare"; similarly, he believes that a 1982 BBC videotape production of the play departs from Olivier's version and is "an interesting restoration of Shakespeare."[18] Hassel differentiates between a director's involvement in a production of a classical text and a scholar's study of the same text. While the director can compare sources, study background material, and direct the cast in a multitude of ways, the scholar has certain luxuries that allow much fuller examination. Though the scholar may engage in the same process of understanding and synthesizing the critical tradition, he or she "can talk about possibilities that might work better for the reader than for the player; the scholar can also suggest several possibilities for the player without having to settle on one of them."

In general, Hassel is accurate, but his conclusion that "the director, the actor, can go only one way" eliminates a director's (or an actor's) option of dramatizing within the performance itself a specific dilemma suggested by the play.[19] The array of interpretive choices presented to performers, too, gives them an edge over scholars, who reach a conclusion and commit it to the printed word, while a performance may, and generally does, change from day to day. An audience's response to a performer's decision to portray a character in a chosen way will influence how that portrayal is carried out during a subsequent performance. It would seem that the performer's possibilities for adaptation and modification are limited only by sensitivity to the text, to the text's reception, and by his or her concept of theatre. In the end, however, both scholar and director must mediate past and present. Both can leave certain problems "delightfully suspended" through the choice made to represent a character one way or another; by eliminating or focusing on one passage, or by adding or explicating another, both make a conscious choice, both deal with questions of history and literature.

History and literature, particularly from the standpoint of Jauss's reception theory, are viewed not strictly as a succession of events or texts following one another, but as a series of influences, each new work exercising an effect on the evolving receptions of its predecessor, and, in turn, serving as a point of departure for further evolution. This is not to eliminate the differences between past and present. As a film character has said, "The past is a foreign country; they do things differently there."[20] The line is a narrative voice-over from Joseph Losey's 1971 *The Go-Between*, and introduces the narrator's recollection of one summer from his prepubescent youth in which he performs the role of "postman" between two star-crossed lovers from opposite social strata in pre–World War I England. His incursion into "foreign" territory as he steps back to heal a long-open wound brings past and present together in a bridge-building effort to recognize and then to close gaps between his youth and premature old age. Losey's character reconstructs one distant summer from within his horizons of experience and understanding. He must recall painful events that circumstances force him to relive in order to deliver one more message; his task, then, is not all so different from that of a recaster who attempts to transform past literary experience in order to appeal to contemporary tastes. The undertaking is intended to evoke, from a theatrical standpoint, specific expectations in new generations of a theatregoing public.

In quite a different context, an actor steps out of character to conclude a short dramatic piece: "Esa . . . esa es otra historia" [That . . . that is another story]. So ends the third of Osvaldo Dragún's *Historias para ser contadas* [Stories to be told], which stops short of introducing yet another story; the statement reflects an awareness, perhaps unconscious, of bridge-building between horizons, particularly if we take "historia" in both of its meanings as "story" and "history."[21] An additional story to be told is "out there," waiting to be linked in some fashion to those that have preceded it. The next story's audience will have incorporated the previous stagings into its collective horizon even though the circumstances of the new story may differ. A similar operation takes place even when great temporal distances exist between performances. We, as late twentieth-century critics, cannot enter the minds of seventeenth-, eighteenth-, or nineteenth-century readers and spectators, yet we do not live in a separate, discrete horizon; to affirm such would deny the continuity of history. Rather, upon receiving a work anew, we draw it back into the present to fuse horizons.[22] Past meets present in continuous mediation through a reading of a past work, or even of an adapted work, in part because of the sustained contact between those texts, in part because the past's traditions are so essential to formulating understanding of both past and present literary works. This fusion of horizons, in turn, is itself a constant process within a "historical consciousness [that] involves the experience of the tension between the text and the present."[23] If tension is relaxed, understanding ceases to evolve, indeed, ceases to function. The essential interplay is what Francisco Ruiz Ramón has called the "allí y aquí" [there and here] of the dramatic text—the past meaning and present significance. It is Jauss's "the here-and-there of reality."[24]

The interplay between past and present is related to the historical nature of both poetry and interpretation which reinforces Frye's "essential facts" that a work of art is contemporaneous to both the period of its production and the period of its later reception. David Hoy explains how these facts function linguistically:

> Once written, the language of the text is freed from the constraints under which it may originally have been conceived. Any action can have conse-

quences that exceed the expectations of the agent, and these consequences may give rise to the necessity for other actions which the agent did not anticipate.[25]

The language of a seventeenth-century dramatic text is elucidated through a variety of interpretations (via scholarly study or theatrical staging); the critic, performer, or spectator experiences a growing awareness of new meanings within the text by means of these interpretations. The text contains the potential (its immanence) of revealing its "truths" to future receivers because of its language's capabilities to transcend the historical moment of creation. This openness is central to the fusion of horizons and is what allows succeeding generations to bring to light, in terms of this book's focus, the seventeenth-century *comedia*. What a later audience will expect or even hear will not necessarily coincide with the reception accorded by its seventeenth-century counterpart. Yet sensitive interpretations will nonetheless render the text eminently intelligible to its new audiences. For this reason, when a critic objects to liberties taken in an adaptation of a well-known classical theatrical text, one type of question often raised is: "Would the playwright have approved?" The question has often been posed especially by literary and performance critics schooled primarily in New Criticism. The supposition of a long-dead playwright's hypothetical approval is an interesting rhetorical exercise, but one that we must go beyond. In this regard it is important to remember that the language with which a creator endows a text—speaking as always of an accomplished work of art—will respond to well-reasoned interpretation informed by the interpreter's horizons.

Adaptations can be viewed, too, within the tradition of literary history as a manifestation of one period's aesthetics superimposed upon another's. Nineteenth-century Spain's frequent *comedia* adaptations reveal considerable incursions by writers of varying talent. Analysis of these *refundiciones*, taking the form of comparisons between, say, the recast text and the seventeenth-century original or, with luck, an actor's copy or prompt book whose notations are clues to the "cut-and-paste" of adaptation, guides us. A dramatic text is an unstable entity precisely because of its malleability from performance to performance, yet this very instability may create a textual quicksand that can engulf the interpreter and make dialogue with the text difficult. Paths to a proper dialogue "will align local detail with the landscape, with the 'tonic' conventions of the work as a whole. But such 'coming to rest' is always provisional. It is a tensed, momentary poise between degrees of established perception and the creative uncertainties, even outright fallacies, which lead to re-vision—literally, to 'a new sighting'."[26] Seeing anew creates pathways, in the "event" of an individual performance, to encourage communication between past and present.

Jonathan Miller, in his book *Subsequent Performances*, discusses the ramifications of a play's performance after the original staging has passed into memory. A play's afterlife, a word Miller has borrowed from Aby Warburg, is its successive recreation on stage.[27] The restaged dramatic text necessarily undergoes modification because it is nearly impossible for a complete and accurate restoration to take place; the director and actors mounting the production clearly will impose their interpretation upon it.[28] Our "here and now," that is, the horizons that condition a reading or staging, are influenced by the period that produced the text, but the text's separate entity imposes individuality as well as originality. A play, Miller correctly asserts, is completed "only when work has been supplied by someone other than the playwright."[29] A dramatic text (a *comedia*, for present purposes) contains myriad allusions mythological and topical that required little explanation during the playwright's lifetime:

> Confronted by classical works . . . it is easy to forget that the author did not write them for posterity. Plays, like any other art form, are created for the artist's contemporaries, which means, to some extent at least, that certain things are understood without having to be explained.[30]

In the movement from a past century's performance to a subsequent staging, it is important to remember that artists are conditioned by the horizons that have given shape to their concept of literature and theatre. Their additions, deletions, and rephrasings become part of the play's performance history.

New sightings, new stagings, "new" texts, horizons, and bridges: to these ends Jauss proposes the decanonization of a classic work so that

> it may be introduced into the horizon of contemporary experience, countering any pretence of timeless validity and being rejuvenated on the modern stage in such a way that the link between past and present experience is not broken, as it undoubtedly is in a naive actualization or rigorous historicization.[31]

One might question if "rigorous historicization" is even possible, because each successive period tends to define history in its own terms,[32] and redefinition often carries with it revisionist overtones. Such are many eighteenth century *comedia* productions which work backwards to force the previous generation's artistic productions to conform to a new set of rules which serve to erase from collective memory the excesses of a past, "uninstructed" time.[33] One principal thrust of the eighteenth century's reception of the *comedia* is its desire to reconstitute one moment in literary history in the light of a more "decorous" theatre. Jauss's idea of a "rejuvenating" reception is important for what the eighteenth century did not do, since, as he says, "The fusion of horizons [must] not be silently presupposed but be consciously achieved as a dialectic mediation of the past and present horizons in a new actualization of meaning."[34] Rejuvenation, in this context, is a positive term, but the *comedia* in the hands of the early *refundidores* (with the exception of Trigueros, Vicente Rodríguez de Arellano, and other *comedia* sympathizers) does not receive substantial new life. Though the effects occasionally produce successful theatre in economic terms (as Tomás Sebastián y Latre achieved in part), the artistic rendering is at a far remove from rejuvenation. Once the Romantics and post-Romantics reappraised their literary and historical past, they were in a much better position than their immediate predecessors to evaluate *comedias* as the texts were transmitted to them. A more complete fusion of horizons yielded, on the whole, greater artistic success in their *refundiciones*. As I discuss below, the *refundición* became acceptable in its function (one of many) of resurrecting widespread interest in the *comedia*.

Just as audience response and reader response approach the reception of an old or modified text in a new time often distant from the moment of original execution, so reworking itself is a reception of the work by specific individuals with an aim toward "updating" and attracting an audience (not to mention *maravedís, reales* and, eventually, *pesetas*).[35] At every moment, artists carry with them the baggage of life and experience, and at the moment of creation fight to be original while recognizing, consciously or unconsciously, many debts to the past. Though that past may be "foreign" and undoubtedly different, its elements struggle to allow horizons to open up to each other in a double operation of decodification and recodification "en donde se conecta o enchufa dialécticamente el 'allí' y el 'aquí,' el significado pasado y el sentido presente del texto clásico" [where the "there" and "here," past significance and present meaning of the classical text, are connected or fit together].[36] Origin and originality confront imitations, reworkings, plagiarism and forgeries. The separation into two overlapping camps of creation and recreation in the final analysis must be artificial, for almost any work of art is in one sense a "forgery," a word, David Quint explains, that suggests something fake as well as "something made or wrought by men."[37] The

Renaissance, almost always with a model in mind, exalted the notion of *imitatio*; and imitation remains an operative concept when analyzing the multifaceted nature of the *refundición*. Kenneth Reckford, in discussing the American playwright Tom Stoppard, states that Shakespeare, for Stoppard, "is . . . a touchstone of art, and of meaning, in a shifting universe."[38] Lope, Tirso, Calderón, and others serve a related function for nineteenth-century recasters.

But a larger concept looms with reception and its attendant horizons. To what extent are reworkings plagiarism? Where does originality enter? What demons, if any, do the reworkers fight when taking on the stature of Calderón or Tirso? Are they attempting to come out of the shadow of the father and thus fight off those now well-documented burdens and anxieties? Is a reworking actually a "strong misreading," as Harold Bloom asks, of an original? We must ask, again with Bloom, "What is the quality of the stolen material?" if indeed a *refundición* is stolen material.[39] Or perhaps it is more conducive to think along the lines of Ian McEwan, who believes that received material for many reasons finds its way into a new work of art: "If writers appear to resemble each other for reasons of history, geography, class, sex or Spirit of the Age, they ameliorate these similarities with their own borrowings, allusions, influences, tributes and pastiches."[40] Deletions from and accretions to a *comedia* alter the text by eliminating specific signifiers whose currency has been spent; with an infusion of material that will lend it greater coetaneity, a recast *comedia* alludes to its source/predecessor. "If the dream of intertextuality culminates in illicit union," Pat Rogers declares, "then allusion aspires to a companionate marriage. . . . You alluded in order not to copy; you imitated, that is, at a conscious distance." Rogers suggests that true imitation allows "the original 'thought' to go on making its own point."[41] In spite of the haziness of what constitutes an original "thought"—itself a center of controversy and focal point of recastings—plays whose performance tradition constitutes a canon in its own right, such as *La estrella de Sevilla* [The star of Seville] and *Sancho Ortiz de las Roelas*, bear this out. The works are able to transmit both new meanings brought out by specific performances and "old" meanings passed on from generation to generation. Horizons of past and present are thus more easily fused. George Steiner details this process with an extraordinary accumulation of data in *Antigones*, a reception-oriented work that studies not only the nearly 2500-year performance tradition of Sophocles's masterpiece, but also the historical and philosophical considerations that condition each generation's reading of the tragedy.[42]

The preceding argument allows the logical conclusion that a reworking becomes the by-product of a collusion between authors regardless of the time and geography that separate them. The horizons of later writers open to the past through allusion so that the product of the "original" creator may collude with another creative mind to enable bridge-building between the *materia prima* and the "copy." This is particularly true given the theatre's foundation in ritual, magic, and religion, three elements that presuppose both continuity and evolution. Theatre is a syncretic religion that develops and metamorphoses with each accretion to it. The dramatic text undergoes a constant process of concretion, that is, of filling in the gaps and indeterminacies of an earlier generation's participation in the theatrical event. A reworker, then, is akin to the readers and spectators discussed above, who, upon rereading a passage with the knowledge gleaned from their present place, are now able to advance significantly toward a redefined concept of understanding. In this way the reworker fills in historical gaps, another way of defining hermeneutical bridge-building, to let the old "thought" live on, to show how that "thought" is received by him from the context of his horizons, and to pass on the old "thought," now modified, to the spectators, who in turn will incorporate the new experience into their horizons.

An adaptation, in its response to new contexts, may offer the continuity of a tradition (that is, it may fulfill certain normative expectations of its genre and period). Equally possible is a rupture with that same tradition, a process that breaks with the horizons of experience. Steiner's *Antigones* approaches the problem from the point of view of a classic and classical text: "The integral authority of the classic is such that it can absorb without loss of identity the millenial incursions upon it, the accretions to it, of commentary, of translations, of enacted variations."[43] One could quarrel with Steiner's view of the classic as a monolithic structure. He suggests that the original *Antigone* remains untouched and unscathed in spite of violent encounters with history; hence Steiner's use of the word *incursions*. Though a classical text may yield adaptations, it is not a rigid, opaque object, but a fluid construct, whose language is freed from original constraints, and it is capable of reaching its receivers through the centuries, yielding new, or at least reformulated, vistas on human behavior.

* * *

The Spanish *comedia*, as critics John Cook and René Andioc have so amply pointed out, could only with difficulty weather social changes or survive the eighteenth century's rules and precepts, as set down by Ignacio Luzán, Bernardo de Iriarte, Tomás Sebastián y Latre, and other *preceptistas*.⁴⁴ Andioc, supported by a considerable body of statistical data, reports a measurable drop in income garnered from performances of Calderón *comedias* in the late eighteenth century; the *comedia* could not keep pace with neoclassical drama, translations of French and German plays, and the burgeoning *comedias de magia*. Reigning aesthetics dictate adherence to neoclassical artistic guidelines that include obeisance to the Aristotelian unities (of time, place, and action) and conformity to a never clearly defined sense of deco -rum. Attempts to redo certain *comedias* within these parameters are clearly informed with the zeal of the converted. Taking this tack in 1772, Tomás Sebastián y Latre opens his *Ensayo sobre el teatro español* with a condemnation of the *comedia*: "los brillantes adornos con que las [i.e., *las comedias*] aliñaron nuestros Poetas, las desfiguran, y confunden" [the brilliant adornments with which our poets dressed up (the *comedias*) disfigure and blur them].⁴⁵ He continues his admonishment by decrying the decadence into which Spanish theatre had fallen through its neglect of the "reglas del Arte" and expresses joy that "unos Genios sublimes . . . consiguieron que amaneciese sobre sus Teatros la hermosa luz de la razón, y del buen gusto" [a few sublime minds . . . were successful in having appear in their theatre the beautiful light of reason and of good taste] (n.p.). He claims, as a good eighteenth-century theorist should, that an uneducated public prevents reasoned discourse from being heard: "[El] vulgo ciego . . . algunas veces no dexa oír las voces de la razón, y ciega a los más linces" [blind masses often do not allow to be heard the voices of reason and blind those with sharpest vision] (n.p.). He lambasts, too, the "Protectores del mal gusto" [protectors of bad taste] who criticize verisimilitude as coldness and decency as lack of poetic fire. Just as a preacher who urges moderation, Sebastián y Latre reaches his peroration:

> Si nuestros poetas hubiesen arreglado su fantasía como era justo, ¡qué perfectos modelos tendríamos hoy para su imitación! Serían menos las piezas, pero mucho más útiles, y conformes a la moderación de un Teatro Christiano, y a la gravedad de la Nación Española.
>
> [If our poets had arranged their imagination as was proper, what perfect models we would have today for imitation! There would be fewer theatrical works, but much more useful ones, and conforming to the moderation of a Christian theatre and the gravity of the Spanish nation.] (n.p.)

Because of the elaborate pains he took to adapt seventeenth-century dramatic works to his period's artistic precepts, Sebastián y Latre has been credited with being the first *refundidor* of the *comedia*.⁴⁶ Given the wide definition of *refundición* that I employ, his role is not as prominent as one might otherwise think. His two *refundiciones* include Rojas Zorrilla's *Progne y Filomena* and Moreto's *El parecido en la corte* [The pretender at court], which he has refashioned not out of admiration for those specific works, but rather "a fin de quitar de nuestro Teatro tantas comedias semejantes a estas de Roxas y Moreto" [with the purpose of removing from our Theatre so many plays like these of Roxas and Moreto](n.p.). The attempt to create a self-destroying artifact arises out of his objection to the moral influence of Rojas's play: "¡Perniciosa enseñanza para jóvenes libres! ¡Y escandaloso espectáculo para doncellas incautas!" [Pernicious lessons for free-thinking young men! And scandalous spectacle for unwary virgins!] (n.p.). A performance history of Sebastián y Latre's version of *Progne y Filomena* remains unknown, but *El parecido en la corte* did enjoy a modicum of success; it played from the last years of the eighteenth century until 1813, and was revived for eighteen performances between 1820 and 1831.⁴⁷

Sebastián y Latre's efforts, his vehement moral indignation at the *comedia*'s evil influence notwithstanding, produced opposite effects from those he had intended. By 1800 recasting the *comedia* had become a recognized, if not fully accepted, practice among playwrights. Cándido María Trigueros and Vicente Rodríguez de Arellano, two of the better known practitioners of the art, believed that the *comedia* could continue to function as a legitimate form of theatre once the excesses of a past age were cast off and at least the outward form made to conform to the Aristotelian unities while the action became more "decorous." Both of these writers were popular in their time, but neither are known particularly for their *refundiciones*. However, Trigueros's interests in the *comedia* were political as well as artistic. The energy that the *comedia*'s detractors spent denouncing Golden Age theatre lent even greater impetus to the *comedia*'s persistence and its ability to withstand incursions. The continued existence of the *refundición*, especially in the face of verbal onslaught, testifies to the *comedia*'s inherent strength.

The virulent anti-*comedia* forces, who often wrote in the *Gaceta de Madrid*, spoke negatively about the form Golden Age plays took. In a 16 June 1811 review of Trigueros's *Sancho Ortiz de las Roelas* (a recast of *La estrella de Sevilla*), the reviewer defines the *refundición* with more than a hint of sarcasm:

> nuevo ramo de literatura inventado en España en el siglo pasado, y al qual se dedicaron con tanto denuedo varios ingenios, que creyeron darnos

un teatro español con solo tomar nuestras antiguas comedias, hacerlas giras, poner al principio lo que estaba al fin, a lo último lo que se hallaba en el medio, cortar tres o quatro relaciones, reformar como extravagante o impropio medio verso antiguo, para embutir otro medio moderno, que no era menos ridículo, y que por lo regular estaba escrito en la lengua franca del día (mal de que ciertamente no adolecen las insinuadas obras, pues son todas modelos más o menos cabales de lenguage y de pureza); y por último, y esta era la operación de empeño, mudar el nombre de jornadas en el de actos, y hacer cinco de tres que todas tienen.

[a new branch of literature invented in Spain in the past century, and to which several writers dedicated themselves with much determination; they intended to give us a Spanish theatre simply by taking our old plays, turning them around, putting at the beginning what came at the end, and at the end what was found in the middle, cutting three or four speeches, rewriting half an old verse considered extravagant or improper to stuff in half a new one that was no less ridiculous, and which generally was written in the popular language of the day (an ill that the suggested works do not suffer, since all are more or less accurate models of language and purity); and finally, and this was the objective, to change the name of "jornadas" to "actos," and make five out of the three that all have.] (683)

This jaundiced view informed by enlightenment poetics could have been learned from Sebastián y Latre's treatise, yet it is accurate in describing the salient characteristics of a *refundición* at the beginning of the nineteenth century.[48] Although it is true that some writers, unhappy with translated plays and imported plots, strove to refashion a Spanish theatre out of Golden Age *comedias*, their efforts consisted of more than simple reorganization of dramatic material.[49] Many *refundiciones* do exhibit the tendencies outlined by the reviewer; just as there are poor plays, so there are recasts of questionable quality. Introductory material is often suppressed (as in the case of *Sancho Ortiz de las Roelas*), long speeches are frequently reduced or excised (as in *Marta la piadosa*), individual verses undergo rewording or recasting into a different strophic form (examples abound in nearly all *refundiciones*), and phrases no longer current are substituted for a vocabulary more easily understood by the audience. The reviewer, of course, wishes to scorn the *refundición* and the *comedia* with it, and has chosen a tone appropriate to his task. Nonetheless, his is but one voice, as other reviews of *Sancho Ortiz de las Roelas* and the reception of still other plays bear out. But definitions and reviews are fine only if understood within their literary-historical context. How and why does the *comedia* speak to the centuries beyond the Golden Age?

What processes are involved in its reception? How did the reception of the *refundición* evolve from the first recast plays? What acceptance did these "reformed" theatrical texts find as their performances became more frequent? These are the questions whose answers we must seek in order to understand the phenomenon of the *refundición*.

* * *

If the early nineteenth century saw sporadic stagings of *comedias* and *refundiciones*, the death of Fernando VII, the concomitant end of the Ominous Decade (1833), and the advent of Romanticism brought a resurgence of literary innovation and fervent gatherings of *literati*. Part of this aperture included reworkings of classical plays to open the season at many Madrid theatres. The newspapers of the time occasionally published performance reviews as well as arguments, written by journalists who were also playwrights and essayists, concerning the value of performing a *comedia* as originally written or the malleable nature of a masterpiece.[50] The tone of the reviews and that of the prologues with which reworkers occasionally prefaced their *refundiciones*, allow an insight into the translation of an earlier culture for a public nearly two hundred years removed from its linguistic and political inheritance.

To qualify *refundiciones* on the whole as *vino añejo en odres nuevos*, as early reviewers imply, is of course a specious generalization. It is one thing to create a new container, yet another to bridge the distance between the 1600s and the 1800s. Linguistic practice and stage conventions evolve, while topical and mythological allusions lose the force of immediacy (as noted in the previous discussion of Jonathan Miller's book). Horizons change and the audience's experience will not include memory, for example, of a military victory two centuries old. (See chapter 3 on Tirso's *Marta la piadosa*.) For a nineteenth-century audience to understand a recast work beyond the level of cape-and-sword action, sexually oriented insinuation, and double entendre, a process of cultural translation within the act of reworking must take place. George Steiner illuminates the encoding and decoding ("el allí y aquí"; "the here-and-there of reality") that occurs in translation within one language to communicate a sense of continuity and a point of familiarity for cultural remembrance. Three principles delineated by Steiner determine the parameters of a *refundición*: emphasis (of some aspect appreciated by a new generation of theatregoers), foreshortening (restructuring of dramatic action), and omission (of that which is no longer culturally current).[51] The result is, in Gadamer's phrase, "effective-history," the force of tradition over those who belong to it. A recast is both culturally and historically rooted. It is at the same time an act of interpretation and criticism not only of the original work of art but also of the culture that produced it. It is also an interpretation of the specific text. Cultural currency, for its part, must be widely defined because traditions are necessarily passed on from generation to generation (cultural inheritance is an important part of historical continuity). The recasters, inheritors of the cultural legacy imbued in them, infuse the *refundiciones* with the spirit generated by their individual horizons.

Frederic Will reinforces this premise: "Translation against one's time-grain almost never works. . . . [T]he translator's language-nature, that to which his honesty must be true, is formed by his whole milieu. It is an artificial nature in which he has come to feel perfectly natural, as a writer feels in his style."[52] However, the debate not only about the quality of the *refundición* but also about its right to exist calls into question the *comedia*'s very translatability. Again Frederic Will lays out an inherent gap created where the recast meets the original:

> Translating, our only legitimate way of querying whether untranslatability exists, by its nature precludes the discovery of what it seeks; . . . translations and the originals they approximate coexist as mutually interflowing circuits of expression, approaching each other but never joining, leaning toward one another yet never quite symmetrically—since the original is privilegedly implicit to the points it wants to make.[53]

Will's remarks about translation fit nicely into the interstices where Jauss's horizons of experience and expectation come together. The fusion of horizons that creates historical continuity between the work of art and the viewer, and which allows continuance of "effective-history," describes the reception of the "interflowing circuits of expression." Though I accept Will's notion of a mutual leaning, I believe his conclusion requires modification. In a case of translation between languages, in which an attempt is made to bridge linguistic gaps and, where possible, cultural ones as well, the original necessarily occupies the privileged position. In the case of cultural translation within one language—as in the *refundición*—a twofold process is at work. Not only may a recaster select a specific seventeenth-century masterpiece to communicate the values in the play chosen to rewrite, he also creates a *refundición* that will displace the *comedia* and thus occupy the privileged position in a new epoch. "The motion of transfer and paraphrase," as George Steiner states, "enlarges the stature of the original."[54] The *comedia* and its *refundiciones* thus develop a symbiotic relationship, each helping the other, and prove La Fontaine's statement that "the old presses on the new with a delicate authority, meshing two levels of time and two styles."[55] Lope's name and quality attract Trigueros and Hartzenbusch (recasters of *Sancho Ortiz de las Roelas*) whose *refundiciones* of well-known plays elicit public as well as critical attention. The original play may become the focal point of discussion, the springboard from which to launch commentary whether of the printed text or of the performed play; the source play (and even the author) may bask in the rising sun of the nineteenth-century's horizons. This far-from-empty theatrical space must be shared, however, by both the recast and recaster, entities equally privileged in the points they attempt to make. Adelardo López de Ayala found in Calderón moral and political qualities applicable to the seventeenth as well as to the nineteenth centuries.[56] Ideas flow between original text and recast just as they flow between the recast and its audience.[57]

Regardless of the century that produces a recast *comedia*, no play is guaranteed a rave review. The normative expectations of the new receiving public may be met by the changes introduced in accordance with the period's aesthetics, or be frustrated either because modifications do not conform to accepted literary or theatrical conventions (setting aside the quality of performances themselves). Though many nineteenth-century critics eventually accepted the *refundición* as a theatrical fact of life required, in the absence of sustained quality performances of original texts, to revive what they saw as a glorious past, others believed that the highest tribute to the Golden Age be reserved for the great dramatists as represented by *comedias* in their "original" form. Frustration and acceptance coexist because both reactions depend upon the degree of openness of each receiver's horizon. Georgia Warnke explains that texts brought forth from the past belong to the tradition from which they deviate, and their "shock quality . . . is contingent upon the traditional expectations [they] obstruct. This art is . . . part of the tradition since it depends upon the assumptions of the tradition for its effect."[58] Though an art form may first meet with hostility for having broken with tradition, once elements of cultural inheritance are discovered and become more familiar—that is, when they cease being innovative and become part of a canon—the new generation is more receptive as it recognizes the elements that compose it. Without being aware of the process, silently, surreptitiously, those elements are incorporated into the subconscious as cultural remembrance; Warnke concludes that "[t]he text that is handed down to us is a fusion of previous opinions about it, a harmony of voices . . . to which we add our own."[59]

As a culturally translated text, then, a reworked *comedia* fuses the horizons within which it exists while attempting to be faithful to two moments in literary history. Yet this double fidelity produces a view of the *refundición* as an art form which is criticized by some for the excesses it exhibits as a *comedia* and by others for not being faithful to its moment of original creation regardless of the adjustments required to make it acceptable to the aesthetics of the period in which its altered form appears. The polemic surrounding the *refundición* arises from its very act of creation. A number of theatre critics, writing throughout the nineteenth century, had rehabilitated Spain's past and believed it unwise to tamper with original texts. As Zeda (pseudonym of Francisco Fernández Villegas) wrote in *El Imparcial* of 12 March 1895:

> Muy laudable es el propósito de la empresa del Español de rendir culto a las glorias de nuestra literatura....
>
> Tampoco estaría demás que... se representasen las obras clásicas tales y como las escribieron sus autores. Por regla general, los arreglos que de las comedias del siglo XVII se han hecho tienen mucho de profanación. Solís... no fue siempre muy escrupuloso en sus adaptaciones; Calixto Boldún cometió verdaderos sacrilegios, y otros escritores de grandísimo mérito literario atendieron más a satisfacer gustos momentáneos del público que a respetar las producciones de los poetas del siglo de oro.
>
> Por talento que tenga un arreglador me parece el colmo de la osadía enmendar la plana a Tirso, a Calderón, Lope o Moreto.... Nadie las mueva... y caso de moverlas muévaselas con todo género de respetos y con todo el estudio que tan delicado trabajo requiere.

> [The Teatro Español's plan to honor the glories of our literature is a laudable proposal....
>
> Nor would it be too much to ask that... the classic works be performed exactly as their authors wrote them. As a general rule, the arrangements that have been made of seventeenth-century *comedias* reveal extensive desecration. Solís was not always scrupulous in his adaptations; Calixto Boldún committed true sacrilege, and other writers of considerable literary merit looked more to satisfying the public's momentary pleasures than to respecting the output of Golden Age poets.
>
> No matter how much talent a reworker may have, for me it is the height of audacity to criticize Tirso, Calderón or Moreto.... Let no one touch them... and if it be necessary to emend them, let it be done with all due respect and with the studiousness required of such delicate work.] (1)[60]

When reviewers of these recast plays find a *refundición* to their liking, they praise the felicitous expression of Lope, Tirso, or Calderón, and comment on the ability of the *refundidor* in question to mesh his "original" verses and structure with those of the seventeenth-century text. Their comments have been conditioned by earlier approaches to and remarks about the *refundición*. In the previously cited 16 June

1811 *La Gaceta de Madrid* review of *Sancho Ortiz de las Roelas*, the reviewer, "J. Ab.," perceives that a recast *comedia* should contain

> asuntos que ... pareciesen dignos de ser manejados con el decoro y arte que el teatro pide, y presentarlos de nuevo, conservando aquellos pensamientos y trozos del autor antiguo, que por su energía, hermosura, propiedad y otras prendas de tal naturaleza pudiesen acomodarse en la moderna composición; pero contra esto hai una objeción de gravísimo peso, y sin réplica alguna, y es que semejante tarea supone el que la emprende buen gusto, sanos principios y mucho pulso, y por consiguiente era imposible que los refundidores de que voi hablando intentasen acometerla.
>
> [subjects that appear worthy of being utilized with the decorum and art that the theatre requires, and presenting them anew, keeping those thoughts and passages of the original author that, because of their energy, beauty, propriety and other qualities of such a nature than can be accommodated in a modern composition; but against this there is a weighty objection, and without possible reply, and it is that such a task supposes in the one who carries it out, good taste, healthy principles and much prudence, and therefore it was difficult for many reworkers to take on the task.] (683)

Earlier, a 1786 issue of *El Censor* had asserted that "es imposible de toda imposibilidad que agraden las comedias arregladas" [it is beyond all possibility that an arranged *comedia* will please] ("Discurso LXXIX" 214). Even Calderón, whose "vasta erudición" [vast erudition] earned the grudging respect of *comedia* detractors, suffered at the hands of an enemy who removed Spain's glories from his plays "substituyendo en su lugar un miserable pedantismo, é introduciendo en ellos infinitísimos errores muy groseros y ridículos" [substituting in their place a pitiful pedantry, and introducing into them an infinite number of vulgar and ridiculous errors] (214). Among the pre-Romantic playwrights, conflicting views regarding Golden Age dramatists abound, yet the method of rectifying their lack of respect for "la razón" [reason] and "las reglas" [the rules] is similar. In the prologue to his *refundición* of Lope's *El anzuelo de Fenisa* [Fenisa's hook] (published in 1803), Cándido María Trigueros explains that "la venerable antigüedad que nos hace mirar con un respeto algo supersticioso aquellas obras cuya cierta bondad consta muchos siglos hace" [the venerable antiquity that makes us look with somewhat superstitious respect at those works whose goodness has been known for many centuries] must yield to a cool, dispassionate study of Lope's play.[61] Trigueros concludes his prologue with a statement both respectful of Lope and aware of the pitfalls awaiting a *refundidor*: "La facilidad con que he podido reducir esta comedia, me ha convencido de la sólida bondad de la invención de Lope: y no será culpa suya si yo no lo he desempeñado bien" [The ease with which I have been able to abridge his play has convinced me of the solid quality of Lope's creativity; and it will not be his fault if I have not carried out my task well] (n.p.). If reduction is viewed as a form of cultural translation, as we may intimate from Steiner, then Trigueros has acted in good faith according to the precepts of his time.

Other *refundidores* are more blatant in condemning the Golden Age dramatists. In 1826 José Fernández Guerra reworked Moreto's *Yo por vos y vos por otro* [I'm for you and you're for another] retitling it *Ir contra el viento* [Going against the grain]. In his prologue he attempts to be solicitous of the intelligent reader and instructive to the less learned: "Ha de permitírseme que, para ahorrar a los inteligentes el minuzioso de hazer la comparazión debida, i para ayudar a los menos doctos a que formen su juizio, toque aquí lijeramente los puntos de contacto que he tenido con el autor." [I am to be permitted, in order to save the intelligent reader the minutiae of making the necessary comparisons, and to help the less learned to form their judgment, to touch upon lightly the points of contact that I have had with the author].[62] Fernández Guerra's attitude is typical of the early nineteenth century: a mixture of humility before the reader (and not spectator; he refers to a "simple y rápida lectura" [a simple and quick reading] as well as to "lectores" [readers]) and disdain for the less instructed writer. Many reworkers preceding him are "destituidos de instruszion y de buen gusto" [completely lacking in instruction and good taste] and therefore let themselves be carried away by "una culpable indolenzia" [a blameworthy indolence] (n.p.). As for Moreto, Fernández Guerra cannot find the words of praise that Trigueros mustered for Lope; rather, Moreto "manchaba i oscurezia sus mismas bellezas" [stained and darkened his own beauties] (n.p.). Furthermore, Moreto as a writer exhibits the weaknesses seen to be characteristic of his time: "Mas como ni la filosofía, ni el buen gusto, ni el conozimiento de las reglas reinaban en aquel siglo, Moreto no prepara el desenlaze, no da caracteres a los personajes, ni trazó una marcha natural i verosímil" [But since neither philosophy, nor good taste, nor knowledge of the rules reigned in that century, Moreto does not prepare the denouement, he does not give personality to his characters, nor does he lay out a natural and likely course of events] (n.p.). The rapid conclusion, too, with which Moreto's *comedia* ends, like so may Golden Age plays, is a "defecto clásico contra la razón y contra el arte" [classical defect against reason and art] (n.p.). Fernández Guerra concludes his diatribe with what has become the enlightenment dramatist's battle cry: "i podrá ser que estos mis ensayos animen a los intelijentes a trabajar con más felizidad en este importante ramo de la literatura española" [and it may be that these essays of mine encourage the intelligent writers to work with greater felicity in this important branch of Spanish literature] (n.p.). He strives, like any good translator, for the essence of his "time-frame," fulfilling Frederic Will's dictum concerning successful translation: "Translating well, like all outreaching knowing, feels good, feeds back into itself confirmingly, but must serve as its own authentication."[63]

Three years after publication of *Ir contra el viento*, Fernández Guerra undertook the recasting of Calderón's *La dama duende*.[64] The prologue, written by Antonio de Miguel, is kinder to the original playwright because of the higher esteem enjoyed by Calderón, viewed as "fecundo i elegante" [fertile and elegant] (n.p.). The recaster is all the more kindly disposed toward this particular *comedia* because, as he sees it, its purpose was to dispel popular belief in "duendes, fantasmas, trasgos, etc." [spirits, ghosts, goblins, etc.] (n.p.) that was held so dearly by the poorly educated segment of the public. Regardless of Calderón's noble intentions, which could have placed his play "en la primera línea de nuestras mejores comedias" [in the first line of our best *comedias*] (n.p.), the eighteenth-century reception of it prohibited outright acceptance. *La dama duende* "se encontraba como eclisado por los defectos propios de la época en que se escribió, i su marcha era tan irregular como la de la mayor parte de las otras obras de aquel injenio" [was eclipsed by the defects of the period in which it was written, and its pace was as irregular as that of the greater part of that brilliant writer's other works] (n.p.). The recaster must follow the guidelines for a proper and decent accordance to good taste: "El desenbarazarla de estos borrones, i presentarla a los ojos del público adornada con todas sus bellezas, era enpresa digna de la ilustrazion i del patriotismo" [Doing away with these smudges, and presenting it to the public adorned with all of its beauties, was an undertaking worthy of the Enlightenment as well as of patriotism] (n.p.). The resulting play has become "regularísima" [quite regular] through strict observation of the three unities and the elimination of unnecessary characters; the final product is a paean to enlightenment and reason: "La eleganzia, la pureza i la naturalidad han suzedido en el estilo a la hinchazón, a la oscuridad i al culteranismo." [Elegance, purity and naturalness in style have replaced swelling, darkness and affectations] (n.p.). Once again "reason" imposes the artificial objectivity with which, it was believed, any work of art must be seen, with which any cultural translation ought to be carried out: "Será mui difízil . . . encontrar el más lijero defecto, si se observa con la fría inparzialidad de la justizia" [It will be very difficult to find the slightest defect if one observes with the cold impartiality of justice] (n.p.).

If "enlightened" aesthetics informed the early years of the nineteenth century, the later decades showed greater tolerance toward the original *comedias* both as literary artifacts and representable theatrical pieces. Reviewers began to judge a *refundición* not on its corrective function, but according to its quality as a discrete work of art. Greater respect for the Golden Age playwrights becomes evident as a later generation learns to appreciate its inherited culture legacy. The condition necessary to foster the rise of the *refundición* is a historicized past, and building bridges to that past requires both honoring it and breaking the foreign-influenced tradition. David Quint analyzes this process, though with respect to the Renaissance and its relation and indebtedness to antiquity:

> To assert the value of individual divergence from a canonic tradition . . . became possible only when that tradition was historicized and ceased to function—on account of its priority—as an absolute standard. The tradition's historicity is recognized in its imitability.[65]

The quest for originality is both a literary and psychological process, and the Golden Age playwrights, from their distant and distanced past, provided the raw material to imitate. The general success of the *refundición* stems, too, from the writers' and public's awareness of the legacy of the Golden Age. The continued production of *comedias* and *refundiciones* reveals the writers' success in transferring and translating cultural identity.

The criticism leveled against *refundidores* speaks as well to the disastrous state of affairs of the nineteenth-century Madrid stage. The precarious economic and political situation of the theatre, which David Gies, Gregorio Martín, Michael Schinasi, and others continue to elucidate, the several attempts at organizational reform, and the desire and need to upgrade the quality of acting also contribute to the battle royal. However, the apologists for the *comedia* and the *refundición* were highly visible.[66] Writing in the newspaper *La España* on 18 November 1855, Aureliano Fernández-Guerra y Orbe (who writes under the alias Pipi) becomes an apologist as well as a theorist for the *refundición* of the *comedia*. He begins by comparing the ancients and the moderns: "Menos escrupulosos que los modernos, allí donde los antiguos encontraban algo que mejorar o variar galanamente, hacíanlo suyo al punto, no atendiendo sino a la perfección y mayor lustre de las obras de ingenio" [Less scrupulous than modern writers, the ancients, where they found something to improve or vary elegantly, made it their own immediately, attending only to the perfection and greater distinction of creative works of art] (1). Fernández-Guerra y Orbe sees the task as one of "corregir la plana al primer inventor y completar su obra . . . puesto que no interesa tanto al público el autor de aquella como que sea modelo de perfección y hechizo" [surpassing the first creator and completing his work . . . since the public's interest resides less in the original author than in its being a model of perfection and charm] (1). The reviewer is cognizant of the ritual aspect of theatre. The magus creates and then relegates to his high priests the task of modeling/reshaping that material into forms recognizable and acceptable to future generations. As the operation affects the Golden Age theatre directly, the reviewer comments both on the changing tastes of the public (their horizons) and on the idea of the source: "Como las costumbres hubiesen cambiado juntamente con el gusto del público, fue preciso aderezar a la moderna la comedia antigua, inagotable y eterno manantial de contentamiento" [As customs had changed together with public taste, it was necessary to adorn in modern dress the old *comedia*, inexhaustible and eternal spring of contentment] (1). In the task of completion set before the reworker, "aderezar" implies a kind of ritualistic preparation[67]; artistic, though not necessarily commercial, success depends upon integration of the new material as well as the degree of "newness" or even originality. Imitation here is not the mimesis of old but, in the definition of Hans-Georg Gadamer, "a transformation that does not simply present again something that is already there. It is a kind of transformed reality in which the transformation points back to what has been transformed in and through it. It is a transformed reality because it brings before us intensified possibilities never seen before."[68]

The reworkers themselves were not in the least abashed in their task, as the quantity of *refundiciones* attests. These writers might have considered their literary operations much as Ben Jonson saw the glorification of Latin or Italian literature: "Nor think it theft, if the rich spoyles so torne / From conquered Authors, be as Trophies worne."[69] Many of them may have been content to be, as Roger Sale states with regard to Thomas Carew's imitations of Ben Jonson, "an excellent minor poet." Others could find contentment in walking "in tracks already trod by another."[70] Such is the appraisal concerning Juan Eugenio Hartzenbusch made in one of the several *Revista de Teatros* of the mid nineteenth century. In the 14 September 1844 issue, announcing the imminent appearance of Hartzenbusch's *El Cid Campeador*, the reviewer notes that the play will be the finest he ever penned: "Creemos muy probable el que así sea porque donde más ha lucido el genio de este poeta ha sido en los asuntos tratados anteriormente por otros escritores" [We believe it likely to be so because where this poet's genius has shone brightest has been in themes treated previously by other writers] (2).

In another review published in *La España* on 14 October 1855, Fernández-Guerra y Orbe verbalizes an appreciation of the *comedia*'s endurance and source of inspiration in a time when originality seems to be at a low ebb:

> En cuaresma de novedades, nos sentamos al opíparo banquete de Moratín, Lope, Tirso, Alarcón, Rojas, Calderón y Moreto. Pero a falta de tortas, rebueno es pan candeal . . . y quien te da lo más que podías desear nada te debe.
>
> [Given the lack of novelty, we sit at the sumputuous banquet of Moratín, Lope, Tirso, Alarcón, Rojas, Calderón and Moreto. But even without cake, white bread is just fine, . . . and anyone who gives you your heart's desire owes you nothing.] (1)[71]

The sumptuous banquet of the Golden Age *comedia* has delights for every need: to "chase away the blues" ("divertir melancolías") the soul of Lope de Vega is ever at the ready; in Juan Ruiz de Alarcón can be found "regalada doctrina" [delightful doctrine]; Tirso emanates spiritual joy ("alborozo del espíritu"); but what reveals the heart of this particular review, and which summarizes the qualities inherent in the Spanish spirit, is the following encomium:

> Pero si buscáis la gala, el tropel y el boato, el honor convertido en nacionalidad . . . , si os agrada una acción llena de alegría o de tristeza, que perturbe y alborote el ánimo, ya por espanto, ya por conmiseración, ya por lo imprevisto y apurado de los lances y el contraste de peregrinos caracteres, acudid al gran don Pedro Calderón de la Barca.
>
> [But if you are looking for grace, the mad rush, pomp, honor become nationality . . . , if what pleases you is an action filled with happiness or sadness, that disturbs and stirs up the soul through fear, through commiseration, through unforeseen and difficult incidents and the contrast of unique characters, turn to the great don Pedro Calderón de la Barca.] (1)

The greater part of the review is dedicated to praising the *comedia* whose representatives are, in the critic's words, "las más hermosas flores del antiguo Parnaso español" [the most beautiful flowers of the old Spanish Parnassus] (1). The reviewer's favorable disposition toward the previous evening's performance of *Casa con dos puertas* is to be expected; he qualifies it as excellent because

> entre los de capa y espada [es] el mejor de Calderón; ameno, regocijadísimo, de efecto sin igual en las tablas, y de estudio profundo para los que aspiren a hacer en dramática verdaderos adelantamientos.
>
> [(It is) the best of Calderón's cape-and-sword plays; pleasing, eminently joyful, of unmatched effectiveness on stage, and ideal for serious study for those who aspire truly to further a career in drama.] (1)

The title of the performed play, too, is especially appropriate for a study of the *refundición*: *comedias* by Lope, Tirso, Calderón, and others enter through one door that opens the passageway between their Golden Age and a new age, and exit through another, either with their original style intact, or perhaps costumed in a style most fitting the artistic conceptions of a modern-day *refundidor*.[72]

Reinforcing Fernández-Guerra y Orbe's fundamental viewpoint but in a more tempered manner is the following anonymous review of Tirso's *Amar por señas* reworked by Narciso Serra:

> [R]econocida la necesidad de refundir, como único medio de dar a conocer en la escena ciertas obras antiguas, muy apreciables, pero de condiciones estrañas al gusto del público actual, que pueden modificarse o suprimirse, es preciso dejar escrúpulos a un lado y desentenderse del respeto; que las obras originales ahí quedan, como han llegado hasta nosotros, por estudio, admiración y recreo de los amantes de nuestra antigua literatura dramática.
>
> [Recognizing the necessity of recasting as the only way of introducing on stage certain older and worthy plays—that can be modified or omitted—foreign to the taste of today's public, we must leave our scruples aside and forget about respect; for the original works remain, as they have come down to us, for study, admiration and amusement for the lovers of our old dramatic literature.] (1)

The reviewer, writing as well in *La España* of 29 December 1855 (the same newspaper in which Fernández-Guerra y Orbe published his reviews), expresses the grudging acceptance, common to many literary commentators, of the *refundición*. He and others recognize that the only way to maintain the cultural inheritance of the *comedia* is to accept it regardless of the form it takes and to view it, in the worst of cases, as a necessary evil (consider the remarks concerning López de Ayala's *refundición* of *El alcalde de Zalamea*, discussed in chapter 4). Still, there is a tendency not to separate within the review the contributions of the *refundidor* from those of the original text's author (in this case, Tirso); the play is characterized by "ligereza y gracia del diálogo" [lightness and grace of the dialogue] (1), but never clarified is the extent of Serra's changes in a recast that retains more than half of the original dialogue. The review both praises Serra for having brought to the stage a long-absent play, and criticizes him for failing to mention the recaster's hand in the production; the result is a privileging of the original text (not surprising given the reviewer's limited tolerance of the *refundición*). The principle of "desentenderse del respeto," however, does stand out as the necessary vehicle for bringing the *comedia* back to the Spanish stage.

* * *

By the end of the nineteenth century, attitudes had come full circle. The *comedia* had found its niche, and respect among reviewers was often a bedrock upon which to build. If the neoclassicists of the late eighteenth and early nineteenth centuries felt the need to undercut the *comedia* to enlighten their period, later writers found in the *comedia* a "touchstone of meaning" to give substance to their own period. The negative as well as positive reception of both the *comedia* and the *refundición* in the nineteenth century, then, obeys the same bridge-building process we in the late twentieth century bring to faithful as well as adapted and reworked *comedia* performances. As Georgia Warnke points out, "We understand [a work of art's] truth . . . from our point of view,"[73] not from any neutral position, not from any strict objectivity. Our experiences as readers or, more particularly, as spectators, together with our circumstances, are what direct our focus to a work of art. Just as Monsieur Jordain of Molière's *Le Bougeois gentilhomme (The middle-class gentleman)*, with all his desires for "culture," is enthralled to learn that he partakes of a long-standing convention of speaking in prose, we, too, are rooted in an interpretive tradition, in how a play or performance has been produced in the past. We are conditioned by what we read; for the theatre critic, a history of theatre or a specific text's performance tradition predetermines, for better or worse, the review of the performance; for the audience, regardless of historical period, past experience in attendance and present expectations often elicited by a performance itself condition those spectators, predispose them toward a specific reception of the text.[74]

2
King Sancho Revisited:
La estrella de Sevilla and
Sancho Ortiz de las Roelas

La estrella de Sevilla has found itself at the center of attention almost continuously since its composition in the 1620s. The bibliography it has generated testifies to its importance, not in the least because of the unresolved question of attribution.[1] This *comedia*'s popularity is proven in its afterlife, its subsequent performances, its resurrection either in its Golden Age form or as a recast. In this last regard, *La estrella de Sevilla* had found its way back in the first years of the nineteenth century and again near the half-way point of the same century after the peak of Spanish Romanticism and once the *refundición* had become well-entrenched in theatrical life.[2]

Cándido María Trigueros and Juan Eugenio Hartzenbusch, both veteran playwrights as well as seasoned *refundidores*, saw in *La estrella de Sevilla* compelling dramatic material that transcends its time of composition. Trigueros recast the play with the new title *Sancho Ortiz de las Roelas*; this version was published in 1800, two years after the playwright's death, and enjoyed performances throughout the nineteenth century.[3] Hartzenbusch reworked Trigueros's play and saw it staged in 1852 to the great expectations of its contemporary reviewers.[4] Critics have elucidated various aspects of the *refundición* process which *La estrella de Sevilla* has undergone. Adams is the first to discuss the *refundición*'s development, though he relies on the fragments originally composed by Hartzenbusch based on the Golden Age play (attributed to Lope); Cook dedicates several pages to the reception of Trigueros's play by the press and the conflicting views it elicited; Andioc limits his comments to the political and social undertones of Trigueros's versions; Aguilar Piñal, in the most all-inclusive study to date on Cándido María Trigueros, discusses the play's reception and Trigueros's introduction to his *refundición*; finally, Caldera outlines both versions in greater detail within an approximation to the *refundición*.[5]

The choice to recast *La estrella de Sevilla* may have been dictated by its popularity and, because of its historical attribution to Lope, by Trigueros's admiration for Lope; as for Hartzenbusch, his love for the *comedia* and admiration of Lope directed his attention to the play. For Trigueros, in particular, his recast of this as well as of several other plays by Lope de Vega allowed him to put into practice his notions of theatrical reform.[6] Trigueros lays out his philosophy of recasting Golden Age plays in the prologue to *Sancho Ortiz de las Roelas*. He admires Lope's "inagotable ingenio" [inexhaustible genius] and praises *La estrella de Sevilla* for its "acción bien escogida, y bien manejada" [well-chosen and well-managed action] that lends the play "un no sé qué de familiaridad" [an indescribable familiarity] (4). Behind this appreciation and critique of Lope's *comedia* is the eighteenth-century writer's instruction in Aristotelian poetics. Even though the recaster states, "Yo no he tenido que hacer mutación alguna en la acción ni en su progreso" [I have not had to make any changes either in the action or in its development] (4) because the necessary elements are present in Lope's original, he does believe it necessary to make "más sensibles estas unidades" [these unities more noticeable] (5). Additionally, Trigueros interpolates new verses and scenes in order to avoid the recast play from being too short, particularly after unnecessary scenes have been removed. In other words, Trigueros has taken a play whose "mérito principal" [principal merit] belongs to the original author and retouches the verses, scenes, and development of dramatic action. Though his modesty forces him (a "corrector") to admit as his own any defects the play now may have, his own claim to a limited role as a recaster of an already good play is somewhat transparent. The tone of the introduction does not allow a reader to accept completely Trigueros's disclaimers and one wishes he had been more open in admitting the fullness of the task he is carrying out.

A comparison of the three plays, as that carried out by Caldera, reveals, beyond the most obvious elimination of the original version's act 1, important changes in language, structure, and focus. Caldera notes that from the beginning Trigueros attempts "di ridurre l'odiosità che necessariamente si addensa sulla figura del re" [to reduce the hatefulness that necessarily gathers around the figure of the king], and cites four lines Trigueros cut from the original's act 1: Viva yo y diga Castilla / lo que quisiere decir / que rey ciego he de seguir / a la Estrella de Sevilla" [Let me live and let Castile say what it will, that I, a blind king, will follow the Star of Seville]. Caldera adds that Trigueros's contributions underline the struggle within the king "fra la passione travolgente e una coscienza che continuamente insorge a contrastare la tentazione" [between overwhelming passion and a conscience that continually rises to face temptation].[7] The supporting evidence from the first *refundición* includes the king's attempt to conquer his passion, his rejection of violence against Bustos's honor and his desire to avoid scandal ("Ay, Don Arias, ser no quiero / escándalo a las edades" [1. 1] [Oh, Don Arias, I do not wish to be remembered as a scandalous king]). Caldera shows, too, how Trigueros learned from one of his contemporaries: "Inoltre Trigueros, forse ammaestrato dall'esempio di García de la Huerta, riesce a scaricare sul consigliere Don Arias—che nell'originale aveva scarso rilievo—la maggior parte della colpa" [Furthermore Trigueros, perhaps having learned from García de la Huerta, dares to shift the blame onto the advisor Don Arias, who in the original had much less visibility].[8] This will be taken up later in a discussion of the final scene of the various versions.

Caldera's introduction leaves room for elaboration. Important differences, for example, become clear by studying the opening speeches of each *refundición*:

Trigueros

Rey. Sé que es vana mi porfía:
   mientras que Bustos Tabera
   guarde a su hermana, o no muera,
   Estrella no será mía.
   Oh! si pudiera vencer,
   Don Arias, esta pasión
   que avasalla mi razón!
   Yo no sé ya qué he de hacer.
Arias. ¡Qué, Señor! romper por todo.
   Antes que todo sois vos,
   y es cosa dura, por Dios,
   que padezcáis de tal modo.

Hartzenbusch

Rey. Sé que sin razón me agravio;
   pero ese desdén prolijo
   no lo mereciera el hijo
   de Alfonso décimo el Sabio.
   Si es ella de buen linaje,
   casi divorciado estoy:
   . . . .
   Yo adoro a Estrella y en vano
   es cuanto mi amor emprende,
   según de mí la defiende
   Bustos Tabera su hermano.
   Ni vencerme ni vencer
   a nadie sé en este lance:
   dime lo que se te alcance,
   don Arias, di qué he de hacer.
Arias. Romper debierais por todo;
   antes que todo sois vos,
   y es cosa dura, por Dios,
   que padezcáis de tal modo.

Trigueros	Hartzenbusch
[*King.* I know that my persistence is in vain; as long as Bustos Tabera keeps watch over his sister or remains alive, Estrella will not be mine. Oh Don Arias, if I could conquer this passion that overcomes my reason. I no longer know what to do. *Arias.* What, my Lord? Break all resistance. Above all you are who you are, and for the love of God it is hard for you to suffer in such a way.] (1.1)	[*King.* I know that I take offence wrongly; but the son of Alfonso X the Wise does not deserve such long-suffering disdain. If she is of noble lineage, I am king, young and loving; I am nearly divorced. To love her is not an insult.... I adore Estrella, and everything my love undertakes is in vain given how her brother Bustos Tabera keeps her from me. I cannot overcome myself nor anyone else in this case; tell me what you advise, Don Arias, tell me what I must do. *Arias.* You should break all resistance. Above all you are who you are, and for the love of God it is hard for you to suffer in such a way.] (1.1)

Trigueros enters into the heart of the plot without the elaboration found in the original. The king's illicit passion overwhelms his reason, but even as the king struggles to overcome the man,[9] he is willing to bend the laws and conventions of the king/subject relationship to fulfill his desire. The conflict of passion against reason in Trigueros's epoch necessarily predetermines the resolution of the king's internal struggle. Trigueros immediately puts the drama into motion as straightforwardly as possible. Arias is quick to offer advice, anxious to be solicitous of his monarch, and eager to find the easiest solution without regard for the consequences. The play on this level is a story of the *privado* who lends questionable advice, and who is punished by the king for it. Arias has evolved from a low-profile character in the original to the advisor who, having fostered the rule of passion, will lose royal protection and will find himself exiled from a kingdom where reason must prevail.

Hartzenbusch, in his opening scene, gives the spectator some historical perspective by recalling the monarch's lineage. This corresponds in part to the nineteenth century's recuperation of Spain's medieval and Golden Age heritage—both historical and literary— and also in part trades on the name of the writer/educator King Alfonso X. More important, though, is Hartzenbusch's justification for King Sancho's pursuit of Estrella: she, too, is of noble blood, worthy of the young and amorous king, and he "casi divorciado." The offense to his ego, however, renders him helpless and, where Trigueros's king states his inability to act and indirectly requests advice from Arias, Hartzenbusch's king puts himself at the mercy of his advisor. The most important difference between the two versions of 1.1 is the king's attitude toward his desire. Hartzenbusch's King Sancho expresses interest only in "vencerme," but he is not convincing; rather he sounds more like the love-sick Calixto eager to seek any recourse to satisfy his wants. Nor is he as abrupt as his immediate literary predecessor in calling for Bustos Tabera's death. Trigueros encapsulates in the king's first speech the entire play; Hartzenbusch offers primarily the impetus to begin forcefully the dramatic action.

Since the original's act 1 has been eliminated in both versions and much of the information contained in that first act needs to be presented (the king's love for Estrella, his attempts to woo her, his use of the slave to gain entry into Estrella's and Bustos's house, the disastrous results of that action), both recasters reduce those incidents to exchanges of information between the king and his advisor. Hartzenbusch follows Trigueros almost word-for-word in the recapitulation: both kings attempt to flatter Bustos to reach his sister, for example. In the original, the king asks Bustos to recommend a successor to a recently deceased general, a task Bustos feels unworthy of yet one he fulfills. Trigueros reduces the verbal exchange to four verses spoken by the king:

> Puestos le di apetecidos,
> que él modesto no admitió,
> y con mi gusto los dio
> donde estaban merecidos.

[I conferred on him coveted appointments that he, modestly, did not accept, and with my blessing he handed them out to the most deserving.]
(1.1)

Bustos is pictured as the wise, faithful servant, a contrast to the sycophant Arias. Hartzenbusch's Bustos is much feistier and makes his independence known from the beginning. The king laments, almost helplessly: "y a emplearlos me obligó / en hombres aborrecidos" [he obliged me to confer them on hated men] (1.1). The fact that Bustos could oblige the king in such a way speaks to the king's awe of his subject (an attitude that anticipates the denouement) as well as to a concept of royal power that differs from the absolutist monarch Trigueros brings forth as a reaffirmation of support for the Spanish king.[10]

A second important discrepancy between the two *refundiciones* is the episode of the king's bribing the slave to gain illicit entry into Estrella's house. Trigueros indicates clearly where blame should lie:

> No alcanzando yo otro medio,
> . . . . .
> me olvidé de mi grandeza,
> Don Arias, al fin me dexo,
> llevado de tu consejo,
> correr hacia la baxeza.
> Seducir logré la esclava,
> que anoche entrada me dio . . .

[Not finding other means . . . I lost sight of my greatness; finally, Don Arias carried along by your advice, I have allowed myself to run headlong toward base action. I succeeded in seducing the slave who allowed me to enter last night . . .] (1.1)

The king has yielded his reason to his advisor and only in the light of day can he realize his lowly course of action. Hartzenbusch, on the other hand, makes it explicit that the king has acted of his own volition:

> No alcanzando yo otro medio,
> . . . . .
> diestro una esclava les gano,
> me avisa anoche, voy, entro,
> y al buscar a Estrella, encuentro
> con Bustos, con espada en mano.

[Not finding other means . . . I deftly win over one of their slaves, last night she sends for me, I go, I enter, and as I search for Estrella, I run into Bustos with sword in hand.] (1.1)

Trigueros concentrates on the mental process of King Sancho's surrender and near resignation to fate whereas Hartzenbusch recapitulates his movements, focusing on the action presented through verbs in the present tense. Both versions coincide in great part on the encounter between the king and Bustos: the king is recognized, though it is not stated explicitly, and he returns to the *alcázar*. The original, of course, dedicates a scene to Bustos's interrogation of his sister and of the servant, whom he hangs at the entrance to the *alcázar*. However, neither Trigueros nor Hartzenbusch include such a scene; rather, the slave's death is reduced to two lines: "la desventurada esclava / con tres puñaladas muerta" [the unfortunate slave stabbed to death] (1.1). Trigueros's concern for decorum impedes the representation of such a grotesque scene; in Hartzenbusch's case it may be a matter of simply following his immediate source closely.

The manipulation of a blameless Tabera is reprehensible to the kings in both plays, yet neither monarch is able to find peace without Estrella. The advice of Don Arias, then, gains the upper hand. Trigueros's king continues to question the suggested course of action; the advisor is cast all the more as a devil who tempts the weak of flesh:

> *Sancho.* Ay, Don Arias, ser no quiero
> escándalo a las edades.
> *Arias.* Y si con sus crueldades
> sigue el Tabera altanero,
> sin que vos rigor mostréis
> que proseguir más le estorbe,
> ¿no dará escándalo al orbe
> que vos no se lo estorbéis?
> A vuestra razón lo dexo,
> mil veces lo dixe ya,
> quizá un día os pesará
> de no seguir mi consejo.
> *Rey.* Duro consejo!.. Ay, Estrella,
> temo tu seguridad.
> Veo que es una maldad,
> Don Arias, mas voy a hacella.

[*King.* Oh, Don Arias, I do not wish to be remembered as a scandalous king.
Arias. And if the proud Tabera remains cruel without your revealing a strong hand to prevent him from being so, will it not scandalize the world that you do not stop him. I leave it to your reason; I have told you a thousand times that one day you may be sorry not to have followed my advice.
King. Harsh advice!... Ah, Estrella, I fear for your safety. I see that it is evil, Don Arias, but I shall follow it.] (1.1)

Sancho is aware of his role as king and as the moral guide of his country, yet his will weakens by the moment. Arias bombards him with rationalizations, and reiterates and twists the king's very word, "escándalo," to describe different effects to related actions. Sancho refers to his forceful seduction of Estrella and the public outcry it will provoke; Arias plays on Sancho's royal stature to signal the affront committed against the king's honor by allowing to pass unpunished Tabera's defense of his own honor, interpreted by Arias as a haughty challenge to the king. Arias further manipulates King Sancho by citing another key word, "razón" [reason], suggesting that while Sancho should rely on reason, that path ironically will lead only to greater emotional distress. Arias has manipulated the discourse so that his is the only viable solution.

Hartzenbusch follows a very different tack:

> *Arias.* Hoy le debéis contener,
> para libraros de sustos:
> ved que es muy capaz el Bustos
> de cuanto podáis temer.
> A vuestra razón lo dejo,
> y dicho lo tengo ya:
> quizá un día os pesará
> de no seguir mi consejo.
> *Rey.* ¡Duro consejo! ¡Ay, Estrella!
> quiero tu seguridad . . .
> Trazamos una maldad:
> pensemos antes de hacella.

[*Arias.* You must contain him today to free yourself from surprises: know that Bustos is quite capable of everything you fear. I leave it to your reason and I have already told you what I think: you may be sorry not to have followed my advice.
King. Harsh advice! Ay, Estrella, I want you to be safe . . . ! We must plan an evil deed; let us think carefully before carrying it out. (1.1)

Here no word of wounded honor or of scandal is spoken; the affair is a matter of political expediency for the king, who must limit the damage his actions create. King Sancho fears for Estrella's life because of her presumed role in sullying the family honor; that is the fear from which the king must free himself. Though both kings act in defense of Estrella, Hartzenbusch's makes the decision without being manipulated into a course of action he finds distasteful. Unlike Trigueros's King Sancho, Hartzenbusch's feels no moral restraints; he formulates a decision on the basis of advice rendered. A difference in *ethos* between the two *refundiciones* is clearly at work.[11]

Act 1, scene 2 in each recast version presents the king alone in soliloquy as he decides Bustos's fate. It is again important to note what Trigueros has created, and, equally important, what Hartzenbusch has cut from Trigueros:

Trigueros

Acaso está arrepentido
de su sangriento rigor,
y el zelo con que el amor
que me abrasa, ha contenido.
Mi poder y dignidad,
le harán sentir, que aunque honrado
fue su proceder osado
mediando la Magestad.

Hartzenbusch

Acaso está arrepentido
de su sangriento rigor
y el celo con que el amor
que me abrasa ha reprimido.
Mi poder y dignidad
le harán sentir que, aunque honrado,
fue su proceder osado
mediando la majestad.
Mas como me engañó! ¿Quién
no tiene su honor en más
al guardarle? ¿Quién jamás
se arrepintió de obrar bien?
O consejo! O pecho mío!
Yo arrepentirme debiera . . .
Infeliz Bustos Tabera,
tu virtud castigo, y brío.

[Perhaps he has repented of his harshness, and zeal has constrained my burning love. My power and dignity will make him feel that although he acted honorably, the means he chose were daring considering that I am King.] (1.2)

[Perhaps he has repented of his harshness, and the zeal has repressed my burning love. My power and dignity will make him feel that although he acted honorably, the means he chose were daring considering that I am King. But how he deceived me! Who does not hold his honor in high esteem when protecting it? Who ever repented of acting properly? Oh Advice! Oh my soul! I should be sorry . . . Unfortunate Bustos Tabera, I punish your virtue and your spirit.] (1.2)[12]

Trigueros's King Sancho hopes against hope that Bustos has repented his rash behavior and will come to beg forgiveness, an eventuality that undoubtedly would allow the king to manipulate Bustos and, he presumes, Estrella. But he knows all too well that Bustos rightfully has defended family honor. Yet the king remains aware that neither his discourse nor his actions are reasoned. Hartzenbusch's king continues to show himself resolute (and perhaps cold-blooded) in his efforts to remove all obstacles between him and Estrella. Though he does hope that Bustos has come to his senses, no moral wavering takes place, no second guessing his actions, no struggle between external advice ("consejo" [advice]) and internal emotion ("pecho mío" [spirit, soul]).

The first meeting between Sancho Ortiz and King Sancho in the original occurs after the king's illicit and frustrated entry into the Tabera household; he has, of course, decided to have Bustos killed for the affront committed. In the *refundiciones,* the scene in which King Sancho enlists Sancho Ortiz to be the instrument of the king's folly, often coinciding verbally with the original, unfolds after the king has told Arias of his encounter with Bustos, and after having met Bustos in the *alcázar*.[13] The king's order to kill Bustos Tabera is more of a direct command for Sancho to take the life of a man whom the king claims has offended him and thus the state. Where the original posits the command as an example of "lesa majestad," the recasts are more specific because the audience has not seen Bustos's defense of his honor, but only knows of it through the king's recapitulation to Arias: "El que contra mí, inhumano / la osada espada sacó / ¿qué merece?" [He who has inhumanly drawn his daring sword against me, what does he deserve?] (1.5). The king's word must stand unchallenged regardless of its reliability.

One other important difference concerns the manner in which Sancho Ortiz intends to comply with the king's orders. Since the two later versions continue to follow at this point the original more or less faithfully, in each the king orders Sancho to kill the marked man "descuidado" ([casually] original and Trigueros) or "En paraje retirado / habéis de lidiar" [In a removed site you must fight] (Hartzenbusch). Sancho's protestations against cowardliness lead the king in the original and in Trigueros to yield to Sancho's insistence on killing face-to-face. In Hartzenbusch, however, the king is insistent:

> *Rey.* No: dad a ese desdichado,
> sin testigos a su lado,
> la muerte que le destino.
> *Sancho.* Le mataré como honrado,
> pero no como asesino.
> *Rey.* En eso libre quedáis.

[*King.* No: kill that unfortunate soul without witnesses by his side.
Sancho. I will kill him like an honorable man, but not like an assassin.
King. That decision I leave to you.] (1.6)

In other words, Sancho is free to face the victim, as long as it is carried out in secret. Hartzenbusch here is preparing his ending, unique to the three versions, in which the king will admit to having committed the murder himself so the love between Sancho and Estrella can flourish. As the king dispatches Sancho Ortiz to his royal duty, violence is much more muted in Trigueros (and in the original) than in Hartzenbusch. The original concludes the scene with the king's words: "obrad, y callemos" [act, and let us keep silent] (1606); Trigueros has the king speak the same lines, but has Sancho, alone, repeat the message that evolved out of his meeting with the king: "obrando sabrá callar, / y callando sabrá obrar / Sancho Ortiz de las Roelas" [Sancho Ortiz de las Roelas will act in silence, and will keep silence in action] (1.6). Hartzenbusch closes his scene without any subtlety: "matad, y callemos"—followed by an (unfortunate) modification of Trigueros: "al herir sabrá callar / y callando pelear / Sancho Ortiz de las Roelas" [Sancho Ortiz de las Roelas will kill in silence and in silence will fight] (1.6; 1.7). The general "obrar" communicates the notion of fulfilling a duty with all the secrecy that that duty might imply; the play on the words "obrar" and "callar," too, with their hint and rhythm of a *refrán*, lend a depth of character to Sancho who at least in this instance faithfully recalls the Golden Age character. "Matad [kill]" however, speaks ill of the king (in a way, perhaps, that Trigueros could not do) and belies the secrecy with which his order is to be carried out. Even though Sancho and the king are alone, the king wishes to leave no doubt about the nature of his subject's duty. Sancho's reply, too, reinforces the violence inherent in the scene, for instead of playing on "obrar" and "callar," his utterances of violence match the king's "herir" and "pelear."

Following the meeting with the king, Sancho is found by his servant Clarindo, who brings him the letter from Estrella announcing that their marriage may now take place. This scene provides an excellent example of the changes in sensibility between the original and Trigueros's version, and between Trigueros and Hartzenbusch. From 1607 to 1682, Sancho's conversation with Clarindo brings together a wonderful mixture of comicality and lyricism. The scene is all the more effective, of course, for what ensues: Sancho's reading the letter from the king declaring that his victim is to be Bustos Tabera.[14]

The letter from Estrella to Sancho, and Sancho's reactions to it, are treated quite differently in the three versions; in this case I believe Caldera offers the best analysis of the passages. Caldera sees the act of recasting as a decoding process in order to make the resulting play more accessible to a new public.[15] He first discusses Trigueros's recast:

> Questo processo di decodificazione è particolarmente avvertibile nella lettera di Estrella, in cui il "venturoso plazo deseado" diviene un semplice "día deseado que esposo pueda llamarte..."[16]

[This process of decodification is particularly noticeable in Estrella's letter, in which the "happily awaited moment" becomes a simple "hoped-for day when I can call you my husband . . . "]

With regard to Hartzenbusch's text, Caldera views the same scene as a recuperation of literariness ("letterarietà") that, though not a return to the tone Lope infused, does manage to include verbal wordplay so dear to Lope ("¡Mi Estrella, mi sol, mi cielo!" [My Star, my sun, my Heaven!]). Hartzenbusch has imposed his unique style on the passage:

> La direzione, tuttavia, è generalmente quella dell'espressione calda dei sentimenti, accompagnata da riflessioni e meditazioni. Su tutto poi si distende un tono generale di incertezza . . . e un bisogno di intimità . . . che conferisce alla pagina una nuova dignità espressiva.[17]

[The direction remains that of a warm expression of sentiment, accompanied by reflection and meditation. Overall, then, a general tone of uncertainty and a need for intimacy that confers a new expressive dignity on the page, are extended throughout the text.]

Caldera, particularly with regard to Hartzenbusch, treats the nature of the changes while leaving aside the question of textual significance. It is true that Sancho's doubts—his eloquence speaks to his well-rounded character and nobility of spirit—lend the passage dignity. Yet they also augment dramatic irony with regard to Sancho's royal duty and contribute to the clandestine nature established by the king's order to Sancho. Hartzenbusch has built the tension admirably in preparation for the following scene, in which Sancho's and Estrella's world is about to crumble.

Sancho's reading the king's order and the subsequent encounter between Sancho and Bustos is the final incident of a series comprising the axis of action in the original, but only the end of the first act in both of the *refundiciones*. The original passage (1683–1764) (including the previous verses in which Sancho sets out to find Bustos and remembers to read the king's written order), reiterates three times the message, "Al que muerte habéis de dar, / es, Sancho, a Busto Tabera" [The one you are to kill, Sancho, is Busto Tabera.] The euphoria Sancho expresses in the original's exclamations ("¡Cómo el amor porfía! / ¡Quién tal Estrella vio al nacer del día!" [1685–86] [How love persists! Whoever saw such a Star at dawn!]) is rendered by Trigueros in a more narrative, and therefore more reasoned and less passionate, statement: "Sancho Ortiz, gran dicha alcanzas: /

todo es hoy felicidades, / amores, y confianzas" [Sancho Ortiz, much good fortune is yours: today everything is happiness, love and intimacy] (1.6). Hartzenbusch offers a curious difference after repeating Trigueros's first verses:

> ¿Todo? ¡Ay, envidiosa suerte!
> ¡Cómo en la mía y en todas
> el mal junto al bien se advierte!
> Bustos ordena mis bodas;
> ¡El Rey me manda una muerte!
> ¿No se pudiera expedir
> ese decreto más tarde?
> Si me paro a discurrir,
> mi brazo, vuelto cobarde,
> no va a saber combatir.

[Everything? Oh, envious luck! How is it that ill always accompanies good! Bustos arranges my wedding. The King orders me to kill! Couldn't he have issued this decree later? If I stop to think my arm will become a coward and will not know how to fight.] (1.8)

Hartzenbusch recovers, in the doubts that haunt Sancho and the awareness that something ill accompanies good fortune, more of the *siglo de oro* sentiment. His contemplative "Si me paro a discurrir" evokes the passage's intertext, Garcilaso's Soneto 1; given Hartzenbusch's knowledge and love of Golden Age literature, Garcilasan echoes should not surprise. Just like the self-questioning lyric voice of an author so influential in the sixteenth and seventeenth centuries, Sancho must soon face the real peril of earning the disdain of his beloved (though he is as yet unaware of this). Sancho's inner voice has already told him "sé que me acabo, y más he yo sentido / ver acabar conmigo mi cuidado" [I know I've reached my end, and I regret the more to see my sufferings end along with me] (7–8).[18] Thus if he thinks too deeply or postpones too long, his ability to fight will be diminished. He seems able to foretell what will befall him.

Sancho's reaction to the king's command undergoes several alterations between the original and the two later versions. The original Sancho does recognize the fleetingness of fortune ("¡Tras una suerte un azar! / Toda esta vida es jugar / una carteta imperfecta . . ." [After good luck such misfortune! All of life is playing an imperfect hand! [1695–96]), which is realized, too, by Trigueros's Sancho: "Quanto bien pensé encontrar / voló, qual si un humo fuera" [All the good fortune I hoped to find blew away like so much smoke] (1.7), and the same sentiment, with only a slight change in wording, is expressed by

Hartzenbusch's characters. In both of the recasts, however, the image of gaming and cards is eliminated. All three versions emphasize the fact that Sancho has given his word to the king. Though the *refundiciones* do not develop to the same extent the struggle between duty and love, they do reflect a shift in focus. Both mention, unlike the original, the specific loss to be suffered: "¿Y he de perder / después de tanto cuidado / a Estrella? No puede ser" [And am I to lose Estrella after having cared so much? It cannot be] (1.6; 1.8). Both restate, too, the impossibility of not fulfilling one's word to the king. However, where the original emphasizes that it is the law "que fuere primero" [that takes precedence] (1750), the recasts are more specific, perhaps to grant Sancho greater moral authority for carrying out what he believes to be a command from an unjust king: "¡La espada sacasteis vos / y al Rey quisisteis herir!" [You drew your sword and attempted to wound the King!] (1.7; 1.8).

The different act division and refocused emphasis of each *refundición* necessarily creates a new center. The Golden Age play turns on Sancho's note from the king ordering him to kill Bustos Tabera. This missive reaches him at the same time as the letter from Estrella confirming their betrothal. The juxtaposition of the two letters emphasizes the conflict between love and honor as well as the nature of writing itself (see Rivers's seminal article on speech acts and *La estrella de Sevilla*). In Trigueros's *refundición* the turning point, between acts 2 and 3, is the death of Bustos at the hands of Sancho Ortiz. This change is important because while it maintains the love/duty conflict and the reading of the two letters, it builds Estrella's character all the more. Her reactions, in a long soliloquy, reveal her not to be simply, as Caldera points out (*Il dramma* 45–48), an undervalued woman who reflects the male point of view. This aspect is highlighted even further in Hartzenbusch's *refundición*, because the axis becomes the encounter between Sancho and Estrella; she determines at that moment to carry out vengeance. It should be noted as well that both Trigueros and Hartzenbusch eliminate Sancho's flight into madness with Clarindo by his side. Indeed, many of Clarindo's scenes are greatly modified and reduced, and after a few brief appearances in Hartzenbusch, the *gracioso* disappears altogether without explanation.

If the portrayal of Sancho's *locura* is removed from the two *refundiciones*, Sancho's loyalty to the monarch even at the cost of friendship is maintained and emphasized. The original *comedia* (2260 ff.) emphasizes Sancho Ortiz's silence as to the reason for his crime as well as his mourning the broken bonds of friendship; both attitudes create the mental strain leading to Sancho's temporary insanity. Trigueros reorients this emphasis by trying to find an acceptable explanation for Sancho's crime; he eliminates Sancho's clear and forthright admission of guilt ("Sí, / y aquí a voces lo confieso . . ." [Yes, and here I will shout my confession; 2262ff.]) and draws a character for whom duty to the monarch—even improper duty—has weakened his capacity for rational action: "Arrojado, y muy cruel, / maté al amigo más fiel" [Rashly, and cruelly, I killed my most faithful friend] (2.5).[19] The key to Sancho's admission is "arrojado," an emotionally charged word that implies a loss of control over reason. Its use at this point vividly recalls the king's passion of 1.1. ("esta pasión / que avasalla mi razón" [this passion which rules my rational thought]), and sets the tone for the anguish later expressed by both Estrella and the king on separate occasions. At the end of act 2 Estrella, attempting to comprehend the tragedy unfolding before her ("¡Válgame Dios, ¡qué delirios / hinchen mi mente de sombras!" [My God, what delirium fills my mind with shadows!; 2.8]), Estrella exclaims in another questioning of her misfortune, "¿Por qué me elevó [el cielo] a la cumbre / para arrojarme al abismo?" [Why has Heaven lifted me to the top to throw me into the abyss?] (2.8). Estrella flounders because she has no control over the events that shape her life. The king, however, in a soliloquy at the end of act 3, recognizes that his "pronta pasión" [quick temper] has been the cause of so much misfortune:

> ¡Quántos daños he causado!
> ¡De esta pronta pasión mía
> quántas veces me ha pesado!
> Yo por ella me arrojé . . .
> aquella infeliz esclava
> por mi arrojo muerta fue . . .
> . . . . . .
> Mi arrojo a Bustos forzó
> a que de su honor se armara
> . . . . . .
> No fuera el riesgo inminente,
> si tuviera yo prudencia;
> con tanto arrojo indecente
> está todo en contingencia
> por no haber sido prudente . . .

[How much pain have I caused! How often I have regretted my quick temper! For her I rushed headlong . . . that unfortunate slave was killed because of my rashness . . . My rashness forced Bustos to arm himself with honor . . . The risk would not be so imminent if I were prudent; with such an indecent quick temper all my plans are in danger because I have not been prudent . . .] (3.8)

King Sancho's anagnorisis serves, too, as a mid-play moral and warning about the necessity of reason's reign over passion (the king has yet to face the *regidores* [councilmen] of Sevilla and admit his complicity). Bustos's death becomes the focal point not only for the traditional love/honor conflict experienced by Sancho but also for the eighteenth century's reason/passion dichotomy, affecting Sancho, Estrella, and the king.

Hartzenbusch dispenses with the questions of reason and passion and recaptures the determination and spirit of the original play. This is not to say that Hartzenbusch's Sancho is driven by maniacal obedience to the king; he laments the sorrow arising out of obligation at the same time that he steadfastly refuses to voice his reasons for murdering his best friend. Sancho's first sentiment is pain expressed in lines from Trigueros:

> ¿Quedan aún más desdichas
> para mí? ¡Bustos! ¡Estrella!
> Dos almas que fueron mías,
> que yo separé sangriento . . .
> (*Aparte*) ¡Ay, palabra, dura, impía!
> ¡Palabra por mi mal dada
> y para mi mal cumplida!

[Is there even more misfortune reserved for me? Bustos! Estrella! Two souls that were mine that I separated cruelly . . . (*Aside*) Oh word of honor, cold, impious! A word given to my detriment and fulfilled to my detriment!] (2.4)

Hartzenbusch eliminates Sancho's twenty-five-line speech about his loss of control ("Arrojado . . . ") and incorporates in its stead a fast-paced interrogation of Sancho by Farfán in which the murderer boldly admits his crime and keeps his word to the king:

> *Farfán.* ¿Quién le dio muerte?
> *Sancho.*   Yo fui.
> *Farfán.* ¿Sin querer?
> *Sancho.*   Con intención.
> *Farfán.* ¿Cuerpo a cuerpo, o a traición?
> *Sancho.* Si otro me lo preguntara,
> ¡vive Dios, que le matara!
> Cuerpo a cuerpo, y con razón.
> *Farfán.* ¿Con qué razón?

Sancho.   Yo la sé.
                . . . . .
Farfán.   Pero la causa, ¿cuál fue?
Sancho.   Una grave, reservada.
Farfán.   Decidla.
Sancho.   No la diré.

[Farfán.   Who killed him?
Sancho.   It was I.
Farfán.   Accidentally?
Sancho.   On purpose.
Farfán.   Face to face, or treacherously?
Sancho.   If one more person asks me the same question, I swear I will kill him! Face to face, and with cause.
Farfán.   What was the cause?
Sancho.   I know what it is. . . .
Farfán.   But what was the cause?
Sancho.   A serious, secret one.
Farfán.   Tell me.
Sancho.   I will tell no one.] (2.4)

It is not surprising for Hartzenbusch to recast this scene with a flavor of the Golden Age, and an additional refinement he adds to his *refundición* further ennobles the character of Sancho Ortiz. After Sancho's refusal to divulge the cause of his actions, the following exchange occurs between Sancho and Farfán:

Farfán.   Si Bustos no dio ocasión,
           asesino, en conclusión,
           sois, por ajena rencilla.
Sancho.   No asesinan los que son
           veinticuatros de Sevilla.

[Farfán. If Bustos gave you no cause, you therefore murdered him at the behest of another.
Sancho. Councilmen of Seville are not murderers.] (2.4)

La estrella de Sevilla uses the verbs "matar" and "dar muerte" to describe Sancho's murder of Bustos Tabera. Hartzenbusch's refinement in his employment of *asesinar* is an important one, because he conveys with it treason or conspiracy. The *Diccionario de autoridades* defines *assasinar* as "matar a alguno, quitarle la vida alevosamente por concierto ò paga" [to kill someone, to take away a life in cold blood through conspiracy or for pay], which, strictly speaking, characterizes the crime. Sancho believes his official position as a "veinticuatro" makes it impossible for him to be an assassin. His refusal to accept Farfán's description speaks to the anger he feels at having fulfilled a demand that violates his duty toward Bustos and love for Estrella. Furthermore, Sancho does not deny an underlying motive for his actions; "ajena rencilla" hints that much is to be learned from what Sancho Ortiz does not say.

The scenes in both *refundiciones* that replace the incident of Sancho's insanity are new to each version, though it is clear that Hartzenbusch modifies Trigueros's interpolations. Both scenes develop Sancho's internal dialogue in which he questions his continued silence and the king's unwillingness to come forward:

Trigueros

¡Fuerte empeño en que he de hablar!
. . . . .
Líbreme, si puede hacerlo;
y si no puede, si acaso
librarme es contra el respeto
de su decoro, salvar
su decoro es lo primero:
no importará que yo muera,
si también le sirvo en esto.
. . . . .
grande causa tener debe;
porque pensar que un excelso
Monarca, de sus ofertas
pueda olvidarse tan presto,
es idea que no puede
caber de Ortiz en el pecho.

[A heavy obligation to speak! . . . Free me, if he can do it; if not, freeing me runs counter to royal decorum, keeping his decorum is most important; it does not matter if I die if I serve him this way as well. . . . He must have sufficient cause, because to think that a lofty monarch can forget his promises so quickly is unfathomable to Ortiz.] (3.8)

Hartzenbusch

Que hable, que hable. No: vileza
fuera eso, y falta de fe:
Obrad y callemos fue
lo que me dijo Su Alteza.
. . . . .
Culpado era Bustos, reo
fue de lesa magestad;
¿cómo, pues, dificultad
para defenderme veo?
Pero ese crimen tan feo
bien pudo calumnia ser.
Si el rey lo llegó a entender,
si fue su mandato error . . .

[Speak, speak. No, that would be a lowly action and reveal a lack of faith. *Complete the task and let us keep silent* was what His Majesty told me. . . . Bustos was guilty, he accused of high treason; why, then, do I see such difficulty in defending myself. But such an ugly crime could well be slander. If the King learned the truth, if his order were in error . . .] (4.3)

In Trigueros, Sancho recognizes the preeminence of royal decorum, even if upholding it implies self-sacrifice. Service to an "excelso" monarch is absolute and unquestioning. The mere thought that the king could renege on a promise is unfathomable. In Hartzenbusch, on the other hand, honor outweighs decorum, a word dropped from Sancho's vocabulary. But Hartzenbusch's Sancho, created in an epoch that no longer subscribes to the concept of an absolute monarchy, does begin to question the king's order. He even begins to suspect the king of transgressing the boundaries of love, friendship, and honor:

> ¡Bustos contra su rey osa
> mano sacrílega alzar!
> ¿Iría el Rey a ultrajar
> a la que hoy fuera mi esposa?
> ¡Joven él, Estrella hermosa,
> Bustos audaz con exceso..!
> De grave, de enorme peso
> tantas conjeturas son.
> ¡Oh, vil imaginación,
> imaginación de preso!

[Bustos dares to raise an unholy hand against his king! Would the king insult the woman who today was to be my wife. He is young, Estrella beautiful, Bustos audacious in the extreme . . . ! So many conjectures weigh heavily on me. Oh vile imagination, a prisoner's imagination!] (3.8)

At first, Sancho cannot believe possible the treachery he imagines, and thus rationalizes it away as a tormented by-product of his incarceration.

Both versions of the soliloquy deal, too, with the question of blame:

Trigueros	**Hartzenbusch**
Ay, Bustos, de ti no dudo,	¡Tabera! Pues donde estás
que si Ortiz, tu amigo tierno	la eterna verdad asiste,
te mató, sufrió en matarte	sabiendo por qué moristes
más que si muriera él mesmo;	a Sancho perdonarás.
que supuso que era justo,	Los brazos me tenderás,
y que debió suponerlo.	cuando este mísero suelo
Sabes bien que tus favores,	deje mañana sin duelo . . .
y tus amistades fueron	
cuchillos que atravesaron	
su corazón . . .	

Trigueros	Hartzenbusch
[Ay, Bustos, I do not doubt you, for if Ortiz, your cherished friend, had killed you, he would suffer for that action more than if he himself had died; he assumed that it was just, and he should think that. You know all too well that your favors and your friendship were knives that pierced his heart...] (3.8)	[Tabera! Wherever you are eternal truth will reside, knowing why you died you will forgive Sancho. You will open your arms to me when tomorrow I leave without grief this wretched earth...] (4.3)

Trigueros's Sancho affirms his belief in his friend, acknowledging paradoxically that his crime was unnecessary. The pain of the murderer, Sancho says, is worse than that suffered by the victim. Hartzenbusch elaborates Sancho's questioning; he believes at first, to assuage his guilt and to justify his act, that Bustos was indeed guilty of no less a crime than "lesa majestad," high treason, a phrase Hartzenbusch recuperates from the original (1513–14). But once Sancho begins to doubt Bustos's guilt, he realizes that his own death is preferable to living with the ever-present memory of his atrocity. Sancho is confident that Bustos forgives him because the crime was committed on the order of the king, an order that cannot be refused, an order that Bustos would comprehend. Friendship goes beyond the grave in the twist that Hartzenbusch gives here; "la eterna verdad asiste" trades on the original's "Las leyes del amistad, / guardadas con lazo eterno, / rompí..." [I broke the laws of friendship that were tied together in eternal bond] (2268–70). The original allows Sancho to expiate his guilt by demanding secret punishment for a secret crime; Hartzenbusch refocuses and recasts the verses so the emphasis falls on friendship ("a Sancho perdonarás. / Los brazos me tenderás..." [3.8]).

The treatment of Sancho's reflections on Estrella likewise vary between the *refundiciones*:

Trigueros	Hartzenbusch
Estrella no está en el cielo; Estrella no ve las almas; Estrella solo ve un reo donde está un héroe... . . . . . Con qué furor irritada de la sangre que está hirviendo, por obligación, por deuda,	Estrella no está en el cielo. . . . . . Yo, que con pasión ardiente la amé cuanto cabe amar, ¡yo con ella he de callar pasando por delincuente! No es el lidiar ser valiente; más valor, más fuerte brío

Trigueros	Hartzenbusch
por un odio justo y recto, ansiando estará por ver en mi vida un escarmiento.	requiere el silencio impío que mantengo contra el llanto que aquélla a quien amo tanto, tanto . . .
[Estrella is not in Heaven; Estrella does not see souls; Estrella sees only a prisoner where there is a hero. . . . Angered by her boiling blood, with what wrath, whether out of obligation, debt, or a just and proper hatred, she anxiously awaits to see an exemplary punishment made of my life.] (4.3)	[Estrella is not in Heaven. . . . I, who with a burning passion loved her as much as one can love, I am to keep silent like a common criminal! Fighting is not the way to be valiant; greater valor, stronger spirit requires the unholy silence I keep against the weeping that she whom I love so much, so much . . .] (3.8)

Trigueros emphasizes Estrella's desire for vengeance, the evidence for which is that his life is "un escarmiento"; all that she can see, according to Sancho, is the "reo" rather than the "héroe" he considers himself for having done his duty even at the cost of sacrificing his love and his life. Hartzenbusch has here borrowed only one line from Trigueros, "Estrella no está en el cielo." Sancho believes Estrella unable to forgive him because she remains, unlike Bustos, an earthbound adversary. Furthermore, Hartzenbusch has Sancho lament the necessary silence that relegates him to the status of delinquent. Important is the absence in Sancho's speech of the word "héroe," for even though he has upheld his side of the bargain, he no longer sees his action as motivated by an overweening sense of loyalty. He draws upon his inner resources and nobility of heart to reinforce his Jericho, the weakening walls of his resolve. True valor, he says, comes not from having fought, nor from not having challenged the king, but from keeping a forced silence. But he does suggest, in the interrupted sentence "que aquélla a quien amo tanto, / tanto . . . ," that his pledge keeps him silent and that if he could talk, Estrella would understand the compelling reasons for his crime. This thought, then, prepares us for the close of the play, when the king assumes sole guilt so that Sancho and Estrella can marry; he wishes to confirm their love and allow it to redeem them as well as him.

Hartzenbusch has ended the soliloquy at this point. Trigueros, however, had continued the speech: Sancho steels himself for death, forcing himself to keep silent, all as a kind of moralizing about his situation: "¡O qué duro es el callar, / quando hablar es de provecho!

Labios míos, de vosotros / se fía mi honor entero . . ." [Oh how difficult it is to keep silent when speaking will resolve so much! Lips, my honor depends on you] (4.3). His apostrophe is reinforced by linking honor—he speaks of "amancillar" [to sully] and "manchar" [to stain]—to his well-wrought yet difficult silence. To close the soliloquy Sancho speaks of his friendship with Bustos, who provided him with assurances that he was a good man: "cómo aprecio estos abrazos / que me acreditan de bueno" [how I appreciate those embraces that confirm my goodness] (4.3). The embraces of friendship recall those of his beloved Estrella, signs of affection that are now "secos" [dry], for "dulces brazos" [sweet embraces], Sancho believes, will now wield the sword of justice. The punishment will come directly from the aggrieved. Unlike Hartzenbusch, Trigueros provides no suggestion of a possible *rapprochement*.

The following fourteen verses comprise Sancho's preparation for execution:

> Calla, y sé digno de ir
> a habitar con tus abuelos
> en el templo de la fama.
> Qué turbado está mi seso,
> qué turbado, al mismo tiempo
> que parezco tan sereno.
> Qual si soñando estuviera
> veo agradables espectros,
> que ahuyentan las negras sombras
> del humano sentimiento:
> una conciencia sin crimen
> no sueña sino contentos.

[Silence, and be worthy of residing with your ancestors in the temple of fame. How confused is my mind, how confused! At the same time I seem so calm. As if in a dream I see pleasing spectres that drive away the dark shadows of human feeling: an innocent conscience dreams only of contentment.] (3.8)

In a passage exemplifying the recaster's art by refocusing the original, Sancho experiences both perturbation and serenity, and the visions he sees, "agradables espectros," are the vestiges of the original Sancho's hallucinations. The spectres are mediated by Sancho's "Qual si soñando estuviera," which portrays him *as if* he were in a dream. Nonetheless, the original scene's suppression in Trigueros is somewhat problematic. I. L. McClelland explains that Trigueros, in modeling his own tragedies after Greek tragedy, "feels the nervous atmosphere that gives a universal tone to classical dramatic passion: the 'arrebatos' in borderline states of mind reconstructed by the Greeks from life . . . for those whose exalted states of mind alienated them from the normal"[20] (126). She then questions why Trigueros does not make use of the "nervous value" of Clarindo's clowning in *La estrella de Sevilla*. Clarindo's mere presence in *Sancho Ortiz de las Roelas* testifies to Trigueros's recognition of his function, though it is not exploited as could be.[21] McClelland offers plausible explanations to account for this:

> Perhaps Trigueros sensed the value of the clown without being able to account for it. Perhaps he did not connect the "extravagances of heroes" with the crisis-extravagances of fools, nor notice how the unbearable restraint of the original Sancho on the main subject was so brilliantly distorted in the curved mirror of his commonplace companion. The Greeks for their nervous purposes did not employ characters readily recognizable as Clarindos. Possibly for the same reason Trigueros did not think of clownish excitability as Chorus-atmosphere. Or perhaps he saw that he could never justify the nervous value of the fool before the devastating literalness of his colleagues.[22]

Or perhaps, in line with McClelland, the suppression of Clarindo particularly as he humors his master, suggests that it would not be decorous for a nobleman of Sancho's stature to be perceived so publicly as near the edge of insanity.[23]

Trigueros maintains much of the flavor of the original in Estrella's attempt to free Sancho and his refusal to flee, opting for execution to avenge Bustos's death and to expiate his guilt. The original underscores Estrella's love for Sancho as a motivating force behind her decision to free him: "Mi amor es más firme y fuerte, / y así la vida te doy" [My love is firmer and stronger, and I give my life to you] (2620–21). Trigueros reconstructs the scene to show Estrella's awareness that Sancho suffers equally over the loss of Bustos, and that his action was not criminal:

> Si no conociera yo,
> que si un hermano perdí,
> tanto pesar te costó
> como el que me cuesta a mí,
> quizá no te libertara;
> pero te conozco, Ortiz:
> todo mi amor lo repara;
> a un criminal no salvara,
> pero salvo a un infeliz.

[Perhaps I would not free you if I did not know that, if I lost a brother, it hurt you as much as it hurts me; but I know you, Ortiz: my love for you makes me aware of this. I would not save a criminal, but I will save an unfortunate man.] (4.6)

"Infeliz," a description accorded Sancho by the king in 1.1, suggests that Sancho obeys a force much greater than himself and over which he has no control. Estella suggests in this way that some political/amorous intrigue forced Sancho's hand:

> Si pudiera imaginarte
> capaz de acción tan impía,
> no pensaría en librarte;
> pero conozco bien yo
> qual es tu proceder justo,
> la pasión no me cegó:
> quando Ortiz mató a Don Busto,
> grande fuerza le obligó.
> . . . . .
> [A] ti forzaron a matar,
> lo conozco, y no te obligo
> a que digas tu pesar.
> Mas yo también sé callar,
> lo conozco y no lo digo.
> Vive, pues, por vida mía.

[If I could imagine you capable of such an impious action, I would not even consider freeing you; but I know well your proper course of action, passion has not blinded me: when Ortiz killed Don Busto, a great power forced his hand. . . . They forced you to kill—I know this—and I do not oblige you to tell me your sorrow. But I, too, know how to keep silent; I know this and I will not say it. By my life, you shall live.] (4.6)

In both speeches Estrella reiterates essentially the same idea: that Sancho is incapable of murder in cold blood. Her allusion to passion refers as well to the king, whom passion has blinded and led to reject reason. She thus recognizes the role of the state in her brother's murder ("grande fuerza"); the repetition of "forzar" and "conocer," this last word uttered five times by Estrella in the first person singular in a space of twenty-eight verses, is her statement of purpose, cognition, and recognition. Right or wrong, the order given to Sancho had to be carried out; yet she *knows* Sancho well enough to understand his mindset, a reflection of the attitudes with which the "ilustrado" Trigueros embeds his text. Finally, Estrella is equal to Sancho in her

inner strength and reserve, for she keeps silent the real motivation—
the King's love for her and the encounter between him and Bustos—
behind King Sancho's orders and Sancho Ortiz's crime. Estrella's
desire to keep Sancho alive is in some measure a way of keeping her
love alive, or at least an attempt to rectify an injustice originated by
the king. The original scene closes with the dialogue between Sancho
and Estrella and his insistence on dying because "te ofendo con
vivir" [I offend you by continuing to live] (2643). Trigueros emphasizes Sancho's heroic stature and so elevates the Golden Age play
into the realm of tragedy. The hero is impotent in face of the decrees
issued by a force greater than the individual:

> *Estrella.* ¡Tan héroe, y es infeliz.
> *Sancho.* ¡Triste y forzoso desliz!

[*Estrella.* So heroic, yet he is unfortunate!
Sancho. Unfortunate and inescapable error.] (4.6)

Hartzenbusch's treatment of the scene dilutes considerably the
heroic stature that Trigueros imparts, and differs as well from the
original. In both the original and in Trigueros, Estrella has veiled her
face and is thus unrecognizable; Hartzenbusch dispenses with this
textual tradition, and in doing so eliminates the dramatic tension
inherent in the scene. Estrella's reasoning for freeing Sancho ostensi-
bly has less to do with love than with honor: "He cumplido con
Tabera, / me falta cumplir contigo" [I have fulfilled my obligation to
Tabera, I must fulfill my obligation to you] (3.10). Again, as in
Trigueros, there is an implication that Estrella knows the reasons why
Sancho Ortiz has killed her brother, an implication that is borne out
in the course of the scene. Estrella has become transformed, in turn,
from "Estrella del alma mía" [Estrella of my soul] in the first two versions, to the quintessential Romantic "Angel adorado mío" [My
adored angel] (3.10) inscribed within his soul.[24] Sancho's heroic
stature is further undercut by the pedantic tone of the conversation
with Estrella which treats the crime as a very human one without the
overtones of Greek tragedy that Trigueros infused. Sancho has just
refused the freedom Estrella wishes to grant him:

> *Sancho.* ... pero tu amante
> debe salir o triunfante
> o muerto, no fugitivo.
> *Estrella.* ¡Cómo! ¿Triunfante salir
> imaginas? De ese modo

>no debiste delinquir.
>Sancho, explícate, habla: todo,
>todo me lo has de decir.

[*Sancho.* But your beloved should leave either triumphant or dead, not a fugitive.
Estrella. What? You think you can leave prison in triumph? Then you should not have broken the law. Sancho, explain yourself, speak: you must tell me everything.] (3.10)

Though Sancho refuses to divulge the reasons for his actions, Estrella feels no compulsion to maintain her silence: "Yo quiero decirte mucho" [I want to tell you so many things] (3.10). The fact that she chooses to speak sets her apart from the code of honor maintained by men and allows her more individuality than in any other version. In addition, her decision transforms Hartzenbusch's *refundición* into an eminently human story. Where one's fate is not decided through heroic restraint (silence) but through the free access to information, an *ethos* quite different from that of half a century earlier, one has greater control to decide these matters. Implicit in this, too, is a decidedly antiabsolutist view of monarchy. The fact that Estrella speaks, the fact that Hartzenbusch's Estrella knows all and volunteers it, would constitute a breach of decorum for Trigueros. Estrella proceeds to detail how the king had learned where she lived, that he had sent her messages, that Bustos had found the king in the house, and that Sancho himself is the straw man who will die for having committed an unpardonable crime at the behest of an immoral—or even amoral—king.

Hartzenbusch, too, is a product of his times. In recasting Sancho's and Estrella's encounter at the prison, Hartzenbusch diverges from his model and prepares the way for the ending. Once armed with the knowledge of King Sancho's duplicity, Sancho refuses to flee, a decision not in consonance with what he has just learned. His acceptance of death would be futile and vain, yet he cannot accept freedom without Estrella, who insists on entering a convent, and without honor: "¿Y quieres que huyendo yo / quede sin honra y sin ti?" [And by fleeing you want me to live without honor and without you?] (3.10). Sancho can allow himself freedom only if the king admits to his order ("Otro ha de hacerme vivir," [My life depends on someone else] 3.10). His further protestations of love, not found in Trigueros, are reminiscent of a Golden Age *comedia*:

> Vivir ausente
> de Estrella, vivir privado
> de su amor, ser de mi ser,
> es mal con que no me atrevo.
> Menos quiero padecer:
> más vale hacer lo que debo,
> y morir si es menester.

[To live without Estrella, to live deprived of her love, being of my being, is a misfortune I cannot withstand. I wish to suffer less; it is better to do what I should and die if need be.] (3.10)

At the close of the scene (the end of act 3 as well), Hartzenbusch repeats Trigueros's additions:

> *Estrella.* ¡Tan noble y tan infeliz!
> *Sancho.* ¡Triste y forzoso desliz!
>
> (3.10)

but no heroic intent can be deduced, no emulation of Greek tragedy is to be found. Sancho and Estrella are two very human individuals caught in the havoc wrought by an eminently human monarch who confuses love and duty. Sancho, for his part, does not permit love to take a subservient slot in a moral hierarchy, particularly given public knowledge of the king's treachery. King Sancho subverts the hallowed notion of royalty; he is "casi divorciado," a fact that removes the taint of adultery and the impropriety of his desire and casts him as an intrusive would-be lover breaking up a betrothed couple. Where Trigueros closes his act 4 with Estrella's and Sancho's mutual command to forget one another, Hartzenbusch's Sancho refuses to accept Estrella's insistent "¡Sancho Ortiz, olvida a Estrella!" [Sancho Ortiz, forget Estrella!] by replying "No, no, mientras viva Ortiz" [No, not while Ortiz lives] (3.10). Once again the possibility that love may conquer in the end is kept open.

Substantial changes inform the denouement of each play; both Trigueros and Hartzenbusch begin act 5 and act 4 respectively after Sancho has refused to accept the freedom offered him by Estrella. The original contains a scene (2646–2745) between the king and Don Arias in which they discuss Sancho's steadfast silence, the king's inability to admit his own wrongdoing, and the possibility of convincing the *alcaldes mayores* to punish Sancho with exile. Trigueros eliminates this scene, opening the act with the *alcalde* Pedro de Caus's recapitulation to King Sancho of Estrella's visit to Sancho Ortiz. Two changes in particular are noteworthy. The king is ever admiring of

Sancho Ortiz's resolve, and when Caus informs the king that it was Estrella who came to free Sancho Ortiz, the king replies that "todos son héroes aquí" [all here are heroes] (5.1), an addition to the original that further ennobles the characters. Hartzenbusch omits the entire scene, it seems, to reduce the length of the play and to quicken the pace, but he also eliminates Trigueros's addition because he does not conceive of the play on the same plane as did Trigueros.

The following scene, original to Trigueros and copied by Hartzenbusch, reveals the king in solitude before his meeting with the *alcaldes* in an attempt to sway their judgment. King Sancho in the first *refundición* rationalizes at length his decision to approach the judges:

> No escusemos diligencia
> que pueda ser empleada
> para librar una vida
> heroyca de tal desgracia:
> libertarle es necesario:
> su causa es mi propia causa:
> salvemos este decoro
> que mis deseos ataja,
> y démosle vida: al fin
> librémosle, y esto basta.

[Let us leave unturned no stone that can be used to rescue a heroic life from such a disgrace; freeing him is necessary; his cause is my own cause; let us save the decorum that cuts short my desire, and let us give him life. Let us free him, once and for all.] (5.2)

The king once again reinforces the heroic stature of Sancho Ortiz and the necessity of avoiding a disgrace that will blemish the king as well; after all, his fate is tied to his subjects'. The king uses three verbs to insist upon the need of saving Sancho Ortiz's life: "libertar," "dar vida," and "librar." The use of the nearly synonymous words highlights the necessity of Sancho's freedom and avoidance of a fate which he only in part has brought upon himself through his heroism (refusal to speak) and through the king's overweening passion. The irony here is that King Sancho, to avoid embarrassment, takes another risk by his attempt to influence the judges' decision on Ortiz's punishment; just as he subverted the code of honor and the laws of decorum through the attempted seduction of Estrella, so he wishes to subvert local civil justice. It is not in the least odd that Hartzenbusch omitted the above-quoted verses from his version. Once again, the word "heroyca" is suppressed, as is the tying together of the two Sanchos' fates.

The closing verses of King Sancho's soliloquy in Trigueros portrays a monarch in awe of both Sancho and justice:

> Mas libertar a Don Sancho
> la misma equidad lo manda:
> si es crimen, fue solo mío,
> y acción mal aconsejada.
> Lo que para Ortiz fue gloria,
> para mí fue ruin venganza.

[Fairness demands that Don Sancho be freed; if a crime has been committed, it was mine alone, and a poorly advised action. What was glory for Ortiz was for me base vengeance.] (5.7)

Hartzenbusch reiterates the passage verbatim except for eliminating two very important verses that affect the interpretation of the passages: "si es crimen, fue solo mío, y / acción mal aconsejada" [4.3]." He does not yet allow his King Sancho to admit so boldly in public his blame in the affair, nor does he imply that the advisor Don Arias is principally responsible for the king's having fallen from the just path. The implication is that King Sancho must assume full responsibility for his actions; he is no longer the absolutist king of the Enlightenment who has let passion rule over reason. Though in many passages cited in this study (and others which have not been brought to bear) Hartzenbusch does not eliminate the play on "razón" and "pasión" so important to Trigueros's play, their meanings take on different shadings. The nineteenth-century audience possibly familiar with Trigueros's *Sancho Ortiz de las Roelas*, as was most likely the case, would see represented the transformation of King Sancho into a very human king whose love for a woman knew no bounds. Once the onus of adultery has been removed, the monarch becomes simply (or not so simply) a man in love who happens to be a king.

The king's attempt to interfere with justice, corresponding to 2805–2923 of the original, carries a slightly different slant in the two *refundiciones*. Farfán's speech, in which he explains the importance of his position and the symbolism inherent in the staff of justice, is spoken in Trigueros's version by Guzmán; and where Farfán says that honor and confidence "nos cargan en nuestros hombros" [weigh on our shoulders] (2817–18), Guzmán adds "sobre nuestros flacos hombros" [on our weak shoulders] (5.3), to enlarge the importance of their jobs, for they as mere mortals must act with caution and judiciousness in a task dedicated to the appropriate fulfillment of justice. Furthermore, Trigueros insists much more than does the original on the necessity of doing right by Sevilla:

> Sabemos quanto Sevilla
> sus Regidores amaba,
> quanto a la clemencia inclina,
> quanto por justicia clama;
> no podemos apartarnos
> en tan duras circunstancias
> de lo que Sevilla hiciera,
> y corresponde a estas varas.

[We know how Sevilla esteems her councilmen, how she is inclined toward clemency, how she clamors for justice; in such difficult circumstances we cannot stray from what Seville would do and what befits these staffs of justice.] (5.3)

Guzmán underscores both local sovereignty and the power invested in his office to contrast with King Sancho's high-handed, illegal, and immoral treatment of Estrella and Sancho Ortiz. The fact that the *alcaldes* are not as yet aware of the king's involvement drives the point home much more clearly both for the king and for the public in attendance. To the king's admonishment that justice be equitable, the *alcaldes* both in the original and in Trigueros's *refundición* claim that the king answers only to God; but Trigueros again elaborates the need for local justice:

> ... si por desgracia nuestra
> perdimos la confianza,
> que a merecer aspiramos,
> tomad, Señor, nuestras varas;
> pero mientras las tenemos,
> por conservarlas intactas,
> solo haremos lo que ordena
> la ley, y exige la causa.

[... if for our disgrace we lose the confidence to which we aspire, my Lord, take our staffs; but while we hold them to keep them whole, we shall do only what the law orders and the cause demands.] (5.3)

Farfán's speech can serve as a warning and a lesson to an enlightened king that he is not exempt from the responsibility of adhering to the laws of the land.

King Sancho's attempt to convince each of the *alcaldes* that to spare Sancho Ortiz's life is a much wiser decision than to condemn him to death carries in Trigueros a greater moralizing tone, suggesting that the king has more at stake. In a way this is true; an eighteenth-century king acting against decorum on stage would be seen quite differently than a seventeenth-century king. Once again the monarch praises the man whom he is coerced into punishing to protect himself; Bustos's death "dexa al reyno privado / de un héroe que le guardara" [leaves the kingdom deprived of a hero to protect it] (5.3), a further repetition of the qualifier that allows Bustos, Sancho Ortiz, and the king to populate the same dramatic space according to the precepts followed by Trigueros. King Sancho, too, emphasizes another moral quality of the prisoner that should free him from punishment: "Este silencio de Ortiz / sin duda el honor lo causa" [Honor is doubtless the cause of Ortiz's silence] (5.4). Sancho Ortiz could speak for himself if unmentioned constraints were not in place. Similarly, when the king attempts to manipulate Farfán, he reiterates "el honor que Ortiz puede / dar, y ha dado ya a su patria" [the honor that Ortiz can confer, and has conferred already, on his country] (5.5). Where the original gives Farfán's response as a simple declaration of loyalty, Trigueros expands to allow and prepare for King Sancho's eventual admission of blame and first cause:

> No hay Regidor en Sevilla
> más capaz que Ortiz de honrarla:
> Farfán de Ribera fue
> siempre muy suyo: y si alcanza,
> quando media vuestra Alteza
> para estorbar su desgracia,
> resquicio de facultad,
> sin que se injurie la vara
> de la justicia, será
> su lealtad asegurada.[25]

[There is not a councilman in Seville more capable of honoring her than Ortiz; Farfán de Ribera was always his own man. And if Ortiz finds, with Your Majesty's mediation to avoid his disgrace, a loophole without compromising the staff of justice, his loyalty will be assured.] (5.5)

Any opening, however slight, will have to be provided by the king, who does not as yet recognize Farfán's subtle offer of a decorous resolution to the king's dilemma; the public, however, could very well keep track mentally of hints leading to the king's necessary admission.

Following the individual meetings with the *alcaldes*, Trigueros inserts a soliloquy, repeated in part by Hartzenbusch, in which the king gloats over his apparent success at persuading the *alcaldes* to spare Sancho Ortiz's life. The original King Sancho states "Bien negocié" [I have negotiated well] (2886), believes it possible to avoid public declaration of his promise to Sancho Ortiz, and decides to exile Sancho and promote him to general; the *refundición* takes up the moral tone presented in the king's arguments to the local officials and develops it further. The judges "son hombres," a point suggested earlier by their own use of "flacos hombros," and they are subject, King Sancho believes, to "el poder quien los manda" (5.6). He still fails to realize that wielding absolute power corrupts absolutely, and that no amount of royal persuasion can force an honest judge to redirect his primary concern away from the merits of a case. The king is further relieved by what he predicts to be a judgment favorable to him because "la causa / no ofrece ningún resquicio / para poder mejorarla" [the case offers no opening to improve it] (5.6). The reiteration of "resquicio," and King Sancho's inability to see that his admission is the crack to admit the light of truth and reason, contribute to the irony of his soliloquy. He repeats the word central to an accurate definition of Sancho Ortiz's stellar qualities: "Es este Ortiz tan heroyco / que los recursos ataja" [Ortiz is so heroic that he limits my options] (5.6). The seemingly unstoppable force indeed has come up against the immovable object. Finally, King Sancho expresses his awareness of the power he does yield, though he has yet to measure his words accordingly:

> ... pero ya veo
> que aun las más flacas palabras,
> quando es un Rey quien las dice,
> reciben grande eficacia.
> ¡Cómo debemos medirlas!
> ¡Cómo debemos pesarlas!
> Una sola de ellas puede
> torcer la mejor balanza.
> Al fin en esta ocasión
> a un hombre inocente salvan,
> porque Ortiz debió sin duda
> hacer lo que yo mandaba. ...

[... but I now see that even the most casual words, when a king speaks them, become all the more effective. How we must measure them! How we must weigh them! Only one of them can pervert justice. On this occasion they have saved an innocent man, because Ortiz without a doubt carried out what I had ordered. ...] (5.6)

There remains in the tone of King Sancho's speech the arrogance associated with him. The force of his words, measured and weighed, he believes has been effective in swaying the judges to his side. He offers his concept of proper action, but the house he has constructed is made of cards and its foundation composed of misused words and abuse of power. Again irony is implicit in his cautionary "torcer la mejor balanza," in that they further the notion, expressed earlier by Farfán, of twisting the staff of justice. King Sancho does wish "equidad" in the sentence against Sancho Ortiz, but does not realize that the resolution/solution is not possible without admitting his own participation. Twisted staffs deflected from proper justice "pecan contra vos" [sin against you], in the words of Farfán (5.8). "Flacas palabras," even those spoken by a king, fall upon "flacos hombros" of human judges who must exercise for that reason all the more caution.

To support their order for Sancho Ortiz's decapitation, the *alcaldes* are again explicit about their duties and about the need for the king to follow their dicta. As in the original, each is willing to lay down his life in service to the king, but in matters of state the staff as symbol of justice holds sway:

> mas faltar a la justicia
> de lo que ofrece la causa,
> es, Señor, tan imposible
> para nuestras nobles canas,
> que ni pudimos hacerlo,
> ni el Rey nos lo demandara.

[But to do ill to the justice of this case is, My Lord, so impossible for our noble heads, that neither could we do it nor could the king demand it of us.]
(5.7)

Trigueros assures his public that the forces of public order adhere to the law particularly when the king errs; after all, as Guzmán says, "somos la misma ley sacra, / y si ella no lo permite / ni empeños, ni riesgos bastan" [we are the sacred law, and if it does not permit (twisting justice), neither insistence nor danger are sufficient cause] (5.7). Thus the king is forced to confront the unreasoned word he has given in passion. He asks Sancho himself for help by asking, "¿Es posible que no hallas / algún resquicio o vereda / para evitar tu desgracia?" [Is it possible that you cannot find any opening or path to avoid your disgrace?] (5.9), searching for the opening of light or path to reestablish truth and reason. Sancho cannot reveal any resolution "mientras mi rey no la encuentre" [as long as my king cannot find it] (5.9); King Sancho has not caught Farfán's earlier suggestion. Again like in the original, the king cannot vacate the *alcaldes*' order. If he urges Estrella to make public the results of her secret prison meeting with Sancho Ortiz (her decision to extend forgiveness), by the same token he must own up to his responsibilities. Consistent to his form, Trigueros's King Sancho reinforces the heroic plane on which the noble characters of this play operate:

> Ya basta:
> todos, menos yo, son héroes
> en esta dichosa patria:
> también yo ser quiero hablando
> tan héroe como el que calla.
> Matadme a mí, Sevillanos,
> que yo solo fui la causa
> de esta muerte . . .

[Enough already: all except I are heroes in this cursed country. I wish to be one, too, speaking as heroic as he who is silent. Kill me, Sevillians, for I alone was the cause of this death . . .] (5.9)

The king has finally learned the only way of ennobling himself, of equalling himself to the heroes who have withstood in silence and with respect the king's word, and who have waited for his truth to prevail.

The original and Trigueros's *refundición* close in similar ways, with the impossibility of marriage between Sancho Ortiz and Estrella. In Trigueros, however, when the king insists that Estrella marry Sancho Ortiz, in keeping with the latter's word to him—the irony of which would not be lost on anyone—Estrella plays on Sancho Ortiz's sympathies by refusing to live with him and requesting permission to enter a convent:

> mas permitid
> que sola y desamparada
> en la lobreguez de un claustro,
> mientras viviere encerrada
> me castigue de querer
> bien al que a Bustos matara.

[but allow me, alone and helpless in the darkness of a cloister, while I live enclosed, to punish myself for having loved too well he who killed Bustos.] (5.9)

Confronted with the dark and mournful adjectives employed by Estrella, Sancho can do no less than release her from the promise of marriage. Her suffering would be his, increased by his love:

> este tormento perpetuo
> mi mismo amor le aumentara,
> y acíbar se convirtieran
> aun las venturas más gratas.

[my very love increases this perpetual torment, and even the happiest of luck becomes embittered.] (5.9)

The "acíbar" or aloe would embitter their lives together, and would render happiness impossible. At the same time, the aloe acts as a *pharmakon* in its capacity to purge or to cleanse the crime committed by Sancho Ortiz.[26] In his relationship with Estrella he becomes the scapegoat who must be purged from society to restore order. He is now free to carry out heroic deeds against "el fiero Moro" as repayment to society.

A word needs now be said about Trigueros's treatment of the king's advisor Don Arias. In the original, Don Arias arranges with the slave Natilde for the king's surreptitious entry into Estrella's house, suggests that the king have Bustos killed in secret, attempts to elicit from Sancho Ortiz the king's promise of protection, and urges King Sancho to make Sancho Ortiz a general and to marry Estrella to a nobleman. In other words, he fulfills the normal role of advisor, but it is the king who carries out the advice. In Trigueros's *refundición,* Arias holds inordinate sway over King Sancho. It is made clear from the beginning that it is Arias who thwarts the good king from the path of reason. Not until the end of the play, however, when the threads of Arias's plans have become unraveled, does King Sancho place blame. Once the Cabildo has issued the death sentence, King Sancho is at a loss for action:

> ¿Qué tengo de hacer, Don Arias?
> ¿Qué he de hacer? ¿Qué me aconsejas,
> entre confusiones tantas,
> tú, que con tu mal consejo
> tantos pesares me causas?
> A muerte le sentenciaron
> sin que mi empeño le valga.

[What must I do, Don Arias? What am I to do? Among such confusion what do you advise, you who with your bad advice cause me such despair? They have sentenced him to death in spite of my insistence.] (5.8)

Only now does King Sancho assert control. He first attempts to pardon Sancho Ortiz in spite of the *alcaldes*' finding, but he realizes, to his shame, the moral impossibility of overruling them. He is concerned, after all, with the "qué dirán" and royal decorum. The only solution is to admit the truth, which in the original is done at the urging of Don Arias, and in Trigueros is carried out by the king's own volition when no other recourse is available to him. Because of Arias's role in thwarting the king from proper action, he must be punished at the same time that Sancho Ortiz's honor is restored:

> *Rey.* Y pues que vos me perdisteis
> con malos consejos, Arias,
> salid luego de Castilla,
> y en vuestro destierro vaya
> el exemplo, y escarmiento
> de los que en lisonjas tratan.
> *Arias.* Por serviros...
> *Rey.* No es servirme
> deslumbrarme: idos, y basta.

[*King.* And since you have done me harm with bad advice, Arias, leave Castille immediately, and let your exile be an example and a lesson for those who traffic in flattery.
Arias. To serve you...
King. Blinding me to reason is not serving me: leave once and for all.]
(5.9)

The compelling force behind the king's decree is the word "deslumbrarme," an accusation against the man responsible for obscuring light of reason from an enlightened king. Arias's crime requires an honorless exile. Though both the advisor and Sancho Ortiz leave the court, the difference in import is clear even in the light of their similar movement. King Sancho repents of having allowed himself be led by passion, and in sending Sancho Ortiz to glory in battle, he can allow his subject to serve the country, expiate his own guilt, and restore lost luster to his tarnished reign. The king's final repentance, "¡O pasión! ¡O mal consejo!" [Oh passion! Oh bad advice!] is met with approval by Farfán, who speaks as an *alcalde* of Sevilla, as a chorus commenting upon the king's words, and as the *vox populi*: "Que vos lo conozcáis, basta" [It is enough that you recognize it] (5.9). Harmony, reason, and decorum are restored after one day filled with so many deeds.

We return now to 4.4 of Hartzenbusch's *refundición*, the scene in which King Sancho meets with the *alcaldes*. Hartzenbusch follows Trigueros nearly word for word, but in Farfán's reply to King Sancho, Trigueros's character's warning that "solo a Dios cuenta dareis, / que él solo en los Reyes manda" [you will give an account to God alone, for He alone has authority over a king] (5.3) has been recast:

> libre es la diestra del rey;
> la ley nuestras manos ata;
> delito en nosotros fuera
> lo que en vos lícita gracia.

[the king's right hand is free; the law ties our hands; actions that constitute a just pardon for you are an offense for us.] (4.4)

The issue is no longer as clear-cut as it had been a half-century earlier. Farfán speaks to a double standard that allows the king freedom to do as he pleases, a condition that may have been true for Trigueros's king, but one that could not be—or would not be—admitted on stage. Farfán must act within the boundaries of law, yet he seemingly gives the king an out if he should need one. One more time it needs be said that Hartzenbusch prepares the audience for his very different resolution.[27]

The last two scenes of Hartzenbusch's *refundición*, 4.9–10, corresponding to Trigueros's 5.8–9, introduce the substantial changes necessary for Hartzenbusch's ending. Hartzenbusch eliminates the verses in which Trigueros's King Sancho deflects the blame for his misguided actions onto Don Arias. Indeed, Arias continues to advise, seeking to avoid fulfillment of the death sentence:

> *Rey.* A muerte le sentenciaron,
>   sin que mi empeño le valga.
> *Arias.* Válgale el poder, y baste
>   con la sangre derramada.
>   Que le indultéis es preciso
>   ya, por una circunstancia
>   que he sabido . . .

[*King.* They have sentenced him to death in spite of my insistence.
Arias. Let your power protect him; enough blood has been spilled. You must pardon him because of an important fact I have learned . . .] (4.9)

Arias wishes to become the peacemaker and is about to introduce an additional element into the denouement before he is interrupted by Sancho's entrance. Hartzenbusch, following Trigueros, has his King Sancho overrule the *alcaldes*' sentence once Estrella agrees to pardon Sancho Ortiz. Farfán, in both versions, objects, but the reasoning is quite different in Hartzenbusch's scene:

Trigueros	Hartzenbusch
Mirad, Señor, os suplico, que la justicia se agravia: pedir la parte por él no es descargo de su falta . . .	[E]n este caso, ved que la justicia se agravia. No es el delito menor porque la parte contraria suplique en favor del reo con piedad, interesada. Sabed, Rey, si lo ignoráis, que Estrella y Sancho se amaban.
[Look, My Lord, I beg you, for justice is aggrieved; to take his side is not an acquittal of the charge . . .] (5.9)	[Notice that in this case justice is aggrieved. The crime is no less because the opposing party appeals with compassion on behalf of the accused. Know, Your Majesty, if you have been unaware, that Estrella and Sancho loved each other.] (4.10)

Not only is no word mentioned in Hartzenbusch of a revenge-minded public, but Farfán's news of Estrella's and Sancho's love takes the king by surprise. King Sancho unwittingly had agreed to the marriage by having promised Sancho Ortiz the hand of a woman of his choosing:

> *Sancho.*   Señor,
> Estrella fue, sin nombrarla,
> con quien casarme ofrecisteis,
> fuera quien fuese la dama.

[Sire, you offered to arrange my marriage regardless of the woman I chose; without my naming her Estrella was my choice.] (4.10)

Silenced speech once again has proven troublesome for the king. At the same time, though, this revelation forces the king's hand; the information Arias was about to impart concerns Sancho Ortiz's and Estrella's mutual affection. Love becomes a reason of state and pre-eminent for King Sancho, who now casts aside his personal interest and is compelled to safeguard love:

> [*Aparte*] (¡Con que a mi propio rival
> encomendé mi venganza,
> y él por cumplir con su Rey,
> a Estrella sacrificaba!
> Salvar su amor es preciso,
> salvarle la vida es nada.)

[(*Aside*) (I entrusted my vengeance to my own rival, and he, to fulfill his king's command, sacrificed Estrella! I must save their love; saving his life is nothing by comparison.)] (4.10)

The king now admits to being the murderer of Bustos Tabera and then ordering Sancho's confession. To say that this new twist to the plot is ingenuous would be an understatement, but it does allow Estrella and Sancho Ortiz to rejoin. To Estrella's desire prove the king's story, his response intimates that, ironically, silence is indeed the wisest course of action:

> Os aconsejo
> que me creáis . . . y os caséis.
> Amparo vuestra beldad
> contra el poder necesita . . .
> Sancho el peligro os evita . . .

[I advise you to believe me . . . and to marry. Your beauty needs protection against power . . . Sancho will protect you from danger . . .] (4.10)

Silence in the service of love and love that allows forgiveness become the standards of this Romanticized version of *La estrella de Sevilla*:

> *Sancho.* Estrella, fuerza es hablar.
> *Estrella.* Callar y huir es mejor.
> *Sancho.* Yo no he de engañar tu amor.
> *Estrella* El se quisiera engañar.
> *Sancho.* No: yo de tu hermano fui . . .
> *Estrella.* Ah, no alces el triste velo:
>   él te perdona en el cielo,
>   y yo te perdono aquí.

[*Sancho.* Estrella, I must speak.
Estrella. It is better to remain silent and to flee.
Sancho. I will not betray your love.
Estrella. It wants to be betrayed.
Sancho. No: I was your brother's . . .
Estrella. Let us not speak of this! He forgives you in Heaven, and I forgive you here.] (4.10)

Earlier, in affairs of state, Sancho Ortiz's silence was a matter of conscience and honor; now, in affairs of the heart, he wishes to be expansive. Estrella, who has lived by declarations of truth, now urges silence because she wants to love Sancho Ortiz and to believe the king. Breaking the silence would eventually force the truth to the surface. The image of the "triste velo" suggests the enmasking of truth that allows her to pardon Sancho for the crime she knows he has committed. The apotheosis of love is clearly a Romantic vision, but, unfortunately, without the etherealness of Zorrilla's play of only eight years before.

* * *

Sancho Ortiz de las Roelas elicited heated reviews in the Madrid press of the nineteenth century. Trigueros's *refundición* in particular is the focus of critical disagreements arising from the author's attempts to adapt a Golden Age *comedia* to the exigencies of neoclassical artistic practices. As the following selections demonstrate, the same qualities considered favorable by one critic are often condemned by another.[28] The first reviews of Trigueros's *Sancho Ortiz de las Roelas*, published in the *Diario de Madrid*, coincide with the play's opening in Madrid.[29] The anonymous critic writing in the 11 February 1800 issue was favorably impressed by the play: "Es una de las mejores tragedias que se han presentado en nuestros teatros" [It is one of the best tragedies presented in our theatres.] (Coe 200). Four days later, on 15 February, 1800 a second reviewer presented a straightforward description of changes introduced by Trigueros: "Yo creo que el refundidor de esta tragedia no la ha tocado en los versos.... Lo que habrá hecho será arreglar la escena cortando algunos episodios con el objeto de que no mudemos de lugar sino en los entreactos...." [I believe that the recaster of this tragedy has not touched the poetry.... What he probably has done is to arrange the scenes cutting some episodes so that changes of place occur only between acts] (Coe 200).[30] This statement cannot be accepted at face value. Assuming the critic actually attended a performance, he seems to have been completely unfamiliar with the text of the original play; even a cursory comparison of the two playtexts would reveal major differences between them. Likewise, the reviewer did not have a printed text before him containing Trigueros's prologue (available in the 1800 edition) wherein he describes the changes made to the original text.

The most detailed review, published in *La Gaceta de Madrid* on 16 June 1811, corresponds to an 1811 performance of Trigueros's *refundición*. The writer, "J. Ab.," whose preface to this critique has been discussed in the previous chapter, differs from the earlier reviews in his opinions about Trigueros's work. His antipathy toward the *comedia* in general establishes a negative tone from the beginning:

Querer hacer una tragedia según las reglas del arte, de una comedia dramática, en que todo es vicioso, plano, artificio, lances y estilo, es empresa algo más que atrevida é imposible de lograr. Así es que D. Cándido María Trigueros al transformar, la *La estrella de Sevilla*, comedia de Lope de Vega, en *Sancho Ortiz de las Roelas*, tragedia, consiguió desbaratar aquella, y hacer, con los retazos que la fue cortando, una monstruo, que ni la obra de Lope, ni un drama en que a lo menos se advierta sentido .... De modo que solo queda una prueba, evidente del mal gusto del refundidor.

[To wish to make a tragedy, according to the rules of art, out of a comedy, in which everything is the pursuit of pleasure, flat, artifice, incidents and style, is more than a daring undertaking and impossible to attain. So it is that D. Cándido María Trigueros, in his transformation of Lope de Vega's *The Star of Seville* into *Sancho Ortiz de las Roelas*, tragedy, succeeded in ruining the first play, and making, with the remnants cut from the original, a monstrous one, that neither in Lope's work nor in a drama can be found any meaning. . . . So that all that remains is evident proof of the recaster's bad taste.] (683)[31]

The critic's negative sentiment about *La estrella de Sevilla* predisposes his attitude toward *Sancho Ortiz de las Roelas*. He concludes his brief plot summary (having chosen five key moments from the plot) by belittling the play: "Es un asunto que podrá ser mui dramático en un teatro de indios bravos; pero que no corresponde seguramente a las costumbres de una nación civilizada" [It is a subject that might be quite dramatic in a theatre of wild indians, but that does not befit the customs of a civilized nation] (683).[32]

The next argument taken up concerns the definition of tragedy, a description the reviewer hesitates to apply to *Sancho Ortiz de las Roelas*:

Ahora, si por tragedia se quiere entender toda cosa en que haya muertes y desmayos, y contorsiones y baldones, y Reyes con ministros o privados que los hagan cometer delitos para contentar sus pasiones, el tal *Sancho* puede, sin el menor escrúpulo, ponerse al frente de todas.

[Now, if by tragedy one wishes to understand anything in which there is death and fainting, and plot twists and insults, and Kings with ministers or advisors who make them commit crimes to satisfy their passions, the so-called *Sancho* can, without the last scruple, lead the way.] (683)

He then launches into a detailed plot summary sprinkled with phrases that leave little doubt concerning his orientation. In act 2, for example, once the *alcaldes* arrive to find Bustos Tabera dead, Estrella faints ("y es mui natural" [and it is very natural]) and revives: "y empieza a requebrar a su querido, a lo que se sigue un duo de palmadas en la frente, entreveradas de suspiros y de exclamaciones sobre si el valiente Sancho había o no tenido razón de matar a su amigo" [and she begins to flatter her beloved, which is followed by a pair of slaps in the face, interspersed with sighs and exclamations about whether the brave Sancho was right or not in killing his friend] (683–84). Sancho's silence is ridiculed ("esto es, en callar el secreto de la muerte de su amigo, pues por lo demás habla que se las pela" [that is, in keeping the secret of his friend's death silent, since as far as anything else is concerned he speaks ceaselessly]) and the king, hearing that the *alcalde*'s verdict does not conform to his wishes,

> Patea, y se da por las paredes de su alcázar, manda traer a Sancho, envía a buscar a Estrella, y la manda que allí mismo, en presencia de todo el mundo, pida la gracia de su amante: ella lo hace de mui buena gana, y el Soberano la concede con no menos voluntad; pero los alcaldes refunfuñan, y gritan que la justicia queda agraviada. En fin la cosa viene a parar en que el bien intencionado D. Sancho el Bravo tiene que cantar de plano, con lo que todo el mundo se muestra tan satisfecho, menos la pobre Estrella, que sin vocación alguna, tiene que meterse monja; solemne y nuevo modo de concluir tragedias.

> [He stamps around, and beats his head on the walls of his castle, orders Sancho brought before him, sends for Estrella, and orders her that right there, in everyone's presence, she beg for her lover's life; she does so gladly, and the Sovereign concedes it no less willingly; but the councilmen complain, and shout that justice is aggrieved. Finally, it all ends that the well-intentioned D. Sancho el Bravo has to admit the truth, with which everyone is satisfied, except poor Estrella who, without any calling at all, has to become a nun; a solemn and new way to end tragedies.] (684)

This last description of the king gives an insight into the performance itself, as least as filtered through the eyes of "J. Ab." Not surprisingly, the 1811 production of this play leaves much to be desired: "porque estoi convencido de que, aunque la saben de memoria, ninguno la entiende, y es imposible expresar lo que el entendimiento no comprehende" [because I am convinced that, although (the actors) know (the play) by heart, not one understands it, and it is impossible to express what the intellect does not comprehend] (684).

A second comment about the performance concerns characterizations of the king and his courtiers:

> Pero no puedo acabar este artículo sin dar cuenta de una observación que llevo hecha de algunos días a esta parte, y es que a todos los Reyes de Castilla han dado los comediantes en transformarlos en Felipes II, vis-

tiéndolos de negro, creyendo sin duda que este color es más decente y magestuoso. También he advertido, en la representación de *Sancho Ortiz*, que todos los cortesanos entran en el quarto del Rei sin sombrero (esto es, en la mano), uso que habrán encontrado en algunas de nuestras antiguas crónicas, como también el anterior.

[But I cannot end this article without relating an observation I have recently made, and it is that playwrights have been given to transform all Kings of Castile into Philip II, dressing them in black, doubtlessly believing that this color is more appropriate and majestic. I have noticed, too, in the performance of *Sancho Ortiz*, that all courtiers enter the King's chamber without a hat (that is, they carry it in their hands), a custom, like the previous one, they probably discovered in some of our chronicles.]
(684)

A conflict between conventions of staging and a text's horizon of expectations has arisen, at least in the mind of the reviewer. If verisimilitude is an important concept for eighteenth-century critics, theatre practitioners, and philosophers, then any suggestion of anachronistic staging will be called into question. A thirteenth-century king in seventeenth-century costume may have been acceptable for the Golden Age stage, but horizons of experience and expectation have changed. Nonetheless, the critic probably found agreement among his readers in his assessment of costume color. Golden Age *comedia* kings may belong to a distant age, but they were not all necessarily humorless.

Hartzenbusch's version of *Sancho Ortiz de las Roelas* debuted in 1852. An October 1857 staging took place at the Teatro de Novedades and may have opened the theatre season; *La Iberia* of 29 October 1857 states that "Representóse anoche en este coliseo, por última vez por ahora" [(It) was performed last night in this theatre, for the last time during this season] (3), indicating that the play had run for at least two weeks (the theatre season normally commenced at the end of September or the beginning of October). The attitudes toward the *comedia* as well as the *refundición* have certainly changed in the more than forty years since "J. Ab." decried Trigueros's recast. The present reviewer, Juan de la Rosa González, avers that *Sancho Ortiz de las Roelas* has been "refundido con notable acierto por el señor Hartzenbusch" [recast with notable success by Mr. Hartzenbusch], an opinion bolstered by the play's success on stage:

Todos los periódicos han hablado del lujo y propiedad con que esta producción ha sido puesta en escena, igualmente que de lo bien interpretada que ha estado.

> [All the newspapers have talked of the richness and propriety with which this production has been mounted; likewise they have spoken of the excellent interpretation.] (3)

The remainder of the brief review concerns the quality of acting.[33]

On 25 September 1880 the Teatro Español opened its season with a revival of Hartzenbusch's recast; though the review makes no mention of it, the staging was timed to honor the eminent writer, who had died on 2 August of the same year. The *refundición* was reviewed by both *La Correspondencia de España* and *La Epoca* the following day. The first of these reviews, too, makes it clear that custom dictated inaugurating the theatre season with plays written by the great playwrights: "Anoche se inauguró el teatro Español. *La estrella de Sevilla*, de Lope de Vega, refundida por el ilustre Hartzenbusch con el título de *Sancho Ortiz de las Roelas*, fue la obra elegida para tal función, siguiendo la costumbre de rendir este tributo a los grandes autores del teatro nacional" [The Teatro Español opened its season last night. *The Star of Seville*, by Lope de Vega, recast by the illustrious Harztzenbusch with the title *Sancho Ortiz de las Roelas*, was the work selected for such an event, following the custom of offering tribute to the great writers of the national theatre] (3). Indeed, the *Correspondencia de España* accepts without complaint the notion of recasting the great works of the Spanish stage: "Hartzenbusch, refundiendo los dramas de Lope, y Ayala las comedias de Calderón, perpetúan las glorias de aquellos genios creadores" [Hartzenbsuch, recasting plays by Lope, and Ayala, recasting Calderón's *comedias*, perpetuate the glory of those creative geniuses] (4). One must keep in mind, however, when reading these reviews specifically that their critical tone is tempered by Hartzenbusch's recent death. Theatrical criticism yields to homage. The decision to stage *Sancho Ortiz de las Roelas* appears to be an astute literary and critical move on the part of the Teatro Español: what better way to praise the man responsible for positive reevaluation of the *comedia* (as well as Golden Age literature in general) than to pair him on a playbill with no one less than Lope de Vega (the question of attribution of *La estrella de Sevilla* postdates Hartzenbusch's *refundición*). The critic, J. de F., places the two writers on the same plane early in the review:

> La refundición está hecha con acabada maestría. Aquellos versos de Lope, de imitación que suspende, de verdad que satisface, de blandura que enamora y de facilidad que encanta, como Hartzenbusch los juzgaba, brotaron con la misma belleza de la pluma y clásica del literato insigno que coleccionó las obras del Fénix de los Ingenios, y ha refundido la que anoche se representó en el Español.

[The recast has been carried out with perfect mastery. Lope's verses—filled with astonishing imitation, satisfying truth, seductive tenderness and enchanting simplicity—burst forth with the same classical style and beauty from the distinguished writer who collected the works of the "Fénix de los Ingenios," and who recast the work performed last night in the Teatro Español.] (3)

The brief summary of the supposed historical source of the original *comedia* and passing comment on the changes introduced in the recast (carried out with "acierto rarísimo" [extraordinarily rare success]) suggests that the critic was unaware of Trigueros's first *refundición* of the play.[34]

The review published in *La Epoca* confirms many of the opinions expressed in *La Correspondencia de España*. While Hartzenbusch's recent death is not given as a reason for the revival of *Sancho Ortiz de las Roelas* by Ramón de Navarrete ("Asmodeo"), the second reviewer, he states unequivocally that the play had not crossed the stage in many years:

¿Cuántos años ha que no se ponía en escena en Madrid *Sancho Ortiz de las Roelas*?
    Yo de mí sé decir que sabiendo casi entera de memoria la admirable composición de Lope de Vega, no recuerdo haber asistido nunca a su representación.

How many years has it been since *Sancho Ortiz de las Roelas* has been staged in Madrid?
    I can say for myself that, knowing Lope de Vega's admirable composition almost entirely by heart, I do not remember ever having attended its performance.] (4)

Enthusiasm characterizes the public reception of Hartzenbusch's *refundición*. The exuberance caused the balcony occupants—those seated in less expensive seats and thus possibly less attuned to the events of the Madrid artistic world—to clamor for the author's appearance on stage. As to the quality of the *refundición*, *La Epoca* is equally laudatory concerning the late playwright's abilities. Asmodeo, too, believes the writer worthy of inhabiting the same space as Lope de Vega: "La refundición que Hartzenbusch hizo de la obra es digna a la par de él y del Fénix de los Ingenios" [The recast that Hartzenbusch has made of the work is worthy both of him and of the "Fénix de los Ingenios"] (4). Additional comments attest to the reviewer's ignorance of Trigueros's earlier reworking that served as the basis for Hartzenbusch's text. The major changes introduced to the recently staged version, according to Asmodeo, include reduction of dramatic action, elimination of useless incidents ("incidentes inútiles"), and overly long dialogues. Finally, comments concerning the quality of acting reflect those stated in the other cited review. After assuring his readers that the Teatro Español's company shows great promise for the coming season, the reviewer understates his praise for the performance of *Sancho Ortiz de las Roelas*: "La representación de ayer es ya una promesa para lo futuro, porque fue en general acertada" [Yesterday's performance is already a promise for the future, because it was on the whole successful] (4).[35]

Five years later the Teatro Español inaugurated its season once again with Hartzenbusch's *Sancho Ortiz de las Roelas*, reviewed now in *La Epoca* of 17 October 1885 by Luis Alfonso. The unstated reason for selecting the play this specific year is to honor the assumed author himself, Lope de Vega, on the 250th anniversary of his death. The critic opens his article not with a discussion of the play, but with a slightly facetious comment regarding the Madrid public's tardiness in arriving at the theatre:

> La sociedad madrileña, que tanto copia de París, no ha copiado todavía, entre otras cosas ventajosas y útiles, la costumbre de asistir a las representaciones teatrales desde el principio, contribuyendo así a que terminaran indefectiblemente antes de media noche, como en París también se acostumbra.
>
> [Madrid society, that copies so much from Paris, still has not copied, among other advantageous and useful ideas, the custom of attending theatre performances from the beginning, thus contributing to the fact that they unfailinginly end before midnight, as one is accustomed to in Paris.] (2)

After dispensing with the other formalities of a newspaper review (that is, the *de riguer* description of the "distinguido y selecto" [distinguished and select] gathering), Luis Alfonso claims that the public is drawn traditionally to the Golden Age cape-and-sword plays due in great measure to the annual performance of Zorrilla's *Don Juan Tenorio*. The reviewer apparently remains unaware of the *comedia's* lack of popularity with the previous generation. However, his statement is an affirmation of a new acceptance enjoyed by the *comedia*, at least on the Madrid stage, as well as a convenient journalistic introduction of the cape-and-sword style of *Sancho Ortiz de las Roelas*.

If Alfonso's fellow reviewers fail to credit Trigueros as the first *refundidor* of *La estrella de Sevilla*, Alfonso commits perhaps a more egregious error in failing to recognize Hartzenbusch as the author of the performance text under review. (One must consider, too, the possibility that the play was not advertised properly. Even so, Alfonso's mistake speaks to his [lack of] knowledge concerning *Sancho Ortiz de las Roelas*.) Three main points reveal Luis Alfonso's error: the play contains four acts, the king's admission of guilt, and Sancho's and Estrella's decision to marry—the latter element having been introduced by Hartzenbusch. Regardless of the oversight, the critic's description of what is believed to be Trigueros's play is more accurate than previous assessments:

> Este Trigueros . . . hizo, más que una refundición, una transformación de *La Estrella de Sevilla*. Dividió en cuatro, para que resultaran más breves y concretos, los tres extensos actos del original; alteró el orden de las escenas; suprimió algún personaje; añadió poco y quitó muchos versos; tachó escenas enteras, y cercenó, hasta reducirlos a la mínima expresión, relaciones y "parlamentos," donde el estro fertilísimo de Lope se desbordaba.
>
> [This Trigueros . . . carried out not simply a recast but a transformation of *The star of Seville*. He divided the three original long acts into four so they would be briefer and tighter; he changed scene order; he eliminated a few characters; he added few and removed many verses; he erased entire scenes and shortened speeches, often reducing them to a minimum, where Lope's fertile inspiration overflowed.] (2)

When the recasting process consists of restructuring the act division, reordering of scenes, and suppression of verses, the reviewer tells us, the play cannot be considered merely a *refundición*. Alfonso does not apply his criteria consistently, though, because he joins with the present text other reworked plays: "Realizó, en suma, un trabajo análogo al de Ayala con *El alcalde de Zalamea*, y al de Moratín con *Hamlet*, si bien con menos rigor, frialdad y espíritu de secta que el último" [In sum he carried out a task similar to Ayala's with *The Mayor of Zalamea* and Moratín's with *Hamlet*, though with less rigor, coldness and overzealousness than the latter] (2). As chapter 4 demonstrates, López de Ayala respects the majority of Calderón's *El alcalde de Zalamea*, including the division of acts; and Moratín's work is first and foremost a translation, a process necessarily accompanied by other operations than those employed in a recast.

Alfonso is unique in defending the *refundición*'s new ending. The marriage of two characters in a situation similar to Sancho Ortiz's and Estrella's has a precedent in Guillén de Castro's *Las mocedades del Cid* and Corneille's *Le Cid*, whose views on the union of Rodrigo Díaz de Vivar and Jimena "demuestra que en el teatro se ha considerado como buena y apropiada unión semejante. Y cuenta que Rodrigo de Vivar mató al Conde Lozano por vengar una afrenta inferida a su propio padre, mientras que Sancho Ortiz mata a Bustos Tabera por orden expresa y terminante del Rey" [shows that in the theatre a similar marriage has been considered good and proper. And it is told that Rodrigo de Vivar killed Count Lozano to avenge an affront directed at his own father, while Sancho Ortiz kills Bustos Tabera in obedience to an express and categorical order of the King] (2). Even King Sancho's admission of guilt finds justification in the reviewer's eyes because in ordering Busto Tabera's death he has transgressed moral law.

This 1885 review is written, then, by a writer whose conservative values inform his deep appreciation of Golden Age drama and the political-moral system it purports to uphold. Sancho Ortiz's fidelity to his king "resalta de una manera hermosa en la comedia de Lope y la refundición de Trigueros" [*sic*] [stands out beautifully both in Lope's *comedia* and Trigueros's *refundición*] (2). The characters and action, too, that populate and comprise the play are worthy of respect. Luis Alfonso's unabashed love for Spain's glorious past and chagrin for the poverty of expression of his contemporary epoch rapturously transport him through his fervent defense of a bygone era in possession of a richness to be mined:

> Sólo caracteres hidalgos y generosos, sólo acciones varoniles y heróicas descuellan en la obra que fue anoche representada. ¡Ah! los autores de aquellos tiempos, o por inspirarse en ejemplos menos ruines, o porque la inspiración naciese sana y pura en ellos, no habían menester como tantos autores (de teatros o de novelas) de estos tiempos, apelar a vicios repulsivos, a pasiones enfermas, a lances de hospital y de mancebía, para producir grandiosos conflictos dramáticos o para crear soberanas obras artísticas.

> [Only noble and magnanimous characters, only manly and heroic actions stand out in the work performed last night. Ah! The authors of bygone days, either because they sought less base examples or because inspiration was born healthy and pure in them, did not need—like so many contemporary authors—to appeal to repulsive vices, sickly passion, hospital or brothel scenes, in order to produce grandiose dramatic conflicts or to create sovereign artistic works.] (2)

Sancho Ortiz de las Roelas, with a sharpness reminiscent of a Toledo sword (as Luis Alfonso suggests later in his review), is an apt starting point, to trace the changing sensibilities with respect to the *comedia*, and an example of how the horizons of experience of two writers (Cándido María Trigueros and Juan Eugenio Hartzenbusch) are formed by their distance from that foreign country that is the past. Their individual interpretations of the Golden Age *comedia* become witnesses to the evolutionary process of literary history;

each reworking creates as well as reaffirms the canonic status of *La estrella de Sevilla* at the same time that each reevaluates, through individual dialogues with the original text, how that canon is critiqued for its contemporaries and how the legacy is to be transmitted to the reviewing public. Implicit in both *refundiciones* is political, social, and literary indoctrination as each author/recaster advances his particular vision concerning the monarch's role in establishing political and social order. The fact of recasting and of performing this play emphasizes, too, its role in reestablishing, for each successive age, how the past is to be interpreted and how tradition is to be incorporated in developing the past's influence on contemporary life.

3
Marta la piadosa:
Tirso at the Hands of Reworkers

Little could Tirso de Molina imagine that his *Marta la piadosa* would eventually produce imitations and recasts within and beyond the borders of Spain. As a tale of hypocrisy and greed, Tirso's comic masterpiece contributed the necessary ingredients for Molière to cook up his *Tartuffe*, and later the eighteenth century initiated a number of "Martas" that took the fundamental characters and plot from Tirso and transformed them into neoclassical and post-Romantic molds to express social concerns of the period. *Marta la piadosa* informed Moratín's vision when he wrote *El viejo y la niña* [The old man and the girl] (1786; first performed in 1790);[1] Tirso's play most likely provided thematic structure to Moratín's *La mojigata* [The pious deceiver] (1791; first performed in 1804), thus leading to a resurgence of interest in the source play.[2] Finally, *El sí de las niñas* [The maiden's consent] (1801; first performed in 1806), the latest of these plays, takes up the theme of arranged marriage.[3] Although the so-called May-December marriages imposed by a father upon an unwilling daughter, is not a motif unique to *Marta la piadosa*, Tirso's popularity beyond the Golden Age argues for his general influence upon Moratín as well as upon other neo classical writers. The presentation in the 1770s on both the Madrid and Seville stages of Molière's *Tartuffe* (in translated and recast form) helped to foster the ambience in which *Marta la piadosa* once again would attract writers' attention. Within this context two *refundiciones* of *Marta la piadosa* appear: one by Pascual Rodríguez de Arellano circa 1790, and another by Dionisio Solís (1819). Solís's popular version in turn greatly influenced an 1865 recast by Calixto Boldún y Conde. The first two *refundiciones*, and to a much lesser extent the third one, are the focus of this chapter.

Teresa de Guzmán printed the *suelta* of *Marta la piadosa* in February 1734, but, like many similar printings, the play was issued for the reading public.[4] Although a *refundición* of Tirso's *comedia* was not to appear until near the end of the century, a translation of *Tartuffe* by Cándido María Trigueros appeared on the Seville stage in 1770, and at the Cruz and Príncipe theatres in Madrid in 1777.[5] Trigueros's play, *La hipocresía castigada, o Juan de Buen Alma* (also known as *El gazmoño*) [Hypocrisy punished, or John Good-Soul], saw only one performance in Madrid, and finally, on 20 June 1779, the Inquisition issued a definitive prohibition against its staging.[6] The translation was forgotten, but Molière's plays continued to evoke considerable interest. It was not until 1802 that a second translation of *Tartuffe* appeared, written by Valles y Codes, under the title *El hipócrita* [The hypocrite]; its performances did not cause the scandal Trigueros's version elicited, but what corrections or changes were made in this latest version are unknown.[7] Coe lists frequent performances of *El hipócrita*, whose variations in title suggest different plays, from 1802 to 1815.[8] The currency that Molière's play had gained in Spain coupled with Moratín's interest in Molière as well as in Tirso, must have contributed to renewed interest in Tirso's *comedia*. The general plot outline of *Tartuffe* would remind writers like Moratín of Tirso's work, and even if the first *refundición* of *Marta la piadosa* was not presented for approval until 1790, it could well have been written earlier to take advantage of Moratín's related plays. The infamous hypocrite was "in the air," and at least two writers attempted to take advantage of both artistic and economic possibilities by trading on the name of one Golden Age writer and on the interest in French plays.

Pascual Rodríguez de Arellano is an obscure eighteenth-century writer related to the better-known playwright and *refundidor* Vicente Rodríguez de Arellano. The scant information available about him reveals his interest in the Spanish theatre and concerns a 1790 petition for financial aid he wrote to a minister of Carlos IV's council:

> Que zeloso del Honor de la Patria, amancillado en el bello ramo de la Literatura Dramática, tomó el empeño de vindicarlo, dedicándose a sugetar varias comedias de nuestros mejores dramáticos a los preceptos del Arte con el intento de formar un Teatro Español arreglado, obra única de que carece la Nación.

> [Zealous of the country's honor—which has suffered dishonor in the noble field of dramatic literature—he has taken the pains to vindicate it, dedicating himself to imposing on several *comedias* by our best play-

wrights the precepts of art, with the intention of forming an ordered Spanish Theatre, a unique form of art lacking in our Nation.][9]

In a summary of the petition, Don Diego Rejón de Silva, a secretary of the Royal Council, mentions that Pascual Rodríguez de Arellano "ha enmendado varias Comedias de Calderón y otros Autores nuestros." [has corrected several *comedias* by Calderón and other authors]. Rejón de Silva adds, too, that he found the prologue to a "Disertación sobre la Dramática" [Dissertation on theatre] "bastante bien escrita" [rather well written] and considered the *comedias No siempre lo peor es cierto* [It's not always as bad as it looks] and *El castigo de la Miseria* [The punishment of misery], "arregladas al Arte con acierto y con mucha felicidad en la imitación del estilo" [skillfully arranged according to the precepts of art and with great felicity in the imitation of the original style].[10] Unfortunately for Rodríguez de Arellano, his request for a subvention to cover printing costs of the *refundiciones*, and thus to work toward a Teatro Nacional, was rejected.

Apart from the writer's attempts to garner a royal subvention, there may have been another reason for Rodríguez de Arellano to recast specifically *Marta la piadosa*. The chronology of Moratín's plays suggests that Rodríguez de Arellano may have been influenced by a performance of *El viejo y la niña* and set himself the task of contributing to an examination of the sociological questions raised by Moratín's plays. He could accomplish this goal by recasting a classical piece that already contained in its essence the concerns about a young woman's right to choose a spouse; the *comedia* could then be easily "adapted" to a form required by a new age. The recast's three acts, however, indicate that the three unities may be imposed on a dramatic text without the necessity of slowing down the pace of the dramatic action in a five-act play (one of the criticisms leveled against Solís's *refundición*). Though it seems that Rodríguez de Arellano's version was never produced, the fact that *La mojigata* was composed in 1791 allows the supposition of reciprocal influence: Moratín may have read some version of *Marta la piadosa*—possibly Rodríguez de Arellano's as well as Tirso's—as he prepared to write *La mojigata*. Doña Clara's deceptions and "beatería"—synonymous less with devotion than with hypocrisy—vividly recall Marta's piety, feigned to avoid an undesired and undesirable marriage. In this regard, *La mojigata* becomes a link as well with Dionisio Solís's 1819 *refundicion* of *Marta la piadosa*.[11] The forced marriages of the other two neoclassical plays certainly owe a debt to Tirso's comedy. Though the thrusts of *El viejo* and *El sí* differ, the arranged marriage between the young woman and the older man was an important social, economic, and cultural phenomenon of the late eighteenth and early nineteenth centuries. Andioc's analysis of the situation of both the single and married woman in late eighteenth-century Spain, to which I will turn in a moment, suggests that Rodríguez de Arellano wished to capitalize on a matter of contemporary importance, and thus he chose *Marta la piadosa* not only to foster a "teatro nacional," but also to show how current and timely Tirso's play could be.[12] In the words of John Cook, many *comedias* "had genuine merit and could, without too great violence, be made to conform to the rules."[13]

Rodríguez de Arellano appears to have been aware of the wide-ranging literary, social, and philosophical debates common to the late eighteenth-century Madrid press. The education of young women and arranged marriages were issues of concern to social reformers of the period, and were reflected in the plays of Moratín and others. A well-educated middle-class young woman "no podía por menos de conformarse con dar el 'sí' que exigía el padre" [could do no less than to comply with her father's demand to agree to the marriage]. In addition, the freedom accorded married women was much greater than that given to single women.[14] Thus the discussion between Marta and her father, Don Gómez, takes on a new currency in the newer age. When Don Gómez scolds Marta, in act 2 of Rodríguez de Arellano's play, for attending to the "asquerosos males" [revolting illnesses] in the hospital, Marta replies that attending to the infirm is a more constructive occupation than idling in front of the window:

>   *Marta.*   A ser liviana
>   y estar siempre a la ventana,
>   ¿qué dixeras? ¿Es delito
>   visitar el hospital
>   que lo riñes como vicio?
>   ¿No se emplea en este oficio
>   la gente más principal?
>   *D. Gómez.* Sé monja.
>   *Marta.*   No determino,
>   aunque este estado es tan santo,
>   estrecharme, padre, tanto.
>   Yo voy por este camino;
>   déxeme con mi opinión.
>   *D. Gómez.* Cásate, pues, y casada
>   más segura y más honrada
>   seguirás tu inclinación,
>   que el Capitán gustará
>   de ese empleo y ese oficio.

[*Marta.* If I were frivolous and always by the window, what would you say then? Is it such a crime to visit the hospital, that you chastise my going as if it were a vice? Do not the most noteworthy people take up this occupation?
D. Gómez. Be a nun.
Marta. Even though that is a saintly position, father, I have not made up my mind to limit myself that much. I am following this path; let me worry about my reputation.
D. Gómez. Get married, then, and once married you can follow your inclinations more safely and honorably, for the Captain will be pleased with that occupation.] (2.2)[15]

The philosophy that condones a married woman's outings, especially for such "pious" purposes, translates well into Rodríguez de Arellano's time. But eliminated from this first recast of Tirso's play is Marta's euphoria at the new-found freedom that her "beatería" has conferred:

> Linda sangre y humor cría,
> Pastrana, la hipocresía.
> Nunca tuve libertad,
> mientras que viví a lo damo,
> como agora; si intentaba
> salir fuera, me costaba
> una riña: ya no llamo
> a la dueña, al escudero,
> ni aguardo la silla y coche,
> ni me riñen si a la noche
> vuelvo: voy a donde quiero.

[I never had the freedom, when I lived the life of a lady, that I enjoy now. If I tried to leave the house, it created an argument; I no longer call the chaperone, the squire, nor do I await the coach, nor do they argue with me if I return late at night. I go where I please.] (2.4)[16]

Marta's free and open admittance of her hypocrisy, communicated to the audience through the word "beata," as well as the notion of unlimited female freedom, become censurable. It seems clear that such an attitude could not be condoned by Rodríguez de Arellano, nor even less by Moratín; in *La mojigata*, for example, at no time does Doña Clara admit that her preparation to take the veil has less than honorable motives. Rather, the focus is on her general unwillingness to follow those steps and on the fact that her father's undue strictness, criticized heavily by Clara's uncle Don Luis, has led to duplicitous behavior. *Marta la piadosa* and *La mojigata* vary greatly and have different aims, but the connection between them is clear.

The potentially deleterious effects of a proposed May-December marriage portrayed in Tirso's play are but one aspect of social criticism, and one that concerned the economists of the time.[17] Other institutions like the honor code, avarice, and false devotion are all the butt of the Mercedarian's critique and are motifs sure to enthrall the public. Moratín looked to his Golden Age predecessor to find valuable source materials, as he had done on other occasions.[18] *La mojigata* shows no evidence of direct textual borrowing, but Doña Clara's hypocrisy takes its impetus from Marta, though the object of critique has been redefined. Clara's deceit, Moratín suggests, grows out of her overly strict upbringing. In *El viejo y la niña*, the marriage between the older Don Roque and the younger Doña Isabel is a *fait accompli*; Isabel rejects her lover (her contemporary) to live up to the social and moral expectations imposed upon her. The marriage evolves out of a question of "interés," a word not uncommon to *Marta la piadosa*. Such interests, be they financial or social, are the calling card for those to whom such superficial qualities are important. The fact that these two plays based on *Marta la piadosa* have taken different aspects of Tirso's *comedia* to expand—hypocrisy and forced marriages—is further testimony to the complexity and the richness of the source.[19]

Pascual Rodríguez de Arellano's *Marta la piadosa* is in many ways a true rewriting. Though the changes he introduced in his manuscript do not reappear in later reworkings, his version eliminates about half of Tirso's original, and appears to be the earliest reworking of Tirso's play. It is shorter than the original (2390 verses as compared to Tirso's approximately 3050). Rodríguez de Arellano could have made use of either Tirso's 1636 *Quinta Parte* or the 1734 *suelta* (almost identical to the *Quinta Parte*). He chose to recast the work into another three-act play, an occasional practice in a period of five-act dramas. The violence often done to the *comedia* by dividing it into five acts is in large part avoided, and thus the pace of the dramatic action is maintained, even with conformity to the "rules." He follows the basic outline of the plot of Tirso's play, yet the great majority of the lines are the recaster's own. Gone are the opening sonnets of Tirso's original, a practice to be followed by the other *refundidores*, as is the Alférez's lengthy account, in act 2, of the battle of the Mámora, another excision continued in the nineteenth-century adaptations. Decorum and verisimilitude found shelter in Rodríguez de Arellano. In Tirso, Marta's love for Don Felipe does not wane in spite of his having killed her brother; in this first recast, the brother is only wounded, and, in fact, returns at the end of the play to find his attacker in his very house. At times, as I shall indicate in the course of the study, Rodríguez de Arellano constructs entire scenes around one or two verses of the original *comedia*. This first *refundición* of *Marta la piadosa* is thus original in many ways and is a good, albeit unexciting, play: because the *refundidor* has prepared the reader/spectator for many of the tricks that Marta and Felipe devise to circumvent Don Gomez's planned marriage for his daughter, the spotlight illuminates not plot twists, but how those turns of events play themselves out.

Two of the major revisions to be found in this version are Rodríguez de Arellano's replacement of the Mámora *relación* and his treatment of women. In the first case, he avoids what would be a boring and unrelated retelling of a distant historical event; Rodríguez de Arellano establishes the relationship between the Alférez and Felipe through a long dialogue between the former and Marta at the structural mid-point of the play corresponding to the original's Mámora verses. The Alférez, too, has been introduced early in the play to make this revision plausible, and thus a logical reordering is brought about by the elimination of the original's verses. As for the second major shift in ideological perspective, the *refundidor* subverts Tirso's playfulness vis-à-vis women, reducing them from astute, psychologically complex characters to "curiosas" who are nevertheless capable, as is Marta, of carrying out a well-wrought plan to thwart Don Gomez's and Capitán Urbina's proposed marital arrangements. In this vein, inconsistencies do arise. Rodríguez de Arellano on the one hand puts Lucía on the same level of intelligence as her sister Marta, while on the other he maintains Marta's references to her sister as "boba" and "necia." The problem occurs because of the desire to change the play to reflect the current theatrical aesthetic while maintaining some of the piquant interest of Tirso's original.

Rodríguez de Arellano follows a procedure similar to Trigueros's in *Sancho Ortiz de las Roelas* in altering the *dramatis personae* and reducing much introductory material from act 1 and condensing it into the characters' opening speeches. The characters of Don Juan and Don Diego from Tirso's original, whose presence has been criticized as unnecessary, have been eliminated.[20] If their function in Tirso is, as I believe, to serve as a kind of Greek chorus commenting upon the action and putting into question the sincerity of Marta's "conversion," Rodríguez de Arellano has shown that their absence does not weaken the structure of the play. More important is the condensation of the ruse Marta and Felipe perpetrate. In this version of *Marta la piadosa*, the first one hundred verses contain important information that Tirso spread over two acts: the learning of Latin, Felipe's reappearance and the use of disguise, a run-in between

Felipe and Marta's brother, the arranged betrothal of Marta with Captain Urbina, the Alférez's interest in Lucía, the theme of "beaterio" (v. 89), and Lucía's prior love for Felipe. How each of these dramatic elements is developed is important to discuss because they describe how the play was recast.

The new *Marta la piadosa* becomes an extended grammar of love, trading on the Latin lesson that Tirso so artfully crafted.[21] Rather than introduce it in the second act, Rodríguez de Arellano opens with Marta on stage, "con un arte en la mano,"[22] pondering the conjugation of the verb "amar":

> Amo, amar, verbo activo
> (y por lo activo cruel);
> ego amo: éste es el
> presente de indicativo.
> (¡Qué bien con mi mal concierta
> esta lección que hoy me plugo!)
> Voy a ver si le conjugo:
> Yo amo, ego amo. La puerta
> parece que abren.

[I love, to love, active verb (and cruel because it is so active); therefore I love: this is the present indicative. (How well today's pleasing lesson harmonizes with my unhappiness!) I love, therefore I love. I think someone is opening the door.] (1.1)

The cause of Marta's concern is twofold: the absence of Felipe and her imminent betrothal to Capitán Urbina. Her grammar drill acts as a password to open a passage to the possibility of love: her servant Sirena—the name certainly is evocative—enters to tell Marta that she has seen Felipe in the marketplace, disguised as a merchant, that he continues to love her, and that the encounter between Felipe and Marta's brother resulted not in death, but in a wound from which he is fast recovering. The use of the particular disguise adopted here by Felipe is another nod to Moratín's *El viejo y la niña*, in which a character, the deceased Don Alvaro de Silva, is a wealthy gentleman from Cádiz.[23] The facts of Felipe's dress as a "comprador" [purchasing agent] and his having left Pastrana in Cádiz suggest not only that city's economic importance but also its popularity in this regard recognized was in the theatre. As for altering the brother's fate, Rodríguez de Arellano lends greater verisimilitude to Marta's continued love for Felipe; if the *siglo de oro* could laugh at the improbability of the "love conquers all" spoof of Tirso,[24] the late eighteenth century would not have the satire within its horizons and would most likely be horrified at the thought. Furthermore, the brother's survival means that the barrier to Felipe's and Marta's hoped-for betrothal has been effectively removed. The lovers' greatest fear is the brother's return. Even this obstacle is easily circumvented, as Felipe explains:

> Si llegan a conocerme
> estando bueno tu hermano,
>   nada se llega a arriesgar,
> porque el mismo pundonor
> ha de elegir por mejor
> el que nos hagan casar;
>   y assí las enemistades
> desde luego cesarán
> y se nos convertirán
> en alegres amistades.

[If they recognize me, since your brother is in good health, nothing will be risked, because honor itself will choose our marriage as the best path; so, enmity will become happy friendship.] (1.12)

We also learn that Marta has already taken on the role of "beata" to thwart any imposed marriage; in the first dialogue with her father, Don Gómez, we learn that Marta has been a "beata" studying Latin for some time:

> D. Gómez.   ¿Marta?
>   Marta. ¿Señor?
> D. Gómez.   ¿Siempre de esa forma?
>   Marta. Soy muy ruda, padre mío,
>   y esta rudeza notoria
>   la ha de vencer el travajo,
>   que todo lo rinde y postra;
>   y como se fue el maestro
>   la aplicación es forzosa.

[D. Gómez. Marta?
Marta. Sir?
D. Gómez. Are you always this way?
Marta. I am very unschooled, father, and hard work, which smoothes all difficulties, will overcome this well-known ignorance. As the teacher has left, I must work at my lessons.] (1.5)

The stage has been set for Felipe's entrance into the household as Dómine Berrío, who will continue Marta's Latin lesson. Her disguise, too, is not invented on the spur of the moment, as in Tirso's original, to thwart her father's wishes for a rich marriage, but has already been put into practice. But the intention behind her interest in learning is discerned in her language:

> que aunque aprendí a declinar
> con facilidad muy pronta,
> en esto del conjugar
> vengo a estar un poco tonta.

[for although I learned how to decline with great facility, I am still somewhat unsure in conjugation.] (1.5)

Not only has she learned to decline nouns and adjectives, but she is working to "decline" the marriage arranged for her by her father. By the same token her weakness in conjugating verbs translates into a lack of desire for a "conjugal" arrangement not of her doing. Rodríguez de Arellano not only has recast much of Tirso's play, he has also adopted some of the felicity in word play and double entendre. Even though Marta has already decided that she will remain faithful to Don Felipe (and she clarifies this to him in her explanation of the "beaterio" that she has devised), she has yet to counter the marriage proposal directly. Unlike Tirso's original in which Marta is not aware of the arranged nuptials until the *comedia* is well under way, in this play she clearly has been preparing for the confrontation. When it does come, she explains her vow to remain ever a virgin because of a narrow escape from a danger she refuses to divulge—a good actress could carry this out with a moment's hesitation upon saying "que no declaro lo que fue" [which I refuse to specify]—in a passage nearly faithful to the original text. The only substantial change occurs at the end of the passage. Tirso wrote:

> Pero los años pasados,
> que agora se cumplen seis,
> por librarme de un peligro,
> que no declaro el que fue,
> hice voto de doncella,
> y pienso que lo he de ser
> hasta que en la virgen tierra[25]
> me entierren a la vejez.

[But six years ago, to free myself from danger—which I refuse to specify—I made a vow to remain a virgin, and I will remain so until in my old age they bury me in virgin land.] (1.16)

After repeating the first five verses Rodríguez de Arellano renders the remainder of the passage in this way:

> y pienso que lo he de ser
> hasta que en el polvo humilde
> me entierren a la vejez.

[and I will remain so until in my old age they bury me in humble dust.]
(1.19)

Rodríguez de Arellano either consulted a source heretofore unknown, an unlikely possibility, or his rewriting reflects contemporary conventions of decorum and "buen gusto." He may have found the use of the word "virgen" sacrilegious, particularly in a *comedia* full of mockery. This is an example of a change that does not alter in any way the sense of the passage or of the play, but does reinforce late eighteenth-century thought about such matters.

The element of disguise, as I mentioned above, is brought out early in the play. Sirena tells Marta, in 1.2, that she has encountered Don Felipe in the marketplace "embozado" [disguised]. He confides in Sirena: ". . . así / no llegue a tomarse susto / porque ha trazado el amor / vestirse de comprador / para feriar tanto gusto . . ." [so do not be afraid, because love has plotted to dress as a buyer to trade for so much pleasure](1.2). After meeting with Marta himself and finalizing the plans of her "beaterio" and desire to learn Latin, he becomes an accomplice with yet another planned disguise:

> y así me voy al instante
> porque todo quede firme,
> hermosa Marta, a vestirme
> de estudiantón vergonzante.
> Y no quieras más saber
> porque la misma ocasión
> nos prestará la instrucción
> del uso que se ha de hacer.

[and so I am going immediately, so that everything is set up, my beautiful Marta, to dress as a shameful begging student. Do not ask any more questions because the plan itself will instruct us in what needs to be done.] (1.12)

If act 1 reveals the protagonists' plans for subverting Don Gomez's wishes to marry Marta off to a wealthy "indiano," act 2 puts the plan into effect. Rodríguez de Arellano continues to follow Tirso in this regard. Indeed, the first three scenes of act 2 follow the plot Tirso laid out: Don Gómez and Capitán Urbina ponder Marta's decision to remain "beata" and "doncella"; they hope that Lucía's marriage to the Alférez will effect a change in Marta's attitude; Marta continues her "good works" at the hospital and refuses to allow a dispensation from her "vows"; Pastrana explains his intention to play the role of an *escribano* [notary] with news of Felipe's supposed capture in order to lure Don Gómez away from home and to allow Felipe's entrance into the household.[26]

The excision of the Alférez's long *relación* of the battle of the Mámora now requires comment. The passage breaks unity of action and therefore is extraneous to the *refundición*, unless Rodríguez de Arellano sought a faithful rendering of the original play, a concept not embraced until the advent of Romanticism. This *refundidior*, to his credit, is the only one to replace the passage with another speech involving the Alférez, who explains to Marta his prior relationship with Don Felipe and the confidences the two share, particularly with regard to Marta. The Alférez deduces that the "Marta" in whose house he presently resides is the same young woman alluded to by Don Felipe and wishes to help further the cause of true love to repay Felipe for having saved his life. The speech's length is reduced (from approximately four hundred verses to approximately seventy-five) and its content modified. The original *Marta la piadosa* is structured around that *relación* and the "máscara de latines" [mask of latinisms] that the Alférez himself consciously parodies at the opening of his speech;[27] Marta's Latin lesson and the various disguises contribute to the "máscaras" that inform the play. The new *relación* is likewise placed at the structural center of the play but, in a not wholly positive reflection on Rodríguez de Arellano's abilities, the dramatic action does not hinge on nor is it heavily influenced by the Alférez's desire to help Marta and Felipe nor by Marta's acceptance of the aid offered. In other words, the rewritten speech at this point serves principally a physical, structural function and secondarily a dramatic one. It prepares the audience (if indeed this version was ever produced on stage) for the Alférez's and Felipe's dialogue later in the play, and in so doing once again reduces the dramatic tension by overpreparation.

Furthermore, the displaced historical event (Mámora) is also a displacement of the role of the Alférez from *juglar*, a teller of an epic tale who parodies Gongoristic language, to a relater of a personal incident. The long passage in Tirso's original lends the *comedia* a wider dimension through Tirso's deft thematic linking; its removal in Rodríguez de Arellano's version reduces the scope of the play. In terms of the "ilustrados," however, such reduction produces a dramatic work that keeps much better to the three unities, especially once the distracting historical references are removed. In this regard, too, the removal of Don Diego and Don Juan serves the purpose of limiting the dramatic action of the play to the ruses Marta invents.

The remainder of act 2 is on the whole taken from Tirso's original with occasional line changes and cuts; none of these seems to be of great moment, but rather reflect Rodríguez de Arellano's desire to shorten the play and eliminate any references and characters not pertaining to the principal plot. With act 3, however, particularly toward the end of the play, numerous changes have been introduced. (Fortunately, one of the best scenes of the entire play, the Latin lesson, is given in its entirety.) Marta's and Pastrana's plans seem to be working, since Don Gómez is to depart for Cádiz, where Felipe is supposedly held prisoner for his wounding of Marta's brother, and Lucía is easily dispatched. Though the details differ from the original, in which Don Gómez rides for Sevilla, the intent remains the same. But instead of Don Gómez's return, after having heard the truth from a friend along the road, Marta's brother, Don Juan, recovered from his wounds, appears.

Don Gómez's avarice, which receives some attention throughout the play, does not enter into the denouement as in Tirso's original though the word "interés" is found frequently throughout both texts. Don Felipe's wealth does not become a factor in the final scene. Marta helps to sort out the differences among the swords (four characters have them drawn, ready for an altercation as Don Juan prepares to defend his family's honor once again), explaining that love is the motivation behind Felipe's presence in the house:

> Amor es la causa solo
> de esta confusión y enredo.
> Yo os pido, señor Urbina,
> mil perdones, si es desprecio
> lo que voy a referiros.
> D[o]n Felipe me amó tierno,
> yo su amor pagaba fina,
> vinisteis vos . . .

[Love is the one cause of this confusion and intrigue. I humbly beg your forgiveness, Mr. Urbina, if what I am about to tell you is disdainful. Don Felipe loved me tenderly, I returned his love politely, you arrived . . .]

(3.15)

Marta has studied well the grammar of love she began to read at the play's opening. Just as the door opens in 1.1 almost magically to the words "ego amo" so the stumbling blocks to her marriage to Felipe are removed once love has effected its spell. Even Capitán Urbina, the rival lover to whom Marta has directed her plea, recognizes that his role is not to be that of husband, but that of an understanding, magnanimous godfather:

> Ya os entiendo;
> basta, no más; y yo alabo
> vuestro juicio y vuestro ingenio,
> y mi necedad corrijo.
> . . . . .
> D[o]n Gómez, es d[o]n Felipe
> muy principal caballero;
> amor es muy poderoso,
> la venganza vil remedio,
> y el honor muy delicado;
> y así también me intereso
> por d[o]n Felipe; y a Marta
> la cantidad misma cedo
> que antes dixe . . .

[I understand; say no more; and I praise your judgment and your inventiveness, and I correct my foolishness. . . . Don Gómez, Don Felipe is a noteworthy gentleman; love is very powerful, vengeance a lowly solution, and honor a very delicate matter; and so I too take an interest in Don Felipe; and I grant to Marta the same amount as before...] (3.15)[28]

Urbina's attitude allows for a peaceful resolution to the conflict because he is the party with the greatest interest in matters of both love and finance, and, even though Marta had not yet become his wife, the one who had to defend his honor. His is the voice of reason who recognizes his foolishness ("necedad") and is willing to correct it. In this he differs considerably from the male protagonist of *El viejo y la niña* at the same time that he shares much with Don Diego of *El sí de las niñas* in recognizing a young woman's decision.

The ending of Tirso's play has been transformed with the addition of a moral. If Tirso is subtle—and biting—in his satire against greed and hypocrisy, Rodríguez de Arellano, true to his age, insists that a moral, or at least a warning, be clearly put forth at the end of the play:

> Pero advirtiendo
> que con capa de virtud
> se cometen mil excesos;

examinad devociones,
madres y padres discretos,
que las hijas muchas veces
afectan el ir al templo
por lograr lo que en sus casas
tal vez lograr no pudieron;
y si hay Dómines en casa,
que validos del pretexto
de enseñar latín, a muchas
las dominan con imperio,
hay dóminas en las puertas
del templo y de tal ingenio,
que hacen declinar a *Musa*
interponiéndole el *sermo*
con *Dominus*, y al instante
pasando a *tempus* de *templum*,
juntan a *Dies*, y al otro,
y dan al través con *sensus*.

[But warning that under the cape of virtue a thousand excesses are committed. Discreet mothers and fathers, examine your children's devotions, for daughters often feign attending mass to do what they are not allowed to do at home; and if there are tutors in the home who, under the pretext of teaching Latin, dominate many daughters imperiously, there are also mistresses at the temple doors and of such inventiveness, that they have you decline "Musa," inserting "sermo" with "dominus," and immediately passing to "tempus" from "templum," they bring together "Dies," and the following day do away with all "sensus."] (3.15; emphasis in original)[29]

The closing speech of *Marta la piadosa* breaks theatrical illusion, as is common to most *comedias*, by having Felipe step out of character to address the audience directly. His warning is more than a simple moral, though, for three reasons: it plays on and with Latinisms created in the manner of Tirso; it introduces additional terminology, related to the Latin lesson, for Marta's "grammar"; and it touches upon the issue of children's education. "Capa de virtud" speaks to more than simple hypocrisy. Marta's behavior as a "beata" is a cover for her intentions; Felipe's disguise as Dómine Berrío cloaks his amorous attentions from Don Gómez and Capitán Urbina. At least these two older characters are forthright about their aims: the father is looking to enrich himself as well as his daughter through her marriage to a wealthy adventurer; the captain offers himself sincerely to Marta, and the fact that he so willingly accedes to her wishes to marry Don Felipe speaks all the more strongly about his honorable intentions and his role as corrector (recall Don Manuel of *La mojigata*).

Felipe's exhortation to parents, particularly in regard to their daughters, takes up the remainder of.this closing speech. The "templo" may be the house of God, but with so many "religious" figures in Don Gómez's household carrying out supposedly virtuous deeds, the home becomes the temple. "Afectar" is especially well chosen, given its *Diccionario de autoridades* definition: "Poner especial cuidado y demasiado estudio y arte en la execución de algún hecho u dicho, para encubrirla u disimularla" [To place special care and excessive diligence and cunning when carryling out some deed or promise for deceitful purposes].[30] Marta's dedication to her "arte," both of disguise and of learning, is her affectation *par excellence* of "devociones" [devotions] that can be carried out only under the "capa de virtudes." (It would not be too outrageous to propose that "capa de virtudes" suggests "varilla de virtudes" [magic wand] for all the "magic" that undoes one betrothal and formulates another.) The ensuing wordplay involving various forms of "dómine" yields multiple signifiers that contribute to a slippage of meaning. The first "dómine" is a clear reference to Dómine Berrío who "dominates" (the direct object pronoun "las" refers to "hijas") the young women with whom they come into contact. To say that such "dómines" simply rule imperiously is to ignore the Latin source of "con imperio": *cum imperio*. The phrase suggests issues of authority, domination, and education because Latin primers often used as their reading passages texts by Caesar, Cicero, and Sallust, late Republicans whose writings are politically and militarily oriented.[31] In other words, if parents do not take care to rear their children (especially daughters) in strict ways, they face an ever-present danger of being supplanted by others (young men who dominate them).

Even this warning has a light tone to counterbalance its seriousness. Not only are "dómines" to be watched but "dóminas" also, the young women who wait in the doorway of their temples (houses of ill-repute?) to trap the unwary in ingenious ways. Just as Marta is unable to decline properly and finally covers her ignorance and possible discovery by feigning anger at "Quis putas," so she makes literal her grammar of love: "Musa" (Marta herself, the creator of the play-within-the-play whose male roles are Dómine Berrío and Don Juan Diego de Hurtado) creates a "sermo" (Marta's ability to improvise speeches and invent situations to suit her purpose) that leads to the appearance of "Dominus" (Felipe as Dómine Berrío). Marta dominates the unfolding of her plan; the fact that, regardless of the ingenuity of her muse, she has difficulty learning the Latin she is supposed to be studying devoutly (though she never gets past "amo") and confuses declensions that plague students of Latin ("tempus" and "templum," both of which are second declension, neuter nouns), is but a minor inconvenience. At the same time, passing from one term to the other is passing from "temple" to "time," from the religious to the quotidian and the creation of the play-within-the-play in its staging within the "templum" or temple of love, which is what her home, and by extension a theatre, has become. The "Dies" or "day" is joined with "tempus," the time needed to carry out her plans (with the suggestion of "dies irae," the day of wrath and Don Gómez's anger at his daughter). The conclusion, then, becomes obvious: "y dan al través con *sensus*," a self-explanatory state of affairs.[32] The entire closing speech, taking in all five possible Latin noun declensions, contains a parody of a parody, that is, of the Latin lesson, as well as a moral for Rodríguez de Arellano's *refundición* about arranged marriages, a daughter's education, and her right to choose a spouse.[33]

* * *

The next known version of *Marta la piadosa*, by Dionisio Solís, opened on 6 May 1819, at the Teatro de la Cruz, and was performed again from the sixth to the eighteenth of December 1819.[34] From 1821 until 1831, the reworked play enjoyed twenty-one performances at Madrid's Cruz and Príncipe theatres, and by 1850 it had been performed nearly fifty times.[35] In addition, it saw at least one performance each in 1851 and 1855.[36] Solís's source, just as Rodríguez de Arellano's, was either the *Quinta Parte* or the *suelta* of Tirso's original play. The version contains approximately 2,900 verses; its actual length is difficult to determine given the large number of interpolations; anywhere from a few verses to entire passages are deleted and replaced with others, often from Tirso's *comedia*. At times, a verse or strophe is emended two or three times, each *apuntador* deciding in favor of a new reading or staying with the "original."

The wholesale changes found in Solís's five-act recast remind us that in 1819 the theatre is still very much in the throes of neoclassical influence: the unities of time, place, and action are maintained at the expense of distorted dramatic action. Solís's decision to remove the opening sonnets, dispense with the *romance* about the Mámora, eliminate the characters Don Juan and Don Diego, and completely restructure the ending obeys a clear desire to "update" what many believed to be a tired genre; the elimination of a historical event two hundred years distant from the audience's horizon follows Rodríguez de Arellano's practice. Judging from Solís's success—at least in the number of performances from 1819 to 1850—he responded accurately to the demands of his public: he mediated, from his historical-cultural standpoint, the heritage in Tirso's play to present values consonant with his time.

Scene rearrangement accompanies recast speeches. The opening of the play corresponds to Tirso's 1.5 with Felipe's and Pastrana's arrival in Illescas. The immediate effect is to displace Marta to a secondary role since Solís's act 1 is overwhelmingly dominated by Felipe and Pastrana. Marta appears only in one scene—her arrival with her sister and father to meet the Capitán in Illescas; she has only eighteen lines to speak and gives only a brief indication of her need to have Felipe close. But her physical presence on stage remains imposing. Felipe's attention is soon attracted by the sight of Marta and her sister on the balcony of a nearby house. His description of her recalls Shakespeare's Romeo and his equation of the rising sun with Juliet:

> ¡Oh sol con madejas de oro,
> que de la noche el silencio
> rompes y enjugas mi lloro,
> desde aquí te reverencio
> y como el indio te adoro!

[Oh sun with golden tufts, you break the night's silence and dry my tears, from here I revere you and like the Indian I adore you.] (1.9)

To this point Solís coincides with Tirso, maintaining the simile of sun worship common to numerous South American Indian peoples; in this play the image is apt because of Captain Urbina's recent return from the New World. The following verses, however, have been removed, an excision which bespeaks a difference in conception of imagery between the two playwrights of two different epochs:

> Desde aquí el alma te escribe
> desta ausencia los enojos,
> en que muere cuando vive.
> Estafetas son los ojos:
> la carta, Marta, recibe,
> y responde el dulce "sí"
> que mi firme amor te ruega.
> Amigo Pastrana, di
> lo mucho que la amo; llega.

[From here my soul writes to you about the anger of this absence in which it dies as it lives. Postmen are my eyes; receive this letter, Marta, and respond with a sweet "yes" to my love's firm request. Pastrana, my friend, go and tell her how much I love her.] (1.9)

The Petrarchan image of the sun as emblematic of a woman's radiant beauty and as worthy idol of the lover's reverence is kept by Solís, but another image peculiar to the Golden Age—the "amor portugués" or the falling in love by the simple meeting of eyes[37]—is not carried into the nineteenth century. Tirso's implicit understanding of inscription both verbal and nonverbal yields the image of writing as well as the transmission of the message; he has applied the means of physical communication (writing) to the nonphysical; the means of the message's conveyance ("estafetas" or eyes as letter carriers) extends the imagery. Solís's elimination of these verses reduces one more scene of the play to a straightforward rendering of dramatic action deprived of the depth and ingenuity conferred by Tirso's imagery. This is not to say that Solís is incapable of creating his own quality text; his abilities as a *refundidor* become clear in the way he refashions the end of the play. But in an effort to appropriate Tirso's text for himself, to translate culturally a seventeenth-century text, he often practices simple reduction.

Solís begins his second act with Tirso's act 1, but adds three *redondillas* that replace the sonnets of Tirso's opening scene. Marta's perplexity at her prospects for marriage—in love with Felipe, but now confronted with two additional possibilities (Capitán Urbina and the Alférez)—is expressed in terms that clearly place this reworked play within its own historical/social context:

> ¡Estamos buenos, amor!
> Santo cielo, ¿qué partido
> tomaré contra el marido
> que ofrecen a mi dolor?
> Que aunque a don Felipe quiero,
> entre el tío y el sobrino
> que están en casa, me inclino
> de preferencia al postrero.
> ¿No basta, niño cruel,
> con un amor a mi pecho,
> que intentas a su despecho
> introducir otro en él?

[We're in fine shape, love! Holy Heaven, what side shall I take against the husband they offer to my chagrin? Although I love Don Felipe, between the uncle and the nephew here in my house, I am inclined toward the latter. Isn't it enough, cruel child, that in spite of the one love in my heart, you attempt to introduce another.] (2.1)

The discussion of Rodríguez de Arellano's *refundición* brought to the forefront the question of forced marriages. Moratín's plays may have suggested Tirso's *Marta la piadosa* to Solís (whether the recaster knew Rodríguez de Arellano's version is impossible to determine; Solís does not quote from it).[38] The steadfastness of the original Marta—who, because she believes for a moment that the Alférez is to be her husband, nevertheless expresses fear at meeting the Alférez's glance ("Miralle temo, / porque a su nuevo amor no me condene" [I am afraid to look at him so I am not condemned to this new love] [1.14])—is placed into question only at this moment. Solís elaborates on Marta's wavering; he writes these lines into his text in order to introduce the logical question that Lucía subsequently asks, the question that immediately follows the sonnets in 1.1 of the original: "¿Quién da materia a las quejas / que tantas formas sin ver / que sabe el temor poner / a las paredes orejas?" [Who gives substance to the many complaints that you set forth without seeing that fear makes the walls hear? (2.2). The remainder of the scene is copied nearly word for word by Solís.[39]

In the ensuing scene, Solís has eliminated the letter Don Gómez has received from his old friend the Capitán, and replaced it with a narration, written in *quintillas* to join with Tirso's versification in 1.2. The informative passage functions to reaffirm that the Capitán is about to ask for Marta's hand in marriage, an event that, for Don Gómez, can do much to soften the emotional loss of his son. The passage also serves to link two scenes taken almost verbatim from Tirso; the first, discussed above, is the discussion and mutual backbiting practiced by the jealous sisters Marta and Lucía; the second develops Marta's deception of Lucía and of her father with "news" of Felipe's supposed arrest in Sevilla in order to buy time to avoid the forced marriage and be reunited with Felipe. In other words, Solís knew a good story when he read one and, given the interest in "mojigatería" in recent theatrical productions, could with a few careful retouches, "update" Tirso's comic play.[40]

Solís has taken for his 2.5–2.7 the end of Tirso's act 1, rewriting the *octavas reales* as a combination of *redondillas* and *romances*. All the elements of Tirso's original are present (the confusion as to the intended husband [the Capitán or the Alférez], Marta's momentary confusion as she tries to invent an incontrovertible reason to delay the wedding, and her ostensible "vow," taken six years earlier, to remain chaste). However, a problem does arise, not so much with regard to Tirso's text, but with different endings to Solís's act 2. The many stagings of this version bring numerous emendations to the text at the discretion of the director in its performance afterlife. It is impossible to know which ending to this act was performed at what date or what possible combination of changes were utilized in any specific performace. Regardless of these problems, some of the rewritings suggest simply a desire to be "different" from the original; indeed, one version of the ending does copy the last two lines of Tirso's act 1: *D. Gómez.* "¿Que castidad prometiste?" / *Marta.* "Sí, señor. (Yo sé con quién)" [*D. Gómez.* You promised chastity? *Marta*: Yes, sir. (I know to whom)] (2.6). Curiously, the other endings avoid Marta's admission, even in an aside, that her vow is nothing more than a ruse. The changes seem to close the act with Don Gómez's need to obey a higher authority (i.e., God) who has dictated his daughter's decision. Further complications for choosing any one ending are the prompter's notes regarding cuts added and later restored; a plethora of "no" and "sí," lines drawn through verses, and bracketed passages litter the manuscript. Nonetheless, the import of all the changes is similar: Don Gómez and the Capitán have decided to defer a decision concerning Marta's status, a closing that differs insubstantially from Tirso's original text.

The first four scenes of Solís's act 3 correspond to the first four scenes of Tirso's act 2; the changes in the text are minor, with one notable exception, a matter of verisimilitude concerning Don Gómez's description of his daughter's clothing that reflects the supposedly pious life she has chosen. Gone are references to an "abanico sin plata," [a cheap fan] and "una estufilla / de felpa o de cabritilla" [a muff made of felt or kidskin] (2.1), apparel not worn in the opening decades of the nineteenth century. But this data suggest, too, that Solís's play is "updated" in more than its formal, textual divisions. The new description of Marta implies the elimination of a vocabulary unfamiliar to the audience as well as a hint about the performance: this version was presented in contemporary costume. Unfortunately the script at hand does not specify set decor, staging, or costumes.

The major change in the opening scene of Solís's act 3 concerns the Alférez. His description of his return from battle at the Mámora has been excised; indeed, no mention is made of his having fought in the battle at all. (This makes the reference to it in act 1 stand out rather clumsily, particularly given Felipe's frustrated desire to join the troops en route to the fort.) Solís replaces all references to this battle and to the Alférez's imminent return (the following scene in the original text) with a bit of Tirso-like humor. Capitán Urbina and Don Gómez have noted the Alférez's love for Lucía and decide to arrange their marriage in order to convince Marta that marriage is acceptable and desirable. Where in the original the Capitán expresses pleasure at the proposed union on behalf of his absent nephew, in Solís's play he voices concern that Lucía may follow in her sister's footsteps:

> ... El a Lucía
> tiene afición y sería
> buen acuerdo por ahora
>   casarlos en el momento;
> no sea que como a mí
> me sucede, al dar el sí
> se le anuble el casamiento
>   y salgamos con que quiere
> ser doncella su muger.

[He has a liking for Lucía and it would make a good arrangement at this point to marry them immediately. I hope what happened to me does not occur again: once the arrangements are made the marriage question clouds over, and it turns out that his wife wants to remain a virgin.] (2.1)

Tirso's character suggests that Lucía's marriage might urge Marta to follow in her footsteps. Solís's Capitán Urbina, on the other hand, expresses a well-founded fear that Marta will exercise undue influence on Lucía. The remainder of the scene details the Alférez's entrance, his desire for Lucía, and Don Gomez's and the Capitán's lamentations over Marta's chosen path; the brief conversation among the three men serves primarily to create a bridge over the excised Mámora description and to cue Marta's entrance in the following scene.

The opening of 3.3 and 2.3, respectively, serves to bring the spectator up to date on the state of Marta's and Felipe's relationship. In Solís, a number of phrases have been crossed out and recast verses written above the original line; the crossed-out passages are from Tirso's original. (Here as elsewhere, it is impossible to ascertain the source and date of the changes.)

Tirso

Vi a Don Felipe en el prado
llegar, la color perdida,
por la mudanza de vida
con que a mi padre he engañado;
  pero viendo que no osaba
hablarme por el respeto
que en este traje prometo,
le dije que le adoraba
  tanto, que por su ocasión
andaba desta manera;
pues si estoy devota, él era
mi imagen de devoción.

Solís

Vi a don Felipe en el prado
llegar, la color perdida,
temerosa que le olvida
mi afición y se ha engañado,
  pero viendo que no osaba
hablarme llena de ceño,
que sólo él era mi dueño,
le dixe, y que le adoraba
  tanto, que por su ocasión
andaba de esta manera,
y que entendiese que a él era
al que amaba mi pasión. ...

Tirso	Solís
[I saw Don Felipe arrive along the promenade, his face ashen because of the change of life with which I have deceived my father. But seeing that he did not dare speak with me out of respect for my clothing, I told him that I adored him so much, that he is the reason that I am dressed in this way. If I am devout, he was the object of devotion.] (2.3)	[I saw Don Felipe arrive along the promenade, his face ashen, fearful that my new interest will replace him and that he has been deceived, but seeing that he did not dare speak with me with the frown on my face, I told him that only he was my master, and that I adored him so much, that he is the reason I am dressed in this way, and that he should understand that my passion was for him . . .] (3.3)

Gone from the recast is Marta's stark admission of deception, softened by her admitted fear that Felipe believes himself forgotten with her feigned metamorphosis. Solís has modified as well the outward signs of Marta's new "profession": it is not the austere clothing of the "beata" which puts Felipe at an emotional distance, but a frown that conveys her supposedly dour attitude toward the joys of life. Finally, and perhaps most importantly, Marta's expression of her unbroken and unmodified affection for Felipe has been altered. Tirso's Marta leaves no doubt about her "devotion" because she continues to hold Felipe as the image of her homage (recall the close of Tirso's act 1 [*D. Gómez.* "¿Que castidad prometiste?" *Marta.* "Sí. (Yo sé con quién")] [*D. Gómez.* You promised chastity? *Marta.* Yes (and I know to whom)]). Curiously, she says "estoy devota" [I am devout] and not "soy devota" [I have taken vows], thus describing the effect of Felipe on her and not a description of any new-found faith. Solís's change—if indeed it was Solís who introduced this specific change—to "y que entendiese que a él era / al que amaba mi pasión" loses the ambiguity imbued by Tirso with "devota" and responds to a "taming" of Tirso.[41]

A new tone brought to things religious affects as well the piquancy suggested by the play's very title.[42] Pastrana ends the exposition of his plan of attack by attributing its ingeniousness to the devil's tricks:

> . . . y quedará
> por este modo segura
>   su vida y nuestra maraña;
> y otras mil cosas que aquí
> han de llover sobre mí,
> porque el demonio me engaña.

[his life and our conspiracy will remain safe; and thousands of other things that will befall me because the devil deceives me.] (2.4)

Solís changes the last word of this speech to "enrreda" to ward off any suspicion of evildoing and complicity with the occult; his interest was certainly more one of propriety than of poetry, because the result destroys the rhyme of the final *redondilla*. Soon thereafter, as Marta realizes the advantage to be gained from this well-wrought plan, Pastrana expresses some fear about what will befall him if they are caught. In the original Pastrana says:

> Por Dios,
> que va temiendo Pastrana
> si por su ocasión le gozas,
> una sarta de corozas ...

[For God's sake, Pastrana fears he will have to wear a convict's cap if you enjoy his pleasure ...] (2.4)

Solís removes the sexual allusion for what may be reasons of decorum; Pastrana no longer claims directly that he fears the "sarta de corozas" for having acted as a go-between,[43] but for some suggestive yet unnamed crime: "por ésta y por otras cosas" (3.4). As is often the case of censorship, self-imposed or otherwise, what is not said often has a stronger impact than direct reference; a skillful actor could convey sexual allusion with gesture and tone of voice and avoid running afoul of propriety and of the censors. This emendation, similar to the immediately preceding one, disrupts the natural rhyme "gozas / corozas" by forcing the rhyme of "cosas / corozas." But this is a wide practice; meter and rhyme have become in the *refundición* secondary to the emendation of text.

The patterns Solís has established early in act 3 continue: a toning down of Marta's more outrageous pronouncements (outrageous perhaps to the audience viewing the *refundición*), and the excision of references, particularly those imbued with irony, to the rosary or other religious practices. In Solís's 3.6, corresponding to Tirso's 2.7, Don Gómez has been informed of Felipe's "capture." To Don Gómez's fervent wish for swift punishment Marta responds, in the original, with a heartfelt desire to avoid such rigor: "Yo, señor, / ... en conciencia, y para abono / de mi alma, le perdono, / y ... el matalle es rigor" [I, sir, in good conscience, and for the peace of my soul, forgive him; killing him is excessive punishment] (2.7). Solís alters Marta's response notably: "Nada digo en este asunto / porque es delicado punto, / mas paréceme rigor" [I say nothing in this matter because it is a fine point of law, but it seems excessive to me] (3.6). The mention of a pardon is removed, perhaps because the notion that a brother's murderer should be forgiven, especially from an aggrieved party, would have been unpalatable to the audience. This interpretation, however, begs the question of the entire *refundición* and the fact that Marta and Felipe do marry in the end. But, as I shall discuss with regard to Solís's act 5, other considerations inform the denouement.

Solís's act 4 corresponds in great measure to a little more than half of Tirso's act 3, eliminating the festivities in the duke's garden as well as the ensuing disguises and the denouement as originally conceived. Solís develops quite a different, yet not altogether original, closure to his play, which will be studied below. The major thrust of act 4/act 3 is maintained. In 4.1, for example, corresponding to Tirso's 3.1, Solís removes additional religious references.[44] In Tirso's opening scene Urbina's expression of love for Marta: "El amor que os tengo es tal, / ya no humano, mas divino" [The love that I have for you is such, no longer human, but divine] (3.1), becomes in Solís's 4.1: "El amor que os tengo es tal / y me ace con vos tan fino" [The love that I have for you is such, and it makes me gallant in your presence]. Again the prompt copy of the *refundición* originally contained Tirso's verses only to have another hand change them, either to tailor the play to a specific performance or to comply with a censor's demands. Marta's reply to Urbina's offer of eight thousand ducats to be put toward her hospital further exemplifies the same process; where Tirso says "Por uno os dé el cielo ciento" [May Heaven increase it one hundredfold] (3.1), the *refundición* reads, "Por uno recibáis ciento" [May you receive one hundred for each one] (4.1). Six verses later Marta adds: "Vendrá a ser, / con tan cristianos motivos, / infinito mi placer" [My pleasure will be infinite if you show such Christian motives] (3.1); "cristianos" becomes "piadosos" in Solís's text (4.1). Describing the building that will result from this generous donation, Marta claims in Tirso's text that "A Salomón / nuevo edificio prevengo" [I foresee a new Temple of Solomon] (3.1) while in Solís's it is simply "a la compasión / nuebo edificio prevengo" [I foresee a new building dedicated to compassion] (4.1).

The Latin lesson remains fundamentally the same in both plays, but Solís's emendations at this juncture are related to invocations of the deity. In the following instances, too, Solís had originally maintained Tirso's wording but rewrote it for undetermined reasons. After Felipe asks Marta to decline "¿Quis putas? ¿Quæ putas?" [What are you thinking about?] she responds in mock horror: "¡Ay que me ha escandalizado! / ¡Jesús! No quiero aprender / gramática, licenciado" (3.2) [Ah! I am scandalized! Jesus! I do not want to learn grammar, Master Licenciate]. Solís's *refundición* is much tamer and evinces a much more controlled response on Marta's part: "¡Sea V[ste]d más bien hablado!" [Watch your tongue!] (4.2). And to her father's attempt to understand why she objects to the "latina costumbre" [Latin custom] Marta's "¡Jesús! ¡Jesús! Ni por lumbre" [Jesus! Jesus! I refuse!] (3.2) becomes an indignant yet essentially calmer "No aumentéis mi pesadumbre" [Do not increase my anger] (4.2).

The ensuing scene presents a further "cleansing" of Tirso. Don Gómez, hearing that the messenger from Seville returns with more news about Felipe's alleged arrest, reaffirms his compelling desire for swift justice. Marta, naturally, finds this attitude frightening, though she cloaks her fear in an expression of compassion. When she refuses to attend the meeting between her father and the messenger (Pastrana as Don Diego Hurtado), Urbina notes, "Es una santa" [She is a saint] (3.3). The *refundición* studiously avoids Tirso's cynicism and yields a lame response; to Don Gómez's "Pues queda en paz" [Peace be with you], Marta replies "Siempre en tanta" [Let it ever be so] (4.3).

Subsequently, Lucía, who in 3.4 (4.4) has espied Marta and Felipe embracing, thereby confirming her suspicions about "Dómine Berrío's" true love, rails in an aside against Don Felipe for having abandoned her in favor of Marta. In Tirso, Lucía's exclamation of anger is in tune with the irony expressed by the other characters with respect to Marta's devotion: "¡Qué divinos tan humanos!" [What divine humans!]. She decides against crying out in order to watch, while hidden, "esta devoción fingida" [this false devotion] (3.5). In the *refundición* Lucía's exclamation is sarcastic but it lacks the necessary irony and venom: "¡Qué derretidos, qué ufanos! / . . . / mejor es ver escondida / esta afición tan creída" [How madly in love, how wrapped up in themselves! . . . It is better to view this arrogant love if I am hidden] (4.5). Even in Don Felipe's speech to Marta, his pronouncements of love, the vocabulary of religion and devotion is replaced by poetically solid but imagistically weak verses:

Tirso

. . . donde está tu hermosura
no es libertad vivir preso:
Como adorarte profeso
por ti profeso clausura.

[to live imprisoned where your beauty resides is not freedom. As I profess to adore you, for you I will take my vows.] (3.4)

Solís

. . .a donde está tu belleza
no es libertad vivir preso.
Y así, mi bien, lo confieso,
por lo tanto con destreza.

[to live imprisoned where your beauty resides is not freedom. And so, my love, I confess it openly.] (4.5)

The verbal game trades on Felipe's disguise as Dómine Berrío and on Marta's as a "beata"; Solís's rendering neutralizes the double entendres with which Tirso subverts his characters' disguises. In the same vein Lucía's response to this part of the conversation, again in an aside, follows the imagery in the lovers' dialogue: "¡Oh qué devotos que están! / ¡Bien rezan, por vida mía!" [Oh how devout they are! My word, how well they pray!] (3.5) Their "devotion" to one another becomes clear in their "prayers," a second reinforcement of the imagery lost in another of Lucía's remarks in the *refundición*: "¡Qué derretidos están! / ¡Qué finos, por vida mía!" [How in love they are! How refined!] (4.5). Two scenes later, once Lucía has confronted Felipe for having abandoned her love, and Felipe, to escape certain entrapment, swears that all has been feigned for Lucía's sake, the same "devotional" language is removed. To Felipe's "Mala Pascua y malos años / la dé Dios a Marta" [May God grant Marta a rotten life], Marta, in an aside as she espies her sister and Felipe in an embrace, exclaims, "Para el cura y sacristán" [For the priest and sacristan], that is, referring to Lucía and Felipe (3.7). The *refundición*, ever striving to neutralize religiously offensive remarks, weakens the retort by having Marta respond, "Llevóse el diablo mi afán" [The devil has robbed me of my desire] (4.7). But the editing process does not end here: this verse in the manuscript has been crossed out and the original "Para el cura y sacristán" is written above it; and below the original "Llevóse" is repeated (act 4, f. 11v). The verse changed, it seems, according either to date or place of performance.

In Tirso's original, this series of scenes also carries with it sexual connotations suggested by three reiterations of "*gozar*"; on each occasion the word has been replaced. As Felipe in Tirso's text explains his disguise to Lucía, he states:

> Todo esto ha sido, mi bien,
> embelecos de tu hermana,
> que no goza, para ti; . . .

[All of this has been, my love, your sister's tricks; she does not have my love . . .] (3.7)

Solís has written "porque no te quiera a ti" [so that I will not love you] (4.7), a shifting of emphasis from Marta (the subject of "goza") to Felipe (that is, to avoid Lucía's and Felipe's seeing each other and thus rekindling their former love). In her ensuing aside, Marta angrily swears to avenge her brother's death on both Felipe and Lucía, "que no gozará" [who will not have me] (3.7); Solís has Marta speak the same lines, but the concluding verse reads "que no lograra" [who will not get me], again a much tamer, though still logical, ending to the thought (4.7). The manuscript reflects shifting reception: "gozará" on folio 12r of act 4 originally is recast as "logrará." Fifty-five verses later, "lograr" again replaces "gozar": Marta now threatens Felipe with exposure: "Que te den la muerte haré. / No pienses, traidor, gozarla" [I will have you killed. Traitor, do not even think about loving her] (3.7). Solís refuses to allow such libertinesque suggestiveness, for Felipe is threatened with "No pienses, traidor, lograrla" [Traitor, do not even think about attaining her] (4.8). This time, however, the manuscript has "lograrla" with no sign of "gozarla" having been written.[45]

Tirso's 3.9 is a clever and important scene for *Marta la piadosa*. In the space of only one hundred verses, some form of the word "jurar" [to swear, to speak an oath] occurs fifteen times, all related to Marta's having shouted out of anger at Felipe "¡Vive Dios!" [My God!]. The play on "jurar" depends on its bisemic value as affirmation and negation (as in an oath against the deity), tied as this is to Felipe's disguise and his having promised to love Lucía, then having switched allegiances, only to confront her—and lie to her—while Marta secretly watches; finally, he has to prove to Marta that his speaking ill of her was but a ruse to prevent Lucía from unmasking him. The passage, then, calls into question Felipe's various oaths, his protestations of love both within and prior to the dramatic action (he had already shifted his affection from Lucía to Marta by the opening of act 1). Solís's corresponding scene—4.9—of 142 verses reduces the number of utterances of "jurar" to fifteen and rewrites several passages. Within his *refundición* Solís has envisioned these oaths as less offensive than the religious references so carefully excised from the previous scenes.

The scene opens as Don Gómez, Capitán Urbina, and the Alférez rush into the room after having heard Marta shout "¡Vive Dios!" The first five verses of Tirso's original from 3.9—

  D. Gómez. ¡'Vive Dios' jurando Marta,
       y dando voces! ¿Qué es esto?
  Urbina. ¿Así una doncella jura?
       No es su virtud muy segura.
Felipe. (Aparte) (¡Ah cruel! Véngate presto).[46]

[D. Gómez. Marta is shouting and swearing "My God"! What is this!
Urbina. A maiden swears like this? Her virtue is not secure.
Felipe. (Aside) Ah, cruel woman! Take your vengeance quickly.] (4.9)

—are deleted in the manuscript of Solís's *refundición*. But Felipe, whose aside to Marta opens the recast scene, makes no mention yet of "jurar": "Aquí están los viejos dos / y te han oído gritar" [The two old men are here and they have heard you shout] (4.9). Marta realizes that to expose Felipe is to condemn him for the murder of her brother; she improvises a play-within-a-play-within-a-play in order to protect both her disguise and Felipe's. The changes Solís introduces, however, are principally in Felipe's response to Marta's chastisement:

Felipe. (Aparte) Dómina, dómina, paso,
 que alborotaré a Madrid
 declarando mi inocencia,
 que es injusta tu impaciencia . . .
 . . . . .
 No obstante, yo me despido
 sin temor y con placer;
 . . . . .
 Ea, Marta, adiós, adiós.

[(*Aside*) Mistress, mistress, take it easy, or I will wake up all of Madrid declaring my innocence, for your impatience is unjust . . . Nevertheless, I take my leave without fear and with pleasure . . . Goodbye, Marta. Goodbye.] (4.9)

Felipe continues to assume the role of teacher, but now he infuses his lesson with a moral tone. The double entendre still informs his response; Marta's impatience is unjust, but she cannot know that yet. Felipe's indignation before false accusation recalls the response of Tirso's character: willingness to leave Don Gómez's house without a second thought, knowing well that Marta is far too enamored of him not to stop him.

Finally, Solís modifies the educational background Felipe ascribes to Dómine Berrío. Instead of the false brother being a "licenciado / en gramática, ordenado / de grados y de corona" [licentiate in grammar, having taken the minor orders] (3.9), with the clerical import of these degrees (clarified by Arellano in his note to 2447), Berrío is now a "Bachiller y doctorado / en leyes en la Sorbona" [Bachelor and doctorate in Law from the Sorbonne] (4.9). He is given considerable stature by allying himself with a prestigious educational institution surely familiar to his audience, yet this same passing reference could easily be a critique of the francophiles who populated the Madrid capital and who attempted to influence the Spanish stage.[47]

In 4.11 (Tirso's 3.11) Solís continues to soften possible affronts to decorum. The Alférez questions "Dómine Berrío" to verify that he is, indeed, the same Don Felipe who saved him earlier in the bullring. Here Solís recasts through both elimination and rewriting, this time changing Tirso's verses "Yo sé que aquí / por Doña Marta trocáis / las galas en la sotana; / ya sé el peligro en que amor / ha puesto vuestro valor" [I know that here you exchange your finery for your cassock; I know the danger in which love has placed your valor] (3.9) to "yo sé que aquí / es a Marta a quien amáis . . ." [I know that you love Marta], a much more straightforward rendering of Felipe's predicament. The more that references to the cassock, swearing, devotion, and the like are removed, the greater the proof that such criticism implied within this context would not or could not pass unnoticed through a censor's hand. Similarly, as Felipe offers help to the Alférez to conquer Inés and garner her love for him, Tirso makes the nature of Felipe's aid clear by having him claim, "no os seré mal tercero" [I will make a good go-between], where Solís writes simply, "me ofrezco por medianero" [I offer myself as your go-between] (3.11; 4.11). The same substitution takes place in the subsequent scene as well.[48]

Act 5 presents a new development and marks Solís's substantial divergence from Tirso's text. He borrows from Lope's *La dama boba* to effect the marriages of Marta and Felipe and of Lucía and the Alférez. The *refundidor*, like his predecessor Rodríguez de Arellano, now dispatches with the original elaborate disguise of a Portuguese noblewoman that Pastrana imposes on Marta and the *fiesta* to be held in a nobleman's private garden. Solís pieces together bits of Tirso's plot while adding a moral to suggest that Marta's deceitful behavior is a result of her father's misguided attempt to arrange an undesired marriage to benefit his own financial standing.

The *gracioso* Pastrana assumes the responsibility to construct a happy ending. It is he who arranges Don Gómez's aborted travel to Seville to witness Felipe's "execution," and who recounts to Marta and Felipe the old man's departure:

> En camino
> de la Puerta de Toledo,
>   que por no pasar el río
>   y escusarte pesadumbres
>   (que lleba sus tres azumbres
>   según el cómputo mío),
>   de su furia temeroso
>   antepuso a su elemento
>   este nuestro; y con acento

> entre resuelto y medroso,
>   entre autorizado y clueco,
> dixo tu padre al borracho
> del cochero: "¡Ola, muchacho!
> ¡Por la puente, que está seco!"

[(I left him) on the road to the Toledo Gate and so as not to pass the river and avoid bothering you with details (because the river has its usual gallon and a half, according to my calculations), fearful of its fury, he opted for land over water; and with a tone of voice between resolute and fearful, between commanding and feeble, your father said to the drunken coachman: "Boy! Take the bridge, it's dry!"] (5.2)

Solís expands on a short passage in Tirso's *Marta la piadosa* in which the characters mock, as was the practice, the shallow and slow-moving Manzanares River. Where in the original the topic arises when Marta wishes to have a dinner by the river, here it is mentioned in conjunction with Don Gómez's need to cross it to leave town. Pastrana quantifies the amount of water the river carries ("azumbres"), an ironic description that reflects the original Pastrana's "Ríome del río yo" [I laugh at the river] (3.13), and describes the mock horror one would feel before the "furia" [fury] of the river's current; for this reason Don Gómez prefers land, a characterization concomitant with the description of the river. Don Gómez is full of bluster and harshness in his dealings with Marta, but fears crossing the river. Pastrana caricatures his tone of voice by describing it as "entre resuelto y medroso" and, more importantly, "entre autorizado y clueco." The father's inconsistencies have allowed Marta the freedom to carry out her plans; his command, too, begins to falter as he becomes *clueco*, old and feeble.[49] Solís implies that the father's stature commands the same respect as does the river and that Marta will have no trouble in carrying out her planned marriage because the major obstacle is no longer a forceful opponent. Nevertheless, Pastrana, Marta, and Felipe all wish to effect the ceremony before Don Gómez's return, as they continue to fear his wrath. This inconsistency points out that Solís may have taken advantage of the opportunity to elicit laughs from the audience through the *gracioso*'s characterization of Marta's father, yet feels constrained to maintain the cultural authority imbued in the father figure. Pastrana remains convinced that, by arranging refuge in a safe house after the marriage to prepare "el remedio conducente / a que su cólera ceda" [the remedy that will best placate his anger] that Don Gómez can be placated: "que es padre aunque está ofendido, / y el título de marido / le ablandará como seda" [because he is a father even though he is offended, and the title of husband will make him as soft as silk] (5.1).

Solís has expanded as well on Marta's final deception of her sister Lucía. Tirso has Marta simply "assure" Lucía that her (Lucía's) marriage to Don Felipe is imminent; she mixes with her lies ("Yo quiero, pues que es razón, / cumplir vuestra vountad, / y que os dé el sí Don Felipe" [Because it is right I want to do as you ask, and have Don Felipe give you his hand in marriage]) just enough truth ("por mi industria / a Guadalquivir se va [Don Gómez] / y en Sevilla busca aquel / que dentro en su casa está. / Casaros pienso esta tarde" [due to my ingenuity Don Gómez is on his way to the Gaudalquivir River, and in Seville he is looking for the man who is in his own house. I will have you married this afternoon] [3.15]) to convince Lucía one more time of her honesty and goodness. Solís creates another situation that calls for Marta to invent an explanation for her embrace of Felipe. Lucía's sarcastic observations end with her threat to inform her father of Marta's deceit and thus put an end to the games. Marta falls back on her "humility" and denies that she would ever try to steal Felipe from her sister. She embarks on a long explanation of her arrangements for Lucía to marry Felipe; his unbounded joy impelled him to embrace her. But within Marta's inventions are grains of truth that attest to Solís's care in the elaboration of Tirso's passage to maintain Marta's essential traits while creating a situation of his own making. To the embrace in question, Marta responds:

> admití su parabien,
> y de él me dexé abrazar
> con el candor e inocencia,
> Lucía, que en mí conoces.
> Tú saliste, y diste voces
> creída de una apariencia
> mentida, y con mal fundado
> y repentino furor,
> afrentas mi pundonor.
> Sea en todo Dios loado.

[I congratulated him and let him embrace me with all the candor and innocence, Lucía, that you know me to possess. You came into the room and reacted vociferously to deceptive appearances, and with a baseless and sudden anger, you insult my honor. Praise God in all things.] (5.3)

The implicit irony naturally is beyond Lucía's ken, and the deception with the truth of an "apariencia mentida" recalls the several layers of lies that Marta has created. As if such forthrightness were not sufficient, Marta indulges in a bit of histrionic foreplay that would tantalize a quality comic actress:

> Lo que quisieres pregona,
> niégame justos loores;
>   insúltame frente a frente,
> huye de mí horrorizada,
> no importa, no importa nada
> que me ofendas impaciente;
>   llámame vil y traidora
> y cuanto quieras celosa;
> trátame de mentirosa,
> que ya llegará la hora
>   en que verás sin disfraz
> la verdad porque yo peno.
> Bomita más, más veneno
> contra tu hermana; más, más.⁵⁰

[Cry out publicly against me, deny me just praise; insult me face to face, flee horrified from me, it does not matter, it does not matter at all that you impatiently offend me; call me to your heart's content vile and a traitor and jealous; treat me like a liar, for soon the hour will come in which you will see clearly the real reason for my suffering. Vomit more and more venom on your sister; more, more.] (5.3)

This performance is certainly consistent with Marta's reactions to the "Quis putas" of the Latin lesson as well as with her forceful and "beatific" rejection of the oath "¡Vive Dios!" in the previous act. Even the present remonstrative passage is not without its element of truth; soon the hour will arive in which the mask is removed and Lucía, along with the public, will see "la verdad por qué yo peno."

Don Gómez's return interrupts the planned festivities; his retelling of how he learned of the multiple deceit carried out within his own house is taken verbatim from Tirso's 3.21, including Urbina's ironic "¿Qué me dais cuenta tan larga, / si estuve presente a todo?" [Why are you giving me all the details if I heard it all myself?] (3.21), which self-reflexively satirizes the recourse of recapitulation. Instead of the rapid resolution of conflict that Tirso presents, Solís postpones the denouement by introducing both social commentary and a situation in which honor can be satisfied only through marriage. Don Gómez must confront Marta with her sins before punishing her:

> ¿Era ésta, embustera Marta,
> era ésta tu castidad?

> ¿Enamorarte en mis barbas
> con tu amante, y regalarle
> a costa mía en mi casa?
> ¿Eran éstos los enfermos
> para quien cada mañana
> pedías los caramelos,
> el chocolate y las pasas,
> y a quien con los mexicanos
> de d[o]n Celedonio labras
> un hospital en el Prado?[51]
> Ynfiel, mentirosa, falsa,
> que como muchas que a sombra
> de la santidad son malas,
> hacías del Beaterio[52]
> a tus liviandades capa.

[Was this your chastity, you liar, Marta? To fall in love with your lover right before my eyes and regale him at my expense in my house? Were these the infirm for whom you asked me for caramels, chocolate and dates every morning, and for whom you are building a hospital in the Prado with Don Celedonio's *pesos*? Faithless, liar, false; like so many who are evil under the guise of saintliness, you used your holiness to hide your lewd behavior.] (5.5)

Marta's tricks have now been given the lie as Don Gómez lists the most minute details of her deception. His invectives recall the final scene of Moratín's *La mojigata*, in which Doña Clara's false humility is revealed. In this case *Marta la piadosa* is, just as it was during Tirso's time, a critique of both Marta's feigned humility and her father's greater interest in money than in the emotional well-being of his daughter.

As punishment, Don Gómez orders Marta to the basement where, unbeknownst to him, Don Felipe is hiding. The recourse from *La dama boba* is given a twist: rather than taking refuge in the *desván* or garret of the house, Marta and Felipe are enclosed together in the basement. The inversion of place is appropriate: in Lope's play, Finea chooses the garret as a hiding-place-turned-love-nest which she volunteers to inhabit when men come to call at her house; the fact that it was reached by climbing *up* a stairwell projects a positive image on it. In Solís's *refundición*, Don Gómez opts for the basement as the site of banishment, and the downward movement connotes punishment and evil. Just as Octavio, Finea's father, learns too late of the dishonor he has unwittingly abetted, so Don Gómez learns through Lucía the horrible truth : "que cuando / presumes que la rescatas / de don Felipe, tu mismo, / tú, cómplice de tu infamia, / la pones entre sus manos" [when you think you are rescuing her from Don Felipe, you yourself, accomplice of your own infamy, put her in his hands] (5.8). In both cases a meddling sister breaks the news of the dishonor, and in both cases an arranged marriage is near the center of controversy.[53] As for Don Gómez, not only is he an accomplice to his shame, he has all along been a cause and an accomplice of Marta's deceit. The irony of both situations resides in the fathers' creation of their own undoing, "forcing" their daughters to "cohabitate," however briefly, with their lovers. The only possible resolution to either predicament is marriage.

The closing scene of Solís's *refundición* coincides once again with Tirso, this time with his 3.21, but with additional interpolations. Pastrana announces the end of the ruse; Marta must now remove "la máscara de la cara" [face mask] (3.21; 5.9), a final uncovering that in the *refundición* does not have the force given it in Tirso's *comedia*.[54] Regardless of minor differences between original text and *refundición* (discovery of Felipe's identity, location of his land holdings and his family name [changed from Ayala to Almeyda y Santillana]), Felipe's wealth and Capitán Urbina's willingness to forgive convince Don Gómez to bless his daughter's marriage. The final speech, spoken by Felipe, rather than the customary Golden Age request for pardon of errors, presents both a moral and a warning, though not as strict nor as detailed as Rodríguez de Arellano's:

> No son todas [las beatas]
> tan embusteras y falsas;
> pero bueno es el guardarse,
> pues tenemos muchas Martas
> con el Remedies[55] en la mano
> y el arte Amandi en el alma;
> a cientos podrán contarse.
> ¡Ojalá no fuesen tantas!

[Not all "devout" women are liars and false; but it is a good idea to be watchful, because we have many Martas with the *Remedies* in their hands and the *Amandi* in their souls; there could be hundreds of them. If only there were not so many! (5.9)

The many "Martas" referred to by Felipe—now the actor stepping forward to address the audience—may suggest a widespread practice in order to seek greater independence in choosing a husband as well as the renown associated with the name "Marta" as found in the *refranero*. The closing verses, then, beyond their comic function at one level of the play, could well be a call for reform in parental consent laws regarding marriage. This reading would place Solís's *Marta la piadosa* squarely in the tradition of Moratín's plays on the same subject. Chronological and thematic coincidence makes it difficult to refute this notion.

* * *

1865 saw the last nineteenth-century *refundición* of *Marta la piadosa* when Calixto Boldún y Conde recast Tirso's play for performance at Madrid's Teatro de Variedades.[56] Its general success does not match that of Solís's *refundición*; in addition to its original performance in 1865, the play was staged in Madrid at least one more time on 20 May 1869 and reached Buenos Aires in the mid-1880s during the South American tour of the renowned Spanish actor José Calvo y Revilla.[57] In his version Boldún borrows heavily from Solís as well as from Tirso; indeed, he follows Solís almost scene for scene, yet in contrast to his immediate predecessor's sense of theatre and comicality, Boldún—a comic actor himself who played the role of Pastrana—makes senseless changes that often verge on slapstick. The printed version does contain an interesting note from the theatre censor Narciso Serra, a playwright and *refundidor* himself,[58] whose approval for performance in the printed version reads: "Examinada esta comedia, no hallo inconveniente en que su representación se autorice, suprimiendo la bajada de Marta al sótano" [Having examined this play, I find no reason not to authorize its performance as long as Marta's descent into the basement is removed]. Following this remark we read, "Queda hecha la supresión indicada. El Autor" [The indicated cut has been made. The Author]. The suggestion of Marta and Fernando in the basement together, a scene that apparently raised no eyebrows in Solís's recast, must have offended the play's censor; whatever titillation the play had was certainly reduced by its removal. This excision alone would not necessarily limit the play's interest were it not for the *refundición*'s poor dramatic writing and construction. The satire against hypocrisy and greed fails in great measure because the characters have become caricatures of themselves. Much of this will be brought forth below in the discussion about Doña Blanca de los Ríos's diatribe against this recast.

Calixto Boldún's three-act *Marta la piadosa* has more in common with Solís's version than with Tirso's original and thus is a recast of a recast, a phenomenon similar to Trigueros's and Hartzenbusch's *refundiciones* of *La estrella de Sevilla*. That play had the fortune of being reworked by two writers well versed in their craft; Tirso's *comedia*, though it did fare acceptably at the hands of Rodríguez de Arellano and of Solís, had the misfortune of falling into Boldún's. The order of scenes follows closely Solís's model, with the most significant changes occurring in act 1 and at the end of act 3. Marta is now Don Gómez's niece; thus the murdered son is not Marta's brother, but her cousin, which seems to have made Marta's continuing love for Fernando (Boldún has changed his name from Felipe for inexplicable reasons) more palatable. Boldún has eliminated both the introduction of Urbina and his nephew into Don Gómez's house (the two are already guests and the marriage is about to take place) and the bullfight scene, thus eliminating a series of events that begins with Fernando's heroism and culminates in the Alférez's recognition of his old friend. Don Juan is no longer an "Alférez"; indeed, Boldún has turned him into a mindless fool, matched in his lack of social graces only by Lucía. Don Gómez says to Capitán Urbina regarding a marriage between Lucía and the Alférez:

>   Ni creáis que le aventaja
>   en discreción mi Lucía;
>   con esta boda, en un día
>   dos jumentos tendrán paja.

[Do not think either that my Lucía is any more discrete; with this wedding two beasts will have a manger together.] (1.6)

Lucía herself contributes to this characterization by her offhand remarks. Marta has just lied about her "voto de doncella" to avoid the arranged marriage, a vow that Lucía exclaims she could never make:

> *Marta.* Hice voto de doncella,
>   y juro que lo he de ser,
>   hasta que en la tierra virgen
>   se cobije mi vejez.
> *Gómez.* ¿Promesa de ser doncella?
> *Lucía.* Jesús, ¡y qué estupidez!
>   Nunca yo...
> *Gómez.*   Calla tú, necia.

[*Marta.*   I made a vow of virginity, and I swear that I will remain so until my old-age takes shelter in the virgin earth.
Gómez. Promise to remain a virgin?
Lucía. Jesus, what stupidity! I would never...!
Gómez. Shut up, fool.] (1.5)

Lucía is even more naive than her predecessors; this example of an abrupt, thoughtless statement is characteristic of many she makes throughout the play. In this regard, as in other areas of this specific recast, Boldún has sought the easy laugh. *Marta la piadosa* certainly provides the material for intelligent as well as less thoughtful treatment. And it is this play that brought the wrath of Doña Blanca on the head of the *refundidor*. For these reasons I omit a detailed study of the changes Boldún has introduced. If, after all, a *refundición* does not result in a quality playtext nor a quality reading text, unless there is a compelling sociocritical argument for its study, it is better left as a footnote to literary and theatre history. However, critical reactions to even a poor recast are worthwhile objects of study if only to understand the effect of the work and the taste of the critics contemporary with the production.

* * *

Performance reviews of the several incarnations of *Marta la piadosa* are not abundant. The material that does exist is important in judging the reception of Tirso's plays to different audiences. I have discovered two reviews specifically of Solís's version; one is merely a notice of the play's presentation indicating the attendance of the queen, the other a detailed review to be discussed shortly. Regardless of this paucity, fifty performances within several revivals indicate Solís's success in a new reading of an old play. Of the Buenos Aires production, a review by the Argentine poet and essayist Calixto Oyuela casts light on changing horizons and evidences that a strict sense of decorum is not limited to the eighteenth-century critics; how much of his negative review is the result of having seen Boldún's version is difficult to determine. Oyuela directs his remarks to the seventeenth-century society depicted in Tirso's *comedia,* thus attacking the essence of the play as well as the recast. Finally, Doña Blanca's ingenious essay occasioned by a late nineteenth-century staging of Boldún's *refundición* produces a stirring defense of Tirso, an acceptance of the *refundición* as a legitimate dramatic form, and a severe critique of Boldún.

Two performances of *Marta la piadosa* took place in 1851 and 1855; as I have just mentioned, the 1851 staging produced little in the way of a review (see Appendix for the complete text), except for *La Iberia*'s noting that "se representó con gran desigualdad y falta de poesía *Marta la piadosa*" [*Marta la piadosa* was performed unequally and with a lack of poetry] (3). Though no author's name is mentioned, the performance history of Solís's *refundición* suggests that it is his. On 18 November 1855, however, *La España* printed an extensive review of Solís's version together with an essay on the nature of *refundiciones*; this first part has been discussed in chapter I. The critique of the performance places emphasis on the texts (Tirso's and Solís's) and describes the actors' performances.

By way of providing a historical context of Tirso's *Marta la piadosa*, the reviewer states that the date of composition is 1614 as gleaned from the "interminable relación" [interminable recounting] of the Mámora spoken by the Alférez (3); it would be impossible to summarize more succinctly than has the critic, Aureliano Fernández-Guerra y Orbe, the principal reasons for this passage's elimination in each of the play's *refundiciones*.[59] He proceeds to outline the purpose of the play and to discuss Marta, a typically Tirsian character but one who suffers from having been drawn by a religious: "lo desvirtúa la malicia del religioso, no nada confiado en cosas de mujeres, manchándole con beleidades e inconsecuencias que le hacen desmerecer. Marta es valiente en presencia de su don Felipe, pero en ausencia está en dos dedos de ceder al gusto de su padre, siendo esposa de otro" [what undercuts (the play's quality) is the maliciousness of the monk, not at all reliable with regard to women's issues, tarnishing it with flightiness and fluff that make it unworthy. Marta is valiant in Don Felipe's presence, but in his absence she is on the verge of giving in to her father's desire for her to marry another man] (3). Even if a real-life Marta displays such filial obedience, Solís's manner of presenting her "sin tamaños lunares" [without so many blemishes] is preferred. The aesthetics of the reviewer, as should be expected, reveal considerable differences from his counterpart of a half-century earlier. Where the so-called enlightened critics prefer a faithful reproduction of nature as a way of imitating the ideal in nature, a writer in the 1850s exhibits a more modern sensibility. An action found in nature need not be faithfully represented on stage for the representation to be appropriate; consistency of characterization and consistency within the play itself are much more important concepts than a strict conceptualization of verisimilitude.

Fernández-Guerra y Orbe provides a general description, noting the elimination "con tino" [wisely] of Don Juan and Don Diego and a denouement carried off "con mayor interés y gracia" [with great interest and elan]. The reviewer recognizes Solís's borrowing from Lope's *La dama boba* and the resulting requirement that the couple be married after Don Gómez has become a kind of "médico de su deshonra" [surgeon of his dishonor]. The borrowed and adapted scene is just as effective today as it was in Lope's time ("no pierde tilde ninguno el poeta moderno para ponerla de bulto" [the modern poet loses nothing by including the entire scene]) and is recast so effectively that the "raudal de sales y chistes . . . no parecen sino caídos de la pluma del buen fraile, eterno regocijo de la española Talía" [flood of wit and jokes . . . seem to have come from the pen of the good friar, eternal delight of the Spanish Thalia] (3). The reviewer's words substantiate the evidence from the prompt copy that this *refundición* was indeed worthy of the popularity it enjoyed.

Just as on other occasions Fernández-Guerra y Orbe has shown himself to be an impartial and fair observer, the criticism underscores his consistency as a reviewer. He complains that the five-act structure of Solís's *refundición* introduces "languidez en el poema" [a slow pace] and slows dramatic action; in this case the reviewer might be accused of ignoring the standard theatrical practice of a previous generation. He may be implying that the director of this specific production restructure the play into three acts (a task carried out some ten years later by Calixto Boldún y Conde) better to marshal the pace. Secondly, the reviewer notes that Don Gómez's avarice is overworked and requires him to sacrifice qualities of gravity inherent in a seventeenth-century gentleman. In the course of explaining his critique on the point, Fernández-Guerra y Orbe allows a view of how at least one scene of *Marta la piadosa* was staged:

> De mucho efecto teatral es sin duda que deje como un rayo caer de la mano la espada asestada contra el pecho del seductor de su hija, al oír que tiene éste diez mil ducados de renta; pero en la composición primitiva se compadecen con más delicado arte la avaricia del viejo y los respetos de un linajudo caballero español.

> [It is doubtless of great theatrical effect to have the sword, pointed at the chest of his daughter's seducer, fall from his hand when he hears that the man has an income of 10,000 ducats; but in the original play sympathy for the old man's avarice and the respect due a high-born Spanish gentleman are more delicately expressed.] (3)

Fernández-Guerra y Orbe's attitude reveals an interesting combination of innovation and tradition. He applauds the *refundición* as an art form in general, and this play in specific, as a means of "aderezar a la moderna la comedia antigua" [dressing up old comedy in modern dress] (3); at the same time he wishes to see a proper gentleman played properly on stage. Finally, the critic questions D. Felipe's status as the murderer of Don Gómez's son as an unfortunate recourse "en una y otra comedia" [in both plays], that is, in both Tirso's original and Solís's reworking. For this last point, Fernández-Guerra y Orbe points to possible differences in ethos between the seventeenth century and the nineteenth:

> Acaso en las costumbres de aquel siglo esto no fuese reparable; pero hoy causa justo desabrimiento la consideración de un padre forzado a tener por yerno al que arrancó violentamente la vida a su hijo, hacia quien sólo respira venganza, gozándose con la idea de verle espirar en afrentoso cadalso. Otro resorte hubiera sido fácil inventar, que supliese a éste con mayor ventaja por todos conceptos.

[Perhaps in that century's customs this was not noteworthy; but today the idea of a father forced to accept as his son-in-law one who violently took away his son's life, toward whom the father breathes only vengeance, relishing the thought of seeing him die on a dishonorable gallows, causes rightful unpleasantness. Another recourse to replace this one, with greater benefit to all concerned, would have been easy to invent.] (3)

This third point is, in the critic's words, "un lunar con que la ofendió Tirso de Molina" [a blemish with which Tirso de Molina disfigured the play] (3), and is closely linked to the second point about Don Gómez's avarice. The reviewer is personally offended by the situation of the two daughters in love with their brother's murderer, and one must admit it is an unusual situation for the *comedia*. To affirm this too rotundly would be to overlook the satire implicit in the play. Tirso, and by extension Solís (because he does not cut the offending scene), lampoons not only arranged marriages and the facility with which women hid behind the veil, but also the overweening concept of honor. By making Don Gómez so overly avarous and thus a caricature, Tirso highlights the ludicrousness of the entire situation. Fernández-Guerra y Orbe's reading fails to take this into account, but it at least is true to its times. It might be too much to expect—and unfair to expect it—for even a critic widely read in the *comedia* to overlook what is to him an egregious error.[60]

When José Calvo y Revilla undertook his South American tour in the 1880s, the Boldún *refundición* formed part of the repertoire; the staging of the play in Buenos Aires elicited important commentary by the poet and essayist Calixto Oyuela, whose review allows us to deduce changes made to Boldún's text in its performed version.[61] Unfortunately, no playscript, actor's or prompt copy has been available to document the full extent of the changes that the director or prompter may have introduced.

The influence of Molière's *Tartuffe* becomes evident; just as Molière may well have borrowed from Tirso, so Boldún's recast of a Tirso play borrows from the borrower. Marta's act 2 speech on the freedom accorded her by a new-found and convenient "piety" has been replaced with a free translation of thirteen verses from Molière's *Tartuffe* (the segment that begins "Oui, mon frère, je suis un méchant, un coupable. . ."[Yes, brother, I am evil through and through]).[62] The use of these verses in Boldún's *Marta la piadosa* changes the character of the play greatly. If Oyuela is accurate—and there is no reason to believe he is not—in reporting that Marta's declaration of freedom has been replaced by the speech in *Tartuffe*, then Marta's hypocrisy is indeed interpreted much more maliciously.

Tartuffe is, as the subtitle of the play indicates, an impostor, a fraud; Marta is simply trying to avoid an odious marriage. Her hypocrisy never crosses into caricature, nor is she guilty of any crime. Boldún's inclusion of the speech—or Calvo's, as may be the case—creates a half-Marta/half-Tartuffe fiction with no relationship to the necessitites of the dramatic action. Oyuela sees no need for supressing the original verses, and one can easily agree with him on this point:

> La traducción libre de estos versos, lejos de producir el efecto que el refundidor imaginó sin duda, rompen la armonía del carácter de Marta. No es aplicable a él todo lo que puede atribuirse a la hipocresía, ideal y abstractamente considerada.

> [The free translation of these verses, far from producing the effect the recaster doubtlessly imagined, break the harmony of Marta's character. Everything that can be attributed to hypocrisy, ideally and abstractly considered, is not applicable to her.] (230)

Neither the manuscript nor the printed version of Boldún's recast contains Molière's verses; the evidence of Oyuela's review leads to the conclusion that the substitution occurred in at least one specific performance, and may very well have been due to Rafael Calvo or to an *apuntador*.

The scene depicting Marta's Latin lesson with Dómine Berrío has been suppressed because of its "shamefulness": "Esta escena, de una gracia extraordinaria, sería hoy imposible de representar, por lo desvergonzado, según dice Marta, de la palabra latina que don Felipe le indica. En la refundición ha sido suprimida" [This scene, extraordinarily witty, would be impossible to represent today because of the shamefulness, according to Marta, of the Latin word don Felipe asks her to decline] (223).[63] The critic, as self-proclaimed protector of morals, does not wish to offend his readers by repeating the phrase in question. Most important, of course, is the fact that Rafael Calvo decided to delete the passage.

Oyuela notes that a "superficial" (his word) observation of the play results in qualifying it as "inverosímil y repugnante" [unlikely and repugnant] (226). If the reviewer's venom were directed solely at Boldún's recast, one could accept his critique with little question. But Oyuela's further commentary suggests his discomfort with Tirso's play as well, if not with the notion of recasts. The critic clearly has no desire either to suspend disbelief willingly or to see the holes Tirso deftly pricks in society's balloon; referring to the intricacies of the plot, Oyuela claims "no es fácil que en la vida real sucedan tales lances" [it is not likely that such events occur in real life] and "no es dable admitir decorosamente ese amor decidido de dos hermanas . . . y mucho menos que le alberguen en su casa con tan atrevidos engaños" [one cannot allow with decorum the resolute love of the two sisters . . . and even less that they house their lover in their home with such daring deception] (226). To dispel these "superficialities," Oyuela explains away the aberrations by considering them as a product of their time. The lack of a regimented police state, he tells us, allowed considerable personal freedom; similarly the Spanish spirit of the early seventeenth century was "aventurero y osado" [adventuresome and daring] a quality found in "casi todas las piezas de costumbres escritas en esa época" [almost all the period pieces written in that time] (226). As a parallel example, Oyuela calls upon a performance of *Hamlet* he must have attended (he gives no specific indication); the critic decries the elimination of the protagonist's dialogue with the gravedigger as "mojigatería retórica" [rhetorical hypocrisy] (227), yet he finds truly grotesque and unlikely Hamlet's run-in with Laertes in Ophelia's tomb. He is unable to reconcile his concept of decorum with Shakespeare's near flawless dramatic design. Through his attempt to discredit another era's concept of art, Oyuela reveals more of his prejudices than he is aware; his idea of verisimilitude is inconsistent and clearly self-serving.

The distant society of seventeenth-century Spain has just been judged and condemned by one nineteenth-century man's values; by the same token, however, we must not be too hard on him and thus commit the same error. Oyuela writes within the literary currents that fostered Menéndez y Pelayo's summary judgments that buried many good plays and playwrights for half a century or more. Nevertheless, Oyuela approves the vitiation of Tirso's text: "Hoy tal cosa [Marta's love for her brother's murderer] nos repugnaría, y por eso el autor de la refundición . . . ha obrado *atinadamente* al hacer que Marta, en vez de ser hija, sea *sobrina* de don Gómez, y por tanto, prima solamente del muerto" [Today (Marta's love for her brother's murderer) would disgust us, and for that reason the reworker . . . has acted wisely in making Marta Don Gómez's *niece* rather than his daughter, and therefore only a cousin of the dead man] (228; emphasis in original). On the whole, the critic's own words will summarize his views on reworking a play belonging to another era:

> Todo cuanto choque de un modo violento al público actual; todo lo que, teniendo razón de ser en el tiempo en que la pieza se compuso, es, para nosotros, o superfluo, o cansado; todo lo que sin perjuicio pueda contribuir al mayor arreglo y regularidad de la representación, puede y debe

suprimirse, modificarse y adoptarse, respectivamente. Todo lo demás es profanación y prurito de lucir ingenio.

[Everything that violently shocks today's public; everything that had a reason for being when the piece was composed and that is for us either superfluous or trite; everything that without prejudice might contribute to better arrangement and regularity of the representation, can and should be suppressed, modified and adopted, respectively. Everything else is profanation and an itchiness to show off.] (232)

Though Oyuela's language belongs to the nineteenth cnetury, the condemnatory tone of voice he employs fits better the *comedia*'s francophile detractors of an earlier part of the century. Similar comments are found, for example, in the introduction Antonio de Miguel wrote to José Fernández Guerra's 1826 *refundición* of Calderón's *La dama duende* (see Chapter 1).

Boldún's recast of Tirso's play was staged for an 1896 performance which had the misfortune (for the play and the then-deceased recaster) of being viewed and reviewed by Doña Blanca de los Ríos.[64] The review carries the signature of "Tirso de Molina" and takes the form of a letter entitled "De Tirso de Molina al refundidor de *Marta la piadosa*" [From Tirso de Molina to the recaster of *Marta la piadosa*] to excoriate Boldún y Conde's reworking. Doña Blanca's letter, too, in her appropriation of Tirso's voice (hers is certainly more informed on one level than that of any reworker) is in itself a kind of adaptation, an attempt to fuse past and present within the horizon of the critic's indisputable experience, her lofty expectations and a nearly two-and-a-half-century-old tradition of Tirso de Molina reception. The article exhibits self-awareness as an artifact, self-awareness in its intertextuality, and it thus points to a horizon in the making, particularly given the quotations from *Marta la piadosa,* the *Cigarrales,* and a tone of an "Arte nuevo para hacer las refundiciones en este tiempo" [New Art for making recasts in this time].[65]

The "playwright's" first reaction to Boldún's version leaves no doubt about the tone she will adapt throughout the article:

¡Y mida agora, si pudiese, qué tanta sería mi sorpresa, y qué tan infinita mi cólera al ver lo que vuesamerced ha osado con esa mi *melindrosa querida*, con esa mi *enamorada beata*, mi taimada y donosísima doña Marta; con ésa, si no la mejor, la más querida y la más mía de todas mis no muy bien conocidas ni mejor estimadas comedias!

[And measure now, if you can, how great my surprise, and how infinite my anger when I see what your grace has dared to do with my beloved prig, with my enamored religious, my astute and very graceful doña Marta; with she who, if not the best, is the most beloved and most mine of my not very well known nor better esteemed plays.] (82–83)

Doña Blanca allows her persona to surface through personal critical beliefs by declaring that *Marta* gave birth to Molière's *Tartuffe* and Moratín's *La mojigata* and is thus an "escuela de los Molières y Moratines" [school of Molières and Moratins] (83). This last phrase is especially felicitous in its Molière-like "L'école de . . ." [School for . . .] tone; recall, too, that Moratín translated a number of the French writer's plays.

The *refundidor*, to Tirso/Doña Blanca, is a "desconocido enmendador de mis aciertos" [unknown emender of my successes] and he and his company are but "comentadores indigestos, los rápsodas de ensamblaje y los críticos intonsos, si no fueren esos zánganos baldíos, robadores de ajena miel, que actualmente se intitulan refundidores de comedias" [undigested commentators, rhapsodists of piecemeal tales and unshorn critics, if not lazy drones, thieves of another's honey, who presently call themselves recasters] (83–84). Doña Blanca, in finding a target with such facility, senses the rupture with the past in a complaint about the plays chosen for revival: "las más intencionadas, picarescas y salpimentadas que produje, para daros el gusto de regalarme y aun calificarme con los epítetos del *picaresco,* el *desenfadado* y hasta del *maleante Tirso*" [the most deliberate, roguish and spicy that I produced to give you the pleasure of granting me and even assessing me with the epithets of *picaresque, carefree* and even *perverse* Tirso] (88; emphasis in original).

Even though the late nineteenth century regarded the *comedia* more favorably than did the opening decades, recasts often vitiated a theatrical text beyond recognition. It is one thing to infuse a play with values that will register within a spectator's horizons (however offensive or disruptive some may find the new text), quite another to introduce changes that are not concordant with the tone of the play nor consistent with themselves, and that impart no kind of unity to the new piece. To correct these faults, the "playwright's" letter at this point becomes an "arte nuevo" for reworkers:

> Bien podéis suprimir en nuestras comedias aquellas copiosas relaciones, verbigracia, la del alférez en *Marta la piadosa,* si . . . las relaciones . . . os parecen tan largas y desmayadas, acórtense en buen hora, suprímanse a quererlo exigencias del gusto nuevo. . . . Acomódense, en suma, a la escena moderna las viejas farsas suprimiendo libertades y cercenando de su opulenta vestidura lo que pareciere ocioso, nunca lo que fuere esencial o

imprimiere carácter. . . . Pero de tales reformas lícitas a lo que *habedes hecho*—y agora me encaro con el refundidor—, ¡ah, mal aconsejado *torcedor de derechos y facedor de agravios*!, con mi *Marta la piadosa*, va tanto— y perdóneseme la arrogancia—como del ingenio de vuesamerced al mío.

[You can easily remove from our plays those copious summaries, v.g., the lieutenant's in *Marta la piadosa*, if the summaries seem so long and worn out, by all means shorten them, remove them if the demands of a new aesthetic require it. . . . In conclusion, let the old farces be adapted to the modern stage, omitting certain liberties and trimming from their opulent costumes what may seem unnecessary, never what may be essential or lend character. . . . But between such permissible reforms and what *you have done*—and now I confront the recaster, ah, poorly advised *twister of rights and committer of offenses*—with my *Marta la piadosa*, is the same gulf— and forgive my arrogance—between your talent and mine.] (89–90; emphasis in original)

Doña Blanca reveals here the acumen of her practiced eye, honed through many years of reading and theatregoing experience. The emendations she suggests to be legitimate are precisely those that a Dionisio Solís or a Juan Eugenio Hartzenbusch have carried out. "Reformas lícitas" is the operative phrase; Boldún is struck down by the lightning bolts tossed by a present-day crusader who is not merely on a quixotic mission.

Finally, the evil eye is cast upon the now infamous *refundidor*. After quoting an 1850 dictionary definition of the verb "refundir"— "Renovar reformando; dar sabor moderno a especies, ideas, escritos o cosas antiguas; arreglar corrigiendo . . . " [To renovate by reforming; to give a modern flavor to old classes, ideas, writings or things; to fix through correction]—comes the curse: "así los literatos del día refunden no pocas piezas de nuestro teatro antiguo, y valiera más, en ocasiones, que se refundieran a sí mismos . . ." [so today's writers recast no few plays of our old theatre, and it would be better if, on occasion, they recast themselves] (96).

Once more the question arises of what the *refundición* is supposed to be, to what extent it must remain "true" to its source. To say that it must remain "true" is too limiting a definition; but when a play centers on a theme that is "universal" in its essence but that, with easy modification, speaks to new generations whose horizons may bear little in common with those of the receivers of the original production, a point of contact, Stoppard's "touchstone of meaning," continues to exist. As the next chapter will show, a seventeenth-century *comedia* in the hands of a capable writer devoted to a cult of Calderón, can become an effective message-bearer for a new social and political climate.

4
Art and Politics: Adelardo López de Ayala and *El alcalde de Zalamea*

Each of the *refundiciones* studied to this point has literary as well as extraliterary dimensions that motivated the respective authors to recast a *comedia*. In the case of *La estrella de Sevilla* and *Sancho Ortiz de las Roelas*, Trigueros and Hartzenbusch focused on the role of the king; the evolving view of monarchic propriety and the role of passion in both public and private life changed materially from the Golden Age through the early nineteenth century and into the post-Romantic era. King Sancho and Sancho Ortiz stand out as examples of the conflict between love and duty and consequently merited reexamination by new generations of playwrights.[1] Social concerns gave rise to three recasts of *Marta la piadosa*. The question of forced marriages infused new life into Tirso's comic masterpiece at the same time that other writers aired related problems in other dramatic texts; the appearance of *El viejo y la niña*, *El sí de las niñas*, *La mojigata*, and *Marta la piadosa* (Rodríguez de Arellano's and Solís's) between the 1780s and 1819, and the arrival of Molière's *Tartuffe* to the Spanish stage, are more than coincidence.

Similar reasons occasioned the recast of Calderón's *El alcalde de Zalamea* by Adelardo López de Ayala. The underpinnings of his *refundición* are perforce political, for it would be naive to ignore the politics that inform Calderón's play and the recast it spawned. The recaster himself is one of the few *refundidores* involved directly with politics and whose political ideology is most explicit in the play he chose to recast. *El alcalde de Zalamea*, for its part, became one of Calderón's most popular plays both inside and outside of Spain.[2] It was first recast in 1810 by Dionisio Solís with the title *El garrote más bien dado o el alcalde de Zalamea* in five acts, and in Cuba in 1856 by Pedro Carreño, who titled it *Pedro Crespo, o El alcalde de Zalamea*, before López de Ayala's three-act version saw its inaugural performance in 1864.[3]

The voice of Pedro Calderón de la Barca is clearly one that has resonated on the Spanish stage and beyond, theatrically and politically, in productions of his original playtexts as well as of recasts for more than three hundred years. Present concerns do not permit a review of the voluminous pages written about the fate of his *comedias* during the eighteenth and nineteenth centuries, nor a study of the *refundiciones* of Calderón's *comedias* as a whole (albeit a worthy and necessary task);[4] his plays were never absent long from the Madrid stage because of both the praise and derogation he received from Ignacio de Luzán's 1737 *Arte poética* onward.[5] As is amply noted in studies on eighteenth-century Spanish literature, Calderón is praised in spite of the "weaknesses" that plague his dramatic works—the Baroque "excesses" of style and lack of regard for the unities, faults which depend more on the epoch of the critic than the writer's capabilities, as his apologists are quick to point out. Well-documented, too, is Calderón's early nineteenth-century return to vogue, thanks to the German Romantics, as Martin Franzbach summarizes: "Sólo a comienzos del siglo XIX se habría realizado el 'descubrimiento' de Calderón. En sus últimos efectos, la entusiasta glorificación del dramaturgo español en el Romanticismo alemán se hace sentir aún hasta el más reciente presente [only at the beginning of the nineteenth century had the "discovery" of Calderón taken shape. The enthusiastic glorification of the Spanish playwright is still felt in his long-lasting effect even today]."[6] Although Franzbach and Sullivan have spurred considerable interest regarding Calderón's reception, many *lacunae* continue to exist:

> Las monografías especiales sobre la influencia de Calderón, se limitan a describir su recepción desde puntos de vista nacionales y no consideran la mediación de los temas calderonianos más allá de las fronteras—contexto en que por ejemplo llega a tener importancia por primera vez el calderonismo italiano. Otra dificultad proviene de la estructura de los textos, cuyos títulos y concisa descripción de contenidos muchas veces sólo pueden conocerse por programas de teatro y datos sobre la representación. Otro problema consiste en la delimitación del modo de la refundición o de la recepción de elementos de la acción, que pueden considerarse todavía como propiedad calderoniana.
>
> [The special monographs on Calderón's influence are limited to describing his reception from national points of view, and they do not consider the mediation of Calderonian themes beyond national boundaries—a

context in which, for example, Italian Calderonianism begins to take on importance for the first time. Another difficulty stems from the structure of the texts, whose titles and concise content description are often learned only through theatre programs and performance data. Another problems consists of delimiting the kind of recast or reception of dramatic action that still can be considered Calderon's.] [7]

Three principal moments of nineteenth-century literary history place Calderón at the forefront of that century's literary discussions: the Böhl de Faber and Mora debates,[8] the reburial of the playwright's remains in 1841, and the Calderón bicentenary celebration in 1881. Nineteenth-century Spain's turbulent politics, too, bring forth an ideological interpretation of a Calderonian *comedia*. *El alcalde de Zalamea* is in many ways a response to the turmoil of the period and to the need, perceived by some, for a model of political behavior and literary form. Two events, one before and one after the 1864 opening of López de Ayala's *El alcalde de Zalamea*, allow a recontextualization of Calderón's play within the practice of writing and staging *refundiciones*: an 1842 performance at the Teatro de la Cruz of Calderón's version, the review of which was published in the *Revista de Teatro* of 1842; and Adelardo López de Ayala's acceptance speech read upon his election to the Real Academia Española.[9] Each of these documents will be discussed below.

Adelardo López de Ayala (1829?–1879), known primarily for developing (with Tamayo y Baus) the *alta comedia*, has been the focus of relatively little critical attention.[10] Because he was both a political and literary figure, his treatment at the hands of his two biographers depends on their respective political stances: the 1891 *Ayala. Estudio político*, by Conrado Solsona, a fellow member of parliament clearly interested in honoring the memory of López de Ayala, was the lone submission in a contest sponsored by the Congreso for a biography of its former president (Solsona n.p.); and *López de Ayala o el figurón político-literario*, by Luis de Oteyza, who made his own Republican tendencies clear in 1932 in a supercilious political and literary denigration of his monarchist subject.[11] (Both Solsona's and Oteyza's comments on the *refundición* of *El alcalde de Zalamea* will be taken into account in the section below dedicated to the play's reviews.) A corrective to Oteyza, as well as the first objective and well-researched analysis of López de Ayala's political life and literary career, are Mabel Harlan's 1935 *Hispania* and 1938 *Hispanic Review* articles; she signals many chronological as well as factual inconsistencies in Oteyza. Two other important studies on this nineteenth-century figure are Castro y Calvo's introduction to the *Biblioteca de Autores Españoles* volumes (180–82), and Edward Coughlin's Twayne overview.[12]

López de Ayala's writings provide the best vantage point from which to judge the mix of politics and literature and to explain the central importance of the Golden Age in the author's literary world (his first four plays are all placed in Golden Age contexts).[13] On 25 March 1870, he delivered his official acceptance speech upon election to the Real Academia Española de la Lengua to occupy the seat vacated by the late Antonio Alcalá Galiano; the document underscores López de Ayala's preoccupation with Calderón de la Barca.[14] Like so many other writers of his generation, López de Ayala had been influenced by Alberto Lista, whose belief in "imitation" over "creation" in the artistic process defines López de Ayala's method in recasting a Calderón *comedia*.[15] His political career, too, is in line with his love for Calderón and the historical kind of drama with which he was successful, and his orientation as a *moderado*, a monarchist, and three times minister for the colonies strongly supports his affection for a similarly monarchical and ultra-Catholic writer like Calderón.

The year 1870 falls between the Glorious Revolution of 1868 and the 1875 Restoration of the Bourbon monarchy, both events of importance for López de Ayala; that year saw the coronation of Amadeus I of Savoy as well as the rise and fall of the First Republic. The recast of *El alcalde de Zalamea* was first staged in 1864 and was performed frequently into the 1880s during periods of uneasy alliances and a variety of governments.[16] López de Ayala recognizes the turmoil of political and literary movements and thus undertakes the task of foregrounding Calderón as a representative of stability: "Entiendo . . . que en un período en que la duda, contaminando todos los espíritus, debilita el alma y hace indecisa la forma de nuestra literatura, no es fuera de propósito fijar una vez más la atención en aquel autor afortunado, que jamás dudó, y cuya fijeza de creencias y miras artísticas presta a sus obras la severa unidad que tanto contribuye a la honda impresión que causa su conjunto" [I understand . . . that in a period in which doubt, contaminating everyone's spirit, weakens the soul and renders undefinable; the form of our literature, it is within our purview to turn once again to that most fortunate author who never doubted, and whose firm beliefs and artistic views lend his works the strict unity that so contributes to the profound impression that they elicit].[17] In this regard, too, López de Ayala criticizes the weaknesses of the theatre of his time, inundated as it is with foreign works "mal disfrazadas de españolas" [poorly disguised as Spanish] (374). His vehemence is noteworthy, and the force of his rhetoric is almost physically palpable; when imported theatrical playtexts produce igual estrago en las conciencias y en el idioma, no me parece inútil insistir en la recomendación del gran poeta, a quien era imposible dejar de ser español ni por un momento, y en cuyas obras palpita entero el corazón de la patria. Cuando invade nuestro teatro una literatura dramática atolondrada y raquítica, que, unas veces frívola y sin ingenio, nos roba el tiempo, sin producir deleite ni enseñanza, y otras, al sentir la frialdad de su pobreza, se finge honrada y católica....

[equal devastation in consciences and in language, it does not seem useless to me to insist on the great poet's recommendation, for whom it was impossible to cease being Spanish for even a moment, and in whose work beats the country's heart. When a confused and rachitic dramatic literature which, at times frivolous and without wit, invades our theatre, it robs us of our time, without producing pleasure nor instruction, and at other times, when we feel the coldness of its poverty, makes itself out to be honorable and Catholic....] (375)

López de Ayala hungers for the standards and greatness to be found in Calderón de la Barca, a poet whose "cristiana modestia" [Christian modesty] is ever apparent (375). The nineteenth-century recaster continually employs a vocabulary that posits strength against weakness within the prevailing political and literary structure: "virilidad" [virility], "nacionalidad" [nationality], "se debilita" [is weakened], "se extingue" [is extinguished] (375). Theatre, after all, constitutes the backbone and the "síntesis de la nacionalidad" [synthesis of nationality] (375); for that reason, argues the playwright, Italy is remembered for its philosophers, painters, and sculptors, but not for its theatre.

The notion of theatre as synthesis of nationality carries with it the identification with one's political and moral grounding; the playwright becomes in this context the ideal spokesman for his people. He is associated with the masses ("la muchedumbre"); his soul merges with that of the group and thus is never found "abstrayéndose del mundo que le rodea" [abstracting itself from the world that surrounds it] (375). This melding of the dramatic poet with the people creates an entity with a heightened aesthetic appreciation: "llevado del dulce placer que producen las infinitas variedades de la belleza, sigue sin esfuerzo los vuelos y caprichos de la fantasía" [carried away by the sweet pleasure that infinite varieties of beauty produce, it effortlessly follows the flights and whims of the imagination] (376).[18] The playwright is unique in expressing the public sentiment (at least the sentiment López de Ayala believes appropriate); he gives voice on stage to the "Espíritu de nacionalidad, intuición de la forma y del efecto" [Spirit of nationality, intuition of form and effect] (375). And the playwright *par excellence* is once again Calderón de la Barca.

From the above exposition it comes as no surprise that in his overview of Calderón's dramatic production López de Ayala finds its center in the *autos sacramentales* [sacramental plays] and the religious *comedias*; what is more, "las comedias religiosas de Calderón son a la vez históricas y políticas" [Calderón's religious plays are at the same time historical and political] (380). Religion and the state, the most important constitutive elements of the Spanish people, find their most fulfilled expression in Calderón. López de Ayala reinforces Calderón's centrality in an extensive historical digression in which he explains why Spaniards dissolve into anarchy "apartados o exentos del yugo de la monarquía" [distanced from or free from the yoke of monarchy] (381);[19] he summarizes incidents that manifest the discord arising in the New World when colonists were left on their own, disharmony that resulted in the death of many less at the hands of the Indians than at those of their fellow countrymen. In his thrice-repeated role as minister for the colonies in various mid-nineteenth-century governments, López de Ayala fought against any appeasement of the insurgents in Cuba and insisted on Spain's strict control of its Caribbean colonies.[20] He was also firmly opposed to the establishment of the republic and could not support a nonmonarchic government precisely because the weak elements of the Spanish character subvert its strong points—faith, customs, blood, common danger, religion: "Fueron nunca poderosos, roto el freno de la monarquía, a contener nuestros espíritus rebeldes en los límites de la templanza . . ." [They were never powerful enough, once the stronghold of monarchy was broken, to contain our rebel spirit within the limits of moderation . . .] (383).

López de Ayala's speech not only represents his political views but also outlines a dramatic theory. It becomes quite logical, then, for this nineteenth-century writer/politician to undertake the recast of *El alcalde de Zalamea*; its main character is a "heroica representación de la honradez y dignidad de los plebeyos" [heroic representation of plebeian honor and dignity] (385) who exercise their rights as individuals always within the authority of the monarch. López de Ayala thus sees the manifestly political orientation of Calderón, and perceives in Pedro Crespo a metonymy for Calderón, a faithful representation of his (Pedro Crespo's) time, who faithfully represents ideals necessary to inspire his countrymen.[21] Through the play he has chosen to recast, López de Ayala subverts the attacks upon Calderón by critics of a previous generation who claim him to be a "soñador extravagante" [extravagant dreamer] (387). Rather, the ideal contains the truth to be spread:

> No es menos nocivo al arte el contrapuesto realismo, hoy proclamado como sistema: temo que pase a contagio; porque es más fácil imitar los groseros modelos que nos rodean, que remontarse a las peligrosas esferas de la fantasía, donde también reside la verdad, pero pura y sublime, y sólo perceptible a la mente inspirada.
>
> [No less dangerous to art (than Romanticism) is the opposing Realism, proclaimed today as a system: I fear it will become a contagion; because it is easier to imitate vulgar models that surround us than to go back to the dangerous spheres of imagination, where, too, truth resides, but pure and sublime, and perceptible only to the inspired mind.] (387)

López de Ayala continues with an apology of Calderón against the playwright's francophile accusers. The rise of Romanticism allowed a reevaluation of Calderón's works, which contributed to the "revolución" that overcame the French influence (389). He agrees that Calderón's style is "incorrecto," but in the sense that so is nature if examined in its individual parts: "Estos detalles defectuosos, sólo vistos desde la altura del conjunto, adquieren sus debidas proporciones" [These defective details, seen only from the perspective of the whole of his work, acquire their due proportions] (389). All in all, Calderón's theatre carries within itself the "sello de grandez y originalidad" [seal of grandeur and originality] difficult to appreciate in its entirety because it is not known widely enough (earlier López de Ayala had lamented that Calderón was "más alabado que leído" [more praised than read] [374]): "Difundida su influencia por todas la venas de la literatura dramática, antes hemos conocido las imitaciones que el modelo, y no percibimos en toda su fuerza la alta novedad, que con su tanto regocijo y asombro gozaron sus primeros espectadores" [Because his influence is diffused through all veins of dramatic literature, we have known the imitations rather than the model, and we do not perceive in all its power the high degree of novelty that with joy and astonishment his first spectators enjoyed] (389). Thus one could argue that López de Ayala's *refundición* imitates Calderón and pushes him to the forefront of recognition; as the ensuing study will show, the recaster leaves large segments of *El alcalde de Zalamea* unaltered in order to produce a text both faithful to the values embodied in Calderón's age and responsive in López de Ayala's view to the nineteenth century's need for political reinforcement.

* * *

Where the principal action of López de Ayala's *El alcalde de Zalamea* follows Calderón quite closely, the recaster interpolates new material to redirect attention to events specific to the *refundición*. Calderón opens with the arrival of the troops to Zalamea, and the rowdy, boisterous Rebolledo's complaints about the constant travel they have endured. Movement toward Zalamea, suggesting the turbulence and trouble about to be stirred up by the soldiers, lends the original play impetus and forcefulness. López de Ayala, on the other hand, begins the action by revealing a "portal grande" at Pedro Crespo's house and by Inés inviting Isabel to enjoy the fresh air of the late afternoon, when they are both surprised by the sound of the soldiers' drums in the distance.[22] The first characterization of the troops, then, is the observation from Pedro Crespo's family and not from the soldiers (the first forty-one verses have been eliminated; Rebolledo's frustration at the forced marches and little rest are picked up later in 1.8). Isabel has no objections to their presence but finds their language offensive. Inés is more open to them and knowledgeable about their ways; she believes, in verses new to the *refundición*, they will be on their way once they find a town unable to bribe them to move on. The remainder of the scene is taken up by Isabel's complaints of the annoying attention given her by "el hidalgote" Don Mendo (1.1).[23]

With the arrival of the troops in Zalamea, López de Ayala emphasizes character description without distraction from intervening scenes. The Captain and the Sergeant discuss their opinions of a "villana" (due to the latter's mention of Crespo's beautiful daughter Isabel); Juan's welcome and the Sergeant's search for Pedro Crespo's daughter are deferred. By presenting the Captain's haughtiness coincident with his first appearance in the play, López de Ayala concentrates his character exposition; Calderón often draws his characters a piece at a time to draw out action. (In this regard recall Rosaura's three major speeches in *La vida es sueño* or Eusebio's often-interrupted *relaciones* in *La devoción de la cruz* [Devotion of the cross] to name but two instances.)

Rebolledo and Chispa first appear in the ensuing scene (1.8) of the *refundición*, obeying López de Ayala's apparent preference for combining what he must have seen as interspersed scenes. The braggart soldier archetype, particularly, loses none of his personality in his 1864 role, even as his relationship to the Captain differs from Calderón's execution of it. Calderón here uses Rebolledo to reveal the Captain's interest in manipulating his soldiers to make them beholden to him:

> *Rebolledo.* Yo vengo a suplicarte...
> *D. Alvaro.* En cuanto puedo
> ayudaré, por Dios, a Rebolledo...
> *Rebolledo.* Yo he perdido
> cuanto dinero tengo y he tenido
> y he de tener, porque de pobre juro,
> en presente, en pretérito y futuro.
> Hágaseme merced de que por vía
> de ayudilla de costa aqueste día
> el alférez me dé...
> *D. Alvaro.* Diga, ¿qué intenta?
> *Rebolledo.* El juego del boliche por mi cuenta;
> que soy hombre cargado
> de obligaciones y hombre al fin honrado.
> *D. Alvaro.* Digo que eso es muy justo,
> y el alférez sabrá que este es mi gusto.

[*Rebolledo.* Grant me a favor...
D. Alvaro. I'll try...
Rebolledo. ... I've lost all that I have, have had And ever shall have, an immense Loss in the present, past and future tense. I'm broke. Captain, you can help me Officially but unofficially.
D. Alvaro. Two reasons and I'll favour you not once, but twice.
Rebolledo. Make me the officer in charge of cards and dice. My reasons: I'm in debt, no joke. My other reason... I'm an honest bloke.
D. Alvaro. You're a persuasive chap. All right. You're gambling officer as from tonight.]²⁴

The Captain then asks Rebolledo to create a false disturbance to give the officer an opportunity to enter the attic room of Pedro Crespo's house, where Isabel and Inés are garreted to keep them from the soliders' sight.

López de Ayala's Rebolledo is much more presumptuous, and the Captain much more manipulative of his soldier, perhaps in the recaster's attempt to paint the officer in as negative a light as possible in preparation for his later abduction of Isabel:

> *Capitán.* ¿Qué hay, Rebolledo?
> *Rebolledo.* Señor,
> hoy quedó vacante el juego
> del boliche, y yo te ruego
> que interpongas tu favor...
> *Capitán.* ¿Para que te den...
> *Rebolledo.* Es llano.
> *Capitán.* Tanta ocasión de porfía,

y andes luego todo el día
con la espadilla en la mano?
No hay prudencia en tus acciones
para bolichero; vete.

[*Captain.* What's up, Rebolledo?
Rebolledo. Sir, today the ball game tender's position became vacant, and I beg you to intercede . . .
Captain. So that they give you . . . ?
Rebolledo. Obviously.
Captain. So much insistence, and then you go around all day with a dagger in your hand? You don't have what it takes to be the game tender; get out of here.] (1.8)

In spite of Rebolledo's, and later Chispa's, pleas, the Captain is not moved and dismisses them summarily from his presence. The scene ends with Rebolledo's insistence that he will get his way. But in 1.9, where López de Ayala reinserts the Sergeant's frustration at being unable to locate Isabel, the Captain has a change of heart, although only to further selfish purposes. He forges a plan to meet with Isabel and requires an accomplice:

Capitán. Sólo por tema la he de ver, y una
invención . . . Rebolledo es despejado
y fingirá muy bien lo que he trazado.
Rebolledo. Yo vuelvo a suplicarte . . .
Capitán. En cuanto puedo
ayudaré, por Dios, a Rebolledo,
que aunque es atolondrado,
me enamora su brío.

[*Captain.* I'm going to see her out of habit, and an idea . . . Rebolledo is quick thinking and he will do a good job of playing along with my plan.
Rebolledo. I'm returning to beg you . . .
Captain. I will help Rebolledo, by God, in any way I can, for although he is scatter-brained, I like his spirit.] (1.9)

The Captain then accedes to Rebolledo's request, but not without an implied obligation for assistance in creating the disturbance that will lead to the Captain's encounter with Isabel, Juan, and Pedro Crespo. The Captain's motives are transparent; he believes Rebolledo to be "atolondrado," a description added by López de Ayala that fosters the lingering impression of an arrogant officer who cares little for his men and much for the satisfaction of his ego.

The Captain's successful ploy leads to the crucial meeting with the Crespo family. Where in Calderón the action takes place in the upstairs room occupied by Isabel and Inés, in the recast the characters converge in a more public area of the house (1.11). López de Ayala imposes an important sense of decorum by refusing to allow the Captain, or any of the men, to enter the upstairs bedroom. By having the women appear downstairs, a greater insult to honor is avoided.[25]

The remaining scenes of act 1 follow Calderón closely, with only minor verbal changes. Crespo maintains his stance of equality in his first meeting with Don Lope and insists throughout their encounter on responding to him oath for oath. The friendship that will form between the two men, the rights of the individual with honor that put Crespo on equal footing with Don Lope, and honor as "patrimonio del alma" [patrimony of the soul] are important social and political statements and hold the same emotional and social importance for both López de Ayala and Calderón.[26]

The opening of the recast's act 2 smoothes the transition to the Captain's long *relación* wherein he expresses his desire for Isabel. The Sergeant comments on Don Lope's and Pedro Crespo's evolving friendship:

> *Sargento.* Si te corre priesa
> lo que tienes que decirle,
> veré si acaso se encuentra
> en el jardincillo: suele
> salir a dar una vuelta
> con Pedro Crespo: se han hecho
> muy amigotes. Le cuenta
> el villano sus costumbres,
> el gobierno de su hacienda
> y sus labranzas: don Lope,
> sus servicios en la guerra
> y sus heridas, y toda
> la familia villanesca,
> especialmente Juanillo,
> le oye con la boca abierta.

[*Sergeant.* If you need to talk with him urgently, I'll see if maybe he's in the garden; he usually takes a walk with Pedro Crespo, they've become quite good friends. The villager tells him of his daily life, how he runs his household and his work; don Lope tells him about his experiences in war and his wounds, and the whole village family—especially Johnny—listens to him open-mouthed.] (2.1)

The use of both diminutive and augmentative suffixes ("jardincillo," "amigote," "Juanillo") linguistically foregrounds the Sergeant's intent to belittle and scorn the attention Don Lope pays to a mere *vil-*

lano. The effect is to denigrate the Sergeant by making him critical and jealous; López de Ayala had already presented the Captain in this way. The two soldiers, changing the subject, discuss Don Lope's plans to meet the king, but the Captain interrupts himself with "¡Si yo lograra / siquiera un momento verla!" [If I could just see her for a moment] (2.1). Both the topics of war and of the Captain's uncontrollable urges are taken from two different scenes in Calderón's original; to López de Ayala's credit he has interwoven them seamlessly to present the picture of a man consumed by his (illicit) passion, who cannot keep his mind on pressing military affairs.

If López de Ayala portrays the Captain in a much more negative light than does Calderón, he shows Isabel to be even more above reproach. The Captain questions the Sergeant about the results of his conversation with the maid, all in an effort to discover some way to meet Isabel:

> *Capitán.* ¿Qué te dijo la criada?
> *Sargento.* ¿No sabes ya sus respuestas?
> Que no quiere que le hablen
> de ti en ninguna manera,
> y que a insistir no se atreve,
> porque, si insiste, la echa
> de su casa.

[*Captain.* What did the maid tell you?
Sergeant. Do I really have to tell you? She doesn't want them to talk to her about you in any way, and [the maid] shouldn't dare insist, because if she does, they'll throw her out of the house.] (2.1)

The speech is a verbalization of what Calderón does not say. In the original act 2, the Captain carries on a conversation with Rebolledo as Don Mendo and Nuño eavesdrop. Rebolledo's "Ya no sabes sus respuestas?" [Do I really have to tell you?] (942; 37) to the Captain's question is followed by Don Mendo's decision to arm himself in order to protect Isabel. The spectator assumes either that the Captain knows well what the maid has replied to Rebolledo and needs no further explanation, or that the Captain and Rebolledo continue the discussion off to the side while Don Mendo and Nuño speak. The latter is more plausible given the Captain's next lines, spoken following Nuño's departure: "¡Que en una villana haya / tan hidalga resistencia, / que no me haya respondido / una palabra siquiera / apacible!" [A peasant girl, but she displays / Aristocratic haughtiness. / I offer passion—she replies / with cold-blooded unfriendliness] (955–59;

37). These same lines follow the Sergeant's detailed explanation of Rebolledo's activities in the recast. No such suspense has been left to the imagination of the nineteenth-century viewer.

The Sergeant's diligence in seeking a way for the Captain to meet with Isabel is soon to pay off. López de Ayala reproduces much of the Captain's eloquent pining for Pedro Crespo's daughter, a moving speech that deceives the spectator into thinking that the Captain is sincere in his feelings toward the young woman.[27] After all, he seems to be saying, if nature can produce day and night in one twenty-four hour period, and if war brings both victory and defeat, why cannot his love for her blossom and wither all in one day. The climax of the Captain's speech in the original, " ¡Ay Rebolledo, / no sé qué hiciera por verla!" [Rebolledo, / I'd do anything to see her] (1027–28; 39), leads to Rebolledo's suggestion that Isabel be serenaded with a *jácara* from La Chispa. López de Ayala creates a new closing :

> *Capitán.*   Y cuando pienso
> que está aquí mismo, y tan cerca
> de mí, que si alza la voz,
> puedo oírla y . . . No hay cadena
> como el respeto. Aquí . . .
> (*Dirigiéndose a la puerta del fondo.*)

[*Captain.* And when I think that she is right here, and so close to me that if she raises her voice, I can hear her and . . . There is no chain like respect. Here . . . (*Moving toward the downstage door*).] (2.1)

The Captain speaks of respect but is easily angered and quick to change his mind. His snap judgments of *villanas* and of small-town life revealed this earlier in the play. Though he has a change of heart brought on by having seen Isabel, he is not a man in whom trust is well placed. At this point, López de Ayala introduces a new plot twist through Rebolledo, who remains an outsider and is clearly not privy to the Captain's thoughts (in Calderón, Rebolledo is the immediate audience of these expressions of desire). To make the Captain appear even more desperate than Calderón paints him, the recast has Rebolledo garner a key to a hidden door leading to Isabel's hideaway. Rebolledo is well drawn in the mold of the typical *gracioso*:

> Un soldado a la criada
> enamora con promesa
> de que, al volver de Lisboa,
> ha de casarse con ella.
>   . . . . .

> (*Saca una llave grande.*)
> y si es muy grande y pesada
> para ser, como quisiera,
> la llave del corazón
> de tu hermosa lugareña,
> es llave de su postigo,
> y en fin . . . por algo se empieza.
> Si logras una ocasión
> en que ella esté sola, entras,
> y Dios te ayude. Esta plaza
> se ha de ganar por sorpresa,
> que para un cerco redondo
> no hay tiempo, señor, ni fuerzas.

[A soldier seduces a maidservant with a promise of marriage upon his return from Lisbon. . . . (*He takes out a large key*) and if it's too big and heavy to be, as you wish, the key to your village girl's heart, it's the key to her door, and finally . . . you have to begin somewhere. If you manage to find her alone, you enter, and may God help you. This fortress will be taken by surprise, because there's no time nor forces for a siege.] (2.2)

Rebolledo's actions and the imagery he employs are well-integrated into the principal dramatic developments. Bribing a servant is, of course, a commonplace in the *comedia*, as is discovering a secret door or passageway. Even the war imagery is appropriate to the Captain's profession and his very reason for being in Zalamea. López de Ayala's incorporation of these elements speaks to his knowledge of Golden Age theatre, and the facility with which the new scene flows testifies to his ability as a dramatist. But even López de Ayala must be true to his time. The choice of Calderón as an author to adapt is both a moral and a political decision; that morality and those politics thus inform the characters. When the Captain insists that he must see Isabel first "para que ella se acostumbre / a verme a su lado, y pierda el temor" [so she can get used to seeing me at her side and lose her fear] (2.1), Rebolledo warns him:

> Muy difícil es que baje
> del desván, y es imprudencia
> que subas tú . . .

[It's unlikely that she will come down from the attic, and it would be imprudent for you to go up . . .] (2.1)

Rebolledo's moralizing tone recalls the first encounter between the Captain and Isabel and Inés; in that scene in act 1, the young women had left their upstairs dwelling to investigate the commotion downstairs. At the same time, Rebolledo's warning is incongruous not only because of his nature (a braggart soldier who cares little for a country girl's honor), but also because the Captain will later abduct Isabel and mistreat her father when she refuses to yield to his advances. Perhaps López de Ayala is attempting to magnify the Captain's crime by highlighting his complete disregard for the mores of the honorable individuals who inhabit Zalamea. To put the voice of consciousness into the mouth of a generally disreputable character like Rebolledo may seem to strain logic; but Rebolledo does play the *gracioso* and has considerable leeway in his pronouncements

As a way to build up to Isabel's abduction by the Captain, López de Ayala augments the scene in which Pedro's son Juan decides to enlist under Don Lope's command. Not all soldiers need be so coarse as Rebolledo, and not all are carried away by the kind of passion the Captain demonstrates. In Calderón, the discussion proper concerning Juan's interest in the military is limited to the four concluding lines of this dialogue:

>   *Don Lope.*   Mal
>   los trabajos de la guerra,
>   sin aquesta libertad [*cantand*],
>   se llevaran; que es estrecha
>   religión la de un soldado,
>   y darle ensanchas es fuerza.
>   *Juan.* Con todo eso es linda vida.
>   *Don Lope.* ¿Fuérades con gusto a ella?
>   *Juan.* Sí, señor, como llevara
>   por amparo a vuecelencia.
>
> [*Don Lope.* Well, you see/The work of war makes such demands/And so does army discipline,/That any soldier must relax [*singing*]/And when he does, he paints the town.
> *Juan*: It seems a good life for a man.
> *Don Lope.* Would you like to see some action?
> *Juan.* I'd immediately join up/If you'd grant me your protection.]
>   (1215–24; 47)

Rebolledo's and La Chispa's serenade of Isabel interrupts the dialogue and leads to Pedro Crespo's and Don Lope's joint skirmish against the offending soldiers. In López de Ayala, however, the expression of Juan's military ambitions becomes the author's undisguised paean to the cause of fighting for God and King. The recast follows the original until 1224, at which point Don Lope describes for the Crespo family qualities inherent in Juan that would make him a good soldier:

> Tenéis limpieza de sangre,
> buena fama y mucha hacienda;
> pues ¿qué os falta? Lo que él puede
> adquirir, y ya lo intenta.
> . . . . .
> . . . el muchacho muestra brío
> y . . . ¿quién sabe? . . . son las guerras
> crisol de los corazones
> y cuna de las noblezas.

[You have pure blood, a good reputation and a considerable fortune; what more could you what? What he can acquire and already attempts to. . . . the boy shows spirit and . . . who knows? . . . war is the melting pot of courage and cradle of nobility.] (2.7)

The development of this scene, on the one hand, has a dramatic function: it heightens the contrast between the Captain and Juan. Where Captain Don Alvaro is a career officer who has made evident his passions and mercurial temper, Juan is hot-headed (consider his later attempt to kill his sister to avenge his family's dishonor) but young; the implication is that he will mature into a responsible adult, perhaps garnering through his deeds the title of nobility that his father refuses, out of pride, to purchase. However, what must be kept in mind is the impulse behind this passage: the active political life its author led. López de Ayala served in the government, supported fully and participated in the Glorious Revolution of 1868,[28] and vociferously opposed republicanism. In 1863 General O'Donnell fell from power after nearly five years of political domination, plunging the Spanish government once again into instability.[29] Domestic political turmoil would be foremost on the public's mind and would affect their perception as well as reception of a play like *El alcalde de Zalamea*. Even though the reviews make no mention of López de Ayala's implied political agenda within the play, the positive response in the Madrid newspapers confirms the audience's affirmation of traditional Spanish, Catholic values. War might be a necessary evil (the Carlist conflicts continued to weigh on mid-nineteenth-century minds)—the "¿quién sabe?" of Don Lope's speech—but war would strengthen the resolve of the country's soldiers and provide for leadership in the aftermath. Don Lope's rhetorical question, too, points to the uncertainty of military stability in 1860s Spain.

Juan may exemplify the wide-eyed idealism of the young, but his father is certainly aware of the military's importance and the need for service on the part of all citizens. As his son prepares to join the departing army, Pedro Crespo communicates to Don Lope that the *villano* learns from the land, distant from the day-to-day politics of the government. Pedro states:

> adonde rejas y trillos,
> palas, azadas y bieldos
> son nuestros mejores libros,
> no habrá podido aprender
> lo que en los palacios ricos
> enseña la urbanidad
> política de los siglos.

[For in this university—/The country—he's a graduate/In ploughshare, thresher, spade, hoe, rake./Wheelbarrow, harness and pitchfork./He's never seen a palace or/Mixed with sophisticated folk,/So if he's ever impolite/Please put it down to ignorance.] (1525–31; 60).

The *refundición* emphasizes less a villager's ignorance of politics than his unfamiliarity with courtly customs:

> adonde rejas y trillos,
> palas, azadas y bieldos
> son nuestros mejores libros,
> de todo punto se ignoran
> los cortesanos estilos.

[For in this university—the country—he's a graduate in ploughshare, thresher, spade, hoe, rakes, wheelbarrow, harness and pitchfork. Here courtly styles are completely unknown.] (2.13)

The modification is small but significant. Pedro Crespo is well aware of the "urbanidad política," as his dealings with Don Lope show, and even though he may be aware of daily life in the capital, he excuses his lack of such social graces. The fact that Pedro Crespo earns Don Lope's respect in short order testifies to the former's political and social savvy. By extension, López de Ayala suggests, Crespo's values could well serve as models of behavior for all Spaniards.

The street battle elicited by the soldiers' rowdy serenade and Don Alvaro's decision to take Isabel by force are pivotal in terms of the original *Alcalde*'s dramatic structure. López de Ayala focuses on place and the importance attached to it. The street site of men's armed conflict (Crespo and Don Lope prepare to chastise the soldiers for their ribaldry) yields to an upstairs room where, in 2.9, Isabel and Inés take refuge. The recaster reorients the dramatic action; Inés states, "Desde arriba / veremos, sin que nos vean, / cuanto pasa" [From above we can see what's going on below without being seen] (2.9), an ironic antecedent to the Captain's ultimate infringement of honor: he invades the women's privacy by appearing in the attic room. Isabel brings to mind *La vida es sueño* and Clarín, who finds death as he attempts to hide from it; dishonor finds her though she has enclosed herself in a private space.

The Captain claims to love Isabel, yet his demonstration of affection leaves much to be desired. Calderón includes no face-to-face encounter between Don Alvaro and Inés. In a confrontation scene from the recaster's pen, the Captain attempts to express his love verbally for the young woman. She is relentless in her rejection because of his brusque behavior toward her; she questions the sincerity of affection that makes her suffer. Though he wishes to ask forgiveness and explain, she silences him with a vociferous defense of her honor:

> *Capitán.*   Perdonad...
> *Isabel.*   No os he de oír,
> ni tenéis que disculparos:
> Yo tardaré en perdonaros
> lo que tardéis en salir.
> Ved que merced al ultraje
> que hacéis a nuestra opinión,
> ya están en contradicción
> la tropa y el paisanaje...
> . . . . .
> ya debéis considerar
> que este empeño puede ser
> deshonra de una mujer
> y perdición de un lugar.

[*Captain.* Forgive me...
Isabel. I will not hear you out, nor do you have a reason to ask forgiveness. My forgiveness will accompany your leaving. Don't you see that thanks to your insult to our honor, the troops and civilians are at odds... you should consider that your determination could well be a woman's dishonor and a town's perdition.] (2.10)

Isabel responds both as a woman and as a villager, allowing her to defend her person as well as Zalamea. The Captain as a soldier previously had offended the village with the raucousness he instigated, and as a man he now offends her. Isabel's identification with the body public implies that any insult the Captain directs to her again affronts the entire village. His language becomes violent as he states unsubtly that no threat is sufficient to deter him:

> Todo lo miro y por todo
> sabe atropellar mi amor
> que es más tirano y más fuerte
> el afán con que te quiero,
> que el rencor de un pueblo entero
> y el peligro de mi muerte.
> Y ya que salir me mandes,
> considera, ingrata bella,
> si es grande amor que atropella
> inconvenientes tan grandes.

[I see everything, and my love will not stand for anything blocking its way, because my desire for you is more tyrannical and stronger than the hatred of an entire village and the danger of my death. And since you order me to leave, consider, my beautiful ingrate, the enormity of love that disregards such great inconveniences.] (2.10)

This interpolation confirms the Captain's intentions and Isabel's firmness in rejecting so ungallant a suitor. He has always shown himself devoid of moderation, and his cant is comprised of extremes: "afán," "rencor," "muerte," and "atropellar." Isabel further elaborates her linguistic control over raw, untempered passion in her response to the Captain's final inquiry about the possibility of love between them:

> ¿Qué amor os puedo tener,
> si antes de haberme mirado
> sufrí caprichos injustos,
> y me habéis dado más sustos
> que letras me habéis hablado?
> . . . . .
> ¿Es que no sale marchando
> con placer un militar,
> si no deja en el lugar
> alguna mujer llorando?
> O así como el caminante
> sin que su dueño lo adiverta,
> coge, al pasar por la huerta,
> la fruta que está delante;
> ¿vos imagináis acaso,

> señor Capitán, que son
> mi honra y mi corazón
> para cogidos al paso?
> Pues ved que de esta victoria
> no es tan posible la palma,
> que Dios no reparte el alma
> conforme a la ejecutoria.

[What love can I have for you if before your having looked at me I suffered your unjust whims, and you have frightened me more than you have spoken with me? . . . Is it impossible for a soldier to leave contentedly if he does not leave some woman crying? Or like the traveler who picks fruit from the orchard without the owner noticing it, do you think, Captain, that my honor and my heart can be "picked" in passing? Just think that the fruits of this victory are not easily won, for God does not grant souls according to one's nobility.] (2.10)

This reply is certainly all-inclusive in its references to every element that impinges upon the relationship between them: the Captain's refusal to abide by convention and decency to court Isabel, her humble social class, the "girl in every port" syndrome often rendered by the refrain of "el amor de un soldado," and the sexually charged image of herself as a fruit to be picked without a thought by any passerby. The last two verses echo her father's definition of honor as a "patrimonio del alma." Her conclusion, too, is stated in military terms (*victoria* and *palma*) that recall Rebolledo's words to the Captain, specifically about the officer's desire for her, earlier in the act:

> Esta plaza
> se ha de ganar por sorpresa,
> que para un cerco redondo
> no hay tiempo, señor, ni fuerzas. (2.2)

He may be an officer, she tells him, but he is no gentleman; his social and military standing impose no obligation upon her to love him. Isabel implies that though she is not noble, her nobility of spirit is much greater than the Captain's.[30] The seed of revenge in the Captain's mind begins to bear fruit. Violence is his final recourse because he is helpless when Isabel betters him in their verbal duel. Two social strata enter in conflict and reflect the discontent brewing within the political scene López de Ayala depicts almost allegorically. The present confrontation becomes the multifaceted axis around which the play turns.

The ensuing scene between Don Lope and the Captain produces a second pivotal moment that will affect the Captain's behavior. In Calderón's version, Don Lope and Pedro Crespo, in order to quiet the soldiers' unruly serenade to Isabel, attack them. To dissemble, Don Alvaro invents a lie about a quarrel among the soldiers themselves. Don Lope's response is to order the troops out of Zalamea; he has no way of knowing about Don Alvaro's involvement in the serenade and melee. In the corresponding recast scene, the Captain's bent toward vengeance, openly displayed to Isabel, is now coupled with insolence. Don Lope, for his part, is keenly aware of the officer's intentions:

> *Capitán.* Mis tropas han recibido
> (porque se estaban holgando
> en esta calle, cantando
> sin alboroto ni ruido)
> de todo el pueblo un ultraje,
> y a que digáis me presento
> qué pena, para escarmiento
> se le impone al villanaje.
> *Lope.* Ya castigados están
> los culpables...
> *Capitán.* Yo...
> *Lope.* Os abona
> el celo; mas mi persona
> suplió la del capitán.

[*Captain.* My troops received (because they were relaxing in the street, singing without bothering anyone) an insult from the entire town, and I present myself for you to tell me what punishment is to be imposed on the villagers.
Lope. The guilty are already punished...
Captain. I...
Lope. Your zeal speaks well of you, but my presence has filled in for the Captain's.] (2.11)

López de Ayala has interspersed effectively his verses with Calderón's. The Captain improvises an explanation by subjecting himself to Don Lope's authority, but he does not convince. Don Lope's reply about punishment meted refers to the toll he and Crespo have just exacted on the other troops; he thus recognizes the Captain's lie about the townspeople having insulted the army. Don Lope, too, replaces the Captain ("suplió") in more ways than one: he steps in to fill the command void created by the Captain's abdication of responsibility. But if Don Lope lets the lie pass, he deals swiftly with the Captain's insubordination:

> *Lope.* Esta insignia habéis de honrarla,
> porque aquí la puso el rey
> para mantener su ley,
> y no para quebrantarla.
> Los que no marchan conforme
> a obediencia y sujeción,
> no son soldados, que son
> bandidos con uniforme.
> . . . . .
> pues donde miro deshecho
> el orden, o relajada
> la obediencia, con la espada
> la imprimo dentro del pecho.

[*Lope.* You are to honor this insignia because the king placed it here to uphold his law and not to break it. Those who do not submit themselves obediently to it are not soldiers, but outlaws in uniform. . . . wherever I see order undone, or obedience relaxed, with my sword I will imprint it within the breast of any who transgress.] (2.11)

The recaster has left no room to doubt the Captain's irrationality, itself a condemnation of action without reason and prudence. Don Lope's imposition of authority not only reminds the Captain of his duty and his place in the hierarchy, it also provides a refrain of Don Lope's praise of the army to Juan Crespo. Once again, readers/spectators hear Calderón's voice claiming respect for the honor of the soul and not only of social rank, and they hear López de Ayala's voice as well. Drawing the contrast between the born ignoble nobleman (the Captain) and he of the noble soul (Juan Crespo), the recaster speaks to his personal political convictions. The tumultuous Spain of the 1860s requires *obediencia y sujeción*. Don Lope's threat to punish with the sword is López de Ayala's warning that order and monarchy are the only effective weapons against anarchy.

The destruction of order through abduction within Pedro Crespo's home—representing the political confusion López de Ayala witnesses—results in Crespo's empowerment not only over personal events but over those in the political arena as well. The *refundición* presents the Captain's incursion even more forcefully than does Calderón, a recasting that makes a great deal of sense given the officer's mercurial temper. Isabel intimates the danger as she comments on the eerie quiet that pervades the town's darkened streets: "¡Qué distinto / aspecto las calles tienen! / Ha un momento, bulla, gritos . . . / y ahora parece un cadáver / el pueblo" [How different the streets look! Just a moment ago movement, shouts . . . and now the town seems like a cadaver] (2.17). With the entrance of the Captain and his men, Isabel's ironic, ominous statement takes on an element of truth. The Captain observes Isabel outside her door; although in Calderón he states simply, "Yo he de llegar y atrevido / quitar a Isabel de allí" [I shall walk over to that door and carry Isabel away] (1705–6; 67), in the *refundición* he emphasizes the forcefulness and cruelty of his decision: "de los brazos mismos / de su padre he de arrancarla, / si no me queda otro arbitrio" [I shall tear her away from his very arms if all else fails] (2.18). (The "otro arbitrio" is another chance to persuade Isabel to love him.)

The abduction itself is carried out much as Calderón had envisioned the action, but the dialogue has been recast, and the ending of the act—the event occurs at the end of act 2 in both plays—has been altered radically. In Calderón, Pedro Crespo defies Rebolledo's warning to flee or risk death, claiming "¿Qué importará, si está muerto / mi honor, el quedar yo vivo?" [You've killed my honour, why, by God, / should I be keen to stay alive?] (1734–35; 68); Inés brings her uncle's sword to him; the Sergeant orders Crespo carried away to the mountain and tied to a tree; and Juan returns, his horse having fallen, to hear the "tristes voces" [a young girl's cry] and "míseros gemidos" [an old man's groan] (1772–73; 70) of his sister and father, respectively. López de Ayala tightens considerably the chain of events, for once Isabel is taken and Rebolledo threatens Pedro Crespo, he replies only, "¿No hay ya rayos en el cielo?" [Are there no lightning bolts left in heaven?] and "Mátame, mátame pronto, / serás menos asesino" [Kill me, kill me quickly, you will be less of a murderer] (2.18); Crespo is left shouting "¡Dadme a mi hija, bandidos!" [Give me my daughter, you outlaws!] as he prepares to follow Isabel's kidnappers. The act ends at this point. López de Ayala's Crespo risks death to take direct action in a most personal crisis that surpasses its immediate context; it becomes a call to arms.

It is noteworthy that the recaster has excised the remaining incidents of Calderón's act 2. From a theatrical perspective, the action in the *refundición* develops much more rapidly than in the original. Attention to the abduction is not deflected, and as a result the emphasis falls more on the crime itself than on tears of stained honor and a brother's implied duty. From the point of view of an 1864 audience's horizons, the cry of lost honor does not ring as forcefully within the social sphere as it had for Calderón's audience two hundred years before. Finally, from a political standpoint, Pedro Crespo's decision to follow the soldiers responds both to his fatherly instincts and to his refusal to allow the forces of destruction to seize the day. Crespo's actions here constitute a personal crusade he must be free to pursue;

any help from the outside, even from his son and niece, would dilute the effectiveness of his attempt. The *villano* must safeguard his *rincón* from the intrusion perpetrated upon it by the court (in the form of a supposedly noble soldier) at the same time that the *villano* himself enters the realm of the court (his subsequent decision to prosecute and execute the Captain without referring the matter to a military tribunal). Crespo may not know the "cortesano estilo" alluded to earlier, but he certainly understands "urbanidad política" and its consequences.

The differences between and motivations behind the two endings do not undercut their dramatic value as closings of an act. Nor does the refocus of the opening of act 3 reduce the effectiveness of Pedro Crespo's resolve to make public the Captain's injustice and of his (Crespo's) official public role and determination to punish the wrongdoer. In both plays Isabel recounts the horrifying events of the previous night. But, as is common to many recasts, the long *relación* she recites is shortened considerably (240 verses in two *tiradas* in Calderón as opposed to 90 verses with interspersed dialogue with her father), and the preparation for her recounting is entirely new to López de Ayala's version. The original act 3 opens with a tearful Isabel imploring the morning star (Venus) and the sun not to shine on her shame; she wanders through the forest where she first hears disconsolate moans and later discovers her father tied to a tree. Once she frees him from his painful bonds she begins to recount her tragedy.

The recast stages none of this, perhaps in order to reduce the loci of action; in fact, Crespo informs his daughter that she had found him tied to a tree because her abducters had taken him there. The act's opening scene takes place in Zalamea's town hall, where Pedro Crespo leads his daughter, in search of the *alcalde*, to sign a formal complaint against the Captain. By placing this scene within the halls of government, the recaster directs the spectator's attention to the place of justice and thus foregrounds its moral preeminence. Common to both plays is Crespo's refusal to hide Isabel's shame and the family's dishonor; public offense demands public vengeance, and for Crespo the ideal of justice rests on a higher plane than personal grievance:

> *Isabel.* ¿Quieres que todos
> se enteren de tu ignominia?
> Pues ya no tiene remedio,
> echémosle tierra encima ...
> . . . . .
> *Crespo.* Calla: no hay tierra que pueda

> cubrir acción tan inícua.
> No, no es posible callar;
> nuestro silencio sería
> encubridor de su infamia,
> cómplice de su malicia.

[*Isabel.* Do you want everyone to know of your shame? Since there is nothing to be done about it, let's bury it forever...
Crespo. Be quiet: there's not enough earth to cover such wicked action. No, it is not possible to keep silent; our silence would hide his vile actions, would be an accomplice of his evil.] (3.1)

Crespo urges Isabel to recall every detail, a procedure opposite that of so many Calderonian—and Golden Age, for that matter—males who silently withstand the pain of such infamy. Where Calderón's Pedro Crespo cries out, "Detente, Isabel, detente. / No prosigas; que desdichas, / Isabel, para contarlas, / no es menester referirlas" [Isabel, please understand this. / There are some stories, Isabel, / Which don't need a story-teller] (1890–93; 73), it is López de Ayala's Isabel who is reluctant to recount her story even to her father:

> *Isabel.* ¿A qué quieres que te cuente
> la más fiera tiranía
> que en vergüenza de los hombres
> quiere el cielo que se escriba?
> Tanto como a mí el contarla
> te ha de pesar el oírla.
> *Crespo.* Estos sucesos crueles,
> estas desgracias impías,
> para los hombres se hicieron,
> y es menester que se impriman
> con valor dentro del alma...

[*Isabel.* To what end do you want me to tell you of the most terrible tyranny ever written to the shame of mankind? Hearing it will hurt you as much as telling it will hurt me.
Crespo. These cruel events, this impious disgrace were made for men, and they must be impressed upon the soul with courage...] (3.1)

There is no shame of writing here, no shame in signing the complaint that will result in Pedro Crespo's brand of justice.

Isabel's abductors take her to a labyrinthine mountain that no longer offers sanctuary for men like the Captain; it is a place that has always inspired terror in Isabel (3.1). Her struggle in the recast is much more violent, her anger more than the "ruegos" and "sentimientos" that the Calderonian Isabel reports having uttered. In López de

Ayala's version Isabel states, "yo me agitaba en los brazos / del vil raptor, convulsiva / y furiosa" [I struggled, with convulsions and rage, in the arms of my vile abductor] (3.1). She becomes so exhausted that "en las puntas de las jaras / se quedaban esparcidas / mis trenzas, sin que el dolor / me diese de ello noticia" [my hair was stuck on the spearheads, but I didn't notice, so great was my pain], a metaphorical rape that precedes the deed carried out by the Captain. Even nature takes action against her: as the light fades from her exhausted eyes, "parecía / cómplice de aquel delito / la naturaleza misma" [Nature herself seemed an accomplice to that crime] (3.1).[31] López de Ayala goes to great lengths to reinforce Isabel's innocence. Not only does he change a "simple corderilla" [simple lamb] to an "inocente corderilla" [innocent lamb] in the above-mentioned quotation, he also allows Isabel an unbreakable will, even if her physical strength is not sufficient to resist the Captain:

> Sólo en mí la voluntad,
> señor, no quedó vencida,
> que en esto el cielo piadoso
> me sacó de tanta ruina,
> sin que la afrenta del cuerpo
> al alma fuera extensiva.

[Only my will was not conquered, for in this a merciful heaven saved me from complete ruin; the affront to my body did not reach my soul.] (3.1)

If nature in the labyrinth of Isabel's dishonor is an accomplice of her abductors, then a pious heaven gives her inner strength to withstand the personal assault. Isabel does not allow the emotional impact of physical violation to corrupt her soul.

The remainder of Isabel's *relación* in López de Ayala is made up of selected verses from the original, with some slight modifications, that give details of her escape and of her brother's wounding of the Captain; this, in turn, is followed by the announcement of Pedro Crespo's election as *alcalde*. Crespo now faces the task of avenging his honor as father of the family and of punishing a criminal who has broken the law. He will carry out his double duty—with his responsibility as *alcalde* taking precedence—resolutely: "Hija, / ya tenéis al padre alcalde: / él os guardará justicia" [Daughter, your father is now the mayor; he will see to justice] (3.2).

Just as López de Ayala recasts for political ends the scene in act 2 involving Juan's decision to enlist in the army, so he includes new verses within Isabel's *relación* to put forward a similar political philosophy. In his Real Academia acceptance speech, López de Ayala digressed to highlight what he considered a character flaw in Spaniards: their inability to function in a civilized manner once distanced from the monarchy. He recalled the annihilation of the first colony, by infighting followed by armed conflict with the indigenous tribes, upon Columbus's return to Spain. Isabel's speech is a reenactment of the underlying principle. She is taken to the mountain whose description as a labyrinth lends it mythic proportions and suggests that it harbors a metaphorical minotaur that devours all who enter. Without an Ariadne to guide her, Isabel is at the mercy of a soulless monster. The placement of the mountain outside the town walls removes it from the protection of civilization and order; the Captain and his men represent the disorder that will prevail once these soldiers are removed from the immediate control of their commander (Don Lope) and away from their monarch (Felipe II). Isabel becomes, then, a symbol of a Spain perilously close to being cut adrift in the troubled seas of republicanism. López de Ayala intends for her story to serve as a warning to the members of parliament and to those charged with the duty of forming a government that the monarchy is the essential lynchpin of order, and that without it Spain will destroy itself. In this context Pedro Crespo becomes the loyal monarchist and the ideal leader who, once integrated into the chain of command, will impose desperately needed order. *El alcalde de Zalamea* becomes, in the hands of Adelardo López de Ayala, a warning to be ignored at the country's peril.

The remainder of the *refundición* is a playing out of the tale. The first in the series of incidents leading to the Captain's execution is the meeting between him and Pedro Crespo. In Calderón's original, Rebolledo announces the unknown mayor's arrival (the public, however, is well aware of the imminent conflict) and a haughty Don Alvaro expresses confidence in the local authority's limited jurisdiction (2156–70). In the recast, the Captain is concerned that Don Lope may notice his absence and Rebolledo insists on the mayor's lack of legal authority:

>   *Capitán.* ¿Si me habrá echado de menos
>   don Lope?
>   *Rebolledo.* Que eso receles
>   es justo, que aquel señor
>   tiene pesadas las manos;
>   mas lo que es de estos villanos
>   y de su estéril rencor,
>   nada tienes que temer,
>   que aunque vuelva y grite el viejo,
>   ya en esta casa, el concejo

> nos tendrá que defender;
> y ni aun prenderte osarán.
>
> *Capitán.* Fuera, por Dios, cosa nueva:
> no hay alcalde que se atreva
> a prender a un capitán.

[*Captain.* I wonder if don Lope has noticed my absence?
Rebolledo. You are right to worry about that, because that gentleman is heavy-handed; but as far as these villagers and their futile resentment are concerned, you don't have anything to worry about. Even if the old man returns and starts shouting, in this house the council will have to defend us; they won't even dare arrest you.
Captain. Good God, that would be unheard of. There isn't a mayor who would dare arrest a captain.] (3.3)

Two elements are at work here. First, López de Ayala heightens the dramatic irony by building the Captain's haughtiness to set him up for a fall, for the audience well knows that Crespo has been elected mayor. Second, the recaster trades on his audience's horizons of expectations. Some segment of the attendant public may have known the original play; its very familiarity would be its attractiveness. It follows, then, that the audience is aware of the Captain's demise and awaits to see how this is handled in the new play. Pedro Crespo will give the lie to Rebolledo's assessment of him. The mayor's supposedly calm demeanor and determination should not be defined as "estéril rencor," empty threats by a powerless individual. And though Crespo has returned, having been long untied from a tree on the deserted mountain, he shouts not one word. There is even a hint of "something in the air" that bothers the Captain: "Inquieto estoy" [I'm worried] (3.3), he says, just before Crespo's entrance.

What follows undermines Rebolledo's prediction. To the soldiers' surprise the new mayor is Pedro Crespo, and he does express "rencor" but it is far from sterile. Calderón has him enter calmly and request politely to speak with Don Alvaro alone (2183–88). López de Ayala reveals the shock in the soldiers' expressions and again portrays Crespo as the man who can match any rival oath for oath:

> *Crespo.* Vive Cristo, que no es buena
> gente que tanto se apena
> de sólo ver la justicia.
> *Capitán.* Yo tengo fuero, y así
> nada tenéis, vive Dios,
> que ver conmigo.
> *Crespo.*   Sois vos

> quien me viene a ver a mí.
> Que sin duda querréis todos
> felicitarme: ¡pardiez! . . .

[*Crespo.* For Christ's sake, innocent people do not get so distressed when they see the authorities.
Captain. The law is on my side, for God's sake, so you have nothing to do with me.
Crespo. You're the one coming to see me. Good Lord, I'm sure you will all want to congratulate me.] (3.4)

Crespo's forcefulness cuts short the soldiers' attempt to intimidate him. His attitude also allows him to operate from a position of strength; when he and the Captain speak alone in the subsequent scene, Crespo reveals the humility inherent in his personality as he begs the Captain to marry his daughter (the scene is copied nearly in its entirety from Calderón). López de Ayala must have thought that if Crespo can establish his authority at the outset and then speak softly in an effort to resolve the dilemma of his honor with diplomacy, he can use the big stick with which he had threatened the Captain (the play on "caballo" and "potro" ["horse," "colt," and "rack"] is quite effective in this regard). Crespo's personality fits López de Ayala's needs to convey his political stance. Crespo as a hand of the king (with reference again to the later metaphor of justice as body) employs diplomacy first and only in its failure resorts to force. But the underlying motive is that the monarchy, through its officially designated representatives, will impose order one way or the other.

This recast raises, especially in the final scenes, the stature of Pedro Crespo; the addition of a few verses to certain speeches is often all that is needed to establish further the balanced personality that López de Ayala develops. After Crespo has ordered the incarceration of the Captain and "requests" the cooperation of Rebolledo and La Chispa, he remembers the king's impending arrival. He begins to enter the chapter house ("sala capitular") to write a request to the neighboring town that he be advised of the king's approach, but remembers that Isabel awaits him there:

> En la capitular
> hay recado de escribir.
> Dejadlos. No han de decir
> que he querido sobornar,
> ni aun con la vista, un testigo.

[There's a writing table in the chapter house. Leave them. No one can say that I have attempted to bribe a witness even by seeing him.] (3.8)

Crespo believes that his impartiality must be beyond reproach, even if this means avoiding the presence of his daughter, the "testigo" to the crime committed by the Captain.

Juan's return further points to Crespo's scrupulous observance of legal and moral decorum. In the original play, Juan's attempted vengeance on his sister ("Vengar así / la ocasión, en que hoy has puesto / mi vida y mi honor" [You risked my life and my good name / And I must be revenged] [2445–47; 90]) implies his belief in her guilt. The recast portrays a much less reflective Juan, who reaches a conclusion that reveals little maturity and knowledge of human nature:

> Si ella [Isabel] culpable no fuera
> de algún modo, cosa es clara,
> ni él al monte la llevara,
> ni al verme tan pronto huyera.

[If Isabel were not in some way guilty, it seems clear, he wouldn't have carried her off to the mountain, nor would he have fled so quickly when he saw me.] (3.9)

Juan's goal in serving in the military is to receive a title of nobility that he can pass on to his heirs; Isabel becomes a potential stumbling block in his path to glory, for avenging dishonor becomes bitter "primeros honores" [first honors] (3.9). Pedro Crespo counterbalances his son's rashness in his own equitable treatment of all; he prevents Isabel's death and arrests Juan for having wounded the Captain, since he is able to put the public good above personal need. Calderón and López de Ayala here coincide, but the added emphasis of the *refundición* allows the new play to support the author's political intentions.

Crespo's intense awareness of office does not efface the warm and loving father. In another important departure from Calderón, López de Ayala creates an encounter between Pedro Crespo and his daughter that would have been unlikely in a Golden Age *comedia*. Calderón's play presents Isabel signing the official complaint against Don Alvaro, but doing so against her better judgment:

> ¿Tú, que quisiste ocultar
> nuestra ofensa, eres ahora
> quien más trata publicarla?
> Pues no consigues vengarla,
> consigue el callarla ahora.

[But it was you who wished to hide/Our family's foul injury,/And now you want to publish it./Either revenge this wrong or quit/And let our shame die silently.] (2489–93; 92)

The one who is silenced is Isabel; this is her last appearance in the play because she will soon enter the convent. López de Ayala's Isabel takes the same path, but her father feels no shame about her. Isabel bids him farewell, but after a brief "Adiós," she turns and painfully addresses him:

Isabel. (Volviendo) ¿Tú también
estás conmigo enojado?
¿Me retiras con enojos
la vista?
Crespo. No la retiro,
Isabel, y no te miro,
porque te afligen mis ojos.
Isabel. ¡Ah! Mírame como sueles;
yo soy la misma.
Crespo. (Abrazándola) ¡Hija mía!
Isabel. ¡Padre! *(Abrazándole con efusión)*

[*Isabel.* (*Turning around*) You are angry with me, too? Do you angrily avert your eyes?
Crespo. I don't avert them, Isabel, and I do not look at you because it makes you suffer.
Isabel. Ah! Look at me as you usually do; I am the same as before.
Crespo: (*Embracing her*) My daughter!
Isabel: Father! (*Embracing him effusively*)] (3.12)

Crespo's embrace affirms visually and physically her innocence as well as her continued acceptance within the family and community bonds. His action is another testament to his ability to separate the public and the personal, almost a representation of "the king's two bodies" on the level of the common man who happens to represent—or perhaps because he represents—monarchic order. The scene is, too, another lesson given by López de Ayala on how to be the perfect prince, on how to rule in the monarch's stead to avoid the disruption that would surely ensue if unruly and unlawful leaders such as the Captain held sway and continued to violate the laws that form the fabric of society.

Pedro Crespo attempts at every turn to justify his decisions, to show that he has not reached them hastily. He is fully aware of the import implicit in condemning the Captain, and he makes it clear just as Don Lope arrives:

Si alguien dice que no es sabio
tan gran apresuramiento,

ART AND POLITICS 157

>   yo diré que más violento
>   entró en mi casa el agravio.
>   (*Hojea el proceso y escribe*)
>   Tal vez si el mozo repara
>   su fin próximo, el espanto
>   consiga ... mas yo entre tanto,
>   he de firmar ...
> Lope. (*Dentro*)   Para, para.

[*Crespo*. If some say that such haste is not wise, I say that the insult entered my house more violently. (*He leafs through the court papers and writes*) Perhaps if the young man reflects on his impending death fear will succeed in ... but meanwhile I must sign ...
Lope. (*Within*) Stop, stop.] (3.14)

Although Don Lope enters too late to save the Captain, as the ensuing scenes prove, the careful thought Crespo has given the matter and the ability to balance public and personal demands reinforce his moral position, seen in his vociferous disagreement over procedure with Don Lope and in his self-defense before the king. The mayor's eloquence and logic result in the king's naming him "alcalde perpetuo" [mayor in perpetuity] of Zalamea.

That the closing scenes of López de Ayala's *El alcalde de Zalamea* in general reflect Calderón does not detract from the integrity of the recast. We have seen time and again how the changes introduced in this nineteenth-century version blend well with the high percentage of verses from the original. The last lines are no exception. Even though the relationship between Don Lope and Pedro Crespo may be strained because Don Lope believes the mayor has overstepped his authority, Pedro Crespo has no regrets. He releases the remaining prisoners—Rebolledo, La Chispa, and his own son Juan—to Don Lope (without the protestations concerning his son's guilt as in the original), and both laments his personal loss (a son to the army and a daughter to the convent) and accepts the heavy responsibilities of his position:

>   *Crespo.* Con dos hijos me encontrasteis: (*A D. Lope*)
>   sin ninguno quedo ya.
>   *Lope.*   Hartos cuidados os quedan
>   con esa vara.
>   *Crespo.*   Es verdad:
>   y administrando justicia
>   y manteniendo la paz,
>   todos los hijos del pueblo
>   su padre me llamarán.

[*Crespo.* (*To Don Lope*) You found me with two children: I have none left.
Lope. You have enough concerns with that staff.
Crespo. It is true: and administering justice and maintaining peace, all of the children of the town will call me their father.] (3.17)

If any doubt existed about viewing López de Ayala's play as a political allegory, this closing should dispel it. Crespo clearly sees himself as a *pater familias* (a position that could be read years later as a very "franquista" interpretation), a man who believes that a kind of benign or enlightened despotism provides the best rule. He will rule in perpetuity much as a monarch rules until death. It is important to reiterate that López de Ayala's participation in the overthrow of Queen Isabel II was not to displace the monarchy in favor of a republic but to place a better-suited ruler on the throne. *El alcalde de Zalamea* is in many ways López de Ayala's answer to the vexing political turmoil facing Spain of the 1860s.

* * *

I now turn to the play's reception in the Madrid press and to how the recast fared vis-à-vis Calderón's *comedia*. The political impetus to recast and stage Calderón seems clear given the writer's political stance. Its performance history in the nineteenth century coincides, not surprisingly, with the important milestones in both Calderón's posthumous career and the ever-changing political climate of nineteenth-century Spanish politics.

Calderón's *El alcalde de Zalamea* was staged at the Teatro de la Cruz on 25 May 1842 on the anniversary of Calderón's death (the Teatro del Príncipe presented *La vida es sueño*) and on the occasion of the reburial of his remains. A review published in the *Revista de Teatro* subsequent to the performance, however, speaks more of the importance of Calderón and the strength of the play than of the performance itself.[32] In the first place, the article points to the sorry state of the Madrid stage in the proliferation of imported and translated plays and emphasizes the importance of custom and tradition:

> A fuer de españoles apegados a nuestros usos y costumbres, preferimos la representación de ellos a la de los que reinan en otros países, con los cuales tienen en general muy poca analogía. Tal vez contribuye a este nuestro modo de pensar cierto espíritu de nacionalidad, que nos hace deplorar la fatalidad porque, pudiendo ser originales y abastecer los teatros con producciones de nuestra propia cosecha, hemos de ir a importar de nuestros vecinos transpirenáicos hasta los artículos de cargazón, que sobre ser por la mayor parte de mala calidad, se averían siempre en el viaje.

[As Spaniards devoted to our traditions and customs we prefer their representation to that of other countries' customs with which there is very little analogy. Perhaps contributing to our way of thinking is a certain spirit of nationality that makes us deplore our fate because, with the capability to be original and supply the theatres with productions of our own making, we must import from our neighbors beyond the Pyrenees all manner of goods that in addition to their being basically of poor quality, are damaged en route.] (52)

The romantic sense of nationalism is clear from the opening lines of the review: Spanish plays should dominate the national stages just as Spanish goods should be preferred over imported ones. The exaltation of everything "local" is indicative of the continued desire to redefine, in the ninth year after the end of the Ominous Decade, battered pride and nationalism.

The anonymous reviewer (who may be Agustín Ferrer del Río, author of another article in the same issue and a regular contributor to the *Revista*) praises the play for its universality as well as for its even construction and fluid movement. The tone is one that contrasts markedly with the scorn still heaped on Calderón, not too many years earlier, for the excesses of his Baroque art:[33]

El alcalde de Zalamea es una de las composiciones dramáticas que más aplausos ha merecido en todas épocas, porque su asunto es también de todos los tiempos y lugares, y porque además tiene bellezas, que resaltan aun a los ojos del vulgo. Difícilmente se hallarán otras muchas, que a la observancia de las unidades, tan cacareadas no hace muchos años, y tan olvidadas hoy, reunan la buena disposición de la trama, la marcha fácil y sencilla, la dignidad de los caracteres, la verdad y franqueza con que están pintados, la armonía de la versificación, y el movimiento y desembarazo de los diálogos.

[*The Mayor of Zalamea* is among the best received dramatic compositions of any epoch, because its theme is likewise universal, and because in addition its beauty is noticeable even to the general public. It is unlikely to find many other plays that, regarding observance of the unities—so highly touted not many years ago and so forgotten today—bring together good plot development, easy and simple pace, dignity of the characters and the honesty and openness with which they are drawn, harmony of versification, and movement and fluidness of the dialogues.] (52)

One can still detect an apologetic note for Calderón, even though these words express true admiration for his dramatic art and although the reviewer exaggerates on claiming that the unities are "tan olvidadas hoy" (one need only to give a cursory reading to a number of *refundiciones*, to conclude that their presence still makes itself felt). But of greater importance than the formalities of dramatic construction are the excerpts of dialogue the reviewer chooses to highlight. If on the whole they exhibit "movimiento y desembarazo," those that occur between Don Lope and Pedro Crespo "no pudieran haber sido mejor concebidos" [could not have been better conceived] (52). The three brief selections quoted in the review concern Don Lope's complaints about his leg "que el diablo me dio" [my infernal leg] (881–90);[34] Pedro Crespo's insistence on being the master in his own house, sitting when he wishes and not when ordered (1118–38); and Don Lope's further problems with his leg and his experiences in Flanders (1151–68). All three dialogues involve the born nobleman, Don Lope, and the nobleman of the soul (recall "patrimonio del alma"), Pedro Crespo. Equality between these two characters in the eyes of the reviewer is the salient conclusion one is forced to reach, or else he would have opted for more stereotypical examples of honor, love, or the comic element represented by Don Mendo and Nuño. The choice clearly implies a rejection of past models of "buen gusto" and an attempt to establish a new canon by which to judge the works of the Golden Age writers. Nonetheless, the reviewer believes it necessary to explain why Don Lope expresses himself so forcefully. He notes that Don Lope's tone of voice, acceptable in the last days of full Romanticism, could not have been condoned only a few years before:

> Aunque Calderón ha querido presentar en don Lope la severidad de un gefe militar acostumbrado al mando, es el hábito que se contrae generalmente en la milicia de espresarse lacónica y desabridamente a favor de interjecciones, más eficaces muchas veces que las frases más pulidas, hubieran sido mal recibidas del público ilustrado las imprecaciones de aquel personage, si en la violencia del mal que le aquejaba, y en la bondad de corazón y rectitud de principios con que le adorna, no hallasen en cierto modo disculpa.

> [Although Calderón wanted to present in don Lope the severity of a military leader accustomed to giving orders, it is customary to learn in the military how to express oneself laconically and gruffly favoring interjections often more effective than the most polished phrases; that character's curses would have been poorly received by an enlightened public if there were not some mitigating circumstances in the violence of his illness and in the goodness of his heart and in his moral uprightness.] (53)

El alcalde de Zalamea, too, is a play free from *culterano* passages, a play that can speak directly to a greater audience; the review insists on this text's "bellezas, que resaltan aun a los ojos del vulgo" [beauties noticeable even by the masses] (52). Not only the quotations selected for the review but also the decision by the impresarios of the Príncipe and Cruz to stage *El alcalde de Zalamea* and *La vida es sueño*, Calderón's best known play, become a literary-political decision, a conscious effort to put forth a specific message to a public still enjoying the openness of liberalism and hoping to glean a sense of "lo español" before a spate of foreign works once again appeared on a national stage.[35] In this sense the review nearly fits within a *costumbrista* category, particularly if the descriptions of Don Lope and Pedro Crespo characterize them as "typically Spanish."

The ambience that produced the attitude toward Calderón reflected in the *Revista de Teatro* indicates the influence of the so-called historical Romanticism favored by Alberto Lista; the values informing the reception of the *comedia* as a whole by this school find continuance in the Golden Age–inspired settings created by López de Ayala in his own plays as well as in his *refundición* (as indicated in the introduction to this chapter). By the 1860s, performances of *comedias* or *refundiciones* opened the theatre season at one or more stages (Príncipe, Cruz, Español, Apolo).

Critiques of the recast's stagings, first at the Teatro de la Zarzuela, are available.[36] Judging from the 26 January 1865 review of the play in *La Iberia*, it would be logical to deduce a performance date of 17 January, Calderón's birthday, as well as the first anniversary of the *refundición*'s opening. The month, though, was not a good one for *El alcalde de Zalamea*:

[L]a ejecución en el teatro de la Zarzuela había sido tan deplorable, que salimos grandemente disgustado de tan horrenda profanación. Muy lejos tendríamos que ir si nos engolfáramos en consideraciones acerca de cómo se suelen interpretar en general las obras de levantadas aspiraciones: concretándonos por hoy a *El alcalde de Zalamea*, muchos y justos anatemas tendríamos también que lanzar sobre los actores de la Zarzuela, por su incapacidad absoluta en interpretar sus papeles . . .

[The performance in the Zarzuela Theatre had been so deplorable that we left greatly disgusted at such a terrible desecration. We would have to go quite far if we were to get involved in thinking about how lofty works are generally played: taking *The Mayor of Zalamea* as our example, we would have to hurl many and well-earned condemnations at the Zarzuela actors for the absolute incapacity to interpret their roles . . .] (1)

The *refundidor* himself escapes the opprobrium heaped upon the infelicitous acting troupe; the reviewer notes that Ayala deserves praise "por la manera con que ha sabido dar unidad al drama sin desvirtuar su espíritu literario, asimilándose en lo posible al estilo y al carácter de la obra" [for the way in which he has been able to lend the drama unity without detracting from its literary spirit, approximating to the extent possible the style and character of the work] (1). The reviewer focuses on two new passages that López de Ayala incorporated into his version of the Calderonian text: Isabel's face-to-face rejection of the Captain (2.10) and Rebolledo's humorous reply to the Captain about the difficulty in finding a horse or mule to carry the wounded officer from Zalamea (3.3).[37] The *La Iberia* reviewer observes that the condensed form of Isabel's long *relación* to her father of her dishonor at the hands of the Captain infuses the *romance* with new life (1). The same critic disagrees with the entire idea of the *refundición*, yet believes López de Ayala deserves praise for a job well done and a "pésame por haber visto destrozar tan inhumanamente su bello trabajo por los actores de la Zarzuela" [condolences for having seen his beautiful work so inhumanely destroyed by the Zarzuela actors] (1).

On 5 February 1865 Gil Carmona published his review of the same performance—at least of the same run—in *El Museo Universal*. In many regards he echoes his colleague's remarks in *La Iberia* by praising the recaster before summarizing the play's development from Lope to Calderón:

> Tan famoso drama bien merecía un refundidor literario que supiera conservar en su primitiva forma, toda la delicadeza incomparable de sus detalles; así ha sucedido y por ello merece parabienes el autor de *El tanto por ciento*.
>
> [Such a famous play well deserved a literary recaster with the ability to conserve in its original form all the incomparable delicateness of its details; thus has it happened and for this reason the author of *The Percentage* deserves congratulations.] (46)

One more time, praise for López de Ayala's recast is tempered by reactions to poor set design and a lamentable performance (with the exception of Carlos Latorre in the lead role), especially on the occasion of a Calderonian anniversary. Gil Carmona is rightfully unforgiving in his critique:

> [Y]o lamento profundamente que exornara una producción tan renombrada con aquel miserable decorado. Allí se emplean cuantiosas sumas en presentar una zarzuela y no deja de causar amargura a los amantes de las viejas tradiciones teatrales, tan indisculpable abandono.

La ejecución de *El alcalde de Zalamea* me causó el mismo efecto que su aparato escénico. . . .

[I profoundly lament that they embellished such a renowned production with that miserable set. They have spent huge sums in presenting a *zarzuela* and this unforgivable neglect does not cease to cause bitterness for the lovers of the old theatrical traditions.
The performace of *The Mayor of Zalamea* produced in me the same effect as its set decor. . . .] (46).

The combination of Pedro Calderón de la Barca and Adelardo López de Ayala must have produced a respectable gathering at the theatres because the same *refundición* opened the season the following fall. The review in *La discusión* of Sunday 1 October 1865 speaks of its production as an "acontecimiento dramático" [dramatic event] due both to the quality of the cast and the effort they put forth on 27 September "para hacer resaltar las bellezas de esta joya literaria" [to make the beauties of this literary jewel stand out] (2).[38] The reviewer shares sentiments with the editorial stance of *La Iberia* with regard to the *refundición* because, as he writes, to present a recast is to subvert "algún tanto de solemnidad al espectáculo" [somewhat the solemnity of the show] and to recast is "quitarle el verdadero sabor de la época" [remove the true flavor of the epoch] (2). Nonetheless, J. (as the reviewer signed the article) believes that the play was well written.

Similar sentiment is expressed in two issues of *La Epoca*, the first in brief mention on 28 September 1865. The play "fue desempeñada a la perfección, y obtuvo un éxito brillante" [was carried out flawlessly and enjoyed a brilliant success] (4). All cast members were "aplaudidos y llamados a la escena diferentes veces al final de cada acto" [applauded and called to the stage several times at the end of each act] (4). In the "Revista de Teatros" section of the same paper, dated 3 October 1865, Julio Nombela gives a much longer review. He begins by noting that three of the principal theatres (Príncipe, Circo, and Variedades) are presenting Calderón, Moreto, and Lope de Vega; he also mentions in passing that the Teatro de la Zarzuela continues with its mediocre offerings, a critique that seconds what reviewers had said in January of the same year about the execution of *El alcalde de Zalamea*. Nombela praises Calderón as one of the great playwrights of the world, enjoys the conceits with which Moreto imbues his "bellas creaciones" [beautiful creations], and finds himself nearly speechless in describing the dramatic output of the "Fénix de los ingenios" (1). Equally important is the recognition granted to these Golden Age writers for their influence on European theatre: "La admiración del mundo es poca para premiar sus méritos. El primero y el último, sobre todo [i.e., Lope and Calderón], arrojaron la semilla, y los teatros de Europa no han hecho desde entonces más que coger el fruto" [the world's admiration is little to praise their merits. The first and the last, over all (i.e., Lope and Calderón), cast the seed, and European theatres since then have done nothing more than reap the fruit] (1).

The comments regarding *El alcalde de Zalamea* itself, "una de las más acabadas creaciones de Calderón" [one of Calderón's most polished creations] (1), include a detailed plot summary, as well as praise for specific actors. Teodora Lamadrid carries out the "escena delicada, difícil" [delicate and difficult scene] of relating to her father the shame she has suffered, "con una verdad admirable" [admirably true-to-life; [José] Valero, in the role of Pedro Crespo, "está sublime; no es posible espresar lo que hace; hay que verlo para saber lo que consigue el verdadero ingenio" [is sublime; it isn't possible to express what he does; you have to see it to know what true genius can do]; and Romea as Don Lope "interpreta con una verdad y un talento que justifican su gran reputación" [acts with a spirit and a talent that justify his great reputation] (1).

Nombela's closing remarks take up the refrain found in another review, the matter of solemnity. But in this case the questioning does not concern the use of a *refundición* as a season-opening production, but of a crowd—rather than the more elite typical theatregoers—seemingly uncontrolled because of the way ticket sales were handled:

> ¿Pero ha solemnizado la empresa como debía el acontecimiento literario y artístico que significaba la inauguración de la temporada en el Príncipe?—No: la primera función debió ser una solemnidad artística; poco hubiera perdido la empresa distribuyendo las localidades entre las corporaciones científicas y literarias, entre las personas notables de todas las clases de la sociedad. Los poetas hubieran celebrado aquel acto, el suceso hubiera adquirido mayores proporciones, y no hubiéramos visto especular en la calle a los revendedores, mientras que en el teatro tenía lugar una reconciliación y un espectáculo, que por lo visto consideraba el público de distinta manera que la empresa.

> [But has management commemorated as it should the literary and artistic event of the Príncipe's opening night?—No: the first performance should be a solemn artistic occasion; management would have lost little by distributing tickets among the scientific and literary societies, among the notable individuals of all social classes. The poets would have celebrated that act, the event would have been much grander, and we wouldn't have seen the scalpers working the street while in the theatre both a reconciliation and a theatrical performance took place, which obviously the public considered differently than management.] (1)

Nombela would like to see theatre openings by invitation only, thus limiting the kind of public who would attend, though the meaning of "entre las personas notables de todas las clases de la sociedad" would seem to be limited to those classes associated with the "corporaciones" who should compose the public. Particularly noxious are the scalpers, whose presence lends an air of rank commercialism that management seemed not to mind.

If Gil Carmona felt saddened by an unprofessional staging of *El alcalde de Zalamea* in January 1865, he could speak more positively about the Príncipe theatre's more rigorous standards. Writing again in *El Museo Universal*, in the 22 October 1865 issue, the reviewer can offer only praise for Valero, who "reproduce con asombrosa exactitud el carácter altivo y severo del labrador Pedro Crespo" [reproduces with astonishing preciseness the arrogant and stern character of the farmer Pedro Crespo] (343). Gil Carmona details specific scenes in which the eminent actor excelled, including the close of the second act and the salient moment ("la situación capital") of the third (the critic unfortunately does not specificy to which scene he refers; it may be Pedro Crespo's encounter with his daughter, or the mayor's self-defense before King Philip). The remainder of his comments concern other cast members, of whom two merit special consideration. Julián Romea, an eminent actor whose best days are behind him, can still elicit a reviewer's praise; Gil Carmona highlights Romea's "comprensión y estraordinario talento" [comprehension and extraordinary talent] although the public may find his abilities wanting (343). He is not as kind with Teodora Lamadrid, who has a history of melodramatic performances: "Añejo achaque es, de la escuela de esta señora actriz, impregnar las palabras de un acento lacrimoso que raya en la monotonía" [It's an age-old complaint concerning this actress's school of thought, to impregnate words with a tearful accent that borders on monotony] (343). Further advice would be useless, the writer tells his readers, because she has chosen to ignore suggestions in the past.

Another important year for López de Ayala's recast, more for political content than literary accomplishiment, is 1868, the year of the Glorious Revolution, in which both López de Ayala and his *El alcalde de Zalamea* played an important role. The biographer Solsona, as prejudiced in his subject's favor as Luis de Oteyza is negative, believes the *refundición* contains "todas las bellezas originales; sin sombras las que no las tenían, pero sin sombras también las que el genio de Calderón dejó veladas y oscurecidas" [all of the original beauties; those without stains remain so, but those that Calderón's genius left veiled or darkened are likewise without stain] (46). In other words, the *refundición* outshines the original; López de Ayala apparently has reworked Calderón's original as favorably as Calderón reworked Lope de Vega's. But there is method to Solsona's madness, considering as he does that this *El alcalde de Zalamea* "ha sido la obra democrática y revolucionaria por excelencia" [has been the democratic and revolutionary work par excellence] (46). He sees the liberal spirit that overcomes Sevilla and Cádiz that year as receiving an infusion from López de Ayala's play during January and February: "Las explosiones del entusiasmo que dominaba a los espectadores no eran otra cosa que síntomas y anuncios de la profunda agitación de los espíritus y del próximo levantamiento nacional" [The explosions of enthusiasm that overcame the public were nothing more than symptoms and signs of profound spiritual agitation and of the coming national uprising] (47). López de Ayala certainly manifests his political beliefs in the person of Pedro Crespo. But while Solsona tends to exaggerate to further the praise heaped on López de Ayala, an argument can be made for the recast's potential effect upon a populace eager for change and feeling the winds of revolution blowing steadily. If Lope de Vega's *Fuenteovejuna* can be transformed into a revolutionary call to justice (as it was for the Bolsheviks), Calderón's *Alcalde* can do double duty to promulgate values the reworker believes necessary to carry out his personal and political agenda. The play's horizons spread over the centuries.

The impetus the play found in the political climate of the 1860s and 1870s carries its popularity throughout the remainder of the century as a cursory look at the remaining reviews will show. A September 1882 performance, again opening the theatrical season, now in the refurbished Teatro de Apolo, is very likely the López de Ayala *refundición*. The review in the newspaper *El Imparcial* indicates only that the play is "la joya del teatro de Calderón" [the jewel of Calderón's theatre] and "la comedia de Calderón" [Calderón's play] (3); however, references to López de Ayala's version of Calderón's play generally state that it is in the standard repertoire as late as the 1930s (see Oteyza). The cast, too, would suggest the same, as it includes José Valero (who now reprises the role of Pedro Crespo he had interpreted in the 1860s) and Elisa Mendoza Tenorio, the actress whom López de Ayala was engaged to marry when he died suddenly in 1879.[39] All in all, this performance seems to have been both a critical and public success: "Los actores recibieron durante la representación, y después de terminar cada acto, pruebas inequívocas de la justa satisfacción del público" [The actors received unequivocal proof of the public's rightful satisfaction during and at the end of each act] (3). The anonymous reviewer then relates a comment directed to him by a "respetable literato" [respectable literary figure]: "Quiera Dios que continúen así.... Tendremos un templo donde refugiarnos contra el temporal de disparates que llueven sobre la escena española desde hace algunos años" [May God let them go on this way.... We will have a temple where to take refuge against the storm of foolishness that has rained on the Spanish stage for several years now] (3). The comment implies that a well-turned *refundición* of a Golden Age play—or even an authentic *comedia*—is better theatre fare than that found on the contemporary stage.[40]

Judging from the frequency of performances, López de Ayala's *El alcalde de Zalamea* was staged in Madrid more or less continuously, though reviews are not always available. A critique in *La Epoca* of 23 October 1887 tells that the play once again opened the season, this year in the Teatro Español, and that the *refundición* indeed provided the standard playtext and attracted the finest actors:

> Calderón de la Barca ha sido el primer autor dramático que se ha alojado este año en el teatro Español.
> Llegó servido por Ayala, el cual lo acicaló hace tiempo acomodándolo al gusto de nuestros días; y nos le presentó respetuosamente cogido de la mano D. Antonio Vico, que es un artista digno de hombrearse con los grandes escritores del siglo XVII.
>
> [Calderón de la Barca is the first dramatic author to take up residence this year in the Teatro Español.
> He arrived attended to by Ayala, who polished him a while ago adapting him to present-day tastes; and he was presented to us respectfully hand-in-hand with D. Antonio Vico, an artist worthy of equal status with the great writers of the seventeenth century.] (2)[41]

This particular critique speaks highly of the artistry of Antonio Vico and of the "excelsitud de nuestro teatro" [loftiness of our theatre] (2), which suggests once more that quality actors such as Vico and a repertoire comprised of the *comedia* and its *refundiciones* ensures the survival and flourishing of the Spanish stage. A phrase from the 1860s reviews—"solemnidad artística"—reappears, but not to criticize the impresarios for having inaugurated the theatre season with a mere *refundición*, but for having chosen specifically this work:

> No hubo error en el pensamiento del público. La función de anoche en el Español revistió todos los caracteres de solemnidad artística. *El alcalde de Zalamea* es una obra que no envejecerá nunca. Se la ve un año y otro, y siempre ostenta su belleza inmarcesible. Nosotros habremos desaparecido ... vendrán nuevas generaciones, y los hermosos caracteres trazados por Calderón seguirán embelesando al público.

[There was no fault in the public's perception. Last night's performance in the Teatro Español took on all the characteristics of a solemn artistic event. *The Mayor of Zalamea* is a work that will never grow old. It is seen year after year, and it always reveals its unfading beauty. We will have disappeared . . . new generations will come, and the splendid characters drawn by Calderón will continue to bewitch the public.] (2)

The reviewer draws no distinction between Calderón and López de Ayala, a tribute to the recaster and to the reception of his play. Although none of the reviews I have seen comments on the political scene of the 1880s, it would not be difficult to surmise that the restored monarchy in the person of Alfonso XII would find favor with *El alcalde de Zalamea* as it has been recast, and that the play and its strong monarchic sentiments would continue to arouse public interest and acclamation.[42]

If López de Ayala's recast was scheduled prominently for September inaugural performances during the 1860s, the 1880s find them scheduled at the end of October, an attractive date because of its proximity to 1 November, the traditional performance slot for Zorrilla's *Don Juan Tenorio*. Although a new staging pleased the reviewer, Pedro Bofull, he took advantage of the forum to remark on the condition of Madrid streets and the lighting used on stage. In *La Epoca* of 31 October 1889, he notes that *El alcalde de Zalamea* was offered "a la manera de un hermoso dechado de autoridades municipales" [in the manner of a perfect model of municipal authority] (4). Nevertheless, Bofull feels the need for social commentary: "Yo no sé cómo dejó establecido ese alcalde el servicio de incendios; ignoro si el empedrado del pueblo de Zalamea era tan malo como el de cierta capital que todos conocemos." [I don't know how that mayor set up street lighting; I am unaware if the street paving in Zalamea was as bad as that of a certain capital that we all know.] (4). At the same time, his critique of stage lighting makes him out to be a curmudgeon unwilling to accept certain material advances in theatre production:

Lo que sí puedo asegurar es que en Zalamea había por aquellos tiempos alumbrado eléctrico, y que hasta la luna servía humildemente a los que estaban en candidatura para el cargo de alcaldes, puesto que cuando la presunta autoridad necesitaba un rayo de luz del astro que brilla por la noche, para ver desde la puerta de su casa el camino por donde se ausentaba su hijo, brotaba de repente, como si obedeciera al mando de un segundo apunte, nada más que para satisfacer el deseo del que iba a recibir la vara de alcalde.

[What I can assure is that during that period in Zalamea there were electric lights, and that even the moon humbly served those running for mayor, for when the would-be mayor needed a ray of moonlight to see from his house the road taken by his son, it suddenly burst forth as if obeying the order of a second prompter only to satisfy the desire of he who was going to receive the mayor's staff of authority.] (4)

Even with his tongue-in-cheek humor and light political satire ("salvo este detalle de *pedir la luna*, lo cual ha transmitido quizá por herencia a los concejales del día un afán de posesión insaciable" [except for this detail of "asking for the moon," which has transmitted perhaps by inheritance to today's councilmen an unquenchable thirst for power]), Bofull believes that the *alcalde* is a man of "rectitud acrisolada, de conciencia pura y estricto cumplidor de la justicia" [proved uprightness, of clean conscience, and a strict fulfiller of justice] and that the play and performance combine to provide a "deleite literario que ya sólo se experimenta en contadas ocasiones, y de unos incidentes dramáticos cuyos moldes se han perdido" [literary delight that is experienced on few occasions, and of dramatic incidents whose models have been lost] (4).

Just as *Don Juan Tenorio* "se impone" [imposes itself] on 1 November, so the *comedia*, even—or perhaps especially—in its recast form, imposes itself on the theatre scene to be enjoyed by public and critics alike. Critical subversion of *refundición* performances appears now to be of the past; López de Ayala, whose posthumous renown seems to emanate from his *El alcalde de Zalamea*, has become a recognized figure in the Plaza de Santa Ana, particularly during the month of October. A second review of the same performance, from *La Iberia* of 31 October 1889, places playwright and recaster on the same plane. The performance was both "brillantísima" and "solemne" (the same word, it bears repeating, employed some twenty-five years earlier to urge *comedia* and not *refundición* performances). The unnamed critic avers that the "público numerosísimo" enjoyed both the struggle of passions and the "choque de caracteres, tan admirablemente trazados, y a los que el autor primero y el *refundidor* de la obra después superion dar tanto relieve" [clash of admirably drawn characters who have been created with sharpness by both the original author and the recaster](4). But the principal emphasis falls here on Antonio Vico as the best interpreter of Calderón in the role of Pedro Crespo. Underscored are the farewell scene between father and son, Isabel's abduction at the end of act 2, and "las más culminantes [escenas]" [the climactic scenes] of act 3.[43]

* * *

The *refundición* of *El alcalde de Zalamea*, like that of *Marta la piadosa*, exemplifies further both the political aims of a recast and the artistic polemic that often accompanies any adaptation of a classical work. Most critics accepted López de Ayala's recast positively while they continued to harbor doubts about the *refundición* as such; comments such as the following one, from the 13 December 1868 *La Epoca*, are not unusual: "Rara vez semejantes profanaciones . . . se han hecho con mano más hábil y delicada" [Rarely have similar desecrations been done with a more capable and sensitive hand] (4). Disrespect for the recast play is not to be considered as disrespect for the writer, provided the *refundidor* is capable not only of understanding the original *comedia* but able to compose verse and to excise judiciously. The judgment of these qualities, we have seen, varies from critic to critic.

Chapters 2, 3, and 4 have focused on recasts that fit a relatively narrow definition of the *refundición* in that the *refundidores* have taken one source text to adapt to the exigencies of new artistic, social, and political realities. Each resulting text is, of course, a new play presented to a new public whose familiarity with the original is not necessarily assured. The same logic dictates, then, that a play which borrows from numerous sources but that may not cite directly the source texts, should fit into a wider category of recasts. The next chapter examines briefly two plays from perspectives that differ from the previous analyses: the Duke of Rivas's *El desengaño en un sueño* and a *Marta la piadosa* performed in 1986. The first of these experienced only a handful of performances, and critiques of it underscore the difficulties in bringing it to the stage; my study aims to clarify how the author subverts the text's most important source (*La vida es sueño*) as well as to augment the conception of what can be considered a *refundición*. The second play's inclusion in a new chapter is intended to signal a new direction that *comedia* studies have begun to take.[44]

5
Future Directions

The title of this chapter is intended to suggest that a study of the *refundición* does not require a univocal approach. It is possible to consider plays that are not, strictly speaking, *refundiciones* as I have defined them in these pages; many playtexts are constituted from a variety of sources, yet a character or an idea borrowed from one play may provide the seed out of which grows not only a new plot but also a renewed conception of theatre. On the other hand, and within a stricter interpretation of recasts, the contemporary stage often sees adaptations and translations of classical theatre that attempt either to communicate the essence of the original text or to adapt according to the reigning aesthetic, or to combine elements of both approaches. These subsequent performances depend, just like a production of a new play, on the quality of rewriting, the ability of a director to see the possibilities inherent in the source text, and the actors' capacity to communicate effectively to their audience what Jonathan Miller calls the "indeterminacy of the text [that] begins to assert itself."[1]

To indicate possible directions I have chosen two plays whose "original" texts date from the seventeenth century, yet whose restagings took place in different periods, one in the nineteenth and one in the twentieth century. The Duke of Rivas's *El desengaño en un sueño* [Disillusionment in a dream] borrows from Calderón's *La vida es sueño* [Life is a dream] as well as a variety of plays both Spanish and non-Spanish. The author has chosen an avenue of expression best suited to a social and political agenda that voices his frustration at the direction Spanish Romanticism has taken. A 1986 production of *Marta la piadosa* by the Centro Universitario de Teatro (Universidad Nacional Autónoma de México) at El Chamizal Golden Age Theatre Festival revived Tirso's masterpiece in a contemporary production that was at once innovative and scandalous (as the reviews will indicate). The critical and performance tradition of the two plays is a testimony not only to the authors/recasters but also to possibilities for future directions inherent in the source texts.

La vida es sueño Refashioned: The Duke of Rivas's *El desengaño en un sueño*

The Duke of Rivas's *El desengaño en un sueño*, written in 1842, translated into French by Jean Gabriel Hugelmann in 1857, and not performed until 1875 (ten years after the duke's death), generally has taken a back seat to the author's more famous *Don Alvaro o la fuerza del sino* [Don Alvaro or the force of destiny].[2] There seems to be little doubt about its Romantic nature, though Richard Cardwell considers the play "a *palinodia* for *Don Alvaro*."[3] The many and varied literary sources of the play reveal the Duke of Rivas's horizons of experience; though *La vida es sueño* clearly influenced *Desengaño*, other sources include the Exemplo XI of *El conde Lucanor* [Count Lucanor]; Alarcón's *La prueba de las promesas* [The proof of the promises]; the eighteenth-century *comedia de magia Sueños hay que lecciones son, o efectos de un desengaño* [Instructive dreams, or effects of disillusionment]; and Shakespeare's *Macbeth, Hamlet,* and *The Tempest*.[4] Grillparzer's *Der Traum ein Leben*, on the other hand, is somewhat problematic. Richard O'Connell argues first that both writers found their source in *Sueños hay . . .* , a plausible explanation given the Austrian writer's penchant for Spanish theatre; O'Connell then suggests that the similarity between the duke's plays and the Austrian's "testifies to a kinship of spirit between the two authors and between the theaters of their respective countries."[5]

The nineteenth-century was not unequivocal in its reception of the Duke of Rivas's play. Manuel Cañete believed it to be, after *Don Alvaro* and *El moro expósito*, "la más original y encumbrada obra poética" [the most original and dignified poetic work] by the Duke.[6] Leopoldo Augusto de Cueto considered it "una magnífica leyenda fantástica" [a magnificent fantastic legend];[7] Padre Francisco Blanco García is highly praiseworthy of the "grandiosa idea" of the play

> donde se adunan la profundidad, el libre vuelo y la lujosa forma calderonianas. No vive Lisardo, es cierto, dentro de la realidad, como vive Segismundo, y por lo mismo no forma un tipo tan humano y tan verdadero; mas, para no ser plagiario de Calderón, apenas tenía otro medio el Duque de Rivas, y aunque al fin resulten ficticios las heroicidades, los crímenes y aventuras del inexperto joven, no brilla menos esplendorosa la enseñanza de que no cabe hallar en esta vida la felicidad.

[where profundity, free flight and luxurious Calderonian forms are brought together. Certainly Lisardo does not live in reality as does Segismundo, and for the same reason he is not as true or as human a being; but, so as not to plagiarize Calderón, the Duke of Rivas had scarcely another means, and although at the end the heroic deeds, the crimes and adventures of the inexperienced young man are fictitious, the lesson that happiness is not to be found in this life shines no less brilliantly.]

Further, it is a "digno remate del grandioso edificio" [worthy crowning jewel of the magnificent edifice] (of the Duke of Rivas's dramatic works).[8] A few years prior to Blanco García's evaluation, Juan Valera had expressed his negative view of the play, condemning it as a contradiction of the Duke himself, and the work "lleno de un espíritu sofístico y verdaderamente pesimista y fatalista" [full of a sophist and truly pessimist and fatalist spirit]; once Lisardo has accepted defeat and returns to his father's arms, according to Valera, [Lisardo] "equipara la realidad con la pesadilla: todas sus maldades soñadas vienen a valer como si fuesen efectivas; y él es un ser abominable, despreciable y vitando" [equates reality and the nightmare: all his dreamed evil-doings carry the same currency as if they were real; and he is an abominable, contemptible and odious being].[9] Enrique Piñeyro, in part, is much more negative as well as pedestrian. *Desengaño* "carece de acción; es una doble alegoría, cuyo objeto y alcance conoce el espectador desde el primer momento y que no puede por consiguiente interesarle. Su radical inverosimilitud va más allá de lo que a la imaginación es permitido corregir o completar" [lacks action; it is a double allegory of whose object and purpose the spectator is aware from the first moment and which thus cannot interest him. Its radical improbability goes beyond what the imagination may correct or complete].[10]

Few twentieth-century studies are dedicated to *El desengaño en un sueño*. Gabriel Boussagol's biography treats the play within the context of a critical biography; E. A. Peers's study in a special number of *Revue Hispanique* contributes only an overview; Richard O'Connell, mentioned above, deals with the question of influence; Rupert Allen published an intriguing archetypal analysis of the play, to which I will return shortly; Richard Cardwell, within an article about Don Alvaro, touches on a crisis of conscience suffered by the Duke of Rivas, occasioned by his inheritance of the dukedom and the more moderate Spanish political climate, that turned him toward a more orthodox stance;[11] Douglas Hilt draws further comparisons between Grillparzer and Rivas, and suggests Rivas's use of Gracián's *El Criticón* and its "world of false appearances, pain, and unhappiness"; Gabriel Lovett's Twayne series book provides a general introduction; and Susan Polansky argues, in a speech-act theory orientation, that "the dramaturgy of destiny . . . constitutes most significantly the textual coherence" of the play.[12]

Although the sources of *El desengaño en un sueño* are patently obvious, a closer look at *La vida es sueño* is revealing. The general thrust of the play—dream world, illusion/reality, *desengaño*—is dependent upon Calderón, and a series of *décimas* spoken by a forlorn Lisardo in act 1 are cast in the mold of Segismundo's first speech:

> Si tal mi destino fue,
> que es imposible lo fuera,
> ¿para qué un alma tan fiera
> dentro de mi pecho hallé?
> ¿Con qué objeto, para qué
> arde esta insaciable llama,
> que toda mi mente inflama,
> de buscar dándome anhelo,
> aún a despecho del cielo,
> oro, amor, poder y fama?

[If such was my destiny, and it is impossible for it to be so, why did I find such a proud soul within my breast? To what end, for what reason does this insatiable flame burn—for it inflames my mind—to seek, giving me desire, even in spite of heaven, for gold, love, power and fame?][13]

The resonances of *La vida es sueño* are clear. The deferred object is the living of the reality that is each son's due; each father (or father-figure, as in the case of Clotaldo and Arbolán) is seemingly omnipotent and all-controlling in the desire to reveal the slippery underpinnings of the life aspired to by each son. (Other instances are detailed in Peer's monograph.) Nevertheless, while the dramatic text at every turn displays romantic sensibility and inclusion of *magia*, it is at the same time conscious of its Calderonian source. Calderón is the most culturally immediate predecessor of the play (the eighteenth-century *comedia de magia* notwithstanding), and thus the writer who must be "overcome." The Duke of Rivas wrote during a period of literary renovation and revolution that accompanied a historical period "agitado, triste y algo estéril" [full of commotion, sad and somewhat sterile].[14] *Desengaño* can be seen within this context as an attempt to recover the lost glorious past and to surpass it. For this reason, the Duke of Rivas, consciously or unconsciously, not only turned away from the kind of desolation leading to suicide found in *Don Alvaro o la fuerza del sino*, he also attempted to outdo Segismundo, even—or perhaps precisely—by turning against the model.

El desengaño en un sueño is not a *refundición* in the strict sense of the word. But Rivas has taken on Calderón beyond the verbal coincidences and recasts to create an interweaving of elements that both pays homage to the Golden Age writer and reduces him to source material in order to supplant him. We can look at the creation of *Desengaño* the same way that we can look at the phenomenon of the *refundición*, that is, as a going beyond, a surpassing, or, in more violent and Derridean terms, a poisoning of the source, the leading astray from the source, to give life, to create something new with the same means with which the original was created: that is, through writing. The new text, in a manner similar to many nineteenth-century *refundiciones*, is a *pharmakon*.

The idea of writing as *pharmakon*, presented in Plato's *Phaedrus* and developed by Derrida "Plato's Pharmacy," has in recent years been used fruitfully by various scholars.[15] James Cowan discusses the notion of *pharmakon* and *pharmakos* in such writers as Sherwood Anderson and William Carlos Williams.[16] In an area closer to present concerns, Frederick de Armas contributes to the rehabilitation of Andrés de Claramonte's dramaturgy by studying the playwright's skillful use of a *pharmakon* in *El secreto en la mujer*.[17] The Duke of Rivas's play lends itself to this kind of interpretation; early in act 1, as Lisardo's father Marcolán, to show his son the error of his ways, casts a spell to make him sleep. If the *pharmakon* functions both as poison and remedy, its presence becomes clear: Marcolán wishes to purge from his son all desire for fame, wealth, and love, corrupt and corrupting as they are, in order to encourage him to continue a life of isolation away from the scourges of the world. The spell is the *pharmakon* whose first stage is hypnosis: "Ya empieza el conjuro a obrar. / Le tocaré con la vara, / y al sueño se rendirá" [The spell already begins to take effect. I will touch him with my staff, and he will fall fast asleep] (221), says his father, while the second is the conjuration of spirits:

> Espíritus celestes e infernales;
> genios del bien y el mal, que los destinos
> por ocultos caminos
> dirigís de los míseros mortales.
>   Al gran poder de mi saber profundo
> obedientes venid, que ya os aguardo,
> y al dormido Lisardo
> mostrad en sueños cuanto encierra el mundo.
>   En vagas vaporosas ilusiones,

> y en fantásticas formas vea su mente
> cuanto anhela imprudente,
> y ancho campo ofreced a sus pasiones.

[Celestial and infernal spirits; genii of good and evil, for you direct the destiny of miserable mortals along hidden paths. Come, obedient, to the great power of my profound knowledge, for I await you; and show in dreams to the sleeping Lisardo what the world has to offer. In hazy, dreamy illusions, and in fantastic forms let his mind see all that he desires so imprudently, and hold no rein to his passion.] (221–22)

It is not necessary for the *pharmakon* to be a poison ingested like the hemlock that Socrates drinks; Derrida tells us that "the *pharmakon* would be a *substance*—with all that that word can connote in terms of matter with occult virtues, cryptic depths refusing to submit their ambivalence to analysis—. . . if we didn't have eventually to come to recognize it as antisubstance itself."[18] Here it may be helpful to recall another of the sources of *Desengaño*—*The Tempest*—in which Prospero holds the island, and particularly Ariel, in the spell worked by his staff; after all, "we are such stuff as dreams are made on."

At this point Rupert Allen's article becomes helpful. The essay underscores the motif of the "'captive son'" and the emasculation of him by the father first in the latter's reluctance to allow Lisardo to go forth into the world, and second in Lisardo's rejection of the world, opting for the security offered by his father's embrace.[19] Even the names of two principal male characters, Marcolán and Arbolán, suggesting pruning hook and tree (211–12), contribute to Lisardo's desire not to abandon Rivas's version of Prospero's island.[20]

It is not my intent to critique Allen's provocative essay,[21] but to demonstrate how his salient points illuminate the concept of the *pharmakon* that subverts the Calderonian Segismundo. Marcolán's working of magic is akin to Clotaldo's giving Segismundo the sleeping potion; both serve to place the sons, either condemned by the stars to an ill-fated life or prevented from experiencing the workings of the world, in "real" situations in order to prove that such protection can be only beneficial. That Segismundo enters the world of his father's palace, coming to question where life ends and the dream begins, while Lisardo embarks upon an allegorical journey in a dream world leading him to the throne, makes no difference at present. The spell as a potion is a *pharmakon* that poisons the mind in order to purge and to offer a cure. It defers reality: the assumption of rightfully inherited power for Segismundo, the struggle to fulfill the inner drive for something greater than a retiring life on the island felt by Lisardo.

Allen describes Lisardo's frustration as that of one who wishes to be initiated into the ways of the world; he is thus "culturally deprived" because he has no imprint on him. In one way, Lisardo is pure, virginal, just like Segismundo, but both know innately that a much different world awaits them, or that they are *destined* to form part of that other world. Marcolán's repression of his son's unconscious powers becomes the instrument of deferral. The effect this has on Lisardo—as it does on Segismundo as well—is to unleash, in Allen's words, "an unreflective male animal for whom only 'external' obstacles exist."[22] The obstacles must be overcome, and whereas Segismundo hesitates ever so briefly before exploiting the power recently conferred upon him, Lisardo questions at first, but soon allows each potential stumbling block—Zora, whose "prior" love he instantly returns; a sumptuous castle and wealth; victory in battle; finally, the throne and the queen's hand—to become part of what is to him a very real world. Whereas Segismundo, however, acts at each step with authority, however overbearing and untempered it may be, Lisardo is content with each new acquisition until the Voz del Genio del Mal (Voice of the Genie of Evil), one of the genii conjured by Marcolán to tempt his son in his oneiric journey, urges him to even greater wealth and glory. This disembodied voice, through the machinations of Marcolán the high priest/father, administers the second and serial *pharmakon* each time Lisardo seems to come to rest. The voice's first "speech," in a polymetric mixture that disrupts the lyricism of the play's versification, leaves no doubt about its poisonous effects:

> Yo marchitaré
> las lozanas flores.
> Yo evenenaré
> los dulces amores.
> Y en horrores
> sus delicias tornaré.
>   La riqueza
>   y grandeza
>   afán
>   serán
>   de su pecho,
> por la avaricia y el terror deshecho.
> Y la indomable ambición
>   su corazón
> al crimen arrastrará,
> y en hondo precipicio lo hundirá.

[I will wither the young flowers. I will poison sweet young love. And I will turn his delights into horrors. Wealth and greatness will be the desire of his breast, undone through greed and terror. And indomitable ambition will drag his heart to crime, and will sink him in a deep precipice.]

(224)[23]

Again like Segismundo during his first stay in the palace, Lisardo receives no direct guidance; though Segismundo is repeatedly warned that he may only be dreaming, Lisardo's complete independence or even alienation from his father's teachings, according to Allen, causes the "disintegration of [his] psyche."[24] Disintegration undermines, subverts, and deconstructs at all times, leading Lisardo to what he believes to be the fulfillment of so many desires pushing him upward in the social strata, but is in effect directing him to his bitter defeat with the death of Zora (who has since abandoned him) and the treason of the queen and Arbolán. But not only is this a subversion or deconstruction of self, but also of the source. Segismundo awakens in his prison to believe that his recent glory was but a dream; he learns soon after to contain his passions. Lisardo is given no such experience, no time or space to reflect upon the hard lessons he is learning. Lisardo is, in other words, a deconstructed Segismundo as the Duke of Rivas undertakes the subversion of the principal thrust of *La vida es sueño*. He does this not simply as a representative of another and a different aesthetic and philosophy (in spite of E. A. Peers's long-refuted belief in Calderonian Romanticism), but also as a creator who feels the anxiety of influence bearing down on him. His cultural closeness to Calderón forces his hand, whereas the distance between Rivas's culture and that of Shakespeare allows him to incorporate the Bard's creations of Hamlet, Macbeth, and Prospero without the need to undercut the foreign elements.

Upon seeing Zora for the first time, Lisardo begins to realize that his dream produces in seemingly flesh-and-blood form all that his imagination told him existed. He exclaims: "¡Ah! que realizando voy / cuanto anheló mi deseo . . ." [Ah! I am only now realizing how much my desire wished for!] (226), unaware of the fact that he is but living a dream. He continues: "Sí, la misma que mis ojos / en ilusión vieron vana . . ." [Yes, the same one that my eyes saw in vain illusion] (226). Once again, because of the dream sequence, the concretization of what has been perceived by the mind's eye is deferred. Although he believes his present experience to be real, he finds himself before an image that he cannot comprehend nor dominate fully. If he were able to do so, he would not let the happiness he finds with Zora escape him to seek the wealth and power that the Voz del Genio del

Mal suggests is within his easy reach: "Lisardo, en el mundo hay más" [Lisardo, there is more in the world than meets your eye] (233). Lisardo continually reacts with awe to his new world—"Nada iguala las dichas que hoy poseo" [Nothing equals the good fortune that I possess today] (240)— until he finds himself compelled to conquer a brave new world:

> ¿Dónde, Zora, estarán
> los tesoros inmensos y riqueza,
> que fundamento dan
> a tanta pompa y sin igual grandeza...?

[Oh Zora, where are the vast treasures and wealth that underlie such pomp and unequalled greatness?] (240)

Lisardo's complacency is always short-lived. Present pleasures satisfy the appetite for but a moment, because satiation, too, is constantly deferred, in spite of Lisardo's statements to the contrary:

> Me enajena el placer, Zora querida.
> Más dicha apetecer fuera demencia,
> que en tus brazos gozar y en la opulencia
> el breve curso de la humana vida.

[Pleasure distracts me, my beloved Zora. It would be madness to desire greater happiness than to enjoy your embrace and in this opulence, the brief course of human life.] (242)

The seduction of wealth and power works insidiously upon him, as his repetition of the word "afán" [zeal] at least a dozen times testifies. "Afán" makes him covet both the throne and the queen, and renders him deaf to the threat of *desengaño* in the words the queen directs to him once he has killed the king:

> ¿Has visto cuán fácilmente
> a los hombres se fascina,
> y a una nación se alucina
> desde una altura eminente?
>   Del rey muerto, como ves,
> ni un vago recuerdo hay ya..."

[Have you seen how easily man is fascinated and a nation is deluded from a prominent height? Not even a vague memory remains of the dead king now.] (279)

The inability to grasp beyond the surface is the effect of the *pharmakon* that continues to work its power. The spell cast over Lisardo has come from a book (hence Prospero again), a written word, and, following Derrida, it "envelops in a single embrace the book and the drug, writing and whatever works in an occult, ambiguous manner open to empiricism and chance, governed by the ways of magic and not the laws of necessity."[25] Such is the impulse behind the regicide, another *pharmakon* now in the hands of Lisardo, for it yields him the throne. He gloats in his glory: "Mi poder es colosal" [My power is colossal] (209), but it is a false victory, one step (so he thinks) in establishing authority, in searching for a personal truth-value. But this in turn is undermined by the working of the *pharmakon*, for this step is the last "upward" movement prior to Lisardo's downfall (recall here *El conde Lucanor* and *La prueba de las promesas*). The *pharmakon* is clearly a two-edged sword. This message becomes all the more forcefully apparent by the placement of the regicide at the end of act 2 and the beginning of act 3, at the middle of the play. It is the axis on which the play turns; the height of power is reached; in other words, the *pharmakon* has yielded its maximum effect. The *desengaño*, hinted at in the death of the king, perhaps another Lisardo who was not so fortunate as to be sleeping, perchance dreaming, is soon to take place. The dead king is now a trace—"vago recuerdo" [vague memory]—and the presence of Lisardo's good fortune will soon become absence because it is supplemental to his life awake. To reinforce this comes the Voz del Genio de Mal, responding with its first negation of Lisardo's apparent good fortune to the question posed by the man who would be king—"¿Quién puede de aquí arrancarme?" "De un asesino el puñal" [Who can pull me away from here? The knife of an assassin.] (282)—his double, his supplement, he who will supplant him. We cannot afford to lose the irony that his replacement is Arbolán, a second father figure whose name echoes that of Marcolán, and whose stature, deriving from "árbol," further suggests nature, solidity, and longevity.

Lisardo's downfall is as rapid as is Segismundo's rehabilitation. He no longer can find a center, an axis for himself: "No sé qué pasa en mi pecho:/ni yo me entiendo a mí mismo" [I don't know what's happening inside of me; I do not even understand myself] (284), a statement that is the reverse of "El placer me enajena" [Pleasure alienates me from myself]. The emptiness in his soul is the place once occupied by Zora (¡Qué soberano hechizo / era para mí!" [What sovereign magic she was for me] [284], he says), who was another manifestation of the *pharmakon*. The second half of the play details Lisardo's fall, both literal and figurative: not only does he lose power, he finds himself magically transported to the *locus amoenus* where he first encountered Zora; when he calls out to her, she appears wearing a death shroud and borne by pall bearers. Lisardo's enemies pursue him, though he never surrenders the now-impossible hope of recovering power, that is, he never learns Segismundo's lesson. After he sees the specter of both the dead king (the ghost of Hamlet's father) and of Zora, he cries out for his father—in *décimas*—to recall once again Segismundo's laments:

> ¡Ay de mí, desventurado!
> ¿Esto he visto, y vivo estoy?
> Me encuentro por doquier hoy
> de crímenes rodeado.
> Mira por mí, padre amado.
> De este mundo de maldad
> vuélveme a la soledad
> del escollo en que nací:
> torne a verme junto a ti,
> ten de Lisardo piedad.

[Ah, unfortunate me! I have seen all this and I remain alive? I am surrounded by crimes on all sides. Look out for me, beloved father. Return me from this world of evil to the loneliness of the mountain where I was born. Let me see myself next to you again. Have pity on Lisardo.] (341)

The *pharmakon* worked by Marcolán poisons Lisardo and thus alters the workings of his mind. By the same token, it "cures" him of his desire to know the world, but quite ironically, for it prevents him from establishing not only his "self" (in terms of ego) but also meaning to his life. The Duke of Rivas's play negates Segismundo's awareness of faith by its very omission. Yet, just as Segismundo returns to the fold, so Lisardo embraces his father, but not to step beyond and learn from the experiences, but to remain in a kind of womb, protected from the vicissitudes of the world that a full maturation would imply. Lisardo becomes a fully deconstructed Segismundo. Segismundo learns from the "dream" and overcomes the factiousness of his personality. Lisardo becomes a fading image of his former real self, having been exposed to constant deferral in his dream world, and making that world as real as any life experience could be. He is the "island-captive," as Allen states (211). He is isolated, insulated, deferred from land but also from the company of man. Both the Duke of Rivas and Marcolán have inscribed a new world, a supplement to the lived reality, of the reality to be lived.

El desengaño en un sueño—the negative is explicit—thus attempts to supplant *La vida es sueño*. By extension, it might be suggested that the Romantic Spanish playwright, taking one of his sources from the Baroque Spaniard *par excellence*, subverts the hegemony of the *comedia* and its influence, and the play is, thus, a kind of *refundición*. The Duke of Rivas's discursive power resides in surpassing the antecedent, in a deconstruction of literary inheritance that at the same time rejects the Romantic hero (recall Richard Cardwell's postulation of the duke's crisis of conscience and his turn to a more conservative viewpoint).[26] He wishes to turn back to Calderón and all that he and his age imply, yet to place his own imprimatur upon the poetic creation. Perhaps the Duke of Rivas sees the Romantic mind as poisoned. Perhaps his *pharmakon*—his act of writing—is an antidote or *palinodia* to Don Alvaro and to Segismundo. Yet I do not wish to detract from the Duke of Rivas's success, for he has created a powerful dramatic work that preys upon the mind and spirit not only of Lisardo but of Romantic Spain itself.

The Duke of Rivas confronted many obstacles in attempting to have a production of his play mounted, and he never lived to see its performance in December 1875. In a letter to the Conde de Morphy dated 13 December 1875 and published in the 15 December 1875 issue of *La Ilustración Española y Americana*, Leopoldo Augusto de Cueto praises *El desengaño en un sueño* and describes its author's frustrations regarding the unwillingness of Madrid's theatres to stage the play. Responding to Augusto de Cueto's 1842 request for a reading, the theatre impresario Juan Lombia kindly but firmly rejects the play because of what he sees as inherent staging difficulties:

> Dejando aparte el inconveniente, también invencible, de que no hay actor, cualesquiera que sean sus facultades físicas, que pueda declamar todo el papel de Lisardo como exige la violencia de las pasiones que de continuo agitan a aquel personaje, la mayor parte de las mutaciones y apariencias que tiene el drama exigen, por su complicación y demás circunstancias, la caída del telón de boca y un blanco de consideración, sin que esto pueda sustituirse con la aparición de una nube pasajera, ni con cualquiera otro medio supletorio.
>
> [Apart from the inconvenient as well as overwhelming fact that no actor, regardless of his stamina, can perform Lisardo's entire role as demanded by the passions that constantly assault that character, most of the play's scene changes and stage devices demand, due to the complications they present and other circumstances, the fall of the house curtain and a focal point, without substituting either of these with the appearance of a passing cloud or any other means.] (374)

Although the play received evaluations from an impressive group of *literati* and theatre personnel, the final judgment qualified the play as *"irrepresentable"* [unrepresentable] (374; original emphasis).27 *El desengaño en un sueño* was admired by many, but none would risk bringing it to the stage until the actor Antonio Vico decided to affirm an *"imposible vencido"* [an impossible task overcome; original emphasis] and perform the title role of Lisardo at the Teatro de Apolo.

Of the performance itself, Augusto de Cueto limits his remarks to formulas repeated in many newspaper reviews.28 He does spend considerable time, however, in a literary evaluation (generally positive and always kind, given the friendship between the late author and the critic) that signals the differences between *Desengaño* and its sources (debunking completely the eighteenth-century *Sueños hay que lecciones son, o efectos del desengaño*) as well as the play's originality. One telling passage, though, indicates that Augusto de Cueto believed it necessary to defend the Duke of Rivas on this last point, a defense formulated in the belief that an artistic creation finds its source not in novelty but in re-creation:

> Usted sabe que el genio no cae nunca en la sandia tentación de inventar nada. Lo que hace el genio es apoderarse de una idea cualquiera, fecunda y luminosa, ya la encuentre en un mal libro, ya en las realidades de la vida, ya en las tradiciones leyendarias, ya en las consejas populares, y una vez escogido este despertador de la fantasía, dar nueva vida, forma más cabal y más bella, y alcance más poderoso a la idea, y levantarla a la altura de los tipos universales. Esa es la verdadera creación del genio.
>
> [You know that genius never falls into the foolish temptation of inventing anything. What genius does is take control of a fertile and luminous idea, whether found in a bad book or in the day-to-day reality of life, whether in legend or in popular tales, and, once this awakener of fantasy is chosen, give the idea new life, a more precise and more beautiful form, and a more powerful reach, and raise it to the height of universal types. That is the true creation of genius.] (375)

The above description could pass in great measure for a wide-reaching definition of a *refundición*; it is reminiscent, too, of the mid-century play reviewers (for example, Aureliano Fernández-Guerra y Orbe) who touted that an accomplished work of art was cast out for others to adapt and improve.

Manuel de la Revilla reviewed *Desengaño* in the same forum two weeks later (30 December 1875), expressing sentiments shared by many who awaited this production: "verdadero acontecimiento teatral" [a true theatrical happening] (248). The staging of the play, though, did not match its expectations, and the critic's words point to the reasons why the Duke of Rivas had been unsuccessful in bringing his play to the stage. In spite of the admiration and respect that other newspapers accorded the late author, says Revilla, "La obra no ha alcanzado el éxito que se presumía" [The work has not reached the success that was expected of it] (248). The ensuing comments underscore the difference between a stageable play and a "poema dramático" [dramatic poem], as some have called *El desengaño en un sueño*:

> *El desengaño en un sueño*, con ser una concepción grandiosamente pensada y gallardamente escrita, no tiene condiciones para la escena. Más que drama es un poema dramático,—algo semejante a esas obras que, como el *Manfredo* de Byron y el *Fausto* de Goethe, no pueden impunemente llevarse a las tablas. Su pensamiento filosófico, desconsolador y pesimista, su acción puramente fantástica, sus personajes apenas bosquejados, sus pasiones apenas desenvueltas, no pueden despertar en el público el interés ni la simpatía.

> [*Disillusionment in a Dream*, because of its being a magnificently well-thought concept and elegantly written, is not a stageable play. More than a drama it is a dramatic poem,—something akin to those works that, like Byron's *Manfred* and Goethe's *Faust*, cannot be brought to the stage with impunity. Its philosophic thought, heartbreaking and pessimistic, its purely fantastic action, its hazily sketched characters, its poorly developed passions, cannot arouse interest nor symphathy in the public.] (248–49)

The episodes that develop rapidly as in a nightmare are doubtlessly awe-inspiring, but they are neither dramatic nor moving. The public was cool to the performance, and although the set was an artistic wonder, it was insufficient to elicit the emotion necessary to appreciate the production. The critic succinctly closes his review:

> Obras de esta clase son para leídas, no para contempladas en escena, porque en el teatro sólo interesa la vida real, nunca las visiones del ensueño ni los caprichosos fantasmas que la mente forja.

> [Works of this kind are to be read, not to be viewed on stage, because in the theatre only real life creates interest, never visions of fantasy nor whimsical ghosts that the mind forges.] (249)

Respect for the author, who had died ten years before, led the critics to temper their remarks. Adulation for the printed text abounded; perhaps the theatre personnel who had rejected *Desengaño* some thirty years earlier had done a kindness to the Duke of Rivas by saving him from certain public embarrassment that would have ensued from a production of his play given the limited technical resources available to the Spanish theatre of the time.

Marta la piadosa in the Twentieth Century: A Brief Performance Review

On 12 March 1986 Raúl Zermeño and the Centro Universitario de Teatro of the Universidad Nacional Autónoma de México brought to the stage at El Chamizal perhaps the most risqué version of *Marta la piadosa* ever produced. Before turning to the review in the 13 March El Paso *Times*, it will be helpful to know the innovations Raúl Zermeño's vision of Tirso produced. The play as Tirso wrote it opens with back-to-back sonnets, a stunning lyric introduction. Such a ploy, to the experienced reader/observer, hints at the deception found in the discrepancy between opening sonnets in which Marta and Lucía lament their brother's death and the ironic and mocking tone characteristic of the play. As a literary practice, and for its purpose of deceiving the reader/viewer into believing that a tragic plot is about to unfold, the recourse is superb, especially because the use of sonnets in an unconventional place calls attention to their presence. Yet theatrically speaking, double sonnets can create a slow pace difficult to alter in ensuing scenes.[29] To avoid "deadly theatre," Zermeño opens the play with a duel between Don Felipe and another man, a swordfight that ends in the death of Marta's and Lucía's brother (the unnamed man). The sisters, who recite the sonnets, are tied to large circular structures as the body is prepared for burial. The two poems now have a context, based on Aztec burial rites, expressed through movement as well as through speech; the ambiguity created by Tirso's use of this specific strophe form is not only maintained, but emphasized. Marta's first two lines, "El tardo buey atado a la coyunda / la noche espera y la cerviz levanta" [The slow-moving ox tied to the yoke awaits the night and lifts his neck] (1. 1–2), become literal as the death of the brother at the hands of Marta's lover weighs her down with a yoke of sadness and despair, all hope for consummating her relationship seeming to vanish. Lucía expresses her loss, incurred for the same reasons as Marta's, a result of inconstant fortune: "Que no puedo esperar ni aun esperanza, / me dice la fortuna, aunque inconstante" [I cannot hope for even hope, inconstant fortune tells me] (1. 15–16). The viewer could imagine the turning of the circular wreath with Lucía attached as a physical sign of fortune's fickleness.[30] Zermeño has taken what Jauss calls the "inner horizon of literature" and has demonstrated its influence on the "outer horizon of everyday life" ("Changing Horizons" 169). The lighter tone of the ensuing dialogue between Marta and her sister regarding their love for Felipe stands out all the more.

Zermeño again reveals his insight into staging in another cleverly mounted series of scenes. Felipe is aware that his actions have made his hoped-for marriage to Marta problematic, and he often crosses the stage in amorous angst. To communicate this melancholy, an affliction that often leaves its victims depressed and helpless, Felipe, when speaking about Marta, collapses under the weight of his love and suffering; his servant Pastrana has no recourse but to carry his master off stage on his back. By visualizing a rhetorical convention whose effect is often expressed verbally but without concomitant actions (at least on the Chamizal stage), Zermeño captures the imagination and captivates the audience. Unfortunately, additional "modernizations" were less felicitous in the eyes of certain members of the audience. The oft-removed Mámora battle spoken by the Alférez was replaced by a multimedia presentation that represented the founding of Tenochtitlán. Aztec warriors, replete with spears, stood before slides of Aztec ruins while pre-Columbian-type music composed for the performance was heard in the background. The director's intention was to counter the imperialism inherent in the Spanish campaign against the Moors by showing the proud Aztecs founding their capital long before the Spanish were to overrun it.[31] Zermeño capitalized on playing to a largely Mexican and Chicano audience who enthusiastically applauded the modification.[32] The thematic link, however, between Tenochtitlán and the Mámora, let alone to *Marta la piadosa*, is difficult to discover. If he had included, for example, the defeat of the *conquistadores* at the hands of the Aztecs during "la noche triste," the scene would have exhibited greater consonance with its anti-imperialist tone.[33]

A final adaptation in the play was even less well received. Once Felipe is introduced into Don Gómez's household and becomes Dómine Berrío, he and Marta engage in various sexual acts. At the end of act 3 in Tirso's original, when Don Gómez and Capitán Urbina are deceived into traveling to Sevilla with the promise of seeing Felipe brought to justice, Marta plans a fiesta by the Manzanares River, where her betrothal to Felipe occurs. Zermeño has replaced the scene by having the two old men, each with Coca-Cola in hand, attend a slide show which, unbeknownst to them, will reveal Marta and Felipe in a variety of copulatory positions. Both men suffer fatal heart attacks, and the way is now clear for Marta's and Felipe's nuptials.

Zermeño's *Marta* quickly became controversial. Tirso de Molina, wrote Diana Washington in the El Paso *Times*, "never envisioned nude scenes in his dramas" (1A). One of the theatre patrons considered the play "in poor taste. Even though it was dark, you could see everything by candlelight. Toward the end they showed a pornographic film, and I had to leave because I didn't want my 13–year-old daughter to see it" (1A). For an official response, the writer interviewed Mr. Franklin G. Smith, then–superintendent of El Chamizal National Park. Mr. Smith made it clear that none of the actors were nude; the actor portraying the brother at the opening of the work "wore a body stocking and G-string and held a large bouquet of flowers in front of him" (1A). Similarly, Marta and Felipe, in their sexual acrobatics depicted on slides, also were wearing body stockings. On the one hand a purist might argue that such vitiation of the text is a profanation of Tirso's memory and his "intentions." Robert ter Horst, in an article published five years before the Chamizal production, has argued convincingly that sexuality is latent within the text from beginning to end; each of several encounters with and escape from death brings with it a release of libidinous energy that seeks satisfaction (441–44). In this respect Zermeño's production becomes an actualization of that which could not be so overtly presented to the seventeenth century. His *Marta la piadosa* is a concrete fulfillment of wish, of desire, of what was suggested. Even proverbs used in the play trade on the sexually suggestive connotations of the name "Marta." Popular culture, as embodied in proverb collections, by definition transcends any one horizon, and is in and of itself a bridge between historical periods. Popular culture, too, may justify such an explicit representation of implied action; the performance then challenges accepted norms of theatrical "behavior."

Though Zermeño's production is not entirely without sin, his staging testifies to a concept of theatre that enlivens a three-centuries-old dramatic text. He reincorporates the opening scene that has been omitted in each of the nineteenth-century reworkings. For 1.1, each of the *refundidores* studied in chapter 3 has attempted to convey past meaning yet satisfy contemporary demands, and has refashioned the opening scene in other ways. Rodríguez de Arellano invents a scene between Marta and her servant in which Sirena (the servant) informs her mistress of an encounter with Don Felipe and his ardent passion for her (Marta) in the plaza; Solís reorganizes the dramatic action and opens with the fifth scene of Tirso's original, a lover's plaint spoken by Don Felipe to his servant Pastrana; Boldún's opening scene shows the servants Pastrana and Inés ushering Fernando (Felipe's name in this version) into Marta's house. Each act 1, scene 1 corresponds to the recaster's notion of theatre; Zermeño's is unique and is often successful precisely because he appeals to a multicultural audience and fuses Mexican, Chicano, and North American horizons of experience.

* * *

Adaptations of classical drama, regardless of the century in which they take place, make it clear that bridge-building opens the past to the present, frees the language of the text from its original constraints so that it appears to us similar to yet different from the text than spoken to its original audience. In the case of both the Duke of Rivas and Tirso de Molina, every adaptation in some way becomes a dialogue with Calderón and Tirso (et al.); it is as well an act of interpretation via adaptation, a reconsideration through reworking. *El desengaño en un sueño* is now fairly relegated to classroom readings and histories of nineteenth-century Spanish theatre, but *Marta la piadosa* carries the tradition. The fact of this *comedia*'s popularity in spite of incursions committed by the occasionally less able writer speaks, naturally, to Tirso's genius, originality, and universality. Catherine Larson has written eloquently on these qualities:

> [T]he elusive nature of Tirso's originality also speaks to his modernity, to his ability to continue to wrest his readers and spectators in the 1990s from complacency so that they might engage in meaningful encounters with a text or a performance. In that sense, the originality of Tirso de Molina relates directly to the efforts of contemporary directors and actors to recapture him in a new age and for new audiences. (1)[34]

Similar statements could be made for any quality playwright of a past era whose works find themselves the object of performance scrutiny on today's stages.[35] Zermeño wielded a double-edged sword vis-à-vis his audience: the interpolation of Mexican culture spanned the horizons of his Hispanic audience, but nudity, even feigned nudity, stretched to the limits its acceptance of innovation. In this last regard, some would say, the director has both de-fused horizons and diffused the play. In the passion to reject values and to impose a new form on old plays, a decanonization does take place, though it might not immediately please the public.

The theatrical experience is a continuum imbued with ritual and magic, and the temporal and aesthetic distance to be mediated condones and even encourages a possible vitiation of the text. In a sentiment expressed by Richard Palmer, José María Díez-Borque, William Gruber, and others, "The locus of happening in a play is in the collective mind of the audience" (Palmer 190). The recreators of the *comedia* clearly find enjoyment in reading the texts that come to us from that "foreign country," and in turn recreate and imbue them with their very different sense of theatre. These new texts derive their authority and validity not just from a quality original text, but from the continuity of theatre experience and the potentially frictional element of innovation. Zermeño's additions to Tirso are certainly no worse than López de Ayala's emendations to Calderón; and the changes brought to bear by Trigueros and Hartzenbusch on their *refundiciones* obeyed specific aesthetics of theatre. All used the theatre to further individual political and social ends and employed the recourses each thought necessary for the task. That, after all, is the purpose of the *refundición*.

Conclusion

A theatrical work is not a closed, hermetic artifact, but a creation ever alive and ever given to change. A recast text yields to the actor, director, and public its "touchstone of meaning" against a background of aesthetic concerns that inform the writer's concept of art.[1] While we *can* appreciate a faithful reproduction of a *comedia*, we are no less interested in what the *refundidor* brings to an interpretation from his or her personal and professional horizons. Likewise today we relish contemporary interpretation with substantially revised texts by actors and directors for whom Spanish may not be their native language. We may disdain specific incursions perpetrated on a *comedia*, but, as is often pointed out, we can always learn from uneven or inconsistent stagings. The fact that Calderón and others retain their vitality and continue to be imitated and reworked affirms that their visions of the world, however anathema to the eighteenth or nineteenth (or twentieth) century, remain as one important source upon which new readings in new contexts develop. The *comedia* is the pretext as well as the pre-text.

The *refundidores,* particularly of nineteenth-century Spain, constitute a generation which inherited the literary richness of their country's Golden Age, perhaps the first of its inheritors to appreciate the legacy. The eighteenth century suffered the trauma of "coming *immediately* after a great creative achievement."[2] The nineteenth century clearly did not face the same burden because it found a source of national pride in the Golden Age's artistic achievements and thus could focus more acutely on what it shared with them.[3] The writers of drama saw their task not as a rendering of "performances whose historically accurate style ha[d] been established by scholars" but as making familiar the strangeness of the past; they presented "the power of fusion that the present possesses as such when it succeeds in elevating past life into presence."[4] They consciously took up the inherited tradition; their process of creation, unbeknownst to most of them, was hermeneutical. According to Gadamer, "The place between strangeness and familiarity that a transmitted text has for us is that intermediate place between being an historically intended separate object and being part of a tradition."[5]

In light of the uneven reception given to the *refundición*, a few general observations from the director Peter Brook are helpful:

> It is vain to pretend that the words we apply to classical plays like 'musical', 'poetic', 'larger than life', 'noble', 'heroic', 'romantic', have any absolute meaning. They are the reflections of a critical attitude of a particular period, and to attempt to build a performance today to conform to these canons is the most certain road to deadly theatre—deadly theatre of a respectability that makes it pass as living theatre.[6]

Brook speaks directly to reproductions that strive toward the director's idea of fidelity to an original performance. At the risk of stretching definitions, it seems clear that though many of these performances adhere to an "original" text, each representation is to a certain extent a recast simply by virtue of re-presentation. Yet recasts often become outcasts due to a director's inability to develop (or an actor's to communicate) the possibilities inherent in the play chosen to stage. In the introduction to his version of Calderón's *El galán fantasma*, José Luis Alonso states that "hay que divertirse con y de Calderón" [we have to have fun with and make fun of Calderón].[7] Alonso's reworking suggests two possible approaches: either as a complete misreading of Calderón (because, as one might argue, the adapted *El galán fantasma* is peppered with lines from many Calderonian works); or as a spoof on Calderón (the characterization of the Duke of Saxony as an effeminate fop runs counter to general expectations of a Calderonian ruler). To accept rigidly the first explanation categorizes us as Peter Brook's "deadly spectator" who takes the task of criticism all too seriously and who fights to maintain a hermetic, unwavering view of theatre by confirming pet theories about staging the classics and not wishing to be shaken by innovation. The second explanation poses other problems, for we as both public and critics must be open to all the possibilities inherent in a text. Just as shifting sands is an apt metaphor for the constant evolution of aesthetic appreciation, so it is for a balanced and intelligent view of theatre. Peter Brook's philosophy—at least from the director's viewpoint—holds up well in this regard: "Hold on tightly, let go lightly."[8] While we should adhere to and fervently defend our beliefs, we should also be willing to allow for innovative readings of the shadows cast from the fire of Plato's cave.

The work of recasting carries implicitly the concomitant counterpart of reception as a practical, "hands-on" approach to the *comedia*. The task compels us to "recrear el teatro clásico español," as Dawn Smith reminds us, "buscando interpretaciones que no sean, por una parte, mera resuscitación de un cuerpo muerto, ni, por otra, una descarada modernización revestida de absurdas libertades" [recreate the classical Spanish theatre seeking interpretations that on the one hand are not a simple resuscitation of a dead body, nor on the other a shameless modernization fashioned with absurd liberties].[9] In our attempts to understand the history of performance and of reception, we must at the same time take care to avoid closed-mindedness just because a work is "different" than its author supposedly "intended" or than what we visualize from the text. As Henry Sullivan explains, "Since the life of a work of art begins only when it leaves its creator's hands, adaptations and translations form part of the widening river of its progress through history. Posterity adds to the dimensions of the masterpiece, while all readers realize the 'virtual' component in what they read, irrespective of its intrinsic or 'immanent' stature."[10]

* * *

It is clear that I have not attempted here a history of the *refundición*, not because the necessity of such an undertaking is in doubt, but rather because the enormity of the task requires first an approximation to the process of recasting. A true history properly carried out would require a study of the aesthetics of eighteenth- and nineteenth-century Spain as well as a recuperation and systematic study of the newspaper reviews that remain to be culled from Madrid's Hemeroteca Municipal; even if that project were to be conducted with a team of investigators, what remains is the state of theatre, of *refundiciones*, and of criticism in the other major cultural centers of Spain. My hope is that the present introduction will provide an impetus for carrying out the arduous yet fulfilling task of compendium and analysis, of a reception history of the Spanish theatre.[11]

Each preceding chapter of this book contains sufficient material for expansion into a separate monograph. Various theoretical approaches would yield illuminating conclusions about the process of rewriting and the resulting plays; much greater detail could be devoted to the reviews themselves for what they say about theatre aesthetics in nineteenth-century Madrid and about the politics of theatre. For each play analyzed other *refundiciones* could come to light and bring forth even more detail about the reception of classical Spanish theatre after the Golden Age, an undertaking that at long last accords recast theatre texts the respect they merit.

Appendix

I have provided in this appendix the full text of the performance reviews relating to the plays studied in chapters 2, 3 and 4; I have also included the review of *Casa con dos puertas mala es de guardar*, cited in chapter 1, because of its inherent importance concerning the *refundición*. By "full text" I mean that part of the review dedicated to the play in question; many of the reviews are quite long and discuss several performances. I recognize that, for a history of nineteenth-century theatre, the complete information provided in the newspapers would be invaluable, but I do not wish to try the reader's patience. Omitted as well are complete reviews for the plays discussed in chapter 5 (*El desengaño en un sueño* and *Marta la piadosa*); in both instances, I have quoted extensively the most germane information.

This appendix does not purport to reproduce every review of each play. As I mentioned above, numerous bound volumes in Madrid's Hemeroteca Municipal are unavailable for consultation. The following critiques, however, do provide an insight into nineteenth-century attitudes toward the *refundición* and the *comedia* as well. In reproducing them I have maintained the original orthography but have modernized the accents; this seeming inconsistency is due to often capricious typesetting that would print, for example, an "á" for the preposition in one line and not in the next. The author's name, if a review is signed, is placed at the end of the corresponding article.

Chapter 1. On the *refundición*

La España, 14 Octubre 1855, pp. 1–2

Hallámonos de ejercicios los devotos de Melpómene, Tersícore y Talía, ni más ni menos como el ratón que dejando el mundo se metió en un queso de bola: y en cuaresma de novedades, nos sentamos al opíparo banquete de

Moratín, Lope, Tirso, Alarcón, Rojas, Calderón y Moreto. Pero a falta de tortas, rebueno es pan candeal, y vale muy más dos toma que un te daré; y quien te da lo más que podías desear nada te debe. Vosotros, amantes de la civilizadora y apacible delectación del teatro, ¿queréis divertir melancolías con escenas que rebosen ternura y amor, rivales de la naturaleza? Dulcemente logrará el fénix de los ingenios dilatar vuestra alma. ¿Gustáis apacentaros en cuadros de lo diario y casero, daguerreotipados de la vida común con tal realce y belleza que a la realidad superan y vencen? De satisfaceros cuidará el buen Inarco Celenio. ¿Os aguija el deseo de regalada doctrina? Ahí tenéis al autor de *La verdad sospechosa*. Al fraile de la Merced si anheláis alborozo para el espíritu; al cantor de *El desdén con el desdén*, si os cautivan el gracejo, los vivos diálogos y sazonados chistes. Pero si buscáis la gala, el tropel y el boato, el honor convertido en nacionalidad (según la felicísima frase de un escelente crítico y poeta moderno), si os agrada una acción llena de alegría o de tristeza, que perturbe y alborote el ánimo, y por espanto, ya por conmiseración, ya por lo imprevisto y apurado de los lances y el contraste de peregrinos caracteres, acudid al gran don Pedro Calderón de la Barca. Ved, pues, como, escogiendo las más hermosas flores del antiguo Parnaso español, y con ello franqueando el palenque a una lid generosa de discreción e ingenio, en la esmerada interpretación de las obras de nuestros dramaturgos se desata un raudal de honesto y provechoso deleite para el indiferente espectador necesitado de solaz y descanso. ¿Y de qué importancia no serán tan altos modelos para quien solícito corre tras la advertencia y la enseñanza?

En hora buena parezcan morlés de morlés estas muestras de pura satisfacción a quien haya olvidado el blanco a que apuntan los intentos de Pipí, que no han sido otros que empeñar a los escritores militantes en coger el agua pura y cristalina, en su fuente; mas no corrompida y encenagada en charcas muy lejanas de su origen; y que los primeros actores de España, dejando a un lado añejas y estériles rencillas, se uniesen para dar a los espectáculos escénicos el realce conveniente, si han de ser enseñanza a los artistas y poetas, y de engrandecimiento a la dramática española.

Acaba de empeñarnos más en nuestra tarea, y de confirmar las esperanzas del público, anheloso de aplaudir siempre con entusiasmo lo bueno y bien hecho, la representación de *Casa con dos puertas mala es de guardar*, escelente, inmejorable por parte de Teodora y Romea, y esmeradísima por la del joven Tamayo (don Victorino).

Es a juicio de muchos, este poema entre los de capa y espada el mejor de Calderón; ameno, regocijadísimo, de efecto sin igual en las tablas, y de estudio profundo para los que aspiren a hacer en dramática verdaderos adelantamientos. La traza, la invención, la disposición de los lances, el concierto de todas las partes entre sí, la versificación y el estilo estímense por inmejorables; pues lejos de ser antes maraña que nudo el enredo dramático, se estrecha y aprieta con suma claridad y verisimilitud en situaciones eminentemente cómicas, y los episodios de la fábula, parecen como hojas de una fragante rosa abierta que la ensanchan y florecen.

[Plot summary with selected quotations from the play have been omitted.]

. . . . . .

Con artificio tan discreto y agradable se aprieta el nudo, y luego con no menor destreza se desata. Colócanse oportunamente en situaciones parecidas, pero no simétricas, para el mayor contraste, las figuras; son discretas en el discurrir, pero no impertinentes ni afectadas; coplan lo verdadero y lo bello de la naturaleza; y combatidas por pasiones diversas, magistralmente pintadas, gracias a un conocimiento prodigioso del corazón humano, dan tal claro oscuro al poema, tanta variedad de matices y de tonos, y tal encanto, en fin, que si durante la representación escénica, entre el auditorio distingue el espectador algún estranjero, no puede menos de llenarse de noble orgullo ufano con las insignes obras que nos legaron nuestros mayores.

Lo difícil en todas las de ingenio es en verdad hallar un buen asunto y el lado porque debe tratarse; pero no basta para ello la fortuna, si faltan las fuerzas de un privilegiado entendimiento. No prodigan este riquísimo tesoro los cielos; mas como venga un siglo en que el hombre aprenda a respetarse a sí mismo respetando a los demás; en que le absorba el anhelo de saber, se familiarice con los monumentos literarios y artísticos de la antigüedad, y haga caudal generoso de los aciertos de sus contemporáneos,—entonces este siglo adquiere el nombre de dorado, y pasa con inmarcesibles laureles a las futuras generaciones. ¿A qué otra cosa debió en todos ramos su esplendor el siglo XVI? A cifrar su solicitud los capitanes no en perder a los valientes, sino en competir con hazañas su gloria; los pintores y escultores, en imitar y hacer propio lo bello moderno y antiguo; los poetas, no en el ageno descrédito, antes en comunicarse recíprocamente generosa doctrina; y de estos, a saber de memoria las escelentes composiciones unos de otros, y los rasgos más felices de su ingenio, pasándolos así al dominio común. Mas luego que las mezquinas pasiones se desataron, y el brutal instinto cegó la razón, y cuando la envidia de las ridículas medianías pretendió con voces oscurecer la verdad, los tiempos de guerras literarias lograron herir de muerte las artes benéficas de la paz. ¿Qué otro fruto sacaron sino de las contiendas de Quevedo, Jáuregui y Montalbán; qué de las de Huerta, Forner y los Iriartes, sino el escándalo y el menosprecio, y al fin la corrupción y el caos?

Raras son las épocas de ingenios inmortales; pero si de los grandes modelos del arte supiesen aprovecharse las medianías, ya que no competirlos, alcanzarían hombrear con ellos. Presente la coyuntura hermosa de estudiarlos con vida en poetas que no viven, sin la opuesta mortificación del amor propio, sepamos aprovecharlo con actividad generosa. Brillar ignorando mucho y desdeñando el aprender, es un imposible; querer suplir con la desvergüenza y osadía la falta de ciencia, locura; meter vano ruido con embelecos y trocar por humo la luz, necedad consumada. Escupir a la agena gloria, a la virtud laboriosa y modesta, téngase por oficio de sapos. Enfatuarse con lo disparatado o trivial que bosteza la pluma, pretendiendo que por reliquia se adore; perder en hablillas de mujerzuelas el tiempo que debía consagrarse a ilustrar y engrandecer el espíritu; y soñar que se ha puesto una pica en Flandes con maldecir de los que le ilustran y engrandecen, es hacer el papel tristísimo de la mosca de Esopo, que yendo en un carro por seco pedregal, esclamaba llena de orgullo: ¡Cuánto polvo levanto!

Pipí [Aureliano Fernández-Guerra y Orbe]

Chapter 2. *Sancho Ortiz de las Roelas*

La Gazeta de Madrid, 16 Junio 1611, pp. 683–84.

Querer hacer una tragedia según las reglas del arte, de una comedia dramática, en que todo es vicioso, plano, artificio, lances y estilo, es empresa algo más que atrevida é imposible de lograr. Así es que D. Cándido María Trigueros al transformar, *La estrella de Sevilla*, comedia de Lope de Vega, en *Sancho Ortiz de las Roelas*, tragedia, consiguió desbaratar aquella, y hacer, con los retazos que la fue cortando, una monstruo, que ni la obra de Lope, ni un drama en que a lo menos se advierta sentido: no solamente no se puede juzgar en la tal producción del ingenio de su legítimo autor, sin que ni aun siquiera por aproximación presentar la menor cosa digna de la alta calificación que se la quiere dar. De modo que solo queda una prueba, evidente del mal gusto del refundidor y de lo ridículo, perjudicial é inútil de las refundiciones, nuevo ramo de literatura inventado en España en el siglo pasado, y al qual se dedicaron con tanto denuedo varios ingenios, que creyeron darnos un teatro español con sólo tomar nuestras antiguas comedias, hacerlas giras, poner al principio lo que estaba al fin, a lo último lo que se hallaba en el medio, cortar tres o quatro relaciones, reformar como extravagante o impropio medio verso antiguo, para embutir otro medio moderno, que no era menos ridículo, y que por lo regular estaba escrito en la lengua franca del día (mal de que ciertamente no adolecen las insinuadas obras, pues son todas modelos más o menos cabales de lenguage y de pureza); y por último, y esta era la operación de empeño, mudar el nombre de jornadas en el de actos, y hacer cinco de tres que todas tienen. Otra cosa les hubiera dado más honra, y sería el haber tomado ciertos asuntos que les pareciesen dignos de ser manejados con el decoro y arte que el teatro pide, y presentarlos de nuevo, conservando aquellos pensamientos y trozos del autor antiguo, que por su energía, hermosura, propiedad y otras prendas de tal naturaleza pudiesen acomodarse en la moderna composición; pero contra esto hai una objeción de gravísimo peso, y sin réplica alguna, y es que semejante tarea supone el que la emprende buen gusto, sanos principios y mucho pulso, y por consiguiente era imposible que los refundidores de que voi hablando intentasen acometerla. No comprehendo en este número ni son dignos de tal nombre algunos escritores de mucha estimación y merecido crédito que, por condescendencia o por motivos particulares, se han visto en la necesidad de *arreglar* dramas antiguos: la repugnancia con que se dedicaban a este trabajo, y lo sobrios que han estado en él, pues no llegarán me parece a tres las comedias refundidas por su pluma, prueba que todavía no les ha faltado el juicio.

Pero ya que nuestra desgracia sea tal que necesitemos tragedias y comedias de taracea; escójanse a lo menos las producciones antiguas, cuyo asunto sea teatral y dramático. Hartas hay de esta especie en nuestros antiguos autores, como lo han reconocido los escritores de otras naciones, particularmente los franceses, que se han apoderado de lo mejor; y a fe que han sabido sacar mui buen partido de su especulación. Tal tragedia, admira y enagena a los espectadores de aquel teatro, que no hubiera quizá existido nunca, si su autor no encontrara en nuestros poetas el asunto de ella, y las mejores escenas y los más sublimes pensamientos que la adornan. Nuestros refundidores, al contrario, han ido eligiendo justamente las composiciones más desatinadas, como esmerándose en sacar del olvido únicamente lo malo de nuestros famosos autores de comedias antiguas, de que tanto se ha hablado, unas veces con demasiado rigor y desprecio, otras con escandalosa parcialidad, y las más sin conocimiento de causa. Que se le antoje a D. Sancho el Bravo requerir de amores a la hermana de un regidor de Sevilla, y que por haber este malogrado sus torpes intentos, le condene a morir a manos de su mayor amigo, del amante correspondido de la niña, y con quien se iba a casar, y que este horrible mandato se execute inmediatamente, quedando la pobrecita sin hermano que la ampare, sin marido que la defienda, y el obediente novio mirado, y con justa razón, como un abominable asesino, y cargado de un delito tan atroz, es un asunto que podrá ser mui dramático en un teatro de indios bravos; pero que no corresponde seguramente a las costumbres de una nación civilizada. Pues tal es en substancia el argumento de la supuesta tragedia intitulada *Sancho Ortiz de las Roelas*. Ahora, si por tragedia se quiere entender toda cosa en que haya muertes y desmayos, y contorsiones y baldones, y Reyes con ministros o privados que los hagan cometer delitos para contentar sus pasiones, el tal *Sancho* puede, sin el menor escrúpulo, ponerse al frente de todas, porque además del inocente homicidio en que está fundada la trama de esta composición, y que el pundonoroso Sancho provoca con tanta suavidad, la pobre Estrella se desmaya (y es mui natural) al ver que su amante es el que ha dado muerte a su hermano; y esto lo hace de discreta, con el fin de dar lugar a los alcaldes de Sevilla a que tomen declaración al reo y confronten el cadáver; y la prueba de ello es que así que se ha acabado de pronunciar la última palabra de la declaración vuelve en sí la desgraciada doncella, y empieza a requebrar a su querido, a lo que se sigue un dúo de palmadas en la frente, entreveradas de suspiros y de exclamaciones sobre si el valiente Sancho había o no tenido razón de matar a su amigo.

Luego empieza el Rei a entrar en cuentas consigo, y quando le dicen que su fiel vasallo está preso, y con una causa criminal encima, ya le parece que no ha andado mui justo en mandar matar a un hombre que no quería que le cortejasen la hermana, y envía a decir a Roelas que si tiene alguna buena disculpa pronta, que no se detenga en darla: Sancho bien la tiene, y más que buena, y es una orden firmada del mismo Rei; pero se la come en vez de hacer uso de ella, quando ve que el benéfico Soberano, en lugar de interponer su autoridad para sacarle de las garras de la justicia, emplea el tiempo en enviarle recaditos, rogándole que declare quién le ha movido a cometer tal delito. Estos recaditos duran nada menos que tres actos, todos viene a decir la misma cosa; pero el arte está en variar cada vez las expresiones. Al Rei todo se le vuelve trazas para dexar cortar la cabeza a Roelas, y al mismo tiempo para no verse obligado a confesar su negra venganza; y como el tal Sancho se ha empeñado en callar (esto es, en callar el secreto de la muerte de su amigo, pues por lo demás habla que se las pela), le hace pasar al Rei tragos de muerte. En esto entierran a Bustos Tavera, que es el nombre del hermano, y acabados los funerales se encamina Estrella al alcázar; está con el Rei, quien la hace muchas cortesías y la dice quatro chuscadas, y ella pide que se la entregue el reo. Don Sancho el Bravo piensa ver el cielo abierto; pues no dudando que la hermosa Estrella, como enamorada y compasiva, tendrá la intención secreta de proteger la fuga de su amante, se halla con un medio mui sencillo de salvar su opinión, y de librar a Sancho de la muerte que iba a padecer por su causa, y así firma la entrega del reo con muestras de grande alegría. Pero el testarudo Roelas, que se ha empeñado en que el Rei solo ha de hablar, dice ahora que el Rei solo es quien le puede sacar de la cárcel y de aquí, otro dúo semejante al pasado, con la diferencia de que este va acompañado de enigmas y quisicosas, todo acerca de la razón o sinrazón de haber enviado al otro mundo al pobre Bustos Tavera, y sobre que habiendo dado Sancho una palabra, debía cumplirla. Estrella contesta en el mismo sentido, y suelta una expresión en que da a entender que sabe mui bien los poderosos motivos que ha tenido el buen Sancho para dar una estocada a su hermano: vuelve a insistir sobre la salida; pero viendo que el regidor de Sevilla se enfada, por no desazonarle más, se vuelve por donde ha venido, diciendo para consuelo de los dos, que si a él le van a cortar la cabeza, ella va a fallecer de dolor.

Don Sancho el Bravo se va ya quedando descolorido a fuerza de cavilar; porque el tal negocio va poniendo mala cara: ensarta otra cáfila de enigmas sobre el caso hablando consigo mismo; y al cabo le ocurre el feliz pensamiento de llamar a los alcaldes separadamente, y de encargarlos que se conmuten la pena de muerte de Sancho en un destierro: ellos le responden a lo gallego, se van a ver la causa, y el Monarca se queda tan contento. Vuelven los dos alcaldes con la sentencia para que el Rei la apruebe, y se halla con que a pesar de sus insinuaciones y coraocas, los tales alcaldes fallan que se le corte la cabeza al regidor Sancho. El Rei patea, y se da por las paredes de su alcázar, manda traer a Sancho, envía a buscar a Estrella, y la manda que allí mismo, en presencia de todo el mundo, pida la gracia de su amante: ella lo hace de mui buena gana, y el Soberano la concede con no menos voluntad; pero los alcaldes refunfuñan, y gritan que la justicia queda agraviada. En fin la cosa viene a parar en que el bien intencionado D. Sancho el Bravo tiene que cantar de plano, con lo que todo el mundo se muestra tan satisfecho, menos la pobre Estrella, que sin vocación alguna, tiene que meterse monja; solemne y nuevo modo de concluir tragedias.

Si a todo lo expuesto se agrega el estar el tal drama escrito en redondillas y quintillas, tendremos la composición más original y graciosa que hayan podido meditar los hombres. Repito que ha sido menester valor para haber emprendido el arreglo de este drama, y una valentía más que de prueba para haberle aplicado el título de tragedia. No hablo del modo con que los actores la han representado, porque estoi convencido de que, aunque la saben de memoria, ninguno la entiende, y es imposible expresar lo que el entendimiento no comprehende. Pero no puedo acabar este artículo sin dar cuenta de una observación que llevo hecha de algunos días a esta parte, y es que a todos los Reyes de Castilla han dado los comediantes en transformarlos en Felipes II, vistiéndolos de negro, creyendo sin duda que este color es más decente y magestuoso. También he advertido, en la representación de *Sancho Ortiz*, que todos los cortesanos entran en el quarto del Rei sin sombrero (esto es, en la mano), uso que habrán encontrado en algunas de nuestras antiguas crónicas, como también el anterior.

J. Ab.

La Iberia, 29 Octubre 1857, p. 3.

Teatro de Novedades: Representóse anoche en este coliseo, por última vez por ahora, el escelente drama trájico, de nuestro teatro antiguo, *Sancho Ortiz de las Roelas*, refundido con notable acierto por el señor Hartzenbusch.

Todos los periódicos han hablado del lujo y propiedad con que esta producción ha sido puesta en escena, igualmente que de lo bien interpretada que ha estado.

María Rodríguez, cuya fe artística y buenas facultades hemos elogiado en distintas ocasiones, ha estado en este drama a toda la altura de una primera actriz, manifestando el concienzudo estudio que de su papel ha hecho, en su actitud siempre digna, y en su acción siempre adecuada al carácter que representaba.

Valero, desplegando su gran inteligencia, y Calvo su aptitud para los papeles que requieren severidad y entonación.

A la conclusión del drama fueron llamados estos actores a la escena como en las noches anteriores.

Juan de la Rosa González

La Correspondencia de España, 26 Septiembre 1880, pp. 3–4.

Anoche se inauguró el teatro Español. *La estrella de Sevilla*, de Lope de Vega, refundida por el ilustre Hartzenbusch con el título de *Sancho Ortiz de las Roelas*, fue la obra elegida para tal función, siguiendo la costumbre de rendir este tributo a los grandes autores del teatro nacional.

La refundición está hecha con acabada maestría. Aquellos versos de Lope, de imitación que suspende, de verdad que satisface, de blandura que enamora y de facilidad que encanta, como Hartzenbusch los juzgaba, brotaron con la misma belleza de la pluma y clásica del literato insigno que coleccionó las obras del Fénix de los Ingenios, y ha refundido la que anoche se representó en el Español.

La estrella de Sevilla es un drama trágico en tres actos, de asunto que se supone ocurrido en tiempo de D. Sancho el Brabo, y que algún crítico suspicaz le creó inspirado en la muerte misteriosa de Escobedo, suponiendo en Sancho Ortiz a Antonio Pérez, en Busta Tavera a Escobedo, en Estrella a la princesa de Eboli y en el rey D. Sancho a Felipe II. La simple lectura del drama desautoriza esta opinión.

El Señor Hartzenbusch al refundir la obra le ha dado el título de *Sancho Ortiz de las Roelas*, modelo de súbditos leales y ciego ejecutor de los mandatos del rey; ha distribuido la novela dramática en cuatro actos, y ha prescendido de la esclava Matilde, que en la obra de Lope representa un triste papel, haciendo estas mudanzas con acierto rarísimo. Hartzenbusch, refundiendo los dramas de Lope, y Ayala las comedias de Calderón, perpetúan las glorias de aquellos genios creadores.

La interpretación de la obra, encomendada a las Srtas. Contreras, Soler y Marín, y a los Sres. Vico, Morales, Luna, Reda [?], Benavides y Moreno, fue escelente por parte del Sr. Vico que en toda la obra dijo su difícil papel con gran verdad, y en la escena con que termina el acto tercero se mostró a gran altura. La frase "que siempre acierta quien piensa una villanía," fue pronunciada por el Sr. Vico de modo inimitable, siendo interrumpido por los aplausos del público en la interesante situación que constituye la escena.

La Srta. Contreras que se encontraba visiblemente afectada, y que además se hallaba enferma, interpretó discretamente el papel de Estrella, poco adecuado a sus facultades. La simpática actriz vistió con gran propiedad, y tuvo momentos felices en los actos segundo y tercero.

El Sr. Morales luchó afortunadamente con las dificultades de su papel, el menos simpático de la obra. Los demás actores celosos del cumplimiento de su deber.

J. de F.

La Epoca, 26 Septiembre 1880, p. 4.

¿Cuántos años ha que no se ponía en escena en Madrid *Sancho Ortiz de las Roelas*?

Yo de mí sé decir que sabiendo casi entera de memoria la admirable composición de Lope de Vega, no recuerdo haber asistido nunca a su representación.

A la mayoría del brillante y escogido auditorio de anoche le sucedía lo mismo; y en las localidades de arriba hubo quien pidiese en los momentos de entusiasmo la presentación del autor en las tablas.

La refundición que Hartzenbusch hizo de la obra es digna a la par de él y del Fénix de los ingenios.

¡Con qué arte y con qué habilidad ha condensado la acción! ¡Con qué inteligencia ha descartado los incidentes inútiles, los diálogos demasiado largos, para que nada distraiga la atención de los espectadores del asunto principal!

Conservando la grandeza de las situaciones y de los caracteres; la versificación rica y armoniosa; las chispas de genio que doquier brillan, logró imprimir al conjunto un carácter de *modernidad*,—perdóneseme por la palabra,—que hace casi disculpar el error de los pobladores de las galerías.

Hartzenbusch ha hecho cuatro actos cortos de las tres jornadas primitivas, distribuyendo de tal modo el argumento, que cada uno de aquellos termina del modo más oportuno:—con una escena de efecto o con un pensamiento profundo.

La compañía del teatro Español presenta este año un personal más numeroso e importante que los anteriores:—guardando los tres artistas a quienes debió en la última temporada tan señalados triunfos,—la Mendoza Tenorio, Calvo y Vico,—ha agregado otros de justa reputación: allí está — y anoche la aplaudimos,— la simpática Contreras, la primera de nuestras damas jóvenes; allí una actriz que en otros tiempos alcanzó alta nombradía por su belleza, por su talento, la Pepita Noriega, a quien todos desean contemplar nuevamente después de su larga ausencia; allí Ricardo Morales; allí en fin Mariano Fernández, completando el cuadro dramático-cómico, que nos promete tantas horas deliciosas en el próximo invierno.

La representación de ayer es ya una promesa para lo futuro, porque fue en general acertada.

La Contreras, que por primera vez ejecutaba un papel de gran responsabilidad, se mostró al principio tímida y recelosa; pero animada por la benevolencia del público, recobró la calma y la seguridad, haciéndose aplaudir, y siendo llamada a la escena en unión de Vico.

Este estuvo a su altura de siempre, especialmente es la escena final del tercer acto, que sintió y dijo de un modo perfecto.

Los otros personajes, muy importantes en el nudo dramático no tienen ocasiones de lucimiento: el Rey, el cual empieza siendo odioso y acaba por hacerse interesante; Bustos Tavera, muerto desde el segundo acto, no pueden sino decir con más o menos acierto los versos de sus respectivas partes.

Un poco más de calor en el Sr. Morales y un poco menos de pasión en el Sr. Luna no habrían estado mal en entrambos caracteres.

Asmodeo [Ramón de Navarrete y Landa]

La Epoca, 17 Octubre 1885, p. 2.

Al levantarse el telón para empezar el primer acto del drama *Sancho Ortiz de las Roelas*, los palcos y butacas del teatro Español hallábanse vacíos en su mayor parte.

La sociedad madrileña, que tanto copia de París, no ha copiado todavía, entre otras cosas ventajosas y útiles, la costumbre de asistir a las representaciones teatrales desde el principio, contribuyendo así a que terminaran indefectiblemente antes de media noche, como en París también se acostumbra. De nueve a nueve y media se llenó la sala, y por cierto de un concurso no menos distinguido y selecto que el de la noche anterior en la Princesa; figurando en primer término la Reina Isabel y sus augustas hijas. La camarera mayor de Doña Isabel, la Duquesa de Hijar, ocupaba también un palco con los Marqueses de Nájera y Villasegura.

El *parterre* lo era de flores vivas, procedentes de aristocráticos invernaderos en gran parte.

Si estuvieran como anoche todas las de la temporada, seguramente que no habría en Madrid teatro más animado que el de la plaza de Santa Ana.

Además de ser inauguración de temporada, la obra elegida para el caso, como respetuoso homenaje al que mereció en su tiempo el epíteto honrosísimo de "Fénix de los Ingenios," era a propósito para atraer al público.

Siéntese el nuestro inclinado siempre a las comedias que antes se decía de "capa y espada;" el entusiasmo anual que produce en toda España dentro de quince días *D. Juan Tenorio*, débese, tanto como a los sonoros versos de Zorrilla, a la *espada* de gavilanes con que D. Juan acuchilla bizarramente a quien se opone a sus intentos, y a la *capa* de grana en que envuelve su airoso talle al marchar en demanda de aventuras.

En *Sancho Ortiz de las Roelas* hay espada también, que esgrimida por un fuerte brazo, tiende sin vida a otro caballero, y hay igualmente versos enérgicos y armoniosos, que vibran como el choque del oro y el cristal.

Nadie ignora que el drama en cuatro actos, con que ayer inauguró sus tareas la compañía del teatro Español, es refundición del que en tres actos escribió Lope de Vega con el título de *La estrella de Sevilla*.

Algunos periódicos, al hablar de esta refundición, la motejan, a mi entender, con escaso fundamento. El arreglo está hecho de mano maestra, y las nobles cualidades que destacan y brillan en ésta como en pocas de las producciones de Lope andaban en la comedia original (comedia entonces se llamaba) diseminadas, revueltas y aun perdidas . . . [part of the review, an introduction to Cándido María Trigueros, is missing] en 1784), y como trabajo curioso las *Poesías de Melchor Díaz de Toledo*, que siendo suyas, atribuyó a un poeta desconocido del siglo XVI.

Este Trigueros, poeta y capellán, como el mismo Lope, hizo, más que una refundición, una transformación de *La Estrella de Sevilla*. Dividió en cuatro, para que resultaran más breves y concretos, los tres extensos actos del original; alteró el orden de las escenas; suprimió algún personaje; añadió poco y quitó muchos versos; tachó escenas enteras, y cercenó, hasta reducirlos a la mínima expresión, relaciones y "parlamentos," donde el estro fertilísimo de Lope se desbordaba. Realizó, en suma, un trabajo análogo al de Ayala con *El Alcalde de Zalamea*, y al de Moratín con *Hamlet*, si bien con menos rigor, frialdad y espíritu de secta que el último.

Persisto, pues, en creer que, sin disputar sobre el desenlace que algunos censuran, por disentir del de Lope—en cuya obra Sancho y Estrella se separan a pesar de su recíproco amor, porque ella considera que el cadáver de Bustos Tavera se interpone entre su hermano y el matador—la refundición de Trigueros da mayor belleza, porque da mayor concisión, a *La Estrella de Sevilla*.

Y aun por lo tocante al desenlace moderno, que semeja preparar las bodas del matador y la hermana de Bustos, el ejemplo del *Cid* de Guillén de Castro y de Corneille demuestra que en el teatro se ha considerado como buena y apropiada unión semejante. Y cuenta que Rodrigo de Vivar mató al Conde Lozano por vengar una afrenta inferida a su propio padre, mientras que Sancho Ortiz mata a Bustos Tabera por orden expresa y terminante del Rey.

Esta fidelidad al Monarca, llevada al heroísmo, resalta de una manera hermosa en la comedia de Lope y la refundición de Trigueros. Sin olvidar un punto la ley del honor, superior a todo en aquel tiempo, lo mismo Bustos cuando sorprende a Sancho, el Rey, en sus aposentos, que Sancho, el veinticuatro de Sevilla, cuando aquél le ordena dar muerte al que ya considera como hermano, que la propia Estrella que conoce las asechanzas del Príncipe, todos muestran un acatamiento al poder real que pasma.

A bien que no implicaba tal respeto violación de la ley, supuesto que los jueces regidores de Sevilla, a pesar de la manifiesta voluntad del Rey, condenan sin piedad a Ortiz de las Roelas, por considerarle homicida, y el Soberano mismo, en suma, admirado de tan bizarras muestras de entereza y lealtad, declárase matador de Bustos, como lo fue, en efecto, para la ley moral, por haber mandado su muerte.

Sólo caracteres hidalgos y generosos, sólo acciones varoniles y heróicas descuellan en la obra que fue anoche representada. ¡Ah! los autores de aquellos tiempos, o por inspirarse en ejemplos menos ruines, o porque la inspiración naciese sana y pura en ellos, no habían menester como tantos autores (de teatros o de novelas) de estos tiempos, apelar a vicios repulsivos, a pasiones enfermas, a lances de hospital y de mancebía, para producir grandiosos conflictos dramáticos o para crear soberanas obras artísticas.

Cuanto a la forma literaria de *Sancho Ortiz de la Roelas*, es de singular gallardía. Si el adjetivo *gallardo*, aplicado a la poesía no existiese, habría que inventarlo para calificar las escenas entre el galán y la dama del segundo y tercer acto. Aquello es de castizo linaje español; aquello es flexible, brillante y bien templado, tal y como eran y son las legítimas hojas de Toledo.

El papel de *Sancho Ortiz* es muy arduo; Vico declaraba anoche francamente que se encontraba un tanto desorientado; era así en realidad; pero su poderoso talento le sacó airoso de las situaciones culminantes.

La Sra. Cirera me sorprendió agradablemente; confieso que no esperaba tanto de ella; no rayó a la altura de las grandes actrices; pero sintió y expresó por lo común bien su parte, y ésta era, nada menos, que la de la *Estrella de Sevilla*.

Cada uno de los demás actores hizo lo que le permitieron sus facultades, sin desentonar sobradamente el conjunto.

Luis Alfonso

Chapter 3. *Marta la piadosa*

La Iberia, 30 Octubre 1851, p. 3.

SS. MM. la Reina [y] el Rey se dignaron anoche honrar con su asistencia la función del teatro del Príncipe, donde se representó con gran desigualdad y falta de poesía la comedia de Tirso titulada *Marta la pidadosa*, y el sainete de don Juan de la Cruz [*sic* for Ramón de la Cruz], *La casa de Tócame Roque*. Como en los carteles y periódicos se había anunciado ayer la asistencia de S. M., la concurrencia fue escogida, y tan crecida, que ocupaba todas las localidades del teatro. A la conclusión de la comedia se dieron algunos vivas a la Reina. Asistieron también a la representación algunos de los señores ministros y autoridades de esta capital. La función concluyó después de las doce.

La España, 18 Noviembre 1855, p. 1.

Menos escrupulosos que los modernos, allí donde los antiguos encontraban algo que mejorar o variar galanamente, hacíanlo suyo al punto, no atendiendo sino a la perfección y mayor lustre de las obras de ingenio. ¡Cuántas joyas muestra la literatura dramática de todos los pueblos, que se han de confesar hijas de agenos ensayos; cuántas que deben a estraña pluma la traza y la idea; cuántos ahidalgados poetas, que dieron ser y vida a composiciones mediadas, las cuales habían perdido sus principios bellísimos, por no saber hallar iguales los fines! Suelen con frecuencia los autores briosos arrimar demasiado las espuelas, y cuando parece que más corren, menos terreno adelantan. No pocos rinden y consumen sus fuerzas todas en el propio ardor de la pujante acometida, al modo de lo que cantó el afamado Hortensio Féliz Paravicino:

> El mismo espíritu ardiente
> que me arrojó a la batalla,
> me redujo a no acaballa;
> corbade fui de valiente.

¿Qué estraño, pues, que escritores pulcros y de noble índole acometan la empresa de andar el camino que aun faltaba a los otros, por espinoso que parezca; y apartar el oro de la escoria; y hacer luz viva de humo denso?

Una ley decía, en la gravedad del derecho romano, estas señaladísimas palabras: "El que enmienda lo que no está sutilmente acabado, merece mayor alabanza que su primer artífice." Y de aquí a no dudar muchos tomaron pie para corregir la plana al primer inventor y completar su obra, sin escrúpulo de conciencia, puesto que no interesa tanto al público el autor de aquélla como que sea modelo de perfección y hechizo. Volviéndola, pues, al yunque y desechando trechos llenos de galas de ingenio, frases bizarras y sentencias briosas, lograron huir la consonancia violenta, la voz humilde, la oración equívoca, y tal desavío que desconcertaba la entereza del metro. Dieron caracteres a los personages y regularidad al plano; y cuidaron fuese natural el desarrollo de la acción, y verosímil el desenlace. De esquisito gusto dotados los poetas del siglo de Luis XIV, y de admirable tino para conocer aquellas composiciones estrañas que necesitaban ser llamadas a juicio y lograr los primeros últimos de la lima,—ya plagiando asuntos inventados por españoles, ya dilatando y acrisolando poemas suyos, un Molière, un Corneille y un Racine, llegaron a ser la admiración del mundo. ¿Pero qué más? ¿No metían su hoz en la mies del prógimo con la mayor frescura nuestros mismos dramáticos del siglo XVII? ¿Cuántos bosquejos de Lope no anduvieron entonces y andan en zancos hoy sin el nombre de su primer autor, y sólo con el del segundo, que les dio mayor ensanche y concertó más regularizadamente la fábula? De él y no de Calderón, v.g., es la traza primitiva de *La vida es sueño* y del *Alcalde de Zalamea*; alguna comedia de Villaizán sirvió para que se ufanase con ella aquel doctor Juan Pérez, discípulo mimado del fénix de los ingenios; y Moreto, revolviendo composiciones viejas y olvidadas, llegó a ser uno de nuestros más famosos dramaturgos. Esto con razón pareció después atentatorio a la propiedad; y como las costumbres hubiesen cambiado juntamente con el gusto del público, fue preciso aderezar a la moderna la comedia antigua, inagotable y eterno manantial de contentamiento. El refundidor pudo hacer tiras y capirotes del enranciado poema, respetando el nombre de su primer autor, ocultando el suyo propio alguna vez, y acompañándole otras.

No siempre cayó en hábiles manos la generosa tarea de enmendar lo que no estaba sutilmente acabado; antes se atrevieron a emplearse en ellos autorcetes ruines, a quienes faltaba tanto el conocimiento del arte, cuanto el ingenio creador de los antiguos; y no es raro encontrar hombre literato que haya estropeado y hecho de peor condición la misma obra que pretendía corregir. Raras parécenme en el siglo anterior las buenas refundiciones, si esceptuamos alguna de Trigueros. Pocas al principio de éste rivalizaron con las de don Dionisio de Solís. Pero a medida que en nuestros días se fue generalizando el buen gusto y despuntando las preocupaciones, ridículamente exageradas contra el teatro español de los siglos XVI y XVII, llegó a conocerse el arte de suprimir lo verdaderamente inútil, suplir lo realmente oportuno y necesario; y por último, llevar el plan por el gusto del tiempo en que se compuso la comedia, sin que repugne al del auditorio que ha de saborearla y aplaudirla. Viose que las restauraciones deben hacerse con tan peregrino artificio, que no difiera el estilo del general de la obra, siguiéndole el genio y el ingenio al inventor; que conviene se limpien las figuras de aquellos lunares que las afean; se descargue la fábula de personages inútiles que la embarazan y embrollan; se completen los caracteres; y no se corte el nudo, antes bien se desate con singular destreza y gallardía. Tales requisitos han procurado llenar en sus refundiciones Bretón, Hartzenbusch, Mesonero, el sabio y modesto refundidor del *Socorro de los mantos*, y otros no menos concienzudos escritores. Y muchas de estas circunstancis se hallan en la refundición de *Marta la piadosa*, del maestro Tirso de Molina, arreglada por don Dionisio de Solís.

Compúsola el fraile de la Merced en 1614, como parece de la interminable relación que puso en boca del Alférez, sobrino del capitán Urbina, pintando la espedición a la Mamora. Los antiguos solían aderezar sus poemas refiriendo bella y magníficamente las hazañas de nuestros guerreros por aquellos días en Flandes, Italia, Africa y América, con lo que se entusiasmaba y solazaba el auditorio, inflamándose en noble ardor de competirlas. Tuvo puesta la mira en pintar un carácter cómico, dejando entrever en ello un objeto moral importante: la mujer de vivo entendimiento que fingiéndose hazañera y mogigata, consigue evitar que la casen a disgusto, y vencer todos los obstáculos que dificultaban su enlace con el hombre de quien vivía enamorada.

Este carácter se halla trazado como de la mano de Tirso. Sin embargo, lo desvirtúa la malicia del religioso, no nada confiado en cosas de mujeres, manchándole con beleidades e inconsecuencias que le hacen desmerecer. Marta es valiente en presencia de su don Felipe, pero en ausencia está en dos dedos de ceder al gusto de su padre, siendo esposa de otro. Quizá esto se halle en la naturaleza, pero es más bella la figura tal como la presenta Solís, sin tamaños lunares. Con tino el refundidor eliminó del drama los personages inútiles de don Juan y don Diego, que en la Fábula no tienen significación ninguna. Y sobre todo, supo desenlazarla con mayor interés y gracia, si ya no con originalidad, ni con la decencia que de esta vez el autor mostró al desatar el nudo del poema. Solís, copiando los resortes con que Lope de Vega preparó el final de su *Dama boba*, dispone que don Felipe se esconda en el sótano de la casa, huyendo del padre de Marta, y que éste encierre allí a su hija por castigo, ignorante de lo que hacía; con lo cual es de todo punto imprescindible el casamiento de ambos enamorados. La situación es ocasionadilla, y no pierde tilde ninguno el poeta moderno para ponerla de bulto, con un tal raudal de sales y chistes, que no parecen sino caídos de la pluma del buen fraile, eterno regocijo de la española Talía. Todo es casi nuevo el último acto. Y no merece menor alabanza el refundidor por el acierto con que trasforma los versos largos del original en preciosas redondillas y galanos romances, salpimentados de ocurrencias picantes e ingeniosas sobre todo encarecimiento.

Tres cargos no obstante deben hacérsele: uno sobre la distribución de la materia dramática; otro sobre el carácter que atribuye al padre de la protagonista; y otro en no haber librado la obra de un lunar con que la ofendió Tirso de Molina: 1º. Convertir en cinco actos los tres del original, es introducir la languidez en el poema, y retardar el desarrollo de la acción, que siendo de suyo muy sencilla, pierde viveza y encanto, dilatada con esceso. Distribuida la fábula en tres miembros únicos, habrían sido los tres de un silogismo verdadero, llenos de movimiento y vida cada uno, de igual importancia y deleite. 2º. El padre de Marta no convenía fuese tan avaro, que a esta pasión repentinamente sacrificase otras consideraciones, graves para un hidalgo del siglo XVII. De mucho efecto teatral es sin duda que deje como un rayo caer de la mano la espada asestada contra el pecho del seductor de su hija, al oír que tiene esta diez mil ducados de renta; pero en la composición primitiva se compadecen con más delicado arte la avaricia del viejo y los respetos de un linajudo caballero español. 3º. Lo que indudablemente en una y otra comedia fue lástima haber imaginado, es hacer a don Felipe matador de un hijo de don Gómez, y por tanto hermano de doña Marta y de doña Lucía, ambas prendadas del galán valiente y discreto. Acaso en las costumbres de aquel siglo esto no fuese reparable; pero hoy causa justo desabrimiento la consideración de un padre forzado a tener por yerno al que arrancó violentamente la vida a su hijo, hacia quien solo respira venganza, gozándose con la idea de verle espirar en afrentoso cadalso. Otro resorte hubiera sido fácil inventar, que supliese a este con mayor ventaja por todos conceptos.

Tales reparos no son ni pueden ser parte para impedir que embelese la comedia, representada con sin igual maestría, como esta vez lo ha sido, atrayendo al coliseo por más de una semana numerosa y escogida concurrencia. La señora Lamadrid, cuya flexibilidad se presta a dar estraordinaria vida a los caracteres más opuestos supo realizar prodigiosamente el de Marta, así como Romea al del dómine Berrío, y Arjona el del avaro don Gómez. Con celo y perfección desempeñaron sus papeles respectivos todos los demás actores.

[The remaining paragraphs cover Narciso Serra's *El todo por el todo* and Eugenio Rubí's *El anillo de la duquesa*.]

Pipí [Aureliano Fernández-Guerra y Orbe]

Chapter 4. *El alcalde de Zalamea*

Revista de Teatro 2ª Serie, Tomo 2º, Enero 1842; pp. 52–53

Hemos visto con mucha satisfacción puesta en escenaen el Teatro de la Cruz la comedia antigua de Calderón que lleva por título, *El Garrote más bien dado y Alcalde de Zalamea*, pues a fuer de españoles apegados a nuestros usos y costumbres, preferimos la representación de ellos a la de los que reinan en otros países, con los cuales tienen en general muy poca analogía. Tal vez contribuye a este nuestro modo de pensar cierto espíritu de nacionalidad, que nos hace deplorar la fatalidad porque, pudiendo ser originales y abastecer los teatros con producciones de nuestra propia cosecha, hemos de ir a importar de nuestros vecinos transpirenáicos hasta los artículos de cargazón, que sobre ser por la mayor parte de mala calidad, se averían siempre en el viaje. Pero vamos a nuestro objeto.

El Alcalde de Zalamea es una de las composiciones dramáticas que más aplausos ha merecido en todas épocas, porque su asunto es también de todos los tiempos y lugares, y porque además tiene bellezas, que resaltan aun a los ojos del vulgo. Difícilmente se hallarán otras muchas, que a la observancia de las unidades, tan cacareadas no hace muchos años, y tan olvidados hoy, reunan la buena disposición de la trama, la marcha fácil y sencilla, la dignidad de los caracteres, la verdad y franqueza con que están pintados, la armonía de la versificación, y el movimiento y desembarazo de los diálogos. Los que pasan entre D. Lope de Figueroa, y Pedro Crespo el Alcalde, no pudieran haber sido mejor concebidos, ni se pudiera tampoco haber desenvuelto ellos con menos palabras, el carácter de entrambos.

>   *D. Lope.*   Yo vengo cansado, y esta
>   pierna, que el diablo me dió,
>   ha menester descansar.
>   *Crespo.*   ¿Pues quien os dice que no?
>   Ahi me dió el diablo una cama,
>   y servirá para vos.
>   *D. Lope.*   ¿Y dióla hecha el diablo?
>   *Crespo.*   Sí.

D. Lope. Pues a deshacerla voy,
 que estoy, vive Dios, cansado!
Crespo. Pues descansad, vive Dios!

Pone luego el poeta a estos dos interlocutores en situación más apacible y suaviza las tintas, que en el diálogo anterior podían aparecer con cierta dureza.

D. Lope. ¿Cómo ayer, sin que os dijera
 que os sentárais, os sentasteis
 y aun en la silla primera?
Crespo. Porque no me lo dijisteis,
 y hoy, que lo decís quisiera
 no hacerlo: la cortesía
 tenerla con quien la tenga.
D. Lope. Ayer todo erais reneigos,
 por vidas, votos y pesias,
 y hoy estáis más apacible,
 con más gusto y más prudencia.
Crespo. Yo, señor, respondo siempre
 en el tono y en la letra
 que me hablan: ayer vos
 así hablabais, y era fuerza
 que fuese de un mismo modo
 la pregunta y la respuesta.
 Demás de que yo he tomado
 por política discreta,
 jurar con aquel que jura,
 rezar con aquel [que] reza.

Y no tarda mucho en acreditar esta verdad poniéndola en evidencia, pues en este mismo coloquio, cambia de tono al ver que lo hace su interlocutor.

D. Lope. ¿No tengo mucha razón
 de quejarme, si ha ya treinta
 años, que asistiendo en Flandes
 al servicio de la guerra,
 el invierno con la escarcha,
 y el verano con la fuerza
 del sol, nunca descansé;
 y no he sabido que sea
 estar sin dolor un hora?
Crespo. ¡Dios, señor, os dé paciencia!
D. Lope. ¿Para qué la quiero yo?
Crespo. No os la dé.
D. Lope.   Nunca acá venga,

>   sino que dos mil demonios
>   carguen conmigo y con ella.
> *Crespo.* Amen, y si no lo hace,
>   es por no hacer cosa buena.
> *D. Lope.* ¡Jesús mil veces, Jesús!
> *Crespo.* ¡Con vos y conmigo sea!

Aunque Calderón ha querido presentar en don Lope la severidad de un gefe militar acostumbrado al mando, es el hábito que se contrae generalmente en la milicia de espresarse lacónica y desabridamente a favor de interjecciones, más eficaces muchas veces que las frases más pulidas, hubieran sido mal recibidas del público ilustrado las imprecaciones de aquel personage, si en la violencia del mal que le aquejaba, y en la bondad de corazón y rectitud de principios con que le adorna, no hallasen en cierto modo disculpa.

Hasta el carácter del capitán que cometió el atentado que forma el asunto de esta pieza, está bosquejado. El rapto premeditado de una doncella honesta cometido de mano armada, a vista y a presencia de su honrado padre, supone una depravación de costumbres y una dureza de corazón en que no puede labrar ya ni el cojo ni el remordimiento. Así Calderón hace al ofendido padre humillarse a los pies del autor de su deshonra, ofrecerle porque la suelde la crecida hacienda que posee, aunque tenga que mendigar con el hijo que le queda la subsistencia, y todo en vano, pues aquel malvado a todo se niega. [Agustín Ferrer del Río?]

La Iberia, 26 Enero 1865, p. 3.

Al ocuparnos, muy a la ligera por cierto, en nuestra anterior Revista de *El alcalde de Zalamea*, comedia de Calderón, refundida por el señor Ayala, no dijimos nada de este importante trabajo literario, porque no teniendo el ejemplar a la vista, no podíamos apreciar debidamente su mérito. Además la ejecución en el teatro de la Zarzuela había sido tan deplorable, que salimos grandemente disgustados de tan horrenda profanación. Muy lejos tendríamos que ir si nos engolfáramos en consideraciones acerca de cómo se suelen interpretar en general las obras de levantadas aspiraciones: concretándonos por hoy a *El alcalde de Zalamea*, muchos y justos anatemas tendríamos también que lanzar sobre los actores de la Zarzuela, por su incapacidad absoluta en interpretar sus papeles; pero queremos apartarnos de este terreno para tributar elogios al señor Ayala, por la manera con que ha sabido dar unidad al drama sin desvirtuar su espíritu literario, asimilándose en lo posible al estilo y al carácter de la obra.

Hay escenas completamente nuevas, entre ellas la X del acto segundo entre Isabel y el capitán, que nos dan la medida del gran talento dramático del señor Ayala. Así hallamos en boca de Isabel, contestando a la funesta y amorosa porfía del capitán, los siguientes versos:

. . . . .
Y ¿cómo os importa nada,
Desdeñosa ni risueña,
Una humilde lugareña
A un tiempo vista y dejada?
¿Es que no sale marchando
Con placer un militar,
Si no deja en el lugar
Alguna mujer llorando?
O así como el caminante,
Sin que su dueño lo advierta,
Coje al pasar por la huerta
La fruta que está delante;
¿Vos imagináis acaso,
Señor capitán, que son
Mi honra y mi corazón
Para cojidos al paso?
Pues ved que de esta victoria
No es tan posible la palma,
Que Dios no reparte el alma
Conforme a la ejecutoria.

El largo, cuanto notable romance, en que Isabel refiere a Pedro Crespo su deshonra, se halla condensado, resultando naturalmente más enérgico y dramático. Merece citarse entre otras cosas el siguiente rasgo cómico en que, sin salirse de la situación, pone de relieve el señor Ayala su mucho ingenio y gracia. Cuando el capitán, herido, trata de huir del pueblo con Rebolledo para unirse con las tropas que se dirijen a Portugal, dice:

Cap. ¿Posible es que ni un vecino,
Por ruego o por amenaza,
Haya sacado a la plaza
Un caballo?
Reb.   Ni un pollino.
Nada pudimos lograr.
Yo le dije a una mujer:
"Patrona, ¿pues no ha de haber
Burros en este lugar?"
Yo que sí y ella que no,
Estábamos disputando,
Cuando un burro rebuznando
La casa entera atronó.
"Escucha,—dije,—y sostén
Que aquí no hay burro escondido."
Y ella dijo: "Es mi marido
Que los imita muy bien."

No somos partidarios de las refundiciones, que por lo común tienden a desnaturalizar las grandes obras de nuestro teatro clásico; pero cuando están hechos con el talento que se adiverte en las que nos ocupan, no podemos menos de aceptarlas gustosos, tributando plácemes a sus autores. Reciba el nuestro el señor Ayala, al mismo tiempo que el pésame por haber visto destrozar tan inhumanamente su bello trabajo por los actores de la Zarzuela.

[The remainder of the anonymous review is taken up with a lengthy discussion of *Una apuesta en la velada de San Juan*, by doña Natividad de Rojas; and of *La espada y el laúd*, by "señor Palou y Coll."]

El Museo Universal, 5 Febrero 1865, p. 46.

[A long review covering several performances at Madrid's theatres. I have excerpted the section on *El alcalde de Zalamea*.]

El teatro de la Zarzuela nos dio a conocer la refundición de *El alcalde de Zalamea* hecho por don Adelardo López de Ayala. Tan famoso drama bien merecía un refundidor literario que supiera conservar en su primitiva forma, toda la delicadeza incomparable de sus detalles; así ha sucedido y por ello merece parabienes el autor de *El tanto por ciento*. Lo único que se observa en el nuevo arreglo de esta magnífica obra, es que la acción camina un tanto apresurada y que pierde su colorido en algunos pasajes a causa de la desaparición de varias mutaciones. Por lo demás, resalta el pensamiento que surgió del fecundísimo ingenio de López [sic!], levantado a inmensa altura por la vigorosa vena del gran poeta don Pedro Calderón de la Barca.

Lope trazó un plan, cuya intención no hubiera llegado a sobrevivir en la memoria de las generaciones; pensó en la figura de Pedro Crespo y le faltaron alientos para completar el cuadro: dificultó el desarrollo de su trama con la acumulación de personajes, puesto que allí eran dos las hijas del labrador y por consiguiente dos los amantes: Calderón había nacido para interpretar los grandes afectos, para idealizar la honra, para pintar la nobleza del alma, para ser el eco, en fin, de las sublimes manifestaciones de la virtud y no plagiando sino identificándose con el maestro, en los rasgos de corazón y subiendo al mismo nivel, los que en el primer *Alcalde* se hallaban empobrecidos, coronó sus esfuerzos, triunfó de todos los vates conocidos y lanzando al glorificado palenque de la literatura de aquella época, uno de los más perfectos modelos de severidad clásica, de forma inspirada y de conceptos profundos, legó a su patria un tesoro en este drama, y muy singularmente en su último acto, digno de señalarse entre los esfuerzos de aquel monstruo de entendimiento. Como Sófocles y Eurípides reprodujeron l[o]s rasgos de Orestes, tratado ya por Esquilo; como Molière siguiendo el impulso que partía de la escena griega, imitó a Plauto en *El Avaro* y *El Anfitrión*, y como Moratín tradujo libremente, introduciendo su inventiva en varias obras del Terencio francés, así Calderón prestó un encanto que no había logrado Lope, a *El alcalde de Zalamea* y por él se reproduce en la escena española la representación de este poema dramático, de cuyo protagonista fue uno de los más atinados intérpretes, el inolvidable don Carlos Latorre. Para solemnizar un aniversario de Calderón, le puso en escena la empresa de la *Zarzuela*, y yo lamento profundamente que exornara una producción tan renombrada con aquel miserable decorado. Allí se emplean cuantiosas sumas en presentar una zarzuela y no deja de causar amargura a los amantes de las viejas tradiciones teatrales, tan indisculpable abandono.

La ejecución de *El alcalde de Zalamea*, me causó el mismo efecto que su aparato escénico: entregados a la señora Tenorio y a Cubero y a Calvet sus principales papeles, dicho se está que sus condiciones artísticas no son bastantes a salir airosas de tan difícil empeño. En cuanto al señor Guerra, aun no ha logrado desprenderse de su amaneramiento provinciano y sus facultades le abandonan. Además no se puede prescindir de la comparación que nos ofrecen los recuerdos y forzoso es confesar que este actor lucha en ella con desventaja.

D. Gil Carmona

La Epoca, 28 Septiembre 1865, p. 4.

Anoche tuvo efecto la apertura del teatro del Príncipe, habiendo asistido una concurrencia numerosísima y escogida a la función inaugural. La famosa comedia del gran Calderón de la Barca, *El alcalde de Zalamea*, refundida por el Sr. López de Ayala, fue desempeñada a la perfección, y obtuvo un éxito brillante. Teodora Lamadrid, la Hijosa, Julián Romea, Valero, Mariano Fernández, Zamora y Morales ejecutaron los principales papeles, siendo aplaudidos y llamados a la escena diferentes veces al final de cada acto.

En nuestra próxima *Revista* describiremos detalladamente esta fiesta artística, que se completó con baile nacional y el sainete *La boda del tío Carcoma*, en el que la Orgaz y Mariano Fernández escitaron constantemente la risa de los espectadores.

La Discusión, 1º Octubre 1865, p. 2.

El miércoles en la noche [27 septiembre] inauguró sus tareas la compañía del teatro del Príncipe, poniendo en escen la escelente comedia de Calderón, titulada: *El alcalde de Zalamea.*

La ejecución de esta notable obra de nuestro teatro antiguo, ha sido verdaderamente un acontecimiento dramático, tanto por el acertado reparto que ha tenido, como por el esmero que todos los artistas que han tomado parte en ella han puesto para hacer resaltar las bellezas de esta joya literaria.

Los intérpretes han sido: las señoras Teodora Lamadrid, Cándida Dardalla y Josefa Hijosa; y los señores Romea, Valero, Pizarroso, Fernández, Zamora y Morales.

La comedia estaba refundida por el Sr. López de Ayala.

Esto ha sido lo único que nos ha parecido mal, y lo que, según nuestra opinión, ha quitado algún tanto de solemnidad al espectáculo.

No vaya a creerse que nos ha parecido mal el que la comedia esté refundida por el Sr. López de Ayala, nada de eso; al Sr. López de Ayala lo juzgamos con bastante talento para poder refundir con acierto una buena comedia del teatro antiguo; lo que nos parece mal es que las comedias del teatro antiguo se representen refundidas, porque es quitarle el verdadero sabor de la época.

Las grandes obras de nuestros antiguos maestros deben mostrarse con sus bellezas y sus defectos; defectos que para nosotros son bellezas, porque nos dejan ver el verdadero carácter de aquella edad de oro para la literatura dramática.

Sin embargo, a pesar de no ser partidarios de las refundiciones, confesamos que la que el señor López de Ayala ha hecho de la comedia *El alcalde de Zalamea* está muy bien.

[Signed by J.; the majority of the review concerns the politics of the Opera theatre and the formation of a company.]

La Epoca, 3 Octubre 1865, p. 1.

Todos los coliseos de Madrid, escepto el Real, han abierto sus puertas al público: el Príncipe, el Circo y Variedades han inaugurado sus tareas rindiendo culto a Calderón, Moreto y Lope de Vega.

El teatro de Novedades no ha querido ser menos; pero necesitando al mismo tiempo justificar su título, ha parado en su mirada retrospectiva en el primer tercio de nuestro siglo, y ha elegido para inaugurar sus tareas el drama del marqués de Molins, *Doña María de Molina*.

Al lado de estos coliseos, que tanto culto rinden a la literatura y al arte, el teatro de la Zarzuela desentona de una manera horrible con sus *Epístolas de San Pablo*, sus *Jardineros*, sus *Consejos de guerra*, etc., etc.; pero esto no es un óbice para que se vea lleno todas las noches. En Madrid, como suele decirse, hay gente para todo.

Grande es nuestro entusiasmo por Calderón: su poderoso genio supo robar a la naturaleza esas creaciones que aparecen en el gran cuadro de sus inmortales obras como la encarnación de los más bellos caracteres del hombre, de los más bellos sentimientos del alma.

Verdadero poeta, si su lenguaje tiene el brillo de las piedras preciosas, los reflejos del sol, los colores que recrean la vista, la música de las aves, de las ramas y de los arroyuelos, bajo esta forma hermosa laten las grandes ideas, las vehementes pasiones, los delicados sentimientos; y de este conjunto de lo bueno y de lo bello, del corazón y de la fantasía, resulta la perfección dramática que ha conquistado para el autor de *La vida es sueño* y *El médico de su honra*, el glorioso título de maestro, no sólo del teatro de España, sino del teatro del mundo.

No poco nos deleita Moreto con su elegante estilo, con sus perfumados conceptos, con la imaginación y el sentimiento con que ilumina sus bellas creaciones.

¿Y qué diremos del gran Lope de Vega, asombro de su siglo, fénix de los ingenios, como le llama la posterioridad?

Gran orgullo nos causa, como españoles, pensar que estos tres poetas han nacido bajo el hermoso cielo de la España, y han hablado el magnífico idioma de Cervantes: gran entusiasmo produce en nosotros la luz del genio que han reflejado en sus creaciones; la admiración del mundo es poca para premiar sus méritos. El primero y el último sobre todo, arrojaron la semilla, y los teatros de Europa no han hecho desde entonces más que coger el fruto.

Después de esta leal declaración, ¿podrá acusársenos de ingratos y descontentadizos si sentimos el caso omiso que han hecho las empresa de los poetas modernos?

¿No hubieran podido Hartzenbusch o García Gutiérrez, Ayala o Eguilaz, Bretón o Rubí, unir su nombre al pacto de alianza que firmaron los artistas rivales el miércoles último al presentarse junto en el teatro del Príncipe? ¿No hubiera sido entonces más completa la reconciliación?

Abandonemos cuanto antes este terreno resbaladizo, porque pudieran fulminar contra nosotros una escomunión los amantes del arte, más dados a contemplar con calma el pasado, que a emplear sus fuerzas en despejar la incógnita del porvenir.

Nos han dado comedias del teatro antiguo: bien venidas sean; han sido en general admirablemente interpretadas; tanto mejor. Demos gracias a las empresas porque han quitado a la crítica el pesar y le han dejado el placer de su tarea: la admiración.

El Alcalde de Zalamea es una de las más acabadas creaciones de Calderón. Todos los caracteres están trazados con una energía, con una verdad, con un colorido sorprendentes. La acción gira sobre dos sentimientos que nadie como el autor de *El médico de su honra* ha sabido comprender y espresar: el honor, el deber.

La fábula es sencilla; pero esta sencillez aumenta la belleza de las grandiosas situaciones a que da lugar el carácter del protagonista, del famoso labrador Pedro Crespo.

Honrado y amante de su familia, sabe inspirar a sus hijos con el ejemplo y [e]l consejo las virtudes que practica. Rico, pero de humilde condición, sabe vivir en su esfera sin traspasar los límites y probar que el hombre, a los ojos de Dios y a sus propios ojos, puede ser grande, cualquiera que sea su nacimiento o su fortuna.

Dulce y afable con los buenos, es rígido y severo con los que desconocen lo que se deben a sí propios; poseído de sus deberes y de sus derechos, no falta a aquellos y no perdona estos; en una palabra, es la imagen viva de la justicia.

Presentado de este modo quiere el poeta colocarle en las situaciones más a propósito para ejercitar sus cualidades. Debe respeto al Rey y le rinde homenaje ofreciendo su casa y hacienda a los soldados que le representan; en cuanto estos le faltan en lo más mínimo su energía los contiene, su dignidad y su discreción los admira.

Ama a su hijo, pero este aspira a ser soldado, a conquistar con su valor la espada que su condición le ha negado: el padre comprende el deseo del hijo, le estimula, le aconseja y le ve partir con lágrimas en los ojos, con heroísmo en el corazón.

Su hija es un modelo de hermosura y virtud. Pedro se mira en ella, pero el capitán a quien aloja en su casa concibe al verla una de esas pasiones culpables que todo lo atropellan. El viejo, con el ánimo que da la indignación, persigue a los que manchan el nombre de su hija con una serenata, y más tarde pasa por la terrible prueba de ver que le arrebata a su hija el infame capitán, mientras que dos soldados le sujetan.

Libre el anciano corre en busca del ladrón de su honra, y los que le ayudan en su inicua empresa le atan a un árbol. Isabel le desata, y el anciano, acompañado de su hija, vuelve al pueblo a pedir justicia.

La escena en que Pedro pide a su hija que le cuente todo lo que ha pasado, escena delicada, difícil y escrita con una maestría pasmosa, es interpretada por Teodora [Lamadrid] con una verdad admirable. Valero está sublime; no es posible espresar lo que hace: hay que verlo para saber lo que consigue el verdadero genio.

El pueblo nombra alcalde al anciano que va a pedir justicia. ¿Pueden reunirse situaciones más interesantes que las que gradualmente inspira a Calderón el asunto de su obra? El capitán que ha mancillado su honra cae en su poder, es alcalde y puede castigarle, pero es al mismo tiempo padre, necesita la honra, la felicidad de su hija, y arrojando la vara de la ley cae de hinojos ante el infame seductor.

La virtud a los pies del vicio, la fuerza postergada a la cobardía, el venerable anciano humillado ante el ladrón de su honra . . . ¡qué situación como ésta ha ideado el genio! Ella sola bastaría para dar a Calderón el puesto que la posteridad le ha dado.

El seductor no cede, las lágrimas no ablandan su empedernido corazón, los ruegos se estrellan en su alma de roca: el padre acaba su misión y empieza la suya el alcalde.

La energía anima aquellas facciones donde había impreso el dolor sus huellas, aquellos ojos húmedos por el llanto se encienden, aquella mano que suplicaba empuña con vigor la vara de la ley.

En vano alega sus fueros el soldado, en vano don Lope de Figueroa pide que le restituyan su capitán, en vano le amenazan . . . la justicia prosigue impasible su obra y la Providencia, representada por el Rey, llega a tiempo para dar el triunfo a la justicia.

El capitán muere ahorcado, Isabel se refugia en un convento, Juan va a la guerra, y Pedro Crespo, después de tantas amarguras, lejos de sus hijos, tiene todavía ánimo para buscar la familia que ha perdido en el amor de los que al darle la vara le han confiado su tutela.

La obra, lo repetimos, es de lo más acabado de Calderón, es una de las obras maestras del teatro universal.

El carácter de D. Lope, que Romea interpreta con una verdad y un talento que justifican su gran reputación, es también admirable; bien es verdad que todos, el del capitán, el de Juan, el de Rebolledo y el de la Chispa, tienen un colorido y una verdad que encantan.

No me despediré del Príncipe sin declarar que la Hijosa y Mariano Fernández compitieron con los tres grandes artistas, Valero, Romea y Teodora, los honores de la representación.

¿Pero ha solemnizado la empresa como debía el acontecimiento literario y artístico que significaba la inauguración de la temporada en el Príncipe?— No: la primera función debió ser una solemnidad artística; poco hubiera perdido la empresa distribuyendo las localidades entre las corporaciones científicas y literarias, entre las personas notables de todas las clases de la sociedad. Los poetas hubieran celebrado aquel acto, el suceso hubiera adquirido mayores proporciones, y no hubiéramos visto especular en la calle a los revendedores, mientras que en el teatro tenía lugar una reconciliación y un espectáculo, que por lo visto consideraba el público de distinta manera que la empresa.

[The remainder of the article reviews a performance of *El desdén con el desdén* with no indication whether it is Moreto's play or a *refundición*.]
Julio Nombela

El Museo Universal, 22 Octubre 1865, p. 343.

Vuelvo la vista a los espectáculos; a la apertura de nuestro histórico y favorecido coliseo del Príncipe, en el cual se han presentado unidos y ganosos de gloria, varios de los primeros actores españoles. La obra elegida para comenzar sus tareas artísticas, fue la refundición hecha por el señor López de Ayala, del vigoroso drama de Calderón *El alcalde de Zalamea*. Acerca de las condiciones de este *arreglo*, ya espresé mi opinión en otra época [see above, *El Museo Universal* of 5 Octubre 1865]; sólo me toca hoy ocuparme de su desempeño y juzgar a los intérpretes de tan apreciada joya literaria con la justicia que guía mi pluma. Valero, considerado siempre como una de las figuras que más sobresalen en nuestra representación escénica, reproduce con asombrosa exactitud el carácter altivo y severo del labrador Pedro Crespo; Valero al presentarse, después de algunos años de ausencia, al público de Madrid, se ha mostrado, como antes, digno de obtener sus mercedes; porque Valero conserva aun viva la fe, encendido el entusiasmo que guía a las grandes conquistas del genio. En el final del segundo acto de *El alcalde de Zalamea* y en la situación capital del tercero, nuestro primer actor renueva sus triunfos del pasado, se sobrepone al natural cansancio de una vida consagrada al penoso esfuerzo de la escena, e inflamado por la inspiración del gran poeta que alienta su palabra y le enaltece con sus ideas, promueve en el auditorio la admiración y logra hacer resonar el estruendo del aplauso. Romea representa el áspero tipo del hidalgo don Lope y dicho se está que Romea comprende sin esfuerzo alguno, toda la rigidez de un carácter duro e impertinente, colocado en la trama para contrastar con el del protagonista: no obstante, el papel resulta tibio, la entonación del artista apagada; deslízanse los versos de sus labios, sin perder ni en concepto ni en sonoridad, pero sí en el colorido y en la espresión; y es que don Julián Romea, cansado ya de sentir y de poseerse del papel, antes de su lamentable enfermedad, aparece hoy desnudo de las facultades que tanto contribuían a ensalzar su comprensión y su estraordinario talento; se encuentra a solas con su esperiencia, con su estudio del arte, con el caudal de su criterio; y estas cualidades desamparadas de la luz poderosa que un día las hizo resplandecer, si pueden y deben conservar el respeto a lo que fue, del sensato espectador, no alcanzan a persuadir al público en general, y mucho menos, si éste no descubre una ráfaga del astro hundido en el ocaso. No negaré que aun existe en Romea, de vez en cuando, algún destello de aquella llama, pero no en verdad representando el drama: para este género, dolor me causa considerar que ha terminado su carrera. Yo prometo aplaudirle representando la tragedia del *César*; yo temo, y ojalá me equivoque, que a la masa general del público no le satisfará. La ejecución del papel de don Lope, ofrece una muestra del porvenir que le aguarda, calzando el coturno.

En *El alcalde de Zalamea* se ha recibido, con la consideración que merece, a Teodora Lamadrid. Añejo achaque es, de la escuela de esta señora actriz, impregnar las palabras de un acento lacrimoso que raya en la monotonía. Si pudiera desprenderse de esta costumbre, Teodora se acercaría aun más a la perfección del arte, pero temo que no influya ya, en su manera de ser este consejo, por las muchas veces que se le he dado y las muchas que lo ha desoído.

En el resto del cuadro de esta obra, merecen especial mención, Pepita Hijosa, Morales y Fernández, Cándida Dardalla y Pizarroso desempeñaron papeles sin recursos; el galán joven señor Zamora no ha correspondido a mis esperanzas; verdad es que su papel era ingrato, pero en tales empresas se prueban los talentos. El tono enfático y la exageración en la frase, envueltos en el natural temor de desmerecer al lado de los dos maestros, perturbaron su espíritu. Espero a juzgarle con mejor conocimiento de causa, en una nueva producción.

D. Gil Carmona

El Imparcial, 15 Septiembre 1882, p. 3

Teatro de Apolo—Desconocida ha quedado la sala después de las reformas practicadas en ella.

Los palcos plateas han quedado reducidos a seis, tres en cada lado; en reemplazo de los demás y de las galerías bajas, se ha colocado nuevas filas de butacas.

El techo, pintado de nuevo, es bueno; el piso donde están las butacas se halla hoy a la altura conveniente para comunicarlas con los palcos plateas, que en otro tiempo se hallaban incomunicadas con dichos palcos.

Los entresuelos se hallan hoy en la línea de los proscenios, y, por consiguiente, desde ellos es visible la escena, cosa que no ocurría anteriormente.

El decorado es de buen gusto, y en general el teatro de Apolo es hoy de los más elegantes de Madrid.

Decir que todas las localidades de la sala estaban ocupadas, que el público era de lo más escogido de Madrid, que había deseos de ver *El alcalde de Zalamea*, que la impresión que produjo la vista del nuevo teatro, que así puede llamarse, en la concurrencia, fue muy satisfactoria, es decir, la verdad.

La joya del teatro de Calderón, salvo mejores opiniones, interpretada por el maestro, por el que es hoy gloria de nuestra escena, lazo de unión entre el arte que terminó y el arte que empieza, D. José Valero; interpretada por el que, con justicia, es considerado hoy como el fiel mantenedor del arte dramático, don Antonio Vico; por Elisa Mendoza Tenorio esa joya de nuestro proscenio; había forzosamente de llevar al teatro de Apolo a los amantes de nuestra patria escena y al mundo elegante.

A éste, porque se anunciaba un acontecimiento teatral, un coliseo nuevo y una temporada, que juzgamos ha de ser brillante para los artistas de dicho teatro, si tienen buen acierto en la elección de obras y no abusan del repertorio.

Cómo interpretaron aquellos actores la comedia de D. Pedro Calderón, no es menester repetirlo.

Hemos tenido ocasión de aplaudir en varias ocasiones al *Crespo* y al *Don Lope*, creados por Valero y Vico, así como a la señorita Mendoza Tenorio.

El resto de los artistas, bien.

D. Ricardo Valero dijo con suma discreción su papel de *Rebolledo*.

Los actores recibieron durante la representación, y después de terminar cada acto, pruebas inequívocas de la justa satisfacción del público.

[Following is a brief review of *Ellas y ellos*, a "recopilación" of Moreto's *Yo por vos y vos por otro*.]

Quiera Dios que continúen así—nos decía saliendo del teatro un respetable literato.—Tendremos un templo donde refugiarnos contra el temporal de disparates que llueven sobre la escena española desde hace algunos años.

[P.]

La Epoca, 23 Octubre 1887, p. 2.

Calderón de la Barca ha sido el primer autor dramático que se ha alojado este año en el teatro Español.

Llegó servido por Ayala, el cual lo acicaló hace tiempo acomodándolo al gusto de nuestros días; y nos le presentó respetuosamente cogido de la mano D. Antonio Vico, que es un artista digno de hombrearse con los grandes escritores del siglo XVII.

Faltóle al primer actor del teatro Español su gallardo y brioso compañero D. Rafael Calvo, que se halla todavía en Berlín, embelesado quizá con las representaciones que se dan en la capital de Alemania de la obra de D. José Echegaray, *El gran galeote*.

Parece que [D. Rafael Calvo] ha escrito diciendo:

—Empezad con las obras del repertorio antiguo. En Alemania también se rinde fervoroso culto a Calderón. Los profes de las Universidades, los directores de los teatros, los artistas, los literatos más insignes comentan y estudian las producciones del gran autor de *El alcalde de Zalamea*. Vosotros representaréis a Calderón mientras yo vivo en una atmósfera calderoniana. Dejadme respirar unos días más ese ambiente. Volveré convertido en un *Don Juan Tenorio*.

* * *

En efecto, *El alcalde de Zalamea*, con que anoche se inauguró el teatro Español, durará hasta el lunes próximo. El martes y el miércoles se pondrá en escena el drama de Lope de Vega *Sancho Ortiz de las Roelas*; el jueves y el viernes se representará la preciosa obra de Rojas *García del Castañar*, y al día siguiente se presentará Rafael Calvo ante el público madrileño con el tradicional drama de D. José Zorrilla.

Entre tanto, el público amante de nuestra gloria escénica acudirá al teatro Español con la avidez y el entusiasmo que demostró anoche.

Regocijaba el alma ver un concurso tan brillante y una expectación tan solemne.

Vico estaba ya en su cuarto vestido de labrador, pensando tal vez en los incidentes que le habían de ocurrir durante las tres horas que duraría la representación escénica. Se acordaba de su honor acrisolado; de su hijo a quien pensaba dedicar a la noble carrera de las armas; de su pobre Isabel, víctima futura de un capitán disoluto; de las tercas disputas que había de sostener con D. Lope de Figueroa, y de las penas y quebrantos que la soldadesca había de introducir en su casa, antes morada apacible y dichosa. Devoraba de antemano su afrenta; suplicaba humildemente al audaz violador que reparase los desgarrones de su honra; se erguía; veíase alcalde; vengaba su honor ultrajado, y recibía de manos del Rey Felipe II su nombramiento de alcalde perpetuo...

Mientras todo esto debía de pasar en tropel por la mente de D. Antonio Vico, pasaban por las puertas del teatro, en gran multitud, los admiradores suyos, todo lo que es más conocido en Madrid, lo más saliente, lo más selecto; y la sala del teatro iba adquiriendo brillantez y animación extraordinarias.

Todo el público sabía también de antemano lo que había de ocurrir. Vico se presentaría profundamente humano. Hallaríase en el teatro Español nuestro grandioso arte dramático. Se respiraría en aquel oasis encantador y deleitoso. Se aplaudiría espontáneamente, sin necesidad de que la *claque* iniciara el entusiasmo, y se proclamaría una vez más la excelsitud de nuestro teatro, reconociendo que todavía nos quedan artistas capaces de interpretarlo dignamente.

* * *

No hubo error en el pensamiento del público. La función de anoche en el Español revistió todos los caracteres de solemnidad artística. *El alcalde de Zalamea* es una obra que no envejecerá nunca. Se la ve un año y otro, y siempre ostenta su belleza inmarcesible. Nosotros habremos desaparecido ... vendrán nuevas generaciones, y los hermosos caracteres trazados por Calderón seguirán embelesando al público.

He aquí por qué anoche nos pareció nueva la obra.

El año pasado la aplaudimos frenéticamente interpretando Rafael Calvo y Antonio Vico los papeles principales: anoche la hemos aplaudido con caluroso fervor, y la aplaudiremos con ahinco análogo el día de mañana.

No volvemos a hablar de la maravillosa interpretación de Vico, porque tendríamos que dar vueltas a la idea que nos domina y repetir en otros términos lo que ya hemos dicho.

Fue llamado al palco escénico infinitas veces, y salió acompañado de los demás artistas, que también se habían esmerado en la interpretación de sus respectivos papeles.

La Iberia, 30 Octubre 1889, p. 3.

Brillantísima al par que solemne era el aspecto que ofrecía anoche el coliseo de la plaza de Santa Ana, que inauguraba sus tareas de la presente temporada con la magnífica obra de Calderón, refundida por D. Adelardo López de Ayala, *El alcalde de Zalamea*.

Desde las primeras escenas, el público numerosísimo que llenaba el teatro comenzó a saborear con delectación las mil bellezas que encierra la soberbia creación del inmortal dramturgo, siguiendo con atención creciente el curso de la acción y los incidentes altamente dramáticos a que da lugar aquella lucha de pasiones y aquel choque de caracteres, tan admirablemente trazados, y a los que el autor primero y el refundidor de la obra después supieron dar tanto relieve.

El papel de protagonista estaba a cargo de Antonio Vico, y el eminente actor, como siempre inspirado, supo decir con tal verdad y sentir tan profundamente, dio tal entonación a su voz, tal expresión a su gesto y a su actitud tal propiedad, que hubo momentos en que hasta el espectador más indiferente parecía decirse, parodiando una frase muy conocida: "Calderón es Calderón y Vico su mejor intérprete."

En todo el primer acto, pero principalmente en la escena de la despedida y en la final del segundo, así como en las más culminantes del tercero, rayó como siempre a gran altura, arrancando en más de una ocasión entusiastas y nutridos aplausos.

Después de Vico, fuerza es citar, en primer lugar, a Donato Jiménez, que desempeñó a la perfección su papel, y a Ricardo Calvo, que estuvo muy bien en el suyo, demostrando que será el fiel continuador de las glorias del insigne artista que llevaba su apellido, y cuya pérdida llora el arte hoy lo mismo que el primer día. [The acclaimed actor Rafael Calvo had died the year before.]

Las señoras Guillén y Sánchez hicieron lo que pudieron por no descomponer el cuadro, a que puso alegre marco Mariano Fernández, felicísimo en la interpretación de su papel de Rebolledo.

[There follow two paragraphs on *Herir por los mismos filos*, and a sextet that played during the intermissions.]

La concurrencia, además de numerosa, era brillante y selecta, viéndose en palcos y butacas hermosas y distinguidas damas.

En suma, la inauguración de la temporada ha sido un éxito, y empezando bajo tan buenos auspicios, no dudamos que el Sr. Vico tendrá motivos para felicitarse en lo sucesivo cosechando nuevos y legítimos triunfos.

La Epoca, 31 Octubre 1889, p. 4.

Apenas se ha abierto el teatro Español, con luz no muy abundante, pero más intensa que el año pasado, cuando ya el libertino *Don Juan Tenorio* echa la zancadilla al grandioso Pedro Crespo y le suspende en sus funciones, ni más ni menos que si fuera un alcalde de nuestros días.

Anoche *El alcalde de Zalamea* se nos ofreció a la manera de un hermoso dechado de autoridades municipales.

Yo no sé cómo dejó establecido ese alcalde el servicio de incendios; ignoro si el empedrado del pueblo de Zalamea era tan malo como el de cierta capital que todos conocemos; y tampoco han llegado hasta mí noticias de si los soldados que mandaba D. Lope de Figueroa entraban, escondidos en sus bagajes, artículos de matute con destino a los pueblos en que se alojaba, a su pase para la capital portuguesa; pero es evidente que los alcaldes de entonces tenían un gran sentimiento de dignidad y una noción del honor extraordinaria.

En cuanto a los adelantos materiales, lo que sí puedo asegurar es que en Zalamea había por aquellos tiempos alumbrado eléctrico, y que hasta la luna servía humildemente a los que estaban en candidatura para el cargo de alcaldes, puesto que cuando la presunta autoridad necesitaba un rayo de luz del astro que brilla por la noche, para ver desde la puerta de su casa el camino por donde se ausentaba su hijo, brotaba de repente, como si obedeciera al mando de un segundo apunte, nada más que para satisfacer el deseo del que iba a recibir la vara de alcalde.

Por lo demás, salvo este detalle de *pedir la luna*, lo cual ha transmitido quizá por herencia a los concejales del día un afán de posesión insaciable, El

Alcalde de Zalamea era un hombre de rectitud acrisolada, de conciencia pura y estricto cumplidor de la justicia.

Pues a ese señor lo desbanca *Don Juan Tenorio*, y no porque se haya visto anoche impedido de celebrar sesión por falta de número, pues todos los escaños y tribunas, vulgo butacas y palcos, se hallaban completamente ocupados de gente distinguida, que aplaudía estrepitosamente los actos (eran tres) del gran alcalde, sino porque el historiador Vico ha tardado en presentarnos aquellos notables hechos, y ya se sabe que en cuanto llega el día de Todos los Santos no hay personaje que se atreva a negar su tablado al bravucón de Sevilla.

* * *

Hemos, pues, gozado anoche, por única vez, de un deleite literario que ya sólo se experimenta en contadas ocasiones, y de unos incidentes dramáticos cuyos moldes se han perdido.

Las fuentes de la emoción estética tienen su origen muy lejos de nosotros, y cuando vemos llegar el raudal de esas aguas purísimas, nos bañamos en ellas y desearíamos que no pasaran con la fugacidad de un solo día.

Pero la costumbre hace ley, y nosotros, hasta en el teatro Español, somos animales de costumbre.

Donde ayer vimos discutiendo a Pedro Crespo y a D. Lope de Figueroa, podremos ver hoy a D. Juan y a D. Luis Mejía alardear de pendencieros. Si anoche nos interesamos por la pobre Isabel, víctima de la sensualidad del capitán D. Alvaro, desde esta misma noche estaremos obligados a interesarnos por Doña Inés, arrancada por su raptor de la celda del convento. Ciutti servirá las profanaciones de D. Juan como Rebolledo sirve las villanías de D. Alvaro; y si la bolichera tomó ayer una buena parte en los atropellos del militar, la dueña será hoy quien preste al seductor su más eficaz auxilio. Anoche, redoble de tambores y toque de pífanos a la aparición del Rey: hoy tañido de campanas y aparición de muertos.

¡El *Tenorio* se impone!

Las esmaltadas décimas del "ángel de amor" vienen a competir con los hermosos conceptos y los esculturales pensamientos que oímos anoche.

Y cuando en la célebre escena del sofá diga D. Juan aquel verso comparativo: "más pura la luna brilla . . ." podremos exclamar:

—Sí; más pura que la de anoche, que aquella luna del segundo acto, centelleante, movediza, lucero de carbones Jablochkoff y astro de guardarropía.

Pedro Bofull

Notes

Preface

1. *Calderón in the German Lands and the Low Countries: His Reception and Influence 1654–1980* (Cambridge: Cambridge University Press, 1981), 5.

Chapter 1. Approaching the *Refundición*

1. The director William Oliver, of the University of California at Berkeley, gave at the 1988 Golden Age Theatre Symposium in El Paso, Texas, a "Scholar's *Comedia* Workshop" in which he taught the basics of acting gestures, movement, and exercises to an audience of scholars. The necessity of understanding the complete theatrical moment became apparent to the attendees, most of whose experience had been limited to written criticism of printed texts. The added dimension of a practical semiotics of acting proved invaluable in discussing the subsequent evening's performance at El Chamizal, a production of Tirso's *El burlador de Sevilla* performed by the Compañía Repertorio Español de Nueva York in contemporary dress but retaining the original language.

2. Northrop Frye, *Anatomy of Criticism* (Princeton: Princeton University Press, 1957), 51.

3. Quoted in *Diccionario de autoridades* (Madrid: Gredos, 1979), 3:540, s.v. "refundición." Corominas (*Diccionario crítico etimológico*, s.v., "refundir") limits his entry to a simple reference reduced from the *Diccionario de autoridades*.

4. A. E. Sloman's superb book, *The Dramatic Craftsmanship of Calderón* (Oxford: Dolphin, 1969) is truly a reception study *avante la lettre* and forms the basis by which to define *refundiciones* within the Golden Age. For a thoughtful and illuminating study on *El rey D. Pedro en Madrid* and related questions of *refundiciones* and transmission, see Carol B. Kirby, "La verdadera edición crítica de un texto dramático del siglo de oro: teoría, metodología y aplicación," *Incipit* 6 (1986): 71–98.

5. John A. Cook, *Neo-Classic Drama in Spain: Theory and Practice* (Dallas: Southern Methodist University Press, 1959), 269–70; Francisco Aguilar Piñal, "Las refundiciones en el siglo XVIII," *Cuadernos de Teatro Clásico* 5 (1990): 41.

6. S.v. "refundición."

7. Nicholas B. Adams, "Siglo de Oro Plays in Madrid, 1820–1850," *Hispanic Review* 7 (1939): 342–57; Sterling A. Stoudemire, "Dionisio Solís's *Refundiciones* of Plays (1800–1834)," *Hispanic Review* 8 (1940): 305–10; Archibald K. Shields, "The Madrid Stage 1820–1850," 3 vols., Ph. D. diss., University of North Carolina, 1933; Ada M. Coe, *Catálogo bibliográfico y crítico de las comedias anunciadas en los periódicos de Madrid desde 1661 hasta 1819* (Baltimore: Johns Hopkins University Press; London: Humphrey Milford, 1935); Seminario de Bibliografía Hispánica de la Facultad de Filosofía y Letras de la Universidad de Madrid, *Cartelera teatral madrileña I: años 1830–39*, *Cuadernos Bibliográficos*, no. 3 (Madrid: CSIC, 1961); Félix Herrero Salgado, *Cartelera teatral madrileña II: años 1840–1849*, *Cuadernos Bibliográficos*, no. 9 (Madrid: CSIC, 1963); Francisco Aguilar Piñal, comp., *Cartelera prerromántica sevillana, años 1830–36*, *Cuadernos Bibliográficos*, no. 22 (Madrid: CSIC, 1968); Seminario de Bibliografía Hispánica de la Facultad de Filosofía y Letras de la Universidad de Madrid, *Veinticuatro diarios: 1845–1900*, 4 vols. (Madrid: CSIC, 1968–75); Pietro Menarini et al., *El teatro romántico español (1830–1850). Autores, obras, bibliografía* (Bologna: Atesa, 1982).

8. For Cook, see note 5; Juan Luis Alborg, *Historia de la literatura española*, vol. 4 (Madrid: Gredos, 1982); Francisco Ruiz Ramón, *Historia del teatro español*, vol. 1 (Madrid: Alianza, 1967); Edward Coughlin, "Neo-Classical *Refundiciones* of Golden Age *Comedias* (1772–1831)," Ph. D. diss., University of Michigan, 1965; René Andioc, *Sur la querelle du théâtre au temps de Leandro Fernández de Moratín* (Tarbes-Burdeos: Saint-Joseph, 1970) and *Teatro y sociedad en el Madrid del siglo XVIII*, 2d ed. (Madrid: Castalia, 1987); Ermanno Caldera, *Il dramma romantico in Spagna* (Pisa: Università di Pisa, 1974). Caldera twice returned to *refundiciones*: "Calderón desfigurado (Sobre las representaciones calderonianas en la época prerromántica)," *Anales de Literatura Española* 2 (1983): 57–81; and "Bretón o la negación del modelo," *Cuadernos de Teatro Clásico* 5 (1990): 141–53. The Italian critic authored, too, an overview of the *refundición* in José María Díez-Borque's *Historia del teatro español*.

9. Aguilar Piñal, "Refundiciones," 33.

10. David Gies, "Notas sobre Grimaldi y el 'furor de refundir' en Madrid (1820–1833)," *Cuadernos de Teatro Clásico* 5 (1990): 114, 120. My summary of Gies's article is limited to a recapitulation of his major points. His *Agustín Durán: A Biography and Literary Appreciation* (London: Tamesis, 1975) and *Theatre and Politics in Nineteenth-Century Spain: Juan de Grimaldi as Impresario and Government Agent* (Cambridge: Cambridge University Press, 1988) discuss attitudes toward the *comedia* as well as the political and artistic struggles of the Spanish stage in the early decades of the nineteenth century. Michael Schinasi, too, has written of Calderón's reception in the nineteenth century, in particular about the views elicited

in the 1841 reburial of the Golden Age writer's remains ("The History and Ideology of Calderón's Reception in Mid-Nineteenth-Century Spain," *Neophilologus* 70 [1986]: 381–95); his ongoing work concerns the foundation of the Teatro Español.

11. Hans Robert Jauss,"The Changing Horizon of Understanding," in *Identity of the Literary Text*, ed. Mario J. Valdés and Owen Miller (Toronto: University of Toronto Press, 1985), 170.

12. Wolfgang Iser, *The Act of Reading: A Theory of Aesthetic Response* (Baltimore: Johns Hopkins University Press, 1978).

13. Hans-Georg Gadamer, *Truth and Method*, trans. and ed. Garret Barden and John Cumming (New York: Crossroad, 1986), 269.

14. Robert C. Holub, *Reception Theory: A Critical Introduction* (New York: Methuen, 1984), 59.

15. Hans Robert Jauss, *Toward an Aesthetic of Reception*, trans. Timothy Bahti (Minneapolis: University of Minnesota Press, 1982), 19.

16. Jauss, "Changing Horizon," 166.

17. I recognize the special problems of interpretation that a theatrical performance poses. It is true that any "reading" of performed theatre is filtered through directors, actors, sets, lighting, and related technical aspects. It is also true that each new performance constitutes a new interpretation, a new text, viewed by a new audience. Yet it is possible for a member of the audience to return to the theatre to witness another staging of the same play; although changes are inevitable, the receiver will now have as part of his or her horizon the previous night's interpretation. In this way can a relationship be drawn between viewing a play and reading a text.

For a thoughtful and concise summary of Gadamer's hermeneutics and its possible application to theatre, see the introduction to Thomas A. O'Connor, *Myth and Mythology in the Theater of Pedro Calderón de la Barca* (San Antonio, Tex.: Trinity University Press, 1988).

18. R. Chris Hassel, *Songs of Death: Performance, Interpretation, and the Text of Richard III* (Lincoln: University of Nebraska Press, 1987), 10.

19. Hassel, *Songs of Death*, 34.

20. Directed by Joseph Losey. Based on the novel of the same title by L. P. Hartley. EMI Films and World Film Services, 1971.

21. Osvaldo Dragún, *Historias para ser contadas* (Ottawa: Girol, 1982).

22. Jauss, *Toward*, 35.

23. Gadamer, *Truth*, 273.

24. Francisco Ruiz Ramón, *Calderón y la tragedia* (Madrid: Alhambra, 1984), 9.

25. David C. Hoy, *The Critical Circle: Literature, History and Philosophical Hermeneutics* (Berkeley and Los Angeles: University of California Press, 1982), 99.

26. George Steiner, *After Babel: Aspects of Language and Translation* (London: Oxford University Press, 1975), 201.

27. Jonathan Miller, *Subsequent Performances* (New York: Viking, 1986), 23.

28. Ibid., 28.

29. Ibid., 33.

30. Miller, *Subsequent*, 30. At this point he discusses authors who write with specific actors in mind. Lope de Vega wrote many of his large-cast plays in the early seventeenth century for specific acting companies. See George Haley ("Gaspar de Porras") and Thornton Wilder's classic articles on Lope de Vega and actors: "Lope, Pinedo, Some Child-Actors and a Lion," *Romance Philology* 7 (1953): 19–25; and "New Aids Toward Dating the Early Plays of Lope de Vega," in *Varia variorum: Festgabe für Karl Reinhardt*, 194–200 (Münster-Köln, 1952).

31. Jauss, "Changing Horizon," 169. I use Jauss's term "decanonization" recognizing that it is problematic here because more often than not the *comedias* whose recasts appear on stage in succeeding epochs have the longest performance tradition. Decanonization might be taken in a wider definition as I used it earlier with reference to literary and stage conventions. In this way an accurate, "historical" representation would not decanonize anything, but innovative stagings can certainly reveal new light on old plays (such as the Brothers Karamazov's production of Shakespeare's *Twelfth Night*) and contribute further to horizons of tradition. The pitfalls of historically rigorous stagings are in part the subject of Peter Brook's *The Empty Space* (New York: Atheneum, 1978). See also my "Peter Brook: Performance Theory and the *Comedia*," *Bulletin of the Comediantes* 43 [1991]: 101–8.

32. One example is the so-called New Historicism, which obeys a late twentieth-century social awareness interpreted, in part, on yet another twist of Marxist criticism. For a concise introduction into this vein of critical thought, see H. Aram Veeser, ed., *The New Historicism* (New York and London: Routledge, 1989).

33. Regardless of the changes imposed, the *comedia* often survives (as we shall see) as a trace that, like disappearing ink, recovers a form similar to the original. While I have opted not to follow this particular critical route, deconstruction could offer another fruitful approach to the *refundición*. See Jacques Derrida, *Of Grammatology*, trans. Gayatri Chakravorty Spivak (Baltimore and London: Johns Hopkins University Press, 1976); and *Dissemination*, trans. Barbara Johnson (Chicago: University of Chicago Press, 1981).

34. Jauss, "Changing Horizon," 169.

35. The term "updating" is often used all too loosely. For example, the 1987 death of Jean Anouilh prompted the Associated Press, in its television report, to note that one of his best-known achievements was his "updating of the Greek classic *Antigone*." This notion of updating reveals a lack of understanding of what adaptation is, what its purposes are, and how to judge it, either from the point of view of a discrete production or from the point of view of the new work's relationship to the original.

36. Ruiz Ramón, *Calderón*, 11.

37. David Quint, *Origin and Originality in Renaissance Literature: Versions of the Source* (New Haven: Yale University Press, 1983), 4.

38. Kenneth Reckford, *Aristophanes' Old-and-New Comedy. Volume 1: Six Essays in Perspective* (Chapel Hill: University of North Carolina Press, 1987), 149.

39. "Plagiarism—A Symposium," *Times Literary Supplement*, 9 April 1982, 413.

40. Ibid.

41. Ibid, 414.

42. George Steiner, *Antigones* (Oxford: Clarendon Press, 1984).

43. Ibid., 296–97.

44. The eighteenth century, as is well known, produced theorists of varying stripes, many of whom defended the *comedia*. Not all writers supported francophile neoclassicism, but to air the debates on eighteenth-century aesthetics is not within the purview of the present study. The interested reader should consult Cook (*Neo-Classic Drama*), Andioc (*Teatro y sociedad*), and Caso González (*Ilustración y neoclasicismo, Historia y crítica de la literatura española, vol. 4,* ed. Francisco Rico *[Barcelona Editorial Crítica, 1983]*), to name but three authors who have dealt with these matters.

45. Tomás Sebastián y Latre, *Ensayo sobre el teatro español* (Madrid, 1775 [1772], n.p.).

46. This attribution, in light of Sloman's and Kirby's work on seventeenth-century *refundiciones,* must now be discounted entirely; see Kirby's "On the Nature of *Refundiciones* of Spain's Classical Theatre in the Seventeenth Century," in *The Golden Age Comedia: Text, Theory and Performance*, ed. Charles Ganelin and Howard Mancing (West Lafayette, Ind.: Purdue University Press, in press). As for Sebastián y Latre's place in literary history as the first neo-classical *refundidor* of a *comedia*, see Joseph Fucilla, "*Menon*: The First Neoclassic 'Refundición' of a Golden Age Play," *Kentucky Romance Quarterly* 23 (1976): 365–75, who argues that an anonymous *refundición* of Calderón's *La hija del aire*, entitled *Menon*, may date from the period 1768–1772 (374). Nonetheless, the undated recast reveals a writer of considerable talent; Fucilla documents (369–72) how the writer successfully rewrote Calderón's verses yet maintained the rhyming word at the end of each line.

47. Cook, *Neo-Classical Drama*, 263.

48. The reviewer's affirmation that the *refundición* was born in the "siglo pasado" [past century] may indeed refer to Sebastián y Latre. However, Tirso's and Calderón's refashioning of earlier plays, as well as of their own, is another form of the *refundición*. For studies of this aspect of recasting, see Catherine Larson, *Language and the Comedia: Theory and Practice* (Lewisburg, Pa.: Bucknell University Press, 1991), particularly the chapter on Calderón's *Cada uno para sí,* and Kirby, "On the Nature . . . ".

49. See the analysis in chapter 3 of Pascual Rodríguez de Arellano's *Marta la piadosa*.

50. The quantity of unstudied material included in veinticuatro diarios is staggering, without counting the many newspapers and periodicals housed in Madrid's Hemeroteca Municipal and not surveyed for *Veinticuatro diarios*. A comprehensive reception study of the nineteenth-century theatre—all aspects of it—is a project in search of authors.

51. Steiner, *After Babel*, 29.

52. Frederick Will, *Thresholds and Testimonies: Recovering Order in Literature and Criticism* (Detroit: Wayne State University Press, 1988), 4.

53. Ibid., 7.

54. Steiner, *After Babel*, 300.

55. Quoted in Steiner, *After Babel*, 351.

56. Material from the original may serve very different ends, as exemplified in the Duke of Rivas's *El desengaño en un sueño* [Disillusionment in a dream]. See chapter 5.

57. Miller has emphasized, regarding plays staged long after the author's death, "the unexpected effect of emphasizing the transferability of the dramatic action" (58).

58. Georgia Warnke, *Gadamer: Hermeneutics, Tradition and Reason* (Stanford, Calif.: Stanford University Press, 1987), 78.

59. Ibid, 90.

60. Because of the extensive use made of newspaper reviews, references to titles, dates, and pages are included in the text.

61. Cándido María Trigueros, *El anzuelo de Fenisa* (Madrid, 1803); subsequent references are given in the text. David Gitlitz recently translated this play into English, giving it the felicitous title *Fenisa's Hook; or Fenisa the Hooker* (San Antonio, Tex.: Trinity University Press, 1988).

62. José Fernández Guerra, *Ir contra el viento* (Málaga: Antonio Fernández de Quincozes, 1826). Subsequent references to this edition are given in the text.

63. Will, *Thresholds*, 14.

64. José Fernández Guerra, *La dama duende* (Málaga: Antonio Fernández de Quincozes, 1829). Subsequent references, cited in the text, are to this edition.

65. Quint, *Origin and Originality*, 4.

66. Gies, *Theatre and Politics*; Gregorio Martín, "Querer y no poder, o el teatro español de 1825 a 1836," in *Studies in Eighteenth Century Spanish Literature and Romanticism in Honor of John Dowling*, ed. Douglas and Linda Jane Barnette (Newark, Del.: Juan de la Cuesta, 1985), 123–31; Schinasi, op. cit., and ed. and comp., "Relación de las producciones dramáticas que se han aprobado por la Junta de Censura, para los Teatros del Reyno desde el mes de Marzo del año prócsimo pasado hasta el 31 de Diciembre del mismo." Typescript. I am grateful to Michael Schinasi for having provided me with a copy of his fascinating work in progress on the nineteenth-century Spanish theatre. The "Relación" contains nearly nine hundred play titles that passed through the censors' hands; among these plays are twenty-five *refundiciones* of Golden Age theatre texts. The small number of *comedias* relative to the entire list does not in any way limit the importance of the *comedia*'s fate in the nineteenth century. As I indicate throughout this study, more and more *comedia* recasts are discovered as research continues on this topic.

67. The idea of ritual-within-theatre may be expanded to include the act of rewriting as a related kind of ritual. For a fundamental approach to ritual and theatre in the sense suggested here, see Richard Hornby, *Drama, Metadrama and Perception* (Lewisburg, Pa.: Bucknell University Press, 1986).

68. Hans-Georg Gadamer, *The Relevance of the Beautiful and Other Essays*, trans.

Nicholas Walker, and ed. Robert Bernasconi (Cambridge: Cambridge University Press, 1986), 64.

69. Quoted in Roger Sale, *Literary Inheritance* (Amherst: University of Massachusetts Press, 1984), 43.

70. Ibid, 45.

71. The complete text of this review is found in the Appendix.

72. The historical trappings a *comedia* often took on, and the reevaluation of medieval and Golden Age Spain in the wake of Romanticism, elicits from Fernández-Guerra nostalgia for a past that never existed. In his review of *García del Castañar* in *La España* of 2 December 1855, he praises the Golden Age's innocence that reigns in García's home:

> Todo el poema respira este ambiente santo; allí no retumban facinerosos gritos engañadores que infernan el corazón; ni se vociferan derechos, antes bien se proclama y galardona el cumplimiento de deberes; . . . con la resignación y la tranquilidad de la conciencia, se dulcifican sus males, abriéndole el pecho a la esperanza de seguros imperecederos bienes.
>
> [The entire poem breathes this holy ambience; deceiving, villanous cries that try the soul do not resound there; nor are rights demanded, rather the fulfillment of duty is proclaimed and rewarded; . . . with resignation and peace of mind, their wrongdoings are softened, opening the heart to the hope of sure, undying goodness.] (1)

He offers a quixotic view of the period, a discourse of arms and letters that exists only in a lyrical dream of wishful thinking.

73. Warnke, *Gadamer*, 74.

74. For an example of a recast that exhibits both its positive and negative quality, see my article, "Rewriting Theatre: A Prolegomenon to a Study of the *Refundición*," *Hispania* 74 (1991): 240–49, wherein I discuss Calixto Boldún y Conde's *A secreto agravio, disimulada venganza*.

As this book went to press I received the special issue of *Bulletin of Hispanic Studies*, "The Eighteenth Century in Spain" (68.1 [1991]); of particular interest is part 2, which covers theatre. The entire issue of *BHS* must be taken into account in further investigations into the phenomenon of the *refundición*.

Chapter 2. King Sancho Revisited

1. A comprehensive bibliography is too long to include here, but the following are among the more recent and important studies of the play: James F. Burke, "*La estrella de Sevilla* and Saturnine Melancholy," *Bulletin of Hispanic Studies* 51 (1974): 137–56; Máximo González Marcos, "El antiabsolutismo en *La estrella de Sevilla*,"

Hispanófila 25, no. 74 (1982): 1–24; William McCrary, "Ritual Action and Form in *La Estrella de Sevilla*," in *Homenaje a William L. Fichter*, edited by A. David Kossoff and José Amor y Vázquez (Madrid: Castalia, 1971), 503–13; Charles M. Oriel, *Writing and Inscription in Golden Age Drama*, Purdue Studies in Romance Literatures (West Lafayette, Ind.: Purdue University Press, 1992); Elias L. Rivers, "The Shame of Writing in *La estrella de Sevilla*," *Folio: Essays on Foreign Languages and Literatures* 12 (1980): 105–17; Alfredo Rodríguez López-Vázquez, "*La Estrella de Sevilla* y Claramonte," *Criticón*, no. 21 (1983): 5–31; idem., "*La Estrella de Sevilla* y *Deste agua no beberé*: ¿un mismo autor?" *Bulletin of the Comediantes* 36 (1984): 83–100; Harlan Sturm and Sara Sturm, "The Astronomical Metaphor in *La Estrella de Sevilla*," *Hispania* 52 (1969): 193–97; Jack Weiner, "Zeus y las metamorfosis de Sancho IV en *La Estrella de Sevilla*," *Explicación de Textos Literarios* 10 (1981): 63–67. Most recently, Alfredo Rodríguez López-Vázquez has published an edition of the play in which he argues for Andrés de Claramonte as author (Madrid: Cátedra, 1991). In April 1992, Pennsylvania State University hosted a symposium dedicated to *La Estrella de Sevilla*; selected papers are currently in press with Bucknell University Press.

2. J. P. Wickersham Crawford, "An Early Nineteenth-Century English Version of *La estrella de Sevilla*," in *Estudios eruditos in memoriam Adolfo Bonilla y San Martín* (Madrid: Viuda e Hijos de Jaime Ratés, 1930), 2: 495–505, discusses a nineteenth-century English translation of *La estrella de Sevilla*.

3. Cándido María Trigueros, *Sancho Ortiz de las Roelas*, Tragedia arreglada . . . (Madrid: Imprenta de Sancha, 1800). The title page adds, too, that the printing costs were borne by "Manuel García Parra, primer actor, que la ha representado en esta corte, en el Coliseo de la Calle de la Cruz." All quotations are from this edition and will be cited in the text according to act and scene. For data on performances see Coe, *Catálogo*, 200–201; Aguilar Piñal, *Cartelera prerromántica*, 40; Seminario, *Cartelera*, 87; and Herrero Salgado, *Cartelera*, 99, indicate dates of performances.

4. The edition I use is Juan Eugenio Hartzenbusch, *La estrella de Sevilla o Sancho Ortiz de las Roelas, Drama trágico de Lope de Vega. Refundido por D. Cándido Mª de Trigueros y arreglado en cuatro actos por* . . . (Buenos Aires: Cabaut y Compañía, 1900); all quotations will be cited in the text according to act and scene. Menarini, *El teatro romántico*, 177, lists this *refundición* as 1834, but all the newspapers of 1852 refer to the "estreno" (opening) to take place. Aguilar Piñal, *Trigueros*, 240, states that the 1834 performance was of Trigueros's version. As for the interest in Hartzenbusch's *refundición*, *El Heraldo* of 22 January 1852 claims that "el público espera con impaciencia el drama *Sancho Ortiz de las Roelas*, refundido por Hartzenbusch" (the public impatiently awaits *Sancho Ortiz de las Roelas*, recast by Hartzenbusch) (Quoted in *Veinticuatro diarios*, 2: 419). Other newspapers reflect similar enthusiasm.

5. Nicholson B. Adams, "Hartzenbusch's *Sancho Ortiz de las Roelas*," *Studies in Philology* 28 (1931): 851–56; Cook, *Neo-Classic Drama*, 263–68; Andioc, *Teatro y sociedad*, 404–7; Francisco Aguilar Piñal, *Cándido María Trigueros: Hombre ilustra-*

do (Madrid: CSIC, 1989), 237–42; Caldera, *Il dramma romantico*, 41–61. In this context see again López-Vázquez's edition (note 1 above), particularly the introduction (20–39). All references to the Golden Age *comedia La estrella de Sevilla* are to verse numbers only from the Frank Reed, Esther Dixon, and John Hill edition (New York: D. C. Heath, 1939).

6. Trigueros's other *refundiciones* include *La moza de cántaro*, *Los melindres de Belisa*, *La buscona* (the title he gave to Lope's *El anzuelo de Fenisa*), *La esclavizada* (*La esclava de su galán*). *El mejor alcalde el rey* (a recast that, to my knowledge, was never completed, nor is there any text available). Aguilar Piñal, *Trigueros*, 235–46, briefly discusses each of these recasts.

7. Caldera, *Il dramma romantico*, 42; the verses cited from Lope's play are 473–76.

8. Ibid., 43.

9. Andioc, *Teatro y sociedad*, 404, speaks to the harmony established between the neoclassical aesthetic and the government's internal policies by eliminating the onstage duel between Sancho Ortiz and Bustos. As for the inconvenience of having King Sancho condone this crime, Andioc writes:

> Consciente de la escasa conveniencia del papel de un rey que se venga de un caballero mandándole matar por el propio cuñado, procura Trigueros compensar una situación de la que no puede prescindir, haciendo que el rey se arrepienta con regularidad de una pasión tan rebelde al influjo de la razón, ¡incluso antes de haber cometido la falta!

> [Conscious of the unsuitability of the role of a king who takes vengeance on a gentleman by ordering him murdered by his own brother-in-law, Trigueros attempts to compensate for an absolutely indispensable scene, by having the king regularly repent, under the influence of reason, of a rebellious passion, even before having commited the crime!] (404)

10. Caldera, *Il dramma romantico*, comments specifically on this exchange as an example of Hartzenbusch's following personal dictates, though at times it is difficult "individuare le ragioni de queste varianti che per lo più sembrano sgorgare istintivamente dal gusto personale di H; tuttavia si può forse scorgere, come nei versi ora riportati, una certa tendenza a toni più discorsivi del pur già discorsivo modello [to specify the reasons for these variants that for the most part seem to flow instinctively from Hartzenbusch's personal taste; it is still possible to perceive, as in the verses cited here, a certain tendency to an even greater discursive tone than found in the already discursive model] (52).

11. Bustos's long, angry threat to Estrella from the original is suppressed from both versions. It is logical for Trigueros to eliminate the passage, as the strong support for an outmoded concept of honor operative in the Golden Age would find little favor among the recaster's critics. Hartzenbusch, again following Trigueros, opted to second his omission.

12. The syntax at the beginning of both passages is confusing. The sense in Spanish, I believe, is this: "el zelo ha contenido el amor que me abrasa." The only changes I have made to Trigueros's text are the first period and capitalization of "Mi." I have translated according to my suggested reading.

13. However, gone from the meeting between the two Sanchos is the underlying tension created by the mention of *estrellas*:

>   *Rey.* Son las virtudes Estrellas.
> *Sancho (aparte).* Si en la Estrella me tocáis,
>   ciertas son mis desventuras;
>   honrándome el rey me ofende;
>   no son sus honras seguras,
>   pues sospecho que pretende
>   dejarme sin ella a escuras.

> [*King.* Stars are virtues.
> *Sancho (aside).* If you speak to me of Estrella, my misfortune is certain. The king offends me by honoring me; his honors are not safe, because I suspect that he wishes to leave me in darkness without her.] (1460–66).

14. By the time of Trigueros's *refundición,* the character of the *gracioso* had been subdued considerably and his role greatly reduced. Clarindo here serves merely as the messenger who delivers the letter and stands quietly and attentively by his master's side:

>   Al ver al Rey que salía,
>   no me detuve y llegué;
>   que este papel os traía.
>   Es de Estrella, y yo bien sé
>   que os es de grande alegría.

[When I saw the king leaving, I didn't stop and came right to you, because I was bringing you this letter. It is from Estrella, and I am quite sure it will make you very happy.] (1.6)

Hartzenbusch does not make Clarindo any funnier—unless a superlative comic actor could give free rein to the imagination—but at least the servant is more than a wooden messenger. Hartzenbusch extends Clarindo's speech by having him recreate the dialogue between himself and Estrella in which she prepares the felicitous message:

>   Al ver al Rey que salía,
>   no me detuve y llegué.
>   Este papel os traía
>   de Estrella; y aunque no sé
>   qué contiene, juraría
>   que soy nuncio de contento;

> pues cruzando por delante
> de su balcón, ha un momento,
> me llamó, y en su aposento,
> menos curiosa que amante,
> preguntó si en casa estabais.
> Le respondí que acababais
> de salir.—"¿A dónde fue?
> repuso. Yo contesté:
> "A palacio: si pensabais
> alguna cosa advertirle...

[When I saw the king leaving I did not stop and came right to you. I was bringing you this letter from Estrella, and although I do not know what it says, I would swear that I am a bearer of glad tidings; as I was passing in front of her balcony, just a moment ago, she called to me, and in her room, less out of curiosity than out of love, asked if you were at home. I responded that you had just left. "Where did he go?" she replied. I answered: "To the palace, if you had something to tell him..."] (1.7)

15. Recall Ruiz Ramón's terminology in *Calderón y la tragedia*, when he speaks of "descodificar" and "recodificar" [decodifying; recodifying] in bringing a seventeenth-century classical play to the contemporary stage.

16. Caldera, *Il dramma romantico*, 57.

17. Ibid.

18. The translation of these verses is from Elias Rivers, ed., *Renaissance and Baroque Poetry of Spain* (1966; Prospect Heights, Ill.: Waveland Press, 1988), 34.

19. This is the first verse of a twenty-five-line speech, new in Trigueros, that contains his admission of guilt:

> Decidlo, y llévenme preso:
> di muerte a Bustos Tabera, .
> y es bien que por ello muera,
> pues que cometí un exceso
> que no le haría una fiera.
> Si honor me obligó a matar,
> amor me obliga a morir.

[Say it, and take me prisoner: I killed Bustos Tabera, and it is right that I die for the crime, for I have committed a wrongful deed that a wild beast would not do. If honor obliged me to kill, love obliges me to die.] (2.5)

20. I. L. McClelland, *Spanish Drama of Pathos*, 2 vols. (Toronto: University of Toronto Press, 1970), 1: 126.

21. Ibid., 128.

22. Ibid., 127.

23. Trigueros could neither condone nor propogate beliefs in the visions the origi-

nal Sancho claims to see, even less that the "diablo cojuelo"—Asmodeus, a product of the mind of the lowly *criado*—could come to the rescue.

24. Hartzenbusch offers a curious recovery of the act of writing: "Estrella, grato recibo / y en mi corazón escribo / tal merced" [Estrella, pleased I receive, and inscribe in my heart, such favor](3.10).

25. Edward Coughlin, in his unpublished 1965 Ph.D. dissertation "Neo-Classical *Refundiciones* of Golden Age *Comedias* (1772–1831)," University of Michigan, comments on Trigueros's having removed Farfán de Ribera's name from Lope's play as an example of reduction carried out by *refundidores*.

25. To define one meaning of "acíbar" the *Dicc. aut.* (s.v., "acíbar") quotes Fray Luis de León: "Con todo esto el acíbar purga las heces de los malos humores" [With all of this the aloe purges the dregs of bad humors]. The drug acts, then, as both poison and remedy; it is, in othe words, a *pharmakon*. For fuller treatment of the *pharmakon* in literature see chapter 5 of this study and the corresponding notes.

27. In the petition King Sancho makes to each of the *alcaldes,* Hartzenbusch follows Trigueros literally, changing only a word or phrase to place his own imprint upon the *refundición*. In the soliloquy following the meeting with Guzmán and Farfán, too, Hartzenbusch remains faithful to his source, with the exception of eliminating six nonessential verses from the end of the king's speech.

28. For the complete text of these reviews, see the Appendix.

29. Where possible I cite directly from the newspapers. Some issues cited were not available at the Hemeroteca Municipal of Madrid either because they were lost or in the process of being microfilmed. In these cases, I have relied on Coe.

30. The *dramatis personae* printed in the 1800 edition of Trigueros's *Sancho Ortiz de las Roelas* contains the names of the actors who most likely performed in the inaugural stagings of the play:

El Rey Don Sancho el Bravo	Sr. Luis Navarro
Don Sancho Ortiz de las Roelas	Sr. Manuel García Parra
Don Bustos Tabera	Sr. Félix Cubas
Doña Estrella Tabera	Sra. Rita Luna
Teodora	Sra. Joaquina Arteaga
Clarindo	Sr. Pasqual Mas
Don Arias	Sr. Antonio Ponce
Don Pedro de Guzmán	Sr. Francisco Vaca
Farfán de Ribera	Sr. Antonio Pinto
Pedro de Caus	Sr. Braulio Hidalgo

Pasqual Mas either performed in and/or was the *apuntador* for Solís's *Marta la piadosa*; his name is written throughout the Biblioteca Municipal manuscript.

31. There follows a general attack on the *refundición*, discussed in chapter 1.

32. The tone recalls that used by Tomás Sebastián y Latre in the prologue to his *refundiciones* of Moreto's *El desdén con el desdén* and Rojas Zorrilla's *Progne y Filomena*. See chapter 1.

33. María Rodríguez, probably in the role of Estrella, "ha estado en este drama a

toda la altura de una primera actriz, manifestando el concienzudo estudio que de su papel ha hecho, en su actitud siempre digna, y en su acción siempre adecuada al carácter que representaba" [has acted in this play like a leading lady, revealing her conscientious preparation for the role in her ever dignified attitude and in her performance always appropriate to the character she would represent]; Valero continues "desplegando su gran inteligencia" [displaying his great intelligence] and [Rafael] Calvo "su aptitud para los papeles que requieren severidad y entonación" [his aptitude for roles that require severity and arrogance] (3).

34. The cast of this production included the renowned Antonio Vico who most likely portrayed Sancho Ortiz. (The reviewer does not state the roles, but the information is easily deduced from the stature of the actors as well as the comments regarding their performance.) Vico spoke with authority and was frequently interrupted by applause. His strong performance may have overshadowed—if not overwhelmed—the actress Contreras in the role of Estrella. Illness seems to have impeded her performance, according to the reviewer, but in any event she may have been miscast: "Interpretó discretamente el papel de Estrella, poco adecuado a sus facultades. La simpática actriz vistió con gran propiedad, y tuvo momentos felices de los actos segundo y tercero" [She performed discretely the role of Estrella, one not well suited to her abilities. The charming actress assumed great propriety, and experienced felicitous moments in Acts 2 and 3] (4). On the whole, the review makes it clear that the play was not given the best possible staging. Care was obviously taken in praise of the late author, and the actors—with the exception of Vico—were treated with kid gloves, perhaps in an effort not to dampen the occasion honoring a writer who deserved a better performance than the Teatro Español gave in September 1880.

35. Estrella was Contreras's first important role, and at first she was "tímida y recelosa" [timid and fearful]; but the public stood behind her, clamoring for her to take a curtain call with Vico. With the exception of the two leading actors, the remainder of the cast, because of their relatively limited roles, "no tienen ocasiones de lucimiento" [do not have the opportunity to shine] (4).

Chapter 3. *Marta la piadosa*

1. Andioc, *Teatro y sociedad*, 420.

2. Alborg, *Historia*, 3: 642. See also María del Pilar Palomo, "Presencia de Tirso en Moratín," *Studi Ispanici* 1 (1962): 165–86. The edition consulted for both *La mojigata* and *El viejo y la niña* is Leandro Fernández de Moratín, *Comedias completas*, ed. Emiliano M. Augilera (Barcelona: Iberia, 1957).

3. Ruiz Morcuende (L) suggests Rojas Zorrilla's *Entre bobos anda el juego* as a possible source of *El sí*, while Dowling (103–4) summarizes accepted opinion that Lope's *La discreta enamorada* may have influenced Moratín.

4. Alice Huntington Bushee, *Three Centuries of Tirso de Molina* (Philadelphia: University of Pennsylvania Press, 1939), 77.

5. Marcelin Defourneaux, "Molière et l'inquisition espagnole," *Bulletin Hispanique* 64 (1962): 33–34.

6. Ibid., 35.

7. Ibid., 36. Together, "Molière . . ." and Defourneaux's "Une Adaptation inédite du *Tartuffe*: *El gazmoño* ou *Juan de Buen Alma* de Cándido María Trigueros," *Bulletin Hispanique* 64 (1962): 43–60, are the only articles, as far as I know, to outline the brief history of *Tartuffe* on the Spanish stage in the late eighteenth and early nineteenth centuries. Both studies are tantalizing in the possibilities they offer for further investigation and contain interesting data pertaining to the Inquisition and the stage both in Spain and in America. For example, in 1818, one of the versions of *El hipócrita* was performed in Lima, Peru; the Holy Office received a request for censorship soon after the staging (the censure itself is dated 25 October 1818) ("Molière . . ." 41). A comparative study including all extant Spanish versions of *Tartuffe* and the *refundiciones* of *Marta la piadosa* is clearly needed.

8. Coe, *Catálogo*, 115.

9. Carmen Pitollet, "Datos biográficos sobre D. Pascual Rodríguez de Arellano y D. Rafael Floranes," *Revista de Filología Española* 10 (1923): 290. Pascual Rodríguez de Arellano's plan to form a Teatro Nacional recalls that of Bernardo de Iriarte (See Cook, *Neo-Classic Drama*, 226–28). Rodríguez de Arellano obviously sides with the *comedia*'s supporters who like to arrange the works according to the newer aesthetic; in this he differs greatly from his contemporary Tomás Sebastián y Latre (discussed in chapter 1), who wished to recast *comedias* with the goal of having them disappear from the stage altogether.

10. Pitollet, "Datos biográficos," 291.

11. Though Solís's *refundiciones* have received some attention, it would be valuable to study the other plays he recast and prevailing social or political conditions. The bibliography on Solís is limited; see Juan Eugenio Harztenbusch, "Don Dionisio Solís, noticia biográfica," in *Biblioteca de Autores Españoles*, vol. 67 (Madrid: Hernando, 1922); Hal Lackey Bailew, "The Life and Works of Dionisio Solís," Ph. D. diss., University of North Carolina-Chapel Hill, 1957; and David T. Gies, "Hacia un catálogo de los dramas de Dionisio Solís (1774–1834)," *Bulletin of Hispanic Studies* 68 (1990): 197–210.

12. Andioc, *Teatro y sociedad*, 419ff.

13. Cook, *Neo-Classic Drama*, 268.

14. Andioc, *Teatro y sociead*, 426 and n. 15, quotes from an anonymous article in the *Diario de Valencia* of 1813 that hints, in short, that Spain is a corrupt country where a single woman's only escape from oppression is marriage.

15. Pascual Rodríguez de Arellano, *La beata enamorada*, MS Leg[ajo] 7° E, Biblioteca Municipal, Madrid (*Marta la piadosa* has been known, too, by this title). This edition is, as far as I know, the only extant version of the play. Marginal notations suggest that the manuscript served as a prompt copy, though I have not uncovered to date any information regarding its performance. I am grateful to Professor Anita Stoll for calling the manuscript to my attention and furnishing me with a

microfilm copy. I have transcribed the text and will refer to act and scene numbers in all quotations.

16. Tirso de Molina, *Marta la piadosa*, in *Obras dramáticas completas*, ed. Blanca de los Ríos, vol. 3, 339–403. 3d ed (Madrid: Aguilar, 1969). All subsequent citations indicate act and scene from this edition.

17. Andioc, *Teatro y sociedad*, 435–36, discusses the economic side effects of these marriages with regard to *El viejo y la niña*. He cites the *Diario de Madrid* of 15 November 1787 which mentions that the number of widows was triple the number of widowers, and quotes Cabarrús in a 1784 speech (436 and n. 33) who complained that such marriages were "'contrarias a la naturaleza e infecundas para el estado'" [contrary to nature and infertile for the state]. The inference, none too subtle, is that fewer children are produced from marital arrangements between older men and younger women, thus reducing the economic base. Also suggested is the avarice (the "interés" that informs Moratín's plays as well as *Marta la piadosa* in its various formulations) of the young women who themselves marry with the hopes of inheriting a comfortable sum in a short time.

18. See Pilar Palomo, "Presencia de Tirso . . . ."

19. Noteworthy in this regard is the fact that Clavijo (*El Pensador*, 18) considers the words "beatas" and "hypócritas" as nearly synonymous (from Andioc, *Teatro y sociedad*, 509, n. 66). This wide meaning given to "beata" explains in part why the word does not appear in Rodríguez de Arellano's *refundición*.

20. For example, see Elvira E. García, ed., *A Critical Edition of Tirso de Molina's "Marta la piadosa"* (Salzburg: Institut für Englische Sprache und Literatur, Universität Salzburg, 1978), 29, for but one opinion.

21. Consider, too, Solís's *refundición* and his ending references to Ovid's *Ars amandi* as well as the *Remedies*, the only indication that Solís may have been aware of Rodríguez de Arellano's version.

22. "Libro que contenía los preceptos de la gramática latina" [Book that contained the precepts of Latin grammar], María Moliner, *Diccionario del uso del español*, s.v. "arte."

23. Andioc, *Teatro y sociedad*, 437–38, details the importance of Moratín's character within the context of *El viejo y la niña*.

24. Consider this particularly in light of Doña Blanca's assessment that *Marta la piadosa* was written to mock Lope's continued interest in affairs of the heart and flesh in spite of his ordainment. See her introduction to the play in the Aguilar edition, 342ff.

25. There is some discrepancy about the reading of this verse. Juliá and others have changed it to "de castidad hice voto" [I made a vow of chastity]. Hartzenbusch had noted in his edition (*BAE* 5: 448) that "Este verso no se halla en la edición original, y sí en el tomo IV del *Tesoro del teatro español*, publicado en París por el señor Don Eugenio Ochoa" [This verse is not in the original edition, but it is in volume 14 of the Treasure of Spanish Theatre, published in Paris by Don Eugenio Ochoa]. Doña Blanca reiterates the quotation (370 n. 1), and in n. 2 suggests the following: "'hasta

que en la tierra virgen / me entierren a la vejez.' Porque la virgen no era tierra" [until they bury me as a virgin / Because the earth was not the virgin]. Her proposed emendation is certainly logical.

26. A substantial change in the text, apart from occasional reductions in speeches and introduction of new verses that serve to carry the imprimatur of the recaster, is the censorship of a mildly risqué passage. Pastrana enters in 1.3—his arrival had been announced at the end of 1.2, with the information that "de tal modo / viene puesto, que en todo / parece un escribano" [he arrives dressed in such a way that he is the spitting image of a notary] (another preparation for disguise and deceit)—initiating a typical *gracioso* dialogue:

> *Pastrana.* Besando a vuesas mercedes ...
> *Sirena.* ¿Qué?
> *Pastrana.*   Las manos.
> *Sirena.*   Socarrón,
> flemática es tu atención
> como en besarlas te quedes.
> *Pastrana.* Pues en qualquiera suceso,
> ¿qué venta puedo yo hallar
> dónde me pueda quedar
> con más gusto que en un beso?
> *Marta.* ¿Siempre de humor?
> *Pastrana.*   Lo que basta
> para no salir de pobre,
> y para que no me sobre,
> liberalmente se gasta.

[*Pastrana.* Kissing your Graces' ...
Sirena. What?
Pastrana. hands.
Sirena. You sly devil. Your attention is very slow moving if you don't go past the hands.
Pastrana. Well, in any event, what inn can I find where I might linger with greater pleasure than in a kiss?
Marta. Do you always trade in humor?
Pastrana. Just enough to stay poor, and in order not to have anything left over, I spend liberally.] (2.3)

The section from "Pues" to the end of the passage has been penned in and later crossed out in the manuscript. The reason for the elimination is not clear, nor can one say if this is a case of self-censorship or if it has been carried out by another reader. In any event, the last lines about Pastrana's humor seem to be completely inoffensive; the only rationale may have to do with the toning down of the *gracioso* in general. Two additional cuts of verses spoken by Pastrana refer to the *Celestina*. After discussing, in Tirso's original, the arrangements for Don Felipe to enter

Marta's house, Pastrana states: "Y yo soy ya / Celestino de Calixto" [And now I am Celestino for Calixto] (2.4). The bawdiness, related in tone to "besos" and the "venta," may have raised some eighteenth-century eyebrows. Recall in this regard the excision of Clarindo's more humorous repartée in Trigueros's *Sancho Oritz de las Roelas*.

27. The Alférez's speech occurs in 2.2:

> Pagaba el sol la posada
> con el oro que se viste
> al signo sexto, que es Virgo
> (si en el sexto hay signo virgen),
> y el antípoda de enero
> a Ceres y a Baco pide
> parias, con cuyos esquilmos
> techos cuelga y trojes hinche
> (quiero decir, que era agosto;
> que no puedo persuadirme
> a que den gusto romances
> con máscara de latines) . . .

[The sun paid for its stay with the gold worn by the sixth sign, which is Virgo, if within the sixth commandment a virgin can be found, and January's antipode requests tributes from Ceres and Bacchus whose fruit hangs from ceilings and fills silos . . . (in other words, it was August, because I am not convinced that ballads enmasked in Latin are enjoyable) . . .]

28. Again Andioc, *Teatro y sociedad*, 438, helps to signal how Rodríguez de Arellano is indebted to Moratín and is as well in tune with the currents of the age. In the detailed discussion of *El viejo y la niña*, Andioc explains how "el dramaturgo los [the old man and his young competitor] enfrenta varias veces para que don Juan evidencie regularmente la 'necedad' o 'tontería' del otro" [the playwright has them face each other several times for Don Juan to reveal regularly the 'stupidity' or 'foolishness' of the other gentleman]. In *Marta la piadosa* the Capitán's declaration that "mi necedad corrijo" [I emend my foolish ways] corresponds to the tone set forth in Moratín's play.

29. The untranslated Latin words are underlined in Rodríguez de Arellano's manuscript and suggest that the Latinisms are intended to produce a specific comic and jocular effect.

30. *Diccionario de autoridades*, s.v., "afectar."

31. For this information, as well as for the ensuing discussion of Latin noun declensions, I am indebted to my colleague Keith Dickson.

32. Dar al través: "Lo mismo que Dar al traste." Dar al traste: "Metaphoricamente vale destruir alguna cosa, abandonarla o perderla" [Metaphorically it means to destroy something, abandon it or lose it] (*Diccionario de autoridades*, s.v. "dar").

33. The moral that Felipe communicates now directly to the audience recalls that spoken by Don Luis of Moratín's *La mojigata* where he chastises his brother's "indiscreet" use of authority that results in Clara's deceitfulness.

34. Dionisio Solís, *Marta la piadosa*, MS Leg[ajo] 2, no. 22, Biblioteca Municipal, Madrid; all citations will indicate act and scene numbers from this manuscript. For performances, see Coe, *Catálogo*, 26–27. For an account of Solís's life and works see Ballew and Gies (cited above in note 11).

35. Archibald K. Shields, "The Madrid Stage 1820–1850, 3 vols., Ph. D. diss., University of North Carolina-Chapel Hill, 1933, 3: 781; Adams, "*Siglo de Oro* Plays," 350. The manuscript carries on the first folio the indications "Sevilla 1829," "1834," "1836," and "Madrid 1847." The second folio contains a list of actors including José Galindo, Jerónimo Lamadrid, Santiago (or Mariano) Casanova, José or Santos Diez, and María del Carmen Concha, among others, performers active in the 1830s (Cotarelo). Additional evidence throughout the manuscript (stage directions, emendations, and the like) indicates that it served as a prompt copy.

36. *Veinticuatro diarios*, 1: 502; 2: 171.

37. See María de Pilar Palomo, "El 'amor portugués' en Tirso de Molina," *Monteagudo* 30 (1960): 4–13.

38. Solís's early work in the theatre as *apuntador* would have brought him into contact with all productions the Madrid stages had to offer, including Moratín's plays. Solís and Moratín were good friends, but when their friendship began is not known; Ballew, "Life and Works," 15ff., reproduces correspondence between Solís and Moratín after 1815, and Solís had written to a friend around this time mentioning his "antigua amistad" [long-time friendship] with the writer.

39. The principal modification occurs in Solís's 2.1, where he replaces "beldad" with "deidad," a description aptly chosen to reinforce Marta's "chastity" and "beatería," as well as to signal that despite her warmth (sexually suggestive?), "ninguno te mira / porque ninguno hasta ahora / hace de servirte caso" [not one man looks at you because no one until now has thought about courting you] (2.1).

40. Coe, *Catálogo*, 233, lists performances of *El viejo y la niña* as late as 16 April 1812, and for *El sí de las niñas* (205) a performance on 17 February 1813. Solís had been working in the theatre since 1798 (Ballew, "Life and Work," 3 et passim).

41. One of the changes to Solís's text in 3.3 from "concierto" to "resuelto" destroys the rhyme of the *redondilla*. Such changes are the inevitable outcome of individual modifications made to a playtext in its transmission. When passages are eliminated or modified for reasons of performance time, of matters of censorship, or of the seemingly whimsical changes that a director may impose, the rhyme scheme receives little or no attention. The metrics of the *refundición* was not a primary concern to the recasters.

42. See Frances C. Hayes, "The Use of Proverbs as Titles and Motives in the *Siglo de Oro* Drama: Tirso de Molina," *Hispanic Review* 7 (1939): 310–23; and Luis Montoto y Rautenstrauch, *Personajes, personas y personillas que corren por las tierras de ambas castillas*, 2 vols. (Sevilla: Librería de San José, 1912), particularly 2: 169–75.

43. See the note to 1619–20 of Ignacio Arellano's edition of *Marta la piadosa* (Kassel: Reichenberger; Barcelona, PPU, 1988).

44. Let us not forget the apparent inconsistencies that such emendations bring to light: Solís may eliminate religious references but recasts and stages a play whose protagonist is a woman who mocks beatitude. Perhaps what Solís suggests is that truly Christian attitudes, such as those demonstrated by Urbina, do not have a place in a theatrical world, meant for the public, populated by purveyors of false virtue.

45. These same two scenes (7 and 8) evidence another manipulation of the original text in references to Marta as hypocrite. When Felipe urges Lucía to participate in the ruse, he refers to the plans conceived by "la hipócrita loca" [the crazy hypocrite] (3.7), a truly nasty (though feigned) remark made banal and gutted of emotional impact by Solís's "esa fea y loca" [that ugly and insane woman] (4.7). The same verse is reiterated in the following scene by Marta who now quotes to Felipe, in anger, these lines that she has overheard (3.7; 4.8) in Felipe's encounter with Lucía.

46. I would correct Doña Blanca's as well as Arellano's punctuation throughout this scene. Both editors have Don Gómez and Marta say, "¡Vive Dios, jurando Marta ..." [Good God, Marta swearing ...] and "¡Vive Dios, ha de jurar un cristiano ... !" [Good God, a Christian is swearing ... !] (3.9), where the exclamation should read "'¿Vive Dios' ... ?" ['Good God' ...] as Don Gómez is reiterating what he believes Marta has said, and Marta is chastising Felipe for his use of that oath.

47. Closure of this scene differs from Tirso's. Felipe agrees to remain in the household provided that Marta, on her knees, kisses his hand. Marta's response to this insistence in Tirso is "Si ello va a decir verdad, 'a la miel me supo el beso'" [If truth be told, the kiss tasted like honey] (3.9), while in Solís her line is much less suggestive, less sensual: "Si vale decir verdad, / esto merece un exceso" [If truth be told, I could get carried away with myself] (4.9). In this case, lost as well is one more layer of the oral tradition found in *Marta la piadosa*'s reliance upon the *refranero*, Tirso's line having come from a traditional song.

48. The remaining scenes of act 4, in which a disguised Pastrana announces the arranged "execution" of Felipe and Don Gómez undertakes the journey to Seville to witness his vengeance, convey the essence of Tirso's action.

49. Corominas (s.v. "clueca") lists "clueco" as a derivative of "clueca" and its definition as "muy débil, achacoso" [very weak, ailing] as employed in *La pícara Justina* of 1605: "porque la persona en este estado se ve obligada a guardar cama y a vivir en la inmovilidad, como la clueca; por lo demás, en ambientes rurales no es raro que se aproveche al enfermo para incubar huevos" [because the person in this state is obliged to stay in bed and remain motionless, like a laying hen; furthermore, in rural areas it is not unusual to make use of the infirm to incubate eggs]. María Moliner, *Diccionario del uso*, s.v. "clueco," following Corominas, defines the word as "caduco" [decrepit, worn out]: "Se aplica a la persona achacosa, débil e inútil, por vejez" [It is applied to the person ailing, weak and useless because of old age]. *Diccionario de autoridades* does not give this definition of the word.

50. Compare Marta's response with a similar scene in Boldún's recast (Madrid: José Rodríguez, 1866) and with *Tartuffe*. Boldún reads:

> Tú me labras la corona
> que de inmarcesibles flores,
> ha de ceñirse mi frente
> en la celeste morada.
> No importa, no importa nada
> que me ofendas impaciente.
> Llámame traidora, y cuantos
> oprobios quieras, celosa;
> táchame de mentirosa,
> que este es el pan de los santos!
> Jesús mío! ya que así
> (*mirando al cielo en ademán de
> arrodillarse*)
> de mi humildad te contentas,
> dame trabajos y afrentas,
> que más pasaste por mí.

[You weave the crown out of unwithering flowers that I will wear in Heaven. It does not matter, it does not matter at all that you offend me impatiently. Call me a traitor and as many insults as you wish, jealous woman; consider me a liar, for this is the bread of the saints! Sweet Jesus, now (*looking heavenward as she kneels*) that you are happy with my humility, heap on travails and affronts, for you suffered much more for me.] (3.5)

In 3.6 of *Tartuffe* (in *Oeuvres complètes*, ed. George Couton, vol. 1 [Paris: Gallimard, 1971]), Tartuffe speaks with Orgon's son Damis and allows him to heap insults which he (Tartuffe) accepts "stoically":

> Oui, mon cher fils, parlez; traitez-moi de perfide,
> D'infâme, de perdu, de voleur, d'homicide;
> Accablez-moi de noms encor plus détestés:
> Je n'y contredis point, je les ai mérités;
> Et j'en veux a genoux souffrir l'ignominie,
> Comme une honte due aux crimes de ma vie.

[Dear son, go on; tell me my crimes are great; / Call me thief, killer, traitor, reprobate; / Load me with epithets still more abhorred: / I won't say no; they are my just reward; After my life of crime, in expiation, / I'll kneel and suffer that humiliation.] (3.6.1101–06)

Translation from *Tartuffe and Other Plays by Molière*, trans. Donald M. Frame (New York: New American Library, Penguin Books USA, 1967), 281.

Although Solís is less subtle than Molière, it seems clear that he had more than a passing familiarity with the French text. It is fair to say, I believe, that Solís has recast the French model.

51. Celedonio, the name given by Solís to Capitán Urbina, suggests Inarco Celenio, the pseudonym of Solís's friend Leandro Fernández de Moratín. The similarity of names between the character and the author of *El viejo y la niña* and *La mojigata* suggests an inside joke; it also reinforces Solís's choice of this Tirso *comedia* due to the currency the topic gained in part through Moratín.

52. This verse and the preceding two are crossed out in the manuscript, and written in their stead by the second hand is "ingrata, vil, fementida / estudiosa y aplicada / al latín, sólo por dar..." [ingrate, vile, treacherous, studious and devoted to Latin, just to give...] (Act 5, f. 15r).

53. Miseno says to Finea in *La dama boba*, "Oye; que hemos concertado / que os caséis" [Listen; we have agreed that you should marry] (ed. Diego Marín, 12th ed. [Madrid: Cátedra, 1989], 3013–14). Another point of contact is the importance of money, given the sizeable dowry Finea has at her disposal. Solís's decision to incorporate an incident from *La dama boba* is a smart one that provides intertextual linking based on a known dramatic convention. What is further suggested, naturally, is a relationship between Lope's play and Tirso's *Marta la piadosa*.

54. The notion of masks and Latinisms is at the center of understanding Tirso's play.

55. The manuscript is difficult to read (it seems to say "Rempies"), but in conjunction with the reference in the following line to "arte Amandi," it is safe to conjecture that Felipe refers to Ovid's two treatises on love.

56. Among Boldún's other contributions to recast Golden Age *comedias* are *A secreto agravio, disimulada venganza* [Secret vengeance for a hidden offense] (Madrid: José Rodríguez, 1867) and *El vergonzoso en palacio* [The shy man in the palace] (Valencia: Francisco Vives Mora, 1910), performed at the Teatro del Circo in 1875. Enrique Funes, in his introductory essay to his own *refundición* of Tirso's *La prudencia en la mujer* [Prudence in the woman] (2d ed. [Santa Cruz de Tenerife: J. J. Benítez, 1889]), states that Boldún "refundió habilidosamente, aunque con imperdonables licencias, *La vida es sueño*" [recast capably, although with unforgivable licences, Life is a dream] (xxxii). Boldún's *Marta la piadosa* calls into question his ability as a recaster, as shall be discussed; as for his version of *La vida es sueño*, Funes adds in a note:

> Refundición inédita, y que solo conocemos por haberla visto representar en América al distinguido actor don Leopoldo Burón; pues la que tantos aplausos ha proporiconado al Sr. Calvo (D. Rafael), Segismundo el más arrogante que hemos conocido, o es refundición de don Dionisio Solís, también inédita, o es un arreglo (que tratándose de *La vida es sueño* resulta muy sencillo) hecho por el mismo Calvo, conocedor ilustradísimo de la escena española, si la fama no miente."

[Unpublished recast, and that we know only from having seen it performed in America by the distinguished actor Don Leopoldo Burón; the one that has garnered great applause for Mr. Rafael Calvo, the most arrogant Segismundo we have known, is either a recast by Dionisio Solís, likewise unpublished, or is an arrangement (which in the case of Life is a dream is very easy to do) done by the same Calvo, learned expert of the Spanish stage, if his fame is not misleading.] (xxxii n. 1)

Funes's 2d edition was published in 1889, one year after the death of Rafael Calvo; he clearly refers to the eminent Spanish actor's South American tour in which Boldún's *Marta la piadosa* was also performed. Curious, too, is the further linking of Solís and Boldún.

57. *Homenaje a José Calvo y Revilla* (Madrid, 1888), 12; *Veinticuatro diarios* 4: 314.

58. In 1855 Serra recast Tirso's *Amar por señas* [Love by signs] (Madrid: José Rodríguez, 1855).

59. A twentieth-century production replaces the speech with a curious substitution (that almost works) of scenes depicting the founding of Tenochtitlán, the capital of the Aztec empire. The production, in March 1986, was performed by the Universidad Nacional Autónoma de México under the direction of Raúl Zermeño. See chapter 5, "Future Directions."

60. Regardless of these three points, Fernández-Guerra y Orbe is favorably inclined toward Solís's recast. Unlike the performance of 1851, the 1855 production was staged "con sin igual maestría" [with unequalled mastery] and attracted an impressive audience for more than a week of performances. The few actors Fernández-Guerra y Orbe mentions in the review suggest, too, the professional quality of the Príncipe theatre: Teodora Lamadrid (who is prominent in an 1864 *refundición* of *El alcalde de Zalamea* [The mayor of Zalamea], the subject of the following chapter) as Marta, Julián Romea as Dómine Berrío (referred to as the character in disguise, and not as Don Felipe), and Arjona as Don Gómez.

61. Calixto Oyuela, "Marta la piadosa," in *Estudios y artículos literarios* (Buenos Aires: Pablo E. Coni e Hijos, 1889), 219–32. All citations will refer to the page numbers of this editon and will be noted in the text.

62. Oyuela points out that Marta's speech from 2.4 of Tirso's play ("Mientras que viví a lo damo . . . ") has been replaced by Tartuffe's famous speech. Although the inclusion merits much greater attention than can be paid here, for the interested reader I include Molière's verses (op. cit.):

> Oui, mon frère, je suis un méchant, un coupable,
> Un malheureux pécheur, tout plein d'inquité,
> Le plus grand scélérat qui jamais ait été;
> Chaque instant de ma vie est chargé de souillures;
> Elle n'est qu'un amas de crimes et d'ordures;
> Et je vois que le Ciel, pour ma punition,
> Me veut mortifier en cette occasion.

De quelque grand forfait qu'on me puisse reprendre,
Je n'ai garde d'avoir l'orgueil de m'en défendre.
Croyez ce qu'on vous dit, armez votre courroux,
Et comme un criminel chassez-moi de chez vous:
Je ne saurais avoir tant de honte en partage,
Que je n'en aie encor mérité davantage.

[Yes, brother, I am evil through and through, / Guilty, full of iniquity and sin, / The greatest scoundrel that has ever been; / Each moment of my life is black with grime; / It is a mass of filthiness and crime; / And I am sure that this mortification / Is just a sign of Heaven's indignation. / Whatever sin they charge against my name, / I won't defend myself, such is my shame. / Believe their stories, everything they say, / And like a criminal send me away: / Whatever ignominy lies in store, / I know that I have merited far more.] (3.6.1074 – 86)

Translation from *Tartuffe and Other Plays by Molière*, 280.

The lack of a playscript is all the more lamentable because it impedes determining the importance of this specific interpolation. Additional changes certainly were introduced to Boldún's basic script; it would be worthwhile to note how the denouement was handled with regard to Solís's original incorporation of the scene from *La dama boba*.

63. I discuss this review in my *Gestos* article, but further reflection has led me to modify somewhat my appraisal of Oyuela's remarks.

64. The article first appeared in the newspaper *El Globo* (December 1896) and was reprinted in a collection of Doña Blanca's essays, *Del siglo de oro* (Madrid: Bernardo Rodríguez, 1910). All quotations are from this edition and will be cited in the text by page number.

65. I have reproduced the full text of the article, as I have done with all the principal newspaper reviews cited in this study, in the Appendix.

Chapter 4. Art and Politics

1. Guillén de Castro's *Las mocedades del Cid* [The youthful deeds of the Cid] explored similar themes, took on new form in France (Corneille's *Le Cid*), but as far as I know has produced no *refundiciones* within Spain.

2. I do not discuss Calderón's recasting of Lope's original *El alcalde de Zalamea*; seventeenth-century recasts, an important aspect of Spanish theatre history, are not within the purview of this book.

Andioc, *Teatro y sociedad*, 19, relates that during the 1764 – 65 theatre season, as a sign of the *comedia*'s decline in popularity, *El alcalde de Zalamea* garnered only 887 *reales*. But the most imporant fact is that Golden Age plays continued to be performed, although it is difficult to determine if in their original form or in some modified, if not entirely recast, version. Andioc does not believe that performances of *refundiciones* are the same as those of *comedias*: "Pero el *conjunto del teatro del siglo de oro* no conoce mejor suerte que el de Calderón, y conviene advertir que no pueden considerarse como auténticas comedias áureas las refundiciones que de varias de ellas hicieron algunos escritores." [But Golden Age theatre as a whole knows no better luck than Calderón's, and one should notice that recasts of several of his plays carried out by some writers cannot be considered authentic Golden Age plays] (20; original emphasis). Needless to say, I do not entirely share Andioc's view. The very existence of the *refundición*, even when intended to "correct" so-called seventeenth-century excesses, highlights the *comedia*'s presence and the fact that it so preoccupied the critics, moralists, playwrights, and impresarios.

3. Ballew, "Life and Works," 102, who notes that *El alcalde de Zalamea* by Solís was performed in 1810. I have not been able to locate a copy of the manuscript. Stoudemire, "Dionisio Solís's *Refundiciones*," 306 –7, notes some twenty performances of the recast in the period from 1810 to 1820; he attributes these more to the personality of the actor Isidoro Máiquez than to the refundición itself. Stoudemire, though, makes no claim to having read or even seen Solís's version. See also the *refundición* by Pedro Carreño, *Pedro Crespo, o El alcalde de Zalamea* (Habana: Manuel Soler, 1856), located in the Harvard University library.

Caldera comments on *comedia* title changes in the *refundición* process: "Se trata de un procedimiento que sólo tenía lugar en casos contados: el ejemplo más típico nos lo ofrece *El alcalde de Zalamea*, que ya a partir del siglo XVIII se representaba con el título de *El garrote más bien dado*, mientras que la denominación primitiva pasaba a subtítulo. Era ésta una obra destinada a afectar profundamente al público más popular y el nuevo título, mucho más emotivo, respondía perfectamente a la misma exigencia" ("Calderón desfigurado," 62). Caldera is, of course, correct in his reasoning, but fails to note que López de Ayala maintained Calderón's original title.

4. Sloman's *The Dramatic Art of Calderón* remains the seminal study on Calderón's practice of recasting earlier *comedias*.

5. For an overview of the field the reader may consult Martin Franzbach's *El teatro de Calderón en Europa*, translated by José Rodríguez de Rivera (Madrid: Fundación Universitaria Española, 1982); Andioc, *Teatro y sociedad*; and Henry Sullivan's definitive *Calderón in Germany and the Low Lands* (Cambridge: Cambridge University Press, 1981). See also González Echevarría, *Calderón y la crítica*, 2 vols. (Madrid: Gredos, 1976); Inmaculada Urzainqui, *De nuevo sobre Calderón la crítica española del siglo XVII* (Anejos del Boces XVIII–2. Oviedo: Universidad de Oviedo, Cátedra Feijóo, 1984); and Caldera, "Calderón desfigurado."

6. Franzbach, *Teatro*, 7.

7. Ibid., 8. For Calderón's influence in Italy, see the fundamental and groundbreaking work by Nancy D'Antuono, "Spanish Golden Age Comedy and the Italian Traveling Players: A Debt Repaid," *Cuadernos de Teatro Clásico*. As noted in chap-

ter 1, the bibliography regarding studies of specific *refundiciones* is indeed limited. See Caldera,"Calderón desfigurado," and Javier Vellón Lahoz, "El proceso de refundición como práctica ideológica: *La dama duende* de Juan José Fernández Guerra," *Cuadernos de Teatro Clásico* 5 (1990): 99–109.

8. Edward Coughlin, *Adelardo López de Ayala* (Boston: G. K. Hall, 1977), 16, points out that Böhl de Faber was a friend of López de Ayala and a coeditorial board member of the political and satirical journal *Padre Cobos*.

9. Couglin, *López de Ayalà*, 30, recalls that, upon López de Ayala's 30 December 1879 death, García Gutiérrez, one of the great dramatists of nineteenth-century Spain, paid homage to the late writer at the Teatro Español, and that the unveiling ceremony for Calderón's statue in the Plaza de Santa Ana coincided with the memorial gathering for López de Ayala. So warmly received was this speech that two years later it was read posthumously by Pedro Antonio de Alarcón at a ceremony commemorating the bicentennary of Calderón's death. See also ibid., 24, and *Obras completas de Don Adelardo López de Ayala*, ed. José María Castro y Calvo, Biblioteca de Autores Españoles, vol. 180, 71 (Madrid: Atlas, 1965).

10. See Conrado Solsona, *Ayala: Estudio político* (Madrid: Hijos de J. A. García, 1891); Luis de Oteyza, *López de Ayala o el figurón político-literario*, Vidas Españolas e Hispanoamericanas del siglo XX, no. 25 (Madrid: Espasa-Calpe, 1932); Mabel M. Harlan, "D. Adelardo López de Ayala, ¿Figura o Figurón?" *Hispania* 18 (1935): 413–36; Castro y Calvo, ed., *Obras completas*, 180: 9-133; and Coughlin, *López de Ayala* for López de Ayala's biography and comments on his *refundición* of Calderón; other articles deal primarily with Ayala's *Consuelo* and touch only in passing on *El alcalde de Zalamea*. In his long study in the *BAE*, Castro y Calvo mentions the *refundición* only briefly within a section dedicated to López de Ayala's dramaturgy (111–133). For generalized views see Ruiz Ramón, *Historia*, 407–10, and Rubio Jiménez, "El teatro en el siglo XIX (II) (1845–1900), in *Historia del teatro en España*, ed. José María Díez Borque, 2: 649 et passim (Madrid: Taurus, 1988). Alborg, *Historia*, 652, mentions his name only once.

11. Oteyza, *López de Ayala*, 55, does contribute to the anecdotal biography of López de Ayala. He reproduces a note written to the playwright and placed within a bouquet of flowers thrown to his feet after a performance of perhaps his most popular play, *El tanto por ciento*:

> Quien estas flores te arroja
> el alma entera te da;
> ¡no serán dignas quizá
> de que Ayala las recoja!
> Ninguno a tu ingenio iguala,
> que se eleva más que el sol.
> ¡Salva el Teatro español,
> y Dios te bendiga, Ayala!

[He who throws you these flowers gives you his entire soul; they may not be worthy for Ayala to gather them! No one equals your brilliance, which rises higher than the sun. Save the Spanish theatre, and God bless you, Ayala!]

12. Mabel M. Harlan,"The Date of *El tejado de vidrio*, with a Bio-bibliographical Note on D. Adelardo López de Ayala," *Hispanic Review* 6 (1938): 236–49; for Harlan's other article as well as bibliographic data on Castro y Calvo and Coughlin, see above, n. 10.

13. Ayala's first four plays are *Un hombre de estado* (1851), *Los dos Guzmanes* (1851), *Castigo y perdón* (1851), and *Rioja* (1854), and have been published in *BAE*, vols. 180–82.

14. See Coughlin (126–31).

15. Donald Shaw, *The Nineteenth Century* (London: Ernest Benn; New York: Barnes and Noble, 1972), 4 (part of *A Literary History of Spain*, general editor R. O. Jones).

16. The *refundición*, published originally in 1864, was again issued in 1881, clearly to coincide with the celebration of Calderón's death. According to Harlan, "The Date...," 248 n. 58, "[t]his *refundición* is the one used when this classic is staged for modern audiences."

17. Adelardo López de Ayala, "Discurso leído ante la Real Academia Española por D. Adelardo López de Ayala en su recepción pública," in *Obras completas de Don Adelardo López de Ayala*, ed. José María Castro y Calvo, *Biblioteca de Autores Españoles*, vol. 182, 374 (Madrid: Atlas, 1965). All subsequent page citations to the "Discurso" will be given in the text.

18. One can read into these lines the influence that Alberto Lista had on López de Ayala, particularly in light of the former's definition of Spanish Romanticism, "entendiendo por 'romántico' lo perteneciente a la literatura cristiana y monárquica, propia de nuestra civilización actual.... La comedia española del siglo XVII pertenece, pues, al género romántico, como el drama de Shakespeare" [understanding as "Romantic" all that pertains to monarchic and Christian literature, belonging to our present civilization.... The Spanish theatre of the seventeenth century belongs, then, to the Romantic genre, like Shakespeare's drama] (Quoted in Donald Schurlknight, "Alberto Lista: 'De la supuesta misíon de los poetas,'" *Dieciocho* 10 [1987]: 169).

19. That these remarks are designed to warn about dangers López de Ayala sees in a republic is clear, but neither literary critics nor biographers of López de Ayala note the coincidence of these statements with the anarchist and socialist movement within Spain in the 1860s and 1870s. For a detailed study, see Raymond Carr, *Spain 1808-1975*, 2d ed. (Oxford: Clarendon Press, 1982), 326–27, 440–41 et passim.

20. Coughlin, *López de Ayala*, 19 et passim.

21. Geography ties him to Pedro Crespo as well; they both share Extremadura as home, and the kindred spirit infuses the writer with admiration for his subject.

22. Adelardo López de Ayala, *El alcalde de Zalamea*, 2d ed. (Madrid: José

Rodríguez, 1881), 1.1. All subsequent references to the act and scene numbers are taken from this edition and will be given in the text.

23. Twenty-five verses of description recast from Calderón are all that remain of Isabel's tireless and tiresome suitor. Crespo's exclamation as he enters in 1.2 ("¡Que nunca / entre y salga yo en mi calle / que no vea este hidalgote / pasearse en ella muy grave!" [Whenever I come in or out / I see that lanky layabout / Sighing and trudging up and down / Like an old boar without a sow]), taken verbatim from Calderón's play, is the final reference to the would-be nobleman and husband. For this translation, see following note.

24. Pedro Calderón de la Barca, *El alcalde de Zalamea*, ed. Angel Valbuena Briones, 5th ed. (Madrid: Cátedra, 1982), 613–18; 628. Subsequent references to Calderón's play refer to verse numbers (Valbuena Briones does not make scene divisions) and are included in the text. Translations of Calderón's text are from Adrian Mitchell's adaptation (*The Mayor of Zalamea or The Best Garrotting Ever Done* [Edinburgh: Salamander Press, 1981]) and refer to the page numbers. Here, pp. 22–23. All subsequent references will be cited in the text immediately after the verse numbers of Calderón's text. Note that Mitchell's text is an adaptation, and often does not follow Calderón literally. Occasional discrepancies may arise between translation of the Golden Age text and that of López de Ayala's recast; important differences will be treated in the notes.

25. López de Ayala also adds to this scene Rebolledo's self-characterization:

> *Rebolledo.* (*Ap. a la Chispa.*) (Fui el hurón
> que saca los gazapillos
> del vivar.) (1.11)

The weasel who robs the rabbit warren is an image of the hunt logically sustainable in the light of the Sergeant's previous search through the residence for the two cousins.

26. For the legalistic aspect of "patrimonio del alma" see Peter N. Dunn, "Patrimonio del alma," *Bulletin of Hispanic Studies* 41 (1964): 78–85. Though Dian Fox, " 'Quien tiene al padre alcalde . . . ': The Conflict of Images in Calderón's *El alcalde de Zalamea*," *Revista Canadiense de Estudios Hispánicos* 6 (1982): 262–68, argues convincingly that Pedro Crespo is a duplicitous man who manipulates justice to attain personal vengeance, her point would not have been remotely possible for López de Ayala to consider. The recaster's identification with Pedro Crespo allows only for a positive view of the play's protagonist.

27. In this speech, as in other long Calderonian speeches, López de Ayala reduces their length by omitting summary verses. Compare how the two writers render one part of the Capitán's *relación* beginning "En un día." First, the original:

> En un día tiene el mar
> tranquilidad y tormenta;

> en un día nace un hombre
> y muere: luego pudiera
> en un día ver mi amor
> sombra y luz, como planeta;
> pena y dicha, como imperio;
> gente y brutos, como selva;
> paz e inquietud, como mar;
> triunfo y ruina, como guerra;
> vida y muerte, como dueño
> de sentidos y potencias.

[All in one day the sun whirls up, / Lights the world, drops into the dark. / All in one day, kingdoms change hands, / Palaces are crushed into dust. / All in one day a city's lost / And gloating victors flood its streets. / All in one day the ocean may / Be level and tumultuous. / All in one day, a man is born. / All in one day, a man must die. / And so, in one day, my love / May view the darkness and the light / As planets do. All in one day, / My love may rise, my love may fall, / Like an empire. All in one day, / My love may harbour animals, / Like a wood people wander through. Tame and angry—like the ocean. / Glorious, ruinous—like the war. / Love's mastered my passions and mind, / My life and death are in its hand.] (975–86; 39)

The recaster has pared down this passage considerably:

> [E]n un día tiene el mar
> calma y borrasca deshecha;
> en un día nace un hombre
> y muere. ¿Por qué no intenta
> amor lo mismo, si es dueño
> de sentidos y potencias?

[All in one day the sea is calm and the storm undone; all in one day a man is born and dies. Why doesn't love do the same if it is master of passions and mind?] (2.1)

28. Even though López de Ayala took an active part in the revolution that forced the abdication of Queen Isabel II (he authored the manifesto urging the rebels to rise up [Coughlin, *López de Ayala*, 22]), he was still a monarchist, and favored not the republic but the crowning of the Infanta Luisa Fernanda and her husband, the Duke of Montpensier. As Harlan explains in "López de Ayala," 417, Ayala "wanted a more worthy occupant on the throne, not a change in the form of government." Also see Carr, *Spain*, 290–319, on the revolution, its build-up and aftermath.

The effect that López de Ayala's *El alcalde de Zalamea* had on its public with regard to the revolution is summarized in Solsona, *Ayala*, 46–47. See the discussion below.

29. Carr, *Spain*, 264.

30. Her attitude brings to mind Pedro Crespo's refusal to purchase a patent of

nobility, as his children had urged him to do, to avoid billeting the army personnel in his house; he believes that opening his home is a patriotic duty shirked only by those who hold themselves above the common citizenry and mundane obligations.

31. In Calisto Boldún y Conde's recast, *A secreto agravio, disimulada venganza*, Don Lope learns of his wife's infidelity in a letter he reads while a storm rages; the light is provided by lightning. For a study of this specific *refundición* see my "Rewriting the *Comedia*."

32. 2ª Serie, Tomo 2°, 1842. In the ensuing references to theatre journals and newspapers, all title and page numbers will be given in the text.

33. See Antonio de Miguel's prologue to Fernández Guerra's 1829 recast of *La dama duende*. Needless to say, much had changed on the intellectual scene between 1829 and 1842. Again, see Vellón Lahoz, "Proceso."

34. Because it it impossible to determine any changes made to the Calderonian text for the performance under consideration, I cannot say whether the playtext had removed the stronger epithets or the reviewer himself softened those shouted by both Don Lope and Pedro Crespo; "Voto a Dios" has been changed here to "Vive Dios," a practice, as we have seen, that López de Ayala adhered to in recasting the play.

35. Carr, *Spain*, 209, provides an interesting insight into how many Spaniards saw themselves at this time:

> Literate Spaniards saw their own country through the eyes of those French Romantic travellers who sought in Spain the contrasts provided by a civilization "untouched by Europe." . . . Spaniards could either glory in their uniqueness and regional diversities or see in this local colour the symbol of Spain's *atraso*—her time-lag behind Europe. There was, therefore, both an aping of foreign fashion to close the cultural gap and a concern to record the lineaments of traditional Spain before it should succumb to Europeanization.

36. The negative review of the 1865 performance at the Teatro de la Zarzuela suggests that the Madrid production was plagued with bad acting from the start. In a letter to Teodora Lamadrid, López de Ayala tells of a request to travel to Barcelona to help with the production: "Olona me há escrito diciéndome que vaya á esa á dirijir el *Alcalde*. Yo en esto, más bien que una súplica, he visto una prueba de cariño que ha querido darme: porque ya puede suponer que la obra no tiene bastante importancia para justificar mi viaje, y que en la compañía de la Zarzuela es más necesaria mi dirección que en la de Barcelona." [Olona has written to tell me to go there to direct the *Mayor*. I've seen in this, rather than a request, a proof of affection that he has wanted to show me: because he can now suppose that the work does not have enough importance to justify my trip, and that my direction is more necessary with the Zarzuela company than with the Barcelona's]. See A. Pérez Calamarte, ed, "Epístolario inédito," *Revue Hispanique* 27 (1912): 576.

The reviews noted in the body of this study do not reflect all announced performances or all the printed reviews. These dates and the bibliographic information about the reviews can be found in the Appendix, along with the complete texts of the excerpted reviews.

37. I have not commented on the passage, but include it here for the reader's information. Although López de Ayala's *El alcalde de Zalamea* is a political artifact, it is not exempt from humor. For the most part, the characters of Rebolledo and La Chispa are toned down considerably—their off-color jokes must have been seen as indecorous—but the recaster has introduced one comic element of his own making. As the Sargento and Rebolledo search for transportation to leave Zalamea, news of the election of a new mayor reaches them; Chispa responds with a metatheatrical play on words: "Con todo, líbreme el cielo / del estreno de un alcalde" [All in all, Heaven free me from a mayor's first day in office] (3.3). One can imagine the reaction this line may have provoked from the play's audience, particularly on opening night. Rebolledo, not to be outdone, responds to the Capitán's question about the impossiblity of finding a horse with which to make an exit from town:

> Nada pudimos lograr.
> Yo le dije a una mujer
> en su casa, ¿no ha de haber
> burros en este lugar?
> Yo que sí y ella que no,
> estábamos disputando,
> cuando un burro rebuznando
> la casa entera atronó.
> "Escucha, dije, y sosten
> que aquí no hay burro escondido."
> Y ella dijo: "es mi marido,
> que los imita muy bien."

[We couldn't get anything. I asked a woman in her house, aren't there any asses in this town? I said yes, she said no, we were arguing, when an ass's bray shook the whole house. "Listen," I said, "and tell me that there is no ass hidden here." And she said: "It's only my husband who imitates them well."] (3.3)

The joke is worthy of Calderón in his lighter moments; nevertheless, it comes across as a gratuitous bit of humor inconsistent with the character as López de Ayala has developed him throughout the play.

38. The cast includes Teodora Lamadrid (López de Ayala's lover to whom he directed the passionate letters edited by Pérez Calamarte, op. cit.), Cándida Dardalla, Josefa Hijosa, Julián Romea, José Valero, Pizarroso, Mariano Fernández, Zamora, and Morales.

39. It is surely more than coincidental that the women involved with the *refundidor*—Teodora Lamadrid and Elisa Mendoza Tenorio—both portrayed Isabel.

40. On the same bill with *El alcalde de Zalamea* is *Ellas y ellos*, a recast by Emilio Alvarez of Moreto's *Yo por vos y vos por otro*, a play that had been recast previously

in 1826 by José Fernández Guerra, with the title *Ir contra el viento*, and again in 1849 by Vicente de Lalama, who used the original title (Schinasi, "Relación," n.p.) (I would like to thank Michael Schinasi for his generosity in providing me with a typescript of the "Relación.") The reviewer considers Alvarez's version "un discretísimo arreglo" [a most circumspect arrangement] and "reducida a un solo acto con acierto y delicadeza en los *engastes*" [reduced to just one act with success and tact in the setting] (3; original emphasis).

41. The following week two other recast *comedias* were to be performed: *Sancho Ortiz de las Roelas* (most likely Hartzenbusch's version) and *García del Castañar* (possibly Solís's); and since 1 November was fast approaching, Zorrilla's *Don Juan Tenorio* was announced.

42. As if further testimony were needed, Rafael Calvo, quoted in this review, writes from Berlin of Calderón's wide acceptance: "Empezad con las obras del repertorio antiguo. En Alemania también se rinde fervoroso culto a Calderón. Los profes de las Universidades, los directores de los teatros, los artistas, los literatos más insignes comentan y estudian las producciones del gran autor de *El alcalde de Zalamea*. Vosotros representaréis a Calderón mientras yo vivo en una atmósfera calderoniana. Dejadme respirar unos días más ese ambiente" [Begin with the works of the old repertoire. Germany, too, renders ferverous homage to Calderón. The university professors, theatre directors, artists, the most noteworthy literary figures comment on and study the productions of the great author of *The Mayor of Zalamea*. You perform Calderón while I live in a Calderonian atmosphere. Let me breathe this ambience for a few days more] (2).

43. Other cast members who received briefer mention are Donato Jiménez, Ricardo Calvo (brother of Rafael Calvo, the eminent actor who had died the year before [see *Homenaje*], Mariano Fernández ("felicísimo en la interpretación de su papel de Rebolledo" [very successful in his interpretation of Rebolledo] [4]), and "las señoras Guillén y Sánchez," whose roles are not mentioned but whose performances must have been marginal: "Hicieron lo que pudieron por no descomponer el cuadro" [They did what they could so as not to detract from the whole] (4).

While the scope of the present study does not take in the twentieth century (where material abounds for many diverse assessments of the *comedia*), one rather severe critic—more of López de Ayala than of his *El alcalde de Zalamea*—is worthy of mention if only to discount him: Luis de Oteyza's 1932 "biography" of Adelardo López de Ayala. Given the author's republican, antimonarchic political stance, his antipathy toward both his subject and the *comedia* should not surprise us. Oteyza first finds fault with translators, and he does so only to further his cause to continue to debunk the literary career of López de Ayala: "Se ha llamado traidores a los traductores—*tradutori traditori*—, y no sé qué cosa terrible habrá de llamarse a los arregladores, pues más que el delito espantoso de traición cometen" [Translators have been called traitors—*tradutori traditori*—, and I don't know what awful thing arrangers will be called, because they commit much more than the frightful crime of treason] (58). More particularly, Oteyza believes that classic works either should be presented exactly as written or not performed at all, "que es lo más sencillo" [which is the easiest thing to do] (58). The biographer assumes a posture intended to keep his criticism of the *comedia* in line with his dislike for Ayala instead of offering a balanced judgment of the *refundición*, the task of which is a "sacrílega labor" [sacrilegious work] (58).

44. For studies on twentieth-century adaptations of the *comedia* see Catherine Larson, "The Uniqueness of Tirso in Contemporary Stagings: Modern Audiences Meet the Master," in *Tirso de Molina: His Originality Then and Now*, ed. Henry W. Sullivan (in press); and *Visualizing Tirso: "El burlador de Sevilla," "Marta la piadosa," and Modern Audiences* (Lubbock, Tex.: Visual Study Series, Association for Hispanic Classical Theater, 1990. Videotape); Dawn Smith, "La comedia a fines del siglo XX: en busca de nuevas interpretaciones escénicas," in *El mundo del teatro español en su Siglo de Oro: Ensayos dedicados a John E. Varey*, ed. José Ruano de la Haza (Ottawa: Dovehouse Editions Canada, 1989), 395–408; Susan Fischer, "*El alcalde de Zalamea o el garrote bien dado* or How to Stage a Play," *Gestos* 7, no. 12 (1991); and my "Peter Brook..."

Chapter 5. Future Directions

1. Miller, *Subsequent*, 49.

2. Regarding notices about the performances, see *Veinticuatro diarios* 2: 290 and 4: 222, 225. There appears, too, a reference to the translation by Hugelmann, which to date I have not seen.

3. Richard A. Cardwell, "*Don Alvaro* or the Force of Cosmic Justice," *Studies in Romanticism* 12 (1973): 576.

4. The listing of these probable sources has become a commonplace in the criticism about *Desengaño*, and I remit the interested reader to Alborg, *Historia*, 4: 508–14, or to Ricardo Navas Ruiz, *Imágenes liberales: Rivas-Larra-Galdós* (Salamanca: Almar, 1979).

5. Richard B. O'Connell, "Rivas's *El desengaño en un sueño* and Grillparzer's *Der Traum ein Leben*: A Problem in Assessment of Influence," *Philological Quarterly* 40 (1961): 574–75. For Grillparzer's relationship with and love for the Spanish *comedia* and theatre in general, see Sullivan, *Calderón in the Low Lands*, 276ff.

6. Manuel Cañete, *Escritores españoles e hispano-americanos* (Madrid: M. Tello, 1884), 71.

7. Leopoldo Augusto de Cueto, "Discurso necrológico literario en elogio del Duque de Rivas," *Boletín de la Real Academia Española* 2 (1870): 565. Augusto de Cueto continues: "Esta obra . . . respira . . . cierto espíritu de generalidad y de grandeza, que pertenece a todos los tiempos y a todas las naciones. *El desengaño en un sueño*, con ser su entonación calderoniana, no está lejos de la inspiración septentrional, y no desdeciría, por cierto, entre las mejores producciones de Goethe y de

Lord Byron" [This work breathes a certain spirit of breadth and grandeur that belongs to all time and to all nations. *Disillusionment in a dream*, with its Calderonian tone, still exhibits its northern inspiration, and certainly would not be unworthy among the best of Goethe's and Lord Byron's productions] (565).

8. Francisco Blanco García, *La literatura española en el siglo XIX*., 2d ed., (Madrid: Sáenz de Jubera Hermanos, 1899), 1:151–52.

9. Juan Valera, *Obras completas*, ed. Luis Araujo Costa (Madrid: Aguilar, 1949), 2: 764.

10. Enrique Piñeyro, *El romanticismo en España* (reprint, New York: G. E. Stechert, 1936), 64.

11. Gabriel Boussagol, "Angel de Saavedra, duc de Rivas. Essai de bibliographie critique," *Bulletin Hispanique* 29 (1927): 5–98; E. A. Peers, "Angel de Saavedra: Duque de Rivas," *Revue Hispanique* 58 (1923): 538–58; Richard B. O'Connell, "Rivas's *El desengaño*"; Rupert Allen, "An Archetypal Analysis of Rivas's *El desengaño en un sueño*," *Bulletin of Hispanic Studies* 45 (1968): 201–15; Cardwell, "*Don Alvaro*," 575–76. Seconding Cardwell's view is Vicente Llorens (*El romanticismo español* [Madrid: Castalia, 1979], 165): "[El] desengaño no corresponde a la desilusión romántica, que en vez de acatar cuerdamente el orden establecido, acaba rebelándose con tal desesperación que puede llegar a la destrucción del propio rebelde, si es que no lo hunde para siempre en dolorosa melancolía. Con *El desengaño en un sueño* Rivas, no menos fiel que Calderón a la moral que le imponía su sentido católico de la vida, se alejaba del romanticismo" [The disillusionment does not correspond to Romantic disillusion, that instead of prudently respecting established order, ends up rebelling with a desperation that can lead to the destruction of the rebel himself, if the disillusionment doesn't sink him forever in painful melancholy. With *Disillusionment in a dream* Rivas, no less faithful than Calderón to the morality imposed by their Catholic sense of life, distanced himself from Romanticism] (165).

12. Douglas Hilt, "Grillparzer and Rivas: The Dreamer Awakened," in *From Pen to Performance: Drama as Conceived and Performed*, ed. Karelisa Hartigan, vol. 3, 61 (Lanham, Md.: University Press of America, 1983); Gabriel Lovett, *The Duke of Rivas* (Boston: Twayne, 1977); Susan Polansky, "Textual Coherence in the Duke of Rivas' *El desengaño en un sueño*: The Dramaturgy of Destiny," *Modern Language Studies* 18, no. 3 (1988): 13.

13. Angel de Saavedra, Duque de Rivas, *Don Alvaro, o la fuerza del sino: El desengaño en un sueño*, ed. José García Templado (Barcelona: Plaza y Janés, 1984), 215. Subsequent citations from this edition will be cited in the text and will refer to page number.

14. Juan Valera, *Obras completas*, 2: 765.

15. Jacques Derrida, "Plato's Pharmacy," in *Dissemination*, trans. Barbara Johnson (Chicago: University of Chicago Press, 1981), 63–171.

16. James Cowan, "The *Pharmakos* Figure in Modern American Stories of Physicians and Patients," *Literature and Medicine* 6 (1987): 94–109.

17. Frederick de Armas, "Balthasar's Doom: Letters that Heal/Kill in

Claramonte's *El secreto en la mujer*," in *The Golden Age Comedia: Text, Theory and Performance*, ed. Charles Ganelin and Howard Mancing (West Lafayette, Ind.: Purdue University Press, forthcoming). See Robert L. Fiore, "Alarcón's *El dueño de las estrellas:* Hero and Pharmakos," *Hispanic Review*, 61.2 (1993): 185–99. I wish to thank Robert Fiore for allowing me to read the typescript of his excellent essay.

18. Derrida, "Plato's Pharmacy," 70.
19. Allen, "Archetypal," 202.
20. Ibid., 211–12.
21. Alborg (*Historia*, 3: 512–13) rejects Allen's thesis out of hand, while Lovett, though accepting it on the whole, makes suggestions to strengthen it.
22. Allen, "Archetypal," 205.
23. García Templado questions the Duke of Rivas's use of meter in this passage:
    "Los excesos polimétricos rompen el ritmo constantemente. Todo el parlamento de la Voz del Genio del Mal destruye la estructura rítmica al variar la posición de los axis fundamentales dentro de la misma estrofa" [The polymetric excesses constantly break the rhythm. The entire speech of the voice of the Genie of Evil destroys the rhythmic structure by varying the position of the fundamental axes within the same strophe] (224). If the rest of the play were not so carefully crafted metrically, I would agree with the editor. However, the Duke of Rivas so carefully mixes strophe forms throughout his play that the violent disruptions in rhythm here add a necessarily strident and jarring tone to the play. A spectator would certainly notice the difference and would probably react with appropriate uncomfortableness.
24. Allen, "Archetypal," 206.
25. Derrida, "Plato's Pharmacy," 72–73.
26. Cardwell, "*Don Alvaro*," 567 n. 17; 575–76.
27. The committee included Luis Pastor, Juan Nicasio Gallego, Eugenio Moreno, José Espronceda, Ventura de la Vega, Antonio Gil y Zárate, Patricio de la Escosura, Julián Romea, and Carlos Latorre.
28. To describe the performance, he employs such phrases as "memorable función" [memorable performance], "trajes magníficos" [magnificent costumes], "decoraciones admirables" [admirable sets], "comparsas pintorescas y numerosas" [many and picturesque extras], and "talento y voluntad sin tasa en los artistas dramáticos" [limitless talent and desire on the part of the actors] (375).
29. The success obtained from opening a play with back-to-back sonnets depends naturally on how they are represented. The nonspeaking actress could perhaps mock the speaker during her recitation (switching roles for the second sonnet) in an effort to dramatize the irony of employing a "weighty" strophe form in a moment of *comedia* self-mockery.
30. The staging of this scene is proof of Zermeño's genius in bringing to life the *comedia*'s theoretical and rhetorical conventions. For another example, and for a general overview of the performance, see Allen 252–53.
31. Zermeño, in a colloquium following the performance, called the *relación* in act 2 a "pegote" and a "rollo espantoso de versos."

32. A similar reaction occurred in Spain during a 1971 *zarzuela* performance when dancers outfitted as contemporary Spanish soldiers marched onto the stage, eliciting from the audience a standing ovation.

33. I am indebted to John J. Allen for this suggestion, made in response to a conference reading of an early draft.

34. I thank Catherine Larson for providing me with a typescript of her essay "The Uniqueness of Tirso in Contemporary Stagings: Modern Audiences Meet the Master." I would also like to draw attention to her videotape analysis, sponsored by the Association for Hispanic Classical Theatre (see Bibliography).

35. A staging need not be revolutionary, as a 1991 performance, at El Chamizal, by Madrid's Compañía Francisco Portes of Moreto's *El lindo Don Diego* so forcefully showed. The costumes were typical of the later Golden Age, props were kept to a minimum, and the text was followed faithfully. Quality marked the production from beginning to end. Less memorable but still worthwhile was Calderón's *El galán fantasma*, performed by the Pequeño Teatro de Madrid under the direction of Antonio Guirau. The text for the performance at the 1985 Golden Age Drama Festival (again, at El Chamizal) had been compiled by the late director José Luis Alonso out of many Calderonian texts. The resulting "pastiche" (for want of a better description) entertained the audience, some *comedia* conventions were subverted in an effort at renovation, and the acting was more than acceptable, yet the production did not "work." For some of the problems experienced in characterization, see my videotape in the Video Study Series.

Conclusion

1. Reckford, *Aristophanes'*, 149.

2. W. Jackson Bate, *The Burden of the Past and the English Poet* (Cambridge: Harvard University Press, Belknap Press, 1970; rpt., New York: Norton, 1972), 12.

3. See Michael Schinasi, "History and Ideology."

4. Gadamer, *Relevance*, 62–63.

5. Gadamer, *Truth*, 262–63.

6. Peter Brook, *The Empty Space* (New York: Atheneum, 1978), 13.

7. *El galán fantasma*, adapt. by José Luis Alonso (Madrid: MK, 1984).

8. Peter Brook, *The Shifting Point: Theatre, Film, Opera, 1946–1987* (New York: Harper and Row, 1987), xiii.

9. Dawn Smith,"La comedia a fines del siglo XX," 404.

10. Henry Sullivan,"Calderón's Appeal to European Audiences in the Enlightenment and Romantic Eras: 1738–1838," *Ottawa Hispanist* 5 (1981), 52.

11. At present David Gies is preparing a history of Spanish theatre in the nineteenth century. While I have not seen this work-in-progress, it undoubtedly will provide additional important information for studying the *refundición*. Even so, Gies's books on Agustín Durán and Juan de Grimaldi, as well as his other articles on theatre

(see Bibliography), do offer an important starting point and theatrical-cultural orientation indispensable for any study on Spanish theatre of the time. Michael Schinasi, too, continues to bring to light fundamental documentation that enhances our knowledge of the nineteenth-century Spanish stage.

Bibliography

Adams, Nicholson B. "Hartzenbusch's *Sancho Ortiz de las Roelas*." *Studies in Philology* 28 (1931): 851–56.

———. "*Siglo de Oro* Plays in Madrid, 1820 –1850." *Hispanic Review* 7 (1939): 342–57.

Aguilar Piñal, Francisco. *Cándido María Trigueros: Hombre ilustrado*. Madrid: CSIC, 1989.

———. *Cartelera prerromántica sevillana, años 1830–36. Cuadernos Bibliográficos*, no. 22. Madrid: CSIC, 1968.

———. "Las refundiciones en el siglo XVIII." *Cuadernos de Teatro Clásico* 5 (1990): 33– 41.

Alborg, Juan Luis. *Historia de la literatura española*. Vol. 4, *El romanticismo*. Madrid: Gredos, 1982.

Allen, John J. "Chamizal '86." *Bulletin of the Comediantes* 38 (1986): 249–54.

Allen, Rupert C. "An Archetypal Analysis of Rivas's *El desengaño en un sueño*." *Bulletin of Hispanic Studies* 45 (1968): 201–15.

Andioc, René. *Sur la querelle du théâtre au temps de Leandro Fernández de Moratín*. Tarbes-Burdeos: Saint-Joseph, 1970.

———. *Teatro y sociedad en el Madrid del siglo XVIII*. 2d ed. Madrid: Castalia, 1987.

Augusto de Cueto, Leopoldo. "Discurso necrológico literario en elogio del Duque de Rivas." *Boletín de la Real Academia Española* 2 (1870): 498– 601.

———. "Carta al señor Conde de Morphy." *La Ilustración Española y Americana*, 15 December 1875, 371–75.

"Aviso al público." "Discurso LXXIX." *El Censor*. (1786): 202–17.

Ballew, Hal Lackey. "The Life and Works of Dionisio Solís." Ph. D. diss., University of North Carolina—Chapel Hill, 1957.

Bate, W. Jackson. *The Burden of the Past and the English Poet*. Cambridge: Harvard University Press, Belknap Press, 1970. Reprinted 1972..

Blanco García, Francisco. *La literatura española en el siglo XIX*. Vol. 1. 2d ed. Madrid: Sáenz de Jubera Hermanos, 1899.

Bloom, Harold. *The Anxiety of Influence*. New York: Oxford University Press, 1973.

Boldún y Conde, Calixto. *A secreto agravio, disimulada venganza*. Madrid: José Rodríguez, 1867.

———. *Marta la piadosa*. Madrid: José Rodríguez, 1866.
Boussagol, Gabriel. "Angel de Saavedra, duc de Rivas. Essai de bibliographie critique." *Bulletin Hispanique* 29 (1927): 5–98.
Brook, Peter. *The Empty Space*. New York: Atheneum, 1978.
———. *The Shifting Point: Theatre, Film and Opera 1946–1987*. New York: Harper and Row, 1987.
Burke, James F. "*La estrella de Sevilla* and Saturnine Melancholy." *Bulletin of Hispanic Studies* 51 (1974): 137–56.
Bushee, Alice Huntington. *Three Centuries of Tirso de Molina*. Philadelphia: University of Pennsylvania Press; London: Humphrey Milford, Oxford University Press, 1939.
Caldera, Ermanno. "Bretón o la negación del modelo." *Cuadernos de Teatro Clásico* 5 (1990): 141–53.
———. "Calderón desfigurado (Sobre las representaciones calderonianas en la época prerromántica)." *Anales de Literatura Española* 2 (1983): 57–81.
———. *Il dramma romantico in Spagna*. Pisa: Università di Pisa, 1974.
Calderón de la Barca, Pedro. *A secreto agravio, secreta venganza*. Madrid: Austral, 1934.
———. *El alcalde de Zalamea*. Edited by Angel Valbuena Briones. 6th ed. Madrid: Cátedra, 1984.
———. *El alcalde de Zalamea*. Adapted by Adrian Mitchell based on a literal translation by Gwenda Pandolfi. Edinburgh: Salamander Press, 1981.
———. *El galán fantasma*. Adaptation by José Luis Alonso. Madrid: MK, 1984.
———. *La vida es sueño*. Edited by Ciríaco Morón Arroyo. 12th ed. Madrid: Cátedra, 1985.
Cañete, Manuel. *Escritores españoles e hispano-americanos*. Madrid: M. Tello, 1884.
Cardwell, Richard A. "*Don Alvaro* or the Force of Cosmic Justice." *Studies in Romanticism* 12 (1973): 559–79.
Carnero, Guillermo. "El teatro de Calderón como arma ideológica en el origen gaditano del Romanticismo español." *Cuadernos de Teatro Clásico* 5 (1990): 125–39.
Carr, Raymond. *Spain 1808–1975*. 2d ed. Oxford: Clarendon, 1982.
Carreño, Pedro. *Pedro Crespo, o El alcalde de Zalamea*. Habana: Manuel Soler, 1856.
Caso González, José Miguel. *Ilustración y neoclasicismo*. Vol. 4 of *Historia y crítica de la literatura española*. Edited by Francisco Rico. Barcelona: Editorial Crítica, 1983.
Checa Beltrán, José. "Los clásicos en la preceptiva dramática del siglo XVIII." *Cuadernos de Teatro Clásico* 5 (1990): 13–31.
Coe, Ada M. *Catálogo bibliográfico y crítico de las comedias anunciadas en los periódicos de Madrid desde 1661 hasta 1819*. Baltimore; Johns Hopkins University Press; and London: Humphrey Milford, 1935.
Cook, John A. *Neo-Classic Drama in Spain: Theory and Practice*. Dallas: Southern Methodist University Press, 1959.
Cossío, José María. "La 'secreta venganza' en Lope, Tirso y Calderón." *Fénix* 4 (27 August 1935): 503–15.
Coughlin, Edward. *Adelardo López de Ayala*. Boston: G. K. Hall, 1977.
Cowan, James. "The *Pharmakos* Figure in Modern American Stories of Physicians and Patients." *Literature and Medicine* 6 (1987): 94–109.

Crawford, J. P. Wickersham. "An Early Nineteenth-Century English Version of *La estrella de Sevilla*." In *Estudios eruditos in memoriam Adolfo Bonilla y San Martíns*. 2: 495–505. Madrid: Viuda e Hijos de Jaime Ratés, 1930.

Crespo, Angel. *El Duque de Rivas*. Madrid: Juca, 1985.

D'Antuono, Nancy L. *Boccaccio's Novelle in the Theater of Lope de Vega*. Madrid: Porrúa, 1983.

———. "La comedia en la Italia del Siglo XVII: *La comedia dell'arte*." *Cuadernos de Teatro Clásico* 8 (1993), in press.

de Armas, Frederick. "Balthasar's Doom: Letters that Heal/Kill in Claramonte's *El secreto en la mujer*." In *The Golden Age Comedia: Text, Theory and Performance*, edited by Charles Ganelin and Howard Mancing. West Lafayette, Ind.: Purdue University Press, in press.

———. "The Four Elemental Jewels in Calderón's *A secreto agravio, secreta venganza*." *Bulletin of Hispanic Studies* 64 (1987): 65–75.

———. *The Return of Astraea. An Astro-Imperial Myth in Calderón*. Lexington: University Press of Kentucky, 1986.

Defourneaux, Marcelin. "Molière et l'inquisition espagnole." *Bulletin Hispanique* 64 (1962): 30 – 42.

———. "Une Adaptation inédite du *Tartuffe*: *El gazmoño ou Juan de Buen Alma* de Cándido María Trigueros." *Bulletin Hispanique* 64 (1962): 43– 60.

de la Fuente Ballesteros, Ricardo. "La pervivencia de la comedia áurea en la zarzuela." *Cuadernos de Teatro Clásico* 5 (1990): 209 –17.

de la Revilla, Manuel. *Críticas*. Burgos: Timoteo Arnáiz, 1884.

Derrida, Jacques. *Dissemination*. Translated by Barbara Johnson. Chicago: University of Chicago Press, 1981.

Dowling, John. *Leandro Fernández de Moratín*. New York: Twayne, 1971.

Dragún, Osvaldo. *Historias para ser contadas*. Ottawa: Girol, 1982.

Dunn, Peter N. "Patrimonio del alma." *Bulletin of Hispanic Studies* 41 (1964): 78– 85.

Durán, Manuel, and Roberto González Echevarría, eds. *Calderón y la crítica: historia y antología*. 2 vols. Madrid: Gredos, 1976.

Eoff, Sherman. "The Sources of Calderón's *A secreto agravio, secreta venganza*." *Modern Philology* 28 (1930): 297–311.

Escobar, José. "El teatro del Siglo de Oro en la controversia ideológica entre españoles castizos y críticos: Larra frente a Durán." *Cuadernos de Teatro Clásico* 5 (1990): 155–70.

Fernández de Moratín, Leandro. *Comedias completas*. Edited by Emiliano M. Aguilera. Barcelona: Iberia, 1957.

———. *Teatro*. Edited by F. Ruiz Morcuende. Madrid: Espasa-Calpe, 1962.

———. *Teatro completo*. Edited by Angeles Cardona de Gibert and Enrique Rodríguez y Vilanova. Barcelona: Bruguera, 1967.

Fiore, Robert. "Alarcón's *El dueño de las estrellas*: Hero and Pharmakos." *Hispanic Review* 61.2 (1993): 185–99.

Fox, Dian. "'Quien tiene al padre alcalde . . . ': The Conflict of Images in Calderón's *El alcalde de Zalamea*." *Revista Canadiense de Estudios Hispánicos* 6 (1982): 262– 68.

Franzbach, Martin. *El teatro de Calderón en Europa*. Translated by José Rodríguez de Rivera. Madrid: Fundación Universitaria Española, 1982.

Frye, Northrop. *Anatomy of Criticism*. Princeton: Princeton University Press, 1957.

Fucilla, Joseph G. "*Menón*: The First Neoclassic 'Refundición' of a Golden Age Play." *Kentucky Romance Quarterly* 23 (1976): 365–75.

Funes, Enrique. *La prudencia en la mujer*. 2d ed. Santa Cruz de Tenerife: A. J. Benítez, 1889.

Gadamer, Hans-Georg. *The Relevance of the Beautiful and Other Essays*. Translated by Nicholas Walker and edited by Robert Bernasconi. Cambridge: Cambridge University Press, 1986.

———. *Truth and Method*. Translated and edited by Garret Barden and John Cumming. New York: Crossroad, 1986.

Ganelin, Charles. "The Art of Adaptation: Building the Hermeneutical Bridge." In *Prologue to Performance*, edited by Louise and Peter Fothergill-Payne, 36–53. Lewisburg, Pa.: Bucknell University Press, 1991.

———. "Breaking Tirso's Codes: '*Cifrar*' in *Palabras y plumas*." *South Central Review* 4 (1987): 1–9.

———. "Peter Brook: Performance Theory and the *Comedia*." *Bulletin of the Comediantes* 43 (1991): 101–8.

———. *Restaging the Comedia: The Case of Calderón de la Barca's "El galán fantasma."* Lubbock, Tex.: Visual Study Series, Association for Hispanic Classical Theater, 1990. Videotape.

———. "Rewriting Theatre: A Prolegomenon to a Study of the *Refundición*." *Hispania* 74 (1991): 240–49.

———. "Tirso de Molina's *Marta la piadosa*: Recasts and Reception." *Gestos* 5 (1990): 57–75.

Gann, Myra. "The Performative Status of Verbal Offenses in *A secreto agravio, secreta venganza*." In *Things Done with Words: Speech Acts in Hispanic Drama*, edited by Elias Rivers, 39–49. Newark, Del.: Juan de la Cuesta, 1986.

Gies, David T. *Agustín Durán: A Biography and Literary Appreciation*. London: Tamesis, 1975.

———. "Glorious Invalid: Spanish Theater in the Nineteenth Century." *Hispanic Review* 61.2 (1993): 213–45.

———. "Hacia un catálogo de los dramas de Dionisio Solís (1774–1834)." *Bulletin of Hispanic Studies* 68 (1990): 197–210.

———. "Notas sobre Grimaldi y el 'furor de refundir' en Madrid (1820–1833)." *Cuadernos de Teatro Clásico* 5 (1990): 111–24.

———. *Theatre and Politics in Nineteenth-Century Spain: Juan de Grimaldi as Impresario and Government Agent*. Cambridge: Cambridge University Press, 1988.

Gil y Zárate, Antonio. *Manual de literatura: Primera parte*. Paris: Garnier, 1865.

Go-Between, The. Directed by Joseph Losey. Based on the novel of the same title by L. P. Hartley. EMI Films and World Film Services, 1971.

González Marcos, Máximo. "El antiabsolutismo en *La estrella de Sevilla*." *Hispanófila* 25, no. 74 (1982): 1–24.

Gruber, William E. *Comic Theaters: Studies in Performance and Audience Response*. Athens: University of Georgia Press, 1986.

Haley, George. "Lope de Vega y el repertorio de Gaspar de Porras en 1604 y 1606." In *Homenaje a William L. Fichter*, edited by A. David Kiossoff and José Amor y Vázquez, 257–68. Madrid: Castalia, 1971.

Harlan, Mabel M. "D. Adelardo López de Ayala, ¿Figura o Figurón?" *Hispania* 18 (1935): 413–36.

———. "The Date of *El tejado de vidrio*, with a Bio-bibliographical Note on D. Adelardo López de Ayala." *Hispanic Review* 6 (1938): 236–49.

Hartzenbusch, Juan Eugenio. "Don Dionisio Solís, noticia biográfica." In *Biblioteca de Autores Españoles*, vol 67. Madrid: Hernando, 1922.

———. "Notas e ilustraciones a varias comedias de Calderón." In *Biblioteca de Autores Españoles*, vol. 14, 687–92. Madrid: Hernando, 1910.

———. *Sancho Ortiz de las Roelas*. Buenos Aires: Cabaut, [1900].

Hassel, R. Chris, Jr. *Songs of Death: Performance, Interpretation, and the Text of Richard III*. Lincoln: University of Nebraska Press, 1987.

Hayes, Frances C. "The Use of Proverbs as Titles and Motives in the *Siglo de Oro* Drama: Tirso de Molina." *Hispanic Review* 7 (1939): 310–23.

Hernández-Araico, Susana. *Ironía y tragedia en Calderón*. Potomac, Md.: Scripta Humanistica, 1986.

Herrera Salgado, Félix. *Cartelera teatral madrileña II: años 1840–1849*. Cuadernos Bibliográficos, no. 9. Madrid: CSIC, 1963.

Hill, Deborah J. "*El alcalde de Zalamea*: A Chronological Annotated Bibliography." *Hispania* 66 (1983): 48–63.

Hilt, Douglas. "Grillparzer and Rivas: The Dreamer Awakened." In *From Pen to Performance: Drama as Conceived and Performed*, edited by Karelisa Hartigan, vol. 3, 51–65. Lanham, Md.: University Press of America, 1983.

Holub, Robert C. *Reception Theory: A Critical Introduction*. New York: Methuen, 1984.

Holzinger, Walter. "Ideology, Imagery and the Literalization of Metaphor in *A secreto agravio, secreta venganza*." *Bulletin of Hispanic Studies* 54 (1977): 203–14.

Homenaje a José Calvo y Revilla. Madrid, 1888.

Hornby, Richard. *Drama, Metadrama and Perception*. Lewisburg, Pa.: Bucknell University Press, 1986.

Hoy, David Couzens. *The Critical Circle: Literature, History and Philosophical Hermeneutics*. Berkeley and Los Angeles: University of California Press, 1982.

Iranzo, Carmen. *Juan Eugenio Hartzenbusch*. Boston: G. K. Hall, 1978.

Iser, Wolfgang. *The Act of Reading: A Theory of Aesthetic Response*. Baltimore: Johns Hopkins University Press, 1978.

Jauss, Hans Robert. *Aesthetic Experience and Literary Hermeneutics*. Translated by Michael Shaw. Minneapolis: University of Minnesota Press, 1982.

———. "The Changing Horizon of Understanding." In *Identity of the Literary Text*, edited by Mario J. Valdés and Owen Miller, 146–74. Toronto: University of Toronto Press, 1985.

———. *Toward an Aesthetic of Reception*. Translated by Timothy Bahti. Minneapolis: University of Minnesota Press, 1982.

Kirby, Carol Bingham. "La verdadera edición crítica de un texto dramático del siglo de oro: teoría, metodología y aplicación." *Incipit* 6 (1986): 71–98.

———. "On the Nature of *Refundiciones* of Spain's Classical Theatre in the Seventeenth Century." In *The Golden Age Comedia: Text, Theory and Performance*, edited by Charles Ganelin and Howard Mancing. West Lafayette, Ind.: Purdue University Press, forthcoming.

Larraz, Emmanuel. *Théâtre et politique pendant la guerre d'indépendance espagnole: 1808–1814*. Dijon: Université de Bourgogne, 1988.

Larson, Catherine. "The Uniqueness of Tirso in Contemporary Stagings: Modern Audiences Meet the Master." In *Tirso de Molina: His Originality Then and Now*, edited by Henry W. Sullivan, in press.

———. *Language and the Comedia: Theory and Practice*. Lewisburg, Pa.: Bucknell University Press, 1991.

———. *Visualizing Tirso: "El burlador de Sevilla," "Marta la piadosa," and Modern Audiences*. Lubbock, Tex.: Visual Study Series, Association for Hispanic Classical Theater, 1990. Videotape.

Linares Rivas, Aureliano. "La primera cámara de la Restauración: Retratos y semblanzas, Don Adelardo López de Ayala." *Revista de España* 61, no. 241 (1878): 97–105.

Llorens, Vicente. *El romanticismo español*. Madrid: Castalia, 1979.

López Anglada, Luis. *El Duque de Rivas*. Madrid: EPESA, 1977.

López de Ayala, Adelardo. "Discurso leído ante la Real Academia Española por D. Adelardo López de Ayala en su recepción pública." In *Obras completas de Don Adelardo López de Ayala*, edited by José María Castro y Calvo. *Biblioteca de Autores Españoles*, vol. 182, 373–90. Madrid: Atlas, 1965.

———. *El alcalde de Zalamea*. 2d ed. Madrid: José Rodríguez, 1881.

———. *Obras completas de Don Adelardo López de Ayala*. Edited by José María Castro y Calvo. *Biblioteca de Autores Españoles*, vols. 180–182. Madrid: Atlas, 1965.

Lovett, Gabriel. *The Duke of Rivas*. Boston: Twayne, 1977.

Lucea García, Javier. *La poesía y el teatro en el siglo XVIII*. Madrid: Playor, 1984.

Lukacher, Maryline F. "Flaubert's Pharmacy." *Nineteenth-century French Studies* 14 (1985/86): 37–50.

Luzán, Ignacio. *La poética, o Reglas de la poesía en general, y de sus principales especies*. Edited by Russel Sebold. Barcelona: Labor, 1977.

Marín, Diego. "El valor de época de Adelardo López de Ayala." *Bulletin of Hispanic Studies* 29 (1952): 131–38.

Martín, Gregorio. "Querer y no poder, o el teatro español de 1825 a 1836." In *Studies in Eighteenth-Century Spanish Literature and Romanticism in Honor of John Dowling*, edited by Douglas and Linda Jane Barnette, 123–31. Newark, Del.: Juan de la Cuesta, 1985.

Martín Fernández, María Isabel. "El lenguaje arcaizante de los dramaturgos posrománticos." *Anuario de Estudios Filológicos* 1 (1978): 93–118.

Maxiriarth [Eugenio Hartzenbusch e Hiriart]. *Unos cuantos seudónimos de escritores españoles con sus correspondientes nombres verdaderos*. Madrid: Sucesores de Rivadeneyra, 1904.

May, T. E. "The Folly and Wit of Secret Vengeance: Calderón's *A secreto agravio, secreta venganza*." *Calderón: Comedias*. Edited by D. W. Cruickshank and J. E. Varey, vol. 19, 37–46. Westmead and London: Gregg and Tamesis Books, 1973.

McClelland, I. L. *Spanish Drama of Pathos*. 2 vols. Toronto: University of Toronto Press, 1970.

McCrary, William. "Ritual Action and Form in *La Estrella de Sevilla*." In *Homenaje a William L. Fichter*, edited by A. David Kossoff and José Amor y Vázquez, 503–13. Madrid: Castalia, 1971.

Menarini, Piero, et al. *El teatro romántico español (1830–1850): Autores, obras, bibliografía*. Bologna: Atesa, 1982.

Menéndez Onrubia, Carmen. "El teatro clásico durante la Restauración y la Regencia (1875–1900)." *Cuadernos de Teatro Clásico* 5 (1990): 187–207.

Menéndez y Pelayo, Marcelino. "*El Alcalde de Zalamea*." *Boletín de la Biblioteca Menéndez y Pelayo* 10 (1928): 193–204.

Meregalli, Franco. "Sur la réception littéraire." *Revue de Littérature Comparée* 54, no. 2 (1980): 134–49.

Miller, Jonathan. *Subsequent Performances*. New York: Viking, 1986.

Molière. *Le Tartuffe ou l'Imposteur*. In *Oeuvres complètes*. Edited by George Couton, vol. 1. Paris: Gallimard, 1971.

———. *Tartuffe and Other Plays*. Translated by Donald M. Frame. 1967; rpt., New York: New American Library, 1981.

Molina, Tirso de. *Marta la piadosa; Don Gil de las calzas verdes*, edited by Ignacio Arellano. Kassel: Reichenberger; Barcelona: PPU, 1988.

———. *Marta la piadosa*. In *Obras dramáticas completas*, edited by Blanca de los Ríos. 3: 339–403. 3d. ed. Madrid: Aguilar, 1969.

Montoto y Rautenstrauch, Luis. *Personajes, personas y personillas que corren por las tierras de ambas castillas*. 2 vols. Sevilla: Librería de San José, 1912.

Navas Ruiz, Ricardo. *Imágenes liberales. Rivas-Larra-Galdós*. Salamanca: Almar, 1979.

O'Connell, Richard B. "Rivas's *El desengaño en un sueño* and Grillparzer's *Der Traum ein Leben*: A Problem in Assessment of Influence." *Philological Quarterly* 40 (1961): 569–76.

O'Connor, Thomas Austin. *Myth and Mythology in the Theater of Pedro Calderón de la Barca*. San Antonio, Tex.: Trinity University Press, 1988.

Oriel, Charles M. *Writing and Inscription in Golden Age Drama*. Purdue Studies in Romance Literatures, no. 1. West Lafayette, Ind.: Purdue University Press, 1992.

Ossorio y Bernard, Manuel. *Ensayo de un catálogo de periodistas españoles del siglo XIX*. Madrid: J. Palacios, 1903–1904.

Oteyza, Luis de. *López de Ayala o el figurón político-literario*. Vidas Españolas e Hispanoamericanas del siglo XX, no. 25. Madrid: Espasa-Calpe, 1932.

Oyuela, Calixto. "*Marta la piadosa*." In *Estudios y artículos literarios*, 219–32. Buenos Aires: Pablo E. Coni e Hijos, 1889.

Palacio Valdés, Armando. "Poetas contemporáneos: Don Adelardo López de Ayala." *Revista Europea* 14, no. 283 (1879): 117–23.

Palacios Fernández, Emilio. "El teatro barroco español en una carta de Bernardo de Iriarte al Conde de Aranda (1767)." *Cuadernos de Teatro Clásico* 5 (1990): 43–64.

———, Ermanno Caldera, Antonietta Calderone, and Jesús Rubio Jiménez. *Siglo XVIII, Siglo XIX*. Vol. 2 of *Historia del teatro en España*. Edited by José María Díez Borque. Madrid: Taurus, 1988.

Palmer, Richard E. *Hermeneutics*. Evanston: Northwestern University Press, 1969.
Palomo, María del Pilar. "El 'amor portugués' en Tirso de Molina." *Monteagudo* 30 (1960): 4–13.
———. "Presencia de Tirso en Moratín." *Studi Ispanici* 1 (1962): 165–86.
Peers, Edgar Allan. "Angel de Saavedra: Duque de Rivas." *Revue Hispanique* 58 (1923): 538–58.
Pérez Calamarte, A., ed. "Epístolario inédito." *Revue Hispanique* 27 (1912): 499–622.
Picón, J. Octavio. *Ayala: Estudio biográfico*. Madrid: Compañía de Impresores y Libreros, n.d.
Piñeyro, Enrique. *El romanticismo en España*. Reprint. New York: G. E. Stechert, 1936.
Pitollet, Carmen. "Datos biográficos sobre D. Pascual Rodríguez de Arellano y D. Rafael Floranes." *Revista de Filología Española* 10 (1923): 288–300.
"Plagiarism—A Symposium." *Times Literary Supplement*, 9 April 1982, 413–15.
Plato. *Phaedrus*. In *The Collected Dialogues of Plato*, edited by Edith Hamilton and Huntington Cairns, and translated by R. Hackforth. Bollingen Series 71, 475–525. Princeton: Princeton University Press, 1963.
Polansky, Susan. "Textual Coherence in the Duke of Rivas' *El desengaño en un sueño*: The Dramaturgy of Destiny." *Modern Language Studies* 18, no. 3 (1988): 3–17.
Profeti, Maria Grazia. "Texto literario del siglo XVII, texto espectáculo del XVIII: la intervención censoria como estrategia intertextual." In *Coloquio internacional sobre el teatro español del siglo XVIII*, edited by Mario Di Pinto, Maurizio Fabbri, and Rinaldo Froldi, 333–50. Abano Terme: Piovan, 1988.
Quint, David. *Origin and Originality in Renaissance Literature: Versions of the Source*. New Haven: Yale University Press, 1983.
Reckford, Kenneth. *Aristophanes' Old-and-New Comedy. Volume 1: Six Essays in Perspective*. Chapel Hill: University of North Carolina Press, 1987.
Reed, Frank Otis, Esther M. Dixon, and John M. Hill, eds. *La estrella de Sevilla*. Boston: D. C. Heath, 1939.
Ríos, Juan A. "La polémica teatral dieciochesca como esquema dinámico." *Cuadernos de Teatro Clásico* 5 (1990): 65–75.
Ríos de Lampérez, Blanca de los. *Del siglo de oro*. Madrid: Bernardo Rodríguez, 1910.
Rivas, Angel de Saavedra, Duque de. *Don Alvaro, o la fuerza del sino; El desengaño en un sueño*. Edited by José García Templado. Barcelona: Plaza y Janés, 1984.
———. *Don Alvaro o la fuerza del sino*. Edited by Donald Shaw. Madrid: Castalia, 1976.
Rivers, Elias. "The Shame of Writing in *La estrella de Sevilla*." *Folio* 12 (1980): 105–17.
———, ed. *Renaissance and Baroque Poetry of Spain*. 1966. Reprint. Prospect Heights, Ill.: Waveland Press, 1988.
Rodríguez de Arellano, Pasqual. *Marta la piadosa*. MS. Leg[ajo] 7° E, Biblioteca Municipal, Madrid.
Rodríguez López-Vázquez, Alfredo, ed. *La Estrella de Sevilla*. Madrid: Cátedra, 1991.

———. "*La Estrella de Sevilla* y Claramonte." *Criticón*, no. 21 (1983): 5–31.

———. "*La Estrella de Sevilla* y *Deste agua no beberé*: ¿un mismo autor?" *Bulletin of the Comediantes* 36 (1984): 83–100.

Rodríguez Sánchez de León, María José. "El teatro español del Siglo de Oro y la preceptiva poética del siglo XIX." *Cuadernos de Teatro Clásico* 5 (1990): 77–98.

Romera Tobar, Leonardo. "Calderón y la literatura española del siglo XIX." *Letras de Deusto* 11, no. 22 (1981): 101–24.

Rubio Jiménez, Jesús. "Notas sobre el teatro clásico español en el debate sobre el realismo escénico." *Cuadernos de Teatro Clásico* 5 (1990): 171–86.

———. "El teatro en el siglo XIX (II) (1845–1900)." In *Historia del teatro en España*, edited by José María Díez Borque, Vol. 2, 625–751. Madrid: Taurus, 1988.

Ruiz Ramón, Francisco. *Calderón y la tragedia*. Madrid: Alhambra, 1984.

———. *Historia del teatro español*. Vol. 1. Madrid: Alianza, 1967.

Sale, Roger. *Literary Inheritance*. Amherst: University of Massachusetts Press, 1984.

Schinasi, Michael. "The History and Ideology of Calderón's Reception in Mid-Nineteenth-Century Spain." *Neophilologus* 70 (1986): 381–95.

———, ed. and comp. "Relación de las producciones dramáticas que se han aprobado por la Junta de Censura, para los Teatros del Reyno desde el mes de Marzo del año prócsimo pasado hasta el 31 de Diciembre del mismo." Typescript.

Schurlknight, Donald. "Alberto Lista: 'De la supuesta misión de los poetas.'" *Dieciocho* 10 (1987): 168–81.

Sebastián y Latre, Tomás. *Ensayo sobre el teatro español*. Madrid, 1773.

Sebold, Russell. *Trayectoria del romanticismo español*. Barcelona: Crítica, 1983.

Seminario de Bibliografía Hispánica de la Facultad de Filosofía y Letras de Madrid. *Cartelera teatral madrileña I: años 1830–39*. *Cuaderno Bibliográficos*, no. 3. Madrid: CSIC, 1961.

———. *Veinticuatro diarios: Madrid, 1830–1900*. 4 vols. Madrid: CSIC, 1968–1975.

Serra, Narciso. *Amar por señas*. Madrid: José Rodríguez, 1855.

Shaw, Donald L. *A Literary History of Spain: The Nineteenth Century*. Edited by R. O. Jones. London: Ernest Benn; New York: Barnes and Noble, 1972.

Shields, Archibald Kenneth. "The Madrid Stage 1820–1850." Ph.D. diss, University of North Carolina–Chapel Hill, 1933.

Sloman, A. E. *The Dramatic Craftsmanship of Calderón*. Oxford: Dolphin, 1969.

Smith, Dawn. "La comedia a fines del siglo XX: en busca de nuevas interpretaciones escénicas." In *El mundo del teatro español en su Siglo de Oro: Ensayos dedicados a John E. Varey*, edited by José Ruano de la Haza, 395–408. Ottawa: Dovehouse Editions Canada, 1989.

Solís, Dionisio. *Marta la piadosa*. MS. Leg[ajo] 2, no. 22, Biblioteca Municipal, Madrid.

Solsona y Baselga, Conrado. *Ayala: Estudio político*. Madrid: Hijos de J. A. García, 1891.

Steiner, George. *After Babel: Aspects of Language and Translation*. London: Oxford University Press, 1975.

———. *Antigones*. Oxford: Clarendon, 1984.

Stoudemire, Sterling A. "Dionisio Solís's *Refundiciones* of Plays (1800–1834)." *Hispanic Review* 8 (1940): 305–10.

Sturm, Harlan, and Sara Sturm. "The Astronomical Metaphor in *La Estrella de Sevilla.*" *Hispania* 52 (1969): 193–97.

Sullivan, Henry W. "*El alcalde de Zalamea* de Calderón en el teatro europeo de la segunda mitad del siglo XVIII." *Letras de Deusto* 11, no. 22 (1981): 15–21.

———. *Calderón in the German Lands and the Low Countries: His Reception and Influence 1654–1980.* Cambridge: Cambridge University Press, 1981.

———. "Calderón's Appeal to European Audiences in the Enlightenment and Romantic Eras: 1738–1838." *Ottawa Hispanist* 5 (1981): 41–58.

ter Horst, Robert. *Calderón: The Secular Plays.* Lexington: University of Kentucky Press, 1986.

———. "'Half in Love with Easeful Death': La comicidad de *Marta la piadosa.*" In *Homenaje a Tirso*, 439–46. Madrid: Revista "Estudios," 1981.

Touron de Ruiz, Mercedes. "El Alcalde de Zalamea en Lope y Calderón." *Cuadernos Hispanoamericanos*, no. 372 (June 1981): 534–50.

Trigueros, Cándido María. *Sancho Ortiz de las Roelas.* Madrid: Sancha, 1800.

Urzainqui, Inmaculada. *De nuevo sobre Calderón en la crítica española del siglo XVIII.* Anejos del Boces XVIII-2. Oviedo: Universidad de Oviedo, Cátedra Feijóo, 1984.

Valera, Juan. *Obras completas.* 3 vols. Edited by Luis Araujo Costa. Madrid: Aguilar, 1949–1958.

Veeser, H. Aram, ed. *The New Historicism.* New York and London: Routledge, 1989.

Vega, Garcilaso de la. *Poesías castellanas completas.* Edited by Elias Rivers. Madrid: Castalia, 1969.

Vega Carpio, Lope de. *El anzuelo de Fenisa; Fenisa's Hook, or Fenisa the Hooker.* Translated by David M. Gitlitz. San Antonio, Tex.: Trinity University Press, 1988.

Vellón Lahoz, Javier. "El proceso de refundición como práctica ideológica: *La dama duende* de Juan José Fernández Guerra." *Cuadernos de Teatro Clásico* 5 (1990): 99–109.

Watson, A. I. "Calderón's King Sebastian: Hero or Fool?" *Bulletin of Hispanic Studies* 61 (1984): 407–18.

Weiner, Jack. "Zeus y las metamorfosis de Sancho IV en *La Estrella de Sevilla.*" *Explicación de Textos Literarios* 10 (1981): 63–67.

Wilder, Thornton. "Lope, Pinedo, Some Child-Actors and a Lion." *Romance Philology* 7 (1953): 19–25.

———. "New Aids Toward Dating the Early Plays of Lope de Vega." In *Varia variorum: Festgabe für Karl Reinhardt*, 194–200. Münster-Köln, 1952.

Will, Frederick. *Thresholds and Testimonies: Recovering Order in Literature and Criticism.* Detroit: Wayne State University Press, 1988.

Wilson, E. M. "La discreción de Don Lope de Almeida." *Clavileño* 2, no. 9 (1951): 1–10.

Zabala, Arturo. *El teatro en la Valencia de finales del siglo XVIII.* Valencia: Instituto Alfonso el Magnánimo, 1982.

Zavala, Iris M. "La poética de lo cotidiano: reflejos de comportamiento en el teatro del siglo XVIII." In *Coloquio internacional sobre el teatro español del siglo XVIII*, edited by Mario Di Pinto, Maurizio Fabbri, and Rinaldo Froldi, 399–415. Abano Terme: Piovan, 1988.

Index

Ab., J., 70, 72, 199
Adams, N. B., 5, 6
afterlife, 12, 100
Aguilar Piñal, Francisco, 31
Alborg, Juan Luis, 6
Alcalde de Zalamea, El, 29, 77, 126–70, 203, 205, 208–23
Alfonso, Luis, 76, 77, 78, 204
Alonso, José Luis, 191
Amar por señas, 29
Andioc, René, 15, 31, 229 n.44, 233 n.9, 239 n.17, 241 n.28, 247 n.2
Augusto de Cueto, Leopoldo, 172, 182, 183, 256 n.7

Blanco García, Francisco, 172
Bloom, Harold, 14
Bofull, Pedro, 168, 169, 223
Boldún y Conde, Calixto, 21, 80, 115–17, 119–21, 187
Boussagol, Gabriel, 173
Brook, Peter, 191, 228 n.31

Caldera, Ermanno, 6, 32, 33, 41–42, 233 n.10, 248 n.3
Cálderon de la Barca, Pedro, 14, 16, 21, 22, 23, 28, 29, 44, 77, 123, 125, 126–70, 176, 188, 189, 194, 205, 212, 213, 214; *Casa con dos puertas mala es de guardar,* 29, 193, 194; *La dama duende,* 25, 123; *El galán fantasma,* 191; *La vida es sueño,* 133, 143, 158, 170, 171–84, 205
canon, 7, 21, 26, 79
Cañete, Manuel, 172

Cardwell, Richard, 173, 182
Carmona, Gil, 162, 165, 213, 218
Carreño, Pedro, 127
Castigo de la miseria, El, 82
Castro y Bellvis, Guillén de, 77, 203
Castro y Calvo, José María, 128
Censor, El, 23
Chamizal, El, 3, 171, 185, 187
Cid, Le, 77
Claramonte, Andrés de: *El secreto en la mujer,* 175
Coe, Ada, 5, 70
Conde Lucanor, El, 172, 180
Cook, John, 6, 15, 31, 83, 229 n.44
Corneille, Pierre, 77
Correspondencia de España, La, 74, 75, 200
Coughlin, Edward, 6
Cowan, James, 175

de Armas, Frederick, 175
decanonization, 12, 188
de la Revilla, Manuel, 183
Derrida, Jacques, 175
Desengaño en un sueño, El, 171–84
Devoción de la Cruz, La, 133
Diario de Madrid, 70
Díez-Borque, José María, 188
Discusion, La, 163
Dragun, Osvaldo, 10

El Paso *Times,* 185, 186
Epoca, La, 74, 75, 76, 163, 167, 168, 170, 201, 202, 213, 214, 219, 222
España, La, 26, 28, 29, 117, 193–96, 204

Estrella de Sevilla, La, 6, 14, 17, 53, 115, 126, 196. See also *Sancho Ortiz de las Roelas*

F., J. de, 74, 200
Fernández de Moratín, Leandro, 28, 77, 80, 81, 82, 83, 85, 99, 124, 196, 203
Fernández Guerra, José, 24 –25, 123
Fernández–Guerra y Orbe, Aureliano, 26 –27, 28, 29, 118–20, 183, 196, 231n.72, 246n.60
Fernández Villegas, Francisco [Zeda], 22
Ferrer del Río, Agustín, 159, 210
Franzbach, Martin, 127
Frye, Northrop, 3, 4, 10
Fuenteovejuna, 166
Funes, Enrique, 245n.56
fusion, 3, 10, 11, 13, 20, 21, 190

Gaceta de Madrid, 17, 23, 70, 196
Gadamer, Hans-Georg, 7– 8, 19, 27
Garrote más bien dado, El, 126
Go-Between, The, 9
Gruber, William, 188

Harlan, Mabel, 128
Hartzenbusch, Juan Eugenio, 6, 21, 27, 28, 31–79, 125, 126, 189, 199 –204, 206, 215, 232n.4, 233n.10, 234n.14, 236n.27; *El Cid campeador,* 28
Hassel, R. Chris, 8, 9
Hilt, Douglas, 173
Hipocresía castigada o Juan de Buen Alma, La [El Gazmoño], 81
Hipócrita, El, 81
Historias para ser contadas, 10
Holub, Robert, 7
horizon, 7– 14, 19, 20, 21, 27, 87, 123, 124, 125, 185, 188, 190; bridge-building, 10, 15, 30, 188; of expectation, 7– 8, 20, 30, 73; of experience, 7– 8, 12, 15, 20, 30, 78, 172; of tradition, 8
Hoy, David, 10
Hugelmann, Jean Gabriel, 172

Iberia, La, 73, 117, 161, 162, 163, 169, 199, 204, 210, 221
Ilustración Española y Americana, La, 182
Imparcial, El, 21, 166, 218
Iser, Wolfgang, 7

Jauss, Hans Robert, 7–9, 10, 13, 185, 228n.31

Kirby, Carol B., 225

Larson, Catherine, 188
Llorens, Vicente, 257n.11
López de Ayala, Adelardo, 21, 29, 77, 126 –70, 189, 203, 210 –23, 250n.18
Losey, Joseph, 9
Lovett, Gabriel, 174

Mámora, battle of, 85, 86, 91, 100, 118, 185, 206
Marta la piadosa, 18, 19, 80 –125, 126, 169, 170, 185– 89, 204 – 8
Martín, Gregorio, 26
McClelland, I. L., 52–53
McEwan, Ian, 14
Menarini, Piero, 5
Mendoza Tenorio, Elisa, 166
Miguel, Antonio de, 25
Miller, Jonathan, 12, 19, 171, 228n.30, 230n.57
Mocedades del Cid, Las, 77
Mojigata, La, 80, 82, 84, 85, 94, 113, 124, 126
Molière [Jean–Baptiste Poquelin], 30, 80, 81, 120, 124, 126, 205
Moreto, Agustín, 163, 194, 205, 214: *El parecido en la corte,* 17; 22, 24, 28; *Yo por vos y vos por otro [Ir contra el viento],* 24, 25, 219
Morphy, Conde de, 182
Museo Universal, El, 162, 165, 212, 217

Navarrete y Landa, Ramón de [Asmodeo], 75, 202
Nombela, Julio, 163, 217
No. siempre lo peor es cierto, 82

O'Connell, Richard, 172, 173
O'Connor, Thomas A., 227
Oliver, William, 225n.1
Oteyza, Luis de, 128, 165, 166, 255n.43
Oyuela, Calixto, 117 120 –22, 246n.62

Palmer, Richard, 188
Pedro Crespo, o El alcalde de Zalameo, 127
Peers, E. A., 173

pharmakon, 65, 175–82, 236 n.25
Piñeyro, Enrique, 173
Polansky, Susan, 174
Portes, Francisco, 259 n.35

Quint, David, 13, 26

Reckford, Kenneth, 14
Rejón de Silva, Diego, 81
Revista de Teatro, 27, 158, 161, 208
Rey D. Pedro en Madrid, El, 4
Richard III, 8
Rivas, Angel Saavedra, Duke of, 170, 171–84, 188; *Don Alvaro, o la fuerza del sino,* 172, 174
Rivers, Elias, 44
Rodriguez, Marla, 199
Rodríguez de Arellano, Pascual, 80–96, 187, 238 n.9
Rodríguez de Arellano, Vicente, 13, 17, 81, 126
Rogers, Pat, 14
Rojas Zorrilla, Francisco, 28, 194, 220; *Progne y Filomena,* 17
Rosa Gonzalez, Juan de la, 73, 200
Ruiz de Alarcón, Juan, 28, 194; *La prueba de las promesas,* 172, 180
Ruiz Ramón, Francisco, 6, 10

Sancho Ortiz de las Roelas, 14, 17, 18, 21, 31–79, 86, 126, 196–204, 220
Schinasi, Michael, 26, 226 n.10, 230 n.66, 260 n.11
Sebastián y Latre, Tomas, 13, 15, 16–17, 18, 229 n.46
Serra, Narciso, 29, 30, 115, 208
Shakespeare, William, 8, 14, 97, 122, 172, 178; *The Tempest,* 172, 176
Shields, Archibald K., 5, 6
Si de las niñas, El, 80, 82, 126
Sloman, Albert E., 225 n.4
Solís, Dionisio, 5, 80, 82, 96–115, 125, 126, 187, 206, 207
Solsona, Conrado, 128, 166
Steiner, George, 14, 15, 20, 24
Stoll, Anita, 238

Stoppard, Tom, 125
Sueños hay que lecciones son, o efectos de un desengaño, 172
Sullivan, Henry, 127, 192

Tartuffe, 80, 81, 120, 124, 126, 238 n.7, 244 n.50, 246 n.62
Teatro de Apolo, 161, 166, 183, 218, 219
Teatro de la Cruz, 81, 96, 128, 158, 161, 208
Teatro de la Zarzuela, 161, 163, 210, 212, 213, 214
Teatro del Circo, 163, 214
Teatro del Príncipe, 81, 96, 158, 161, 163, 204, 213, 214, 217
Teatro de Novedades, 73, 199
Teatro de Variedades, 115, 163, 214
Teatro Español, 74, 76, 161, 167, 200, 202, 219, 220, 223
ter Horst, Robert, 187
Tirso de Molina, 14, 22, 28, 29, 30, 80–125, 171, 188, 189, 194, 206
Traum ein Leben, Der, 172, 173
Trigueros, Candido María, 6, 13, 17, 21, 23, 24, 31–79, 81, 86, 126, 189, 196–204, 206, 234 n.14; *El anzuelo de Fenisa,* 23

Vallés y Codes, Carlos [?], 81
Vega, Lope de, 14, 20, 23, 28, 29, 32, 42, 71, 74, 77, 78, 109, 113, 163, 166, 194, 196, 201, 202, 207, 212, 214, 220; *La dama boba,* 109, 113, 118–19, 207, 245 n.53
Viejo y la niña, El, 80, 82, 85, 86, 126, 241 n.28

Warnke, Georgia, 21, 30
Washington, Diana, 186
Will, Frederic, 20, 25

Zermeño, Raúl, 185–89
Zorrilla, José de, 76, 168, 202, 220; *Don Juan Tenorio,* 76, 168, 169, 202, 220, 222, 223